Developing
Clarion for Windows™
Applications

Ross A. Santos
David Harms

SAMS
PUBLISHING

201 West 103rd Street
Indianapolis, Indiana 46290

This book is dedicated to all computer professionals who are diligent and vigilant in the search of that special one-of-a-kind software development tool.

Trademarks

Publisher

Richard K. Swadley

Acquisitions Manager

Greg Wiegand

Managing Editor

Cindy Morrow

Acquisitions Editors

Greg Croy
Rosemarie Graham

Development Editor

Bradley Jones

Software Development Specialist

Kim Spilker

Editor

Kitty Wilson

Copy Editors

Kimberly K. Hannel
Tonya Simpson

Editorial Coordinator

Bill Whitmer

Editorial Assistants

Carol Ackerman
Sharon Cox
Lynette Quinn

Technical Reviewer

Danny Joe

Marketing Manager

Gregg Bushyeager

Assistant Marketing Manager

Michelle Milner

Cover Designer

Nathan Clement

Book Designer

Alyssa Yesh

Director of Production and Manufacturing

Jeff Valler

Imprint Manager

Kelly Dobbs

Manufacturing Coordinator

Paul Gilchrist

Support Services Supervisor

Mary Beth Wakefield

Production Analysts

Angela Bannan
Dennis Clay Hager
Bobbi Satterfield

Graphics Image Specialists

Teresa Forrester
Clint Lahnen
Tim Montgomery
Dennis Sheehan
Greg Simsic
Craig Small
Susan VandeWalle
Jeff Yesh

Page Layout

Charlotte M. Clapp
Judy Everly
Shawn MacDonald
Casey Price
Tina Trettin
Mark Walchle
Dennis Wesner

Proofreading

Mona Brown
Michael Brummit
Jama Carter
Kevin Laseau
Donna Martin
Kim Mitchell
Cheryl Moore
Brian-Kent Proffitt
Beth Rago
SA Springer

Indexer

Chris Cleveland

Overview

Contents

III   Hand Coding in Clarion for Windows

14   Hand-Crafted Code: A Language Primer   221

15   Hand-Crafted Code: Principles and Approaches   247

16   Hand Code, Reuse, and the Application Generator   261

Acknowledgments

We owe a debt of gratitude to the many people who helped make this book possible, not the least of whom are friends, co-workers, and families, who put up with the long hours it has taken from our so-called normal lives. Deepest thanks to Sandy, Ashley, Sydney, and Sheldon Santos for their understanding, love and sacrifice, and to Bonnie Reimer for her patience, encouragement, and shameless admiration. Warren McKay of Memex Software, Inc., graciously allowed Dave time away from other responsibilities so the book could be finished (more or less) on time. Danny Joe provided skilled technical editing, Brad Jones and Kitty Wilson beat our prose into shape, and Greg Croy and Rosemarie Graham made it all happen.

We'd also like to thank the many who reviewed our manuscript and offered their comments, corrections, and suggestions. They include Danny Joe, Susan Lemieux, Will Fastie, Brad Feld, David Jung, James K. Smith, Bartee Lamar, Robert Gove, Kurt Gengenbach, John Golka, Gino Creglia, John Hearsey, David Shewmaker, Stephen Bottomly, Nigel Moss, Andy Stapleton, Bob Butler, Nik Johnson, Todd Seidel, Roy Rafalco, Scott Ferret, David Bayliss, Richard Chapman, Thomas Mosely, and Nigel Hicks. Special thanks to the CompuServe Clarion community and the members of Team TopSpeed.

Most of all, we are indebted to Bruce Barrington, architect of the Clarion language and CEO of TopSpeed Corp., who not only supported us throughout this work but gave us something to write about.

About the Authors

Ross Santos is an independent consultant specializing in large-scale commercial and corporate application development, object-oriented technologies, and client/server computing. He has more than 15 years of software development experience and has been the lead beta tester and technical consultant "guru" on CompuServe for the Clarion for Windows product. Ross has a unique relationship with TopSpeed Software—he is considered the "insider" or "friend of TopSpeed," having intimate knowledge of the company, its products, and its future. Ross is also a member of the Clarion for Windows division of Team TopSpeed on CompuServe.

David Harms is a private consultant specializing in systems analysis and software design for the broadcast industry. An avid Clarion user, he is also leader of the Clarion for Windows division of Team TopSpeed on CompuServe.

Foreword

It has been suggested that software development is a pre-industrial art, that programmers are really craftsmen—master craftsmen, perhaps, but craftsmen nonetheless—building one-of-a-kind applications from hand-crafted parts. Available evidence would seem to support this notion. Every new project offers the same business risk as the last. The best development teams succeed, buoyed by their intellectual prowess. Less gifted development efforts face less certain outcomes. Certainly, the best predictor of software quality is the aggregate talent and experience embodied in its development team. The same can be said of the process of composing a concerto or building a musket. Such creations necessarily reflect the skills of their creator.

What is it that traps programming in the pre-industrial age? What is the common ground beneath software developers and musket makers? Why haven't software developers achieved the productivity gains enjoyed by other industries? They lack machine tools!

Machine tools opened the door of the Industrial Revolution. Rifles can be manufactured on an assembly line because machine tools produce interchangeable parts. Today, no one doubts that automated manufacturing produces better products cheaper and faster. If we are to make better software, cheaper and faster, we will need better tools to automate and control the process of software development. We will need tools such as Clarion for Windows.

Clarion for Windows employs the same technology that launched the industrial revolution: Standardize and simplify the process of building software components. Then automate the process of assembling those components into custom applications. Like a machine tool, Clarion for Windows *manufactures* your applications for you!

Now you can become a software industrialist—you can be in control of a wonderful software factory that produces applications faster than you dreamed possible. We call it fast applications...fast! You will call it just plain fun!

It will take you less than an hour to "Quick Start" your first Clarion application. Then you will be hooked. Your application expands as the fill-in-the-blanks templates write your code for you. When you need it, you will find the Clarion language to be expressive (easy to read), compact (easy to write), and conventional (easy to learn). The Windows grammar and messaging model is built into the Clarion language so gracefully that that you will feel like an "old hand" in no time.

So get ready for an adventure—an exciting journey into a bright new world of high-powered Windows programming. Your guides will be Ross Santos and Dave Harms. There are none better. Ross and Dave are old friends and great Clarion gurus who have played a major role in developing and testing Clarion for Windows.

Read on. You are in for the time of your life.

Bruce D. Barrington
Chairman, TopSpeed Corporation

Introduction

Choosing a development environment for Windows programming can be a difficult task, because programming for Windows is considerably more complex than programming for DOS. Vendors of programming languages tend to choose one of two routes: Either they make it possible to create small, powerful applications through extensive use of low-level language statements (C++ is a good example), or they create a more comprehensive environment (such as Visual Basic) that makes it easier to create programs, at the expense of speed and low-level control over the program.

The former approach burdens the programmer with learning a difficult language, and the latter burdens the user with a painfully slow end product. If you've been waiting for a third alternative, one that combines ease of use with remarkable speed and power, your wait is over.

Clarion for Windows (CW) is a rapid application development environment that enables you to create C++-quality programs with remarkable ease. And that's not just an idle boast. As this book demonstrates, you can create a working application in minutes, a decent prototype in hours, and complete products in days and weeks, while other products take weeks and months.

The comment about C++ speed is not just marketing hype. Clarion for Windows is heir to the vaunted TopSpeed compiler technology, which produces fully optimized, true Windows executables. The standard Sieve of Eratosthenes benchmark (a program designed to test raw processing ability), written in Clarion for Windows, runs only 20 percent slower than the comparable code in MS Visual C++. It runs 36 times faster than a Visual Basic application, and 1300 times faster than Powersoft's PowerBuilder 3.0a.

Clarion for Windows really is fast, but that's not its only (some would even say primary) appeal. CW code is almost as fast as C++, and it is far easier to read, learn, and maintain. The language itself is expressive, elegant, and comprehensive, but what really makes CW a productive development environment is its templates.

Templates, like objects, enable a programmer to organize code and data without rewriting commonly used components. Templates can both incorporate objects and organize them within a larger code framework. The Application Generator, which is one of the tools you can use to create (or to assist in the creation of) your programs, is itself defined by a set of templates. This means that for the first time you not only have a tool that can write your programs for you, you have access to the source code (templates) for that tool. You can literally redefine the CW development environment to suit your particular needs and programming style.

All of this translates into a new level of productivity. Although Clarion for Windows is a programmer's tool rather than an end user's tool, it adapts well to both the novice programmer and the expert coder. You can get more done in a shorter period of time, and produce small, fast, royalty-free EXEs while you're at it.

As you've probably gathered, we're quite excited about the potential for application development using Clarion for Windows. You probably wouldn't use it to write something like an operating system (even here some hard-core CW programmers might disagree, given that they can easily integrate C++ and Assembler), but for the vast majority of projects (particularly business software) now written in languages such as C++ and Visual Basic, we believe CW is the best choice.

How to Use This Book: The Four-Part Plan

We've divided the book into four parts. Part I, "A Clarion for Windows Primer," looks briefly at the development environment. It discusses some of the concepts behind both the Clarion for Windows approach to application development and the Windows way of doing things, particularly compared to DOS. If you've never used Clarion (in any of its previous DOS versions), and if you've never programmed for Windows, you'll find plenty of useful background here.

Part II, "Developing with the Application Generator," covers the Application Generator, which is the approach most CW programmers (and virtually all new ones) will use to create Windows programs. If you're already familiar with Clarion for DOS 3.0, you may be able to skim through most of these chapters, because the basic principles of application generation in CW are, for the most part, similar. If you're new to Clarion, this section of the book will give you the most immediately practical information on creating applications.

Part III, "Hand Coding in Clarion for Windows," looks at programming using the Clarion language somewhat more directly, in what might be called a traditional programming style. It then explores what we like to think of as the "second" Clarion language: the template language. The template language is at the heart of the application generation system; in fact, almost everything the Application Generator does is driven by the templates it uses, and you can modify those for your own purposes. This part of the book explores the synergy of the Clarion language and the template language. There are some advanced topics here, geared toward the developer wishing to make the most of the development environment. Beginning users may safely skip this part of the book for now.

Part IV, "Advanced Topics," covers a variety of specialized topics, most of which are alluded to earlier in the book. Unlike the earlier parts of the book, the chapters in this section are not designed to be read in any particular order. They by no means exhaust the advanced topics of Clarion for Windows programming, but they provide a useful reference for some of the challenges that will come your way. Even if you're a beginning CW programmer and don't have an obvious need for the information in these chapters, you might find that you have some new ideas for approaching development after you read them.

Part I: The Details

Chapter 1, "Introduction to the Development Environment," is an overview of the Clarion for Windows development environment. It discusses the major parts of the environment and their relationships with each other. If you're new to Clarion, you should read this chapter.

Chapter 2, "Choosing a Development Style," covers some of the possible approaches to development. Because of Clarion for Windows' great flexibility, you actually have a number of development paths available to you. Will you stay strictly within the Application Generator? Will you use a more traditional hand coding approach? Will you use some combination of the two? Key factors here are your experience level and the type of application you are creating.

Chapter 3, "Choosing Databases Wisely," discusses the database driver technology and offers some suggestions for which drivers may be appropriate for your application. You don't need to concern yourself with this chapter if your applications don't read or write data files, but developers of business software and other database-related programs will want to read this material.

Chapter 4, "Concepts You Should Know," and Chapter 5, "Unlearning DOS: Old Habits Die Hard," take the basic information already presented about the Clarion for Windows development environment and apply it to the unique challenges presented by the transition from DOS to Windows. If you're an experienced Windows programmer, you may want to skim this section for only those areas where CW differs from other Windows tools. If you've never programmed for Windows, these chapters will give you a good foundation for understanding how and why CW does what it does.

Part II: The Details

Chapter 6, "Quick Start: The Two-Minute Application," is an introduction to rapid application development using the Application Generator. This is the starting point for most application development. Quick Start is also a handy tool for creating small test applications, and is recommended throughout the book as a learning aid.

Chapter 7, "Defining Your Data," covers one of the often-neglected aspects of application development: analyzing and designing the database your application will use. As with Chapter 3, if your application doesn't read or write data files, you won't need to concern yourself with this chapter, but if you write business or database applications, there are some concepts here that can really speed your development and save you a lot of grief.

Chapter 8, "Creating Procedures," discusses the basics of how to create procedures (functions) in the Application Generator.

Chapter 9, "Refining Procedures: Code and Control Templates," looks in more detail at how procedures can be constructed and enhanced in the Application Generator. Chapter 8 uses some predefined procedure templates to accomplish much of the work, and Chapter 9 takes a more object-oriented approach.

Chapter 10, "Assigning and Building Your Help Files," examines the issues involved in creating hooks in your programs for Windows help files. It also discusses some of the tools available for actually creating help files.

Chapter 11, "From Here to EXE: The Project System," looks at how all the source code, icons, libraries, and optional components such as graphics files are tied together. You'll need at least a basic knowledge of this part of CW to turn your applications or source code into working programs.

Chapter 12, "Testing and Debugging," reviews the use of the integrated Windows-hosted debugger, and Chapter 13, "Distributing Your Application," examines some important issues you need to consider when you are creating a program for limited or general distribution.

Part III: The Details

Chapter 14, "Hand-Crafted Code: A Language Primer," is an introduction to the Clarion language. You'll find this useful if you're new to the Clarion language and you want to know what's happening "under the hood."

Chapter 15, "Hand-Crafted Code: Principles and Approaches," is a style guide to CW language programming. The basic knowledge of the Clarion language covered in Chapter 14 is assumed.

Chapter 16, "Hand Code, Reuse, and the Application Generator," begins a transition from hand coding to using the Application Generator in a variety of ways. Although CW does have some object-oriented aspects (and they are becoming more prominent with time), it primarily accomplishes code reuse through the template system. This chapter gives you a good background on how the Application Generator accomplishes code reuse.

Chapter 17, "Creating Code Templates," looks at ways to incorporate often-used hand code into the Application Generator templates. Chapters 18, "Creating Procedure Templates," Chapter 19, "Creating Control Templates," and Chapter 20, "Creating Extension Templates," extend this concept of reuse in the templates to several other template types. A basic understanding of code, procedure, control, and extension templates, as outlined in these four chapters, will enable you to make significant revisions to the appearance and function of the Application Generator. These chapters, probably more than any other chapters in this book, are a gateway to making CW the most productive development environment in which you've ever worked.

Chapter 21, "The AppGen: The Ultimate Hand Coding Tool," explores the potential for re-creating the Application Generator so that it codes the way you do. Only you can really decide how you would like such an Application Generator to work, so this chapter concentrates on principles, and makes some specific suggestions about which templates are universally applicable.

Part IV: The Details

Chapter 22, "Using Dynamic Data Exchange," looks at Clarion for Windows' rather tidy implementation of dynamic data exchange (DDE). If you've ever used DDE in another language, you're probably in for a very pleasant surprise.

Chapter 23, "Using Drag and Drop," discusses how to add Drag and Drop capability to a CW application. This is quite easy to do. Chapter 20 also contains source for an extension template to make the entire job even simpler.

Chapter 24, "Using Open Database Connectivity," covers the basics of using the Open Database Connectivity (ODBC) driver. ODBC enables you to use any file system that has an ODBC driver available for it. If Clarion's impressive array of file drivers isn't enough for you, chances are you can find your answer through ODBC.

Chapter 25, "Using the Windows API," uses a phone dialer example to illustrate how to call Windows API functions. Most API calls are quite easy to make; usually, the biggest problem is getting the prototypes right. This chapter will give you a good start on the process.

Chapter 26, "Using VBXs and Non-CW DLLs," has some issues in common with Chapter 25, because all Windows API calls are also calls to DLLs. Most functionality that you purchase for integration into your program will probably come as VBXs and/or DLLs, however, so these are examined and compared.

Chapter 27, "Using Initialization Files," looks at the concept and use of .INI files, including WIN.INI. Almost all programs can benefit from the proper use of an .INI file, and this chapter explains the key issues.

Chapter 28, "Multithreading and Thread Management," will sooner or later interest just about all CW programmers. This detailed discussion of the subject also includes the complete source for Ross's now-famous Thread Manager, which lets you keep track of how many copies of a procedure you open, gives you a way to iconize and restore windows at will, and more.

Chapter 29, "Multiple-Document Interface Versus Non–Multiple-Document Interface," discusses the issues of the multiple-document interface (MDI), its relationship to threading as implemented in Clarion for Windows, and the alternatives to using MDI. This chapter is best read in conjunction with Chapter 28.

Chapter 30, "Clarion for Windows and Client/Server Computing," covers the use of CW programs in a client/server environment. If one chapter seems like a relatively small contribution to this subject, it's only because client/server is a relatively painless effort under Clarion for Windows.

Chapter 31, "Sharing Code: Source, OBJs, and LIBs," is an overview of the various options available to the programmer who wants to avoid code duplication. This is a companion approach to the template system, but it also applies to hand coders who are not using templates at all.

Chapter 32, "Sharing Code: Creating Clarion DLLs," takes up where Chapter 31 leaves off, but raises some of the special issues that pertain only to DLLs. There's some good information here on how to manage large and multiprogrammer application development.

Conventions Used in This Book

The following typographic conventions are used in this book:

- Code lines, commands, statements, variables, and any text you type or see on the screen appears in a `computer` typeface.
- Placeholders in syntax descriptions appear in an *`italic computer`* typeface. Replace the placeholder with the actual filename, parameter, or whatever element it represents.
- *Italics* highlight technical terms when they first appear in the text and are sometimes used to emphasize important points.

The printed page sometimes isn't wide enough to accommodate long code lines. At the beginning of some code lines in this book you will see a code continuation character (➥), which indicates that the code line was too long. When you see this, you are to enter the code that follows the ➥ on the preceding line.

In Summary...

In this book we've tried to cover those areas that are essential to making CW as effective a development environment as it can be. If you're a DOS programmer with no Clarion experience, you'll want to pay particular attention to Parts I and II. If you're a skilled Clarion programmer looking to move up to the Windows product, Parts I and III will probably offer you the most meat. And whatever your level, you'll probably find at least a few chapters in Part IV that will help you get around some of the programming challenges Windows presents.

We hope that you learn as much reading this book as we did writing it!

I

A Clarion for Windows Primer

1

Introduction to the Development Environment

A Brief History of Clarion

Clarion for Windows is a language with a remarkable pedigree. It originated in the early 1970s, when Bruce Barrington, who would go on to found Clarion Software, became disenchanted with available business programming languages. In the early 1980s he saw in the IBM PC an opportunity for a new programming language that was powerful and expressive, yet easy to read and maintain. Unlike many who only dream of such a tool, Barrington created his.

Clarion 1.0 was remarkable not just for the elegance of its language, but for the introduction of two tools: the Screen Formatter and the Report Formatter. The Screen Formatter greatly simplified interface design by letting the programmer design screens interactively, placing text and fields exactly as they would appear to the user. This approach to screen design took full advantage of the IBM PC's memory-mapped video, allowing direct program access to data onscreen. Programmers no longer needed to go through endless cycles of coding, compiling, and testing the interface.

With Clarion 2.0, Clarion programming took another huge leap forward. This version introduced Designer, an early application-generation tool that integrated the screen and Report Formatters with a type of Data Dictionary and a procedure-design aid. Designer enabled the programmer to generate common types of procedures by doing little more than specify which files to use and where to place fields from those files on the screen. Designer then blended this information with standard code from a "model" file and created commented source code.

Clarion 2.0 was also one of the first development environments to provide "one-stop shopping"—in addition to Designer, the product included a source editor, a runtime processor, a compiler and linker to create royalty-free EXEs, file maintenance utilities, an integrated help authoring system, and even a file and directory management tool.

A key limitation of Clarion 2.x, and a common gripe among experienced programmers, was the large amount of "magic" code in the model file. Although you could greatly extend the functionality of Designer with custom model files, there were many aspects of code generation that were hidden inside Designer itself. Furthermore, as programmers developed larger and larger applications with Clarion, limitations in the compiler and linker technology also became apparent.

In 1989, the company began a complete rewrite of the Clarion programming language. Clarion entered into a technology licensing agreement with JPI, creators of the TopSpeed compilers (and, incidentally, the original founders of Borland) to give Clarion a speed boost. JPI's TopSpeed compiler technology represented a somewhat unique approach in the industry. All the languages created by JPI were designed as front ends to "plug in" to the same object code back end. This meant that a given function written in C++, Modula 2, or Pascal would always result in the same highly optimized object code.

If the licensing of the JPI technology proved successful, Clarion would become yet another front end (like Modula 2 or C++), and would gain all the speed and size benefits usually associated with 3GL programming languages. To the many devoted Clarion programmers accustomed to Clarion 2.x, the promise of new speed, better memory management, and new features was enticing.

As it turned out, the fit between Clarion and JPI was so good that the companies eventually agreed to merge, with the new entity ultimately going by the name TopSpeed Corporation.

Clarion 3.0 was somewhat longer in coming than most people expected. This was not due to difficulties in grafting in a new compiler and linker, but resulted from a complete redesign of the product. Mindful of the changes going on in operating systems, Clarion set out to make the new version portable. Although it would be a DOS product, there was to be nothing in the design or the libraries that would impede a port to a GUI platform such as Windows.

Along the way, Clarion 3.0 also sprouted a number of significant new features. Where Clarion 2.x supported only its native data file format, ASCII and binary DOS files (Btrieve and dBASE support could be had through add-on products), 3.0 employed a brand new database driver technology.

The purpose of this technology was to make file processing statements such as SET, PUT, ADD, and GET independent of the actual data files being used. This meant that a programmer could write the code once, and then only need to change drivers to support different file formats or mix file formats within an application.

Clarion 3.0 also introduced a much more flexible alternative to the model file, called the *template system*. Templates, like model files, provided the basis for code generation and embodied much more of the intelligence formerly embedded in the Designer program. Features such as conditional generation and code embed points were now controlled from the template system itself. Additionally, default procedure characteristics could be added and maintained through a special application file, allowing the developer even more control over the application generation process.

Clarion 3.0 was also the first version of Clarion to run in, and create programs for, a protected mode environment. With the addition of the TopSpeed DOS extender, developers could create massive DOS applications (up to 16MB in size on machines equipped with 286 and better processors).

Clarion 3.0 first shipped in 1992, but by this time work had already been started on the Windows version of Clarion (which is often referred to as CW). At the Clarion Developers Conference in 1993, developers were given a sneak preview of the new system. Compiler author David Bayliss not only demonstrated most of CW's salient features, but used a CW program to create his presentation graphics. This demo program shipped with CW 1.0, and is substantially unchanged since that first demonstration, indicating not only that CW was, from the start, a remarkably stable programming language, but that the developers have stayed true to their original vision.

With that brief background (Bruce Barrington has written a more detailed discussion of the language's origins in the foreword to the CW Language Reference), let me introduce you to Clarion for Windows.

Clarion for Windows

Like its DOS predecessors, Clarion for Windows is a somewhat difficult product to describe because it presents several faces to developers. It is, fundamentally, a programming language that produces true native Windows EXEs. As a language, it is comparable to C++ in speed and efficiency, yet far easier to read and learn.

Clarion for Windows is also a full suite of tools designed to smooth the development process. The development environment main window is shown in Figure 1.1. For fast, easy application creation, there is the Application Generator.

NOTE

A very important feature of this arrangement is that you do not lose any access to the language when you use the application development tools. They are there to serve you, not to limit you.

FIGURE 1.1.

The Clarion for Windows integrated development environment.

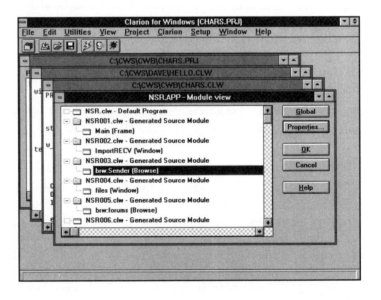

To support multiple file formats, there is the file driver technology that lets you "plug and play" (and even mix and match) different file systems; for general-purpose coding, there is the elegance and power of the Clarion programming language. The Windows-hosted debugger gives you full access to the internal workings of your program, and fast compiling and intelligent linking produce compact EXEs.

CW is its own best recommendation. If you really want to see a CW application in action, look at the screen. Much of the CW development environment is itself written in Clarion for Windows.

A Practical Overview

At the heart of every CW app is the programming language. When you create a program, whether you know it or not, CW code is generated, compiled, and linked into an EXE. In this respect, CW is no different from a language such as C++. The difference is that CW provides a number of tools to automate as much of this process as possible.

In CW, for instance, you do not need to maintain source code listings of your file definitions. You can design the files visually in the dictionary editor. You do not need to write source code to view records from those data files. You can visually design these procedures in the Application Generator, or AppGen, using the capabilities of the Window Formatter.

You do not need to maintain complex project information to make your application into an EXE. You can let the Project System do this automatically. And if you want to extend your system, using Visual Basic controls for instance, you do not need to know the intricacies of using VBXs. Again, you can let the system manage this for you.

Note that I have used the phrase "you do not need to," as opposed to "you cannot" CW imposes very few restrictions on you, the programmer. If you want to do everything at a low level, you can. You can write all that source code, you can handcraft your project files, if you really want to. The more accomplished you get with CW, the more you may find you want to get down and dirty, just for the sheer pleasure of having absolute control over the application you are building. But you don't have to.

Much of this ability to move between generated code and hand code is due to the new template technology, which includes code templates (for inserting fragments of code), control templates (which embody the logic required to process a given control), and extension template (which allow you to enhance existing templates without actually modifying the original template code).

CW also introduced the new TopSpeed file driver. This driver, written especially for CW, represents a breakthrough in database technology, and is the subject of patent action. It is designed to work both as single user and client server (although the server engine is not available at the time of this writing), and to provide data compression and security. It can optionally keep all data files and indexes in one physical file, and for certain operations it is very fast.

The end result of all of these enhancements is a development environment that covers virtually all the bases, from fast-and-easy application generation to down-and-dirty coding.

The following chapters discuss the fundamental building blocks of the CW development environment, and then examine the various development paths you can take to creating your own Windows programs with CW.

With the release of CW 1.0, TopSpeed corporation is in the enviable position of having created application development technology that is second to none. The future is bright indeed, and I trust you will find this product as exciting and enjoyable to use as I do.

Now it's time to take a look at some of the pieces that make up CW.

The Data Dictionary

Computer programs have traditionally been understood as being composed of two parts—data and code. Data is the information that gets manipulated, and code is the set of instructions that tells the computer how to manipulate the data. In many applications, much of the working data is kept on disk in data files of one format or another, and it is the job of the Data Dictionary to help you (and the AppGen) keep track of the format of these files. Figure 1.2 presents CW's dictionary editor.

FIGURE 1.2.

The dictionary editor.

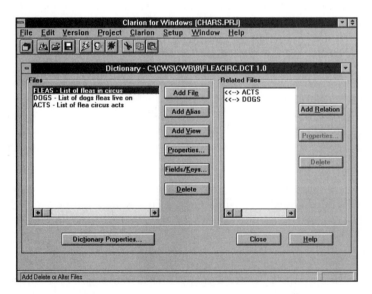

Not all applications will make use of the dictionary editor. For instance, if your only purpose in buying CW was to write the ultimate Windows alarm clock program, it's quite likely you won't need to bother with any data files (beyond, perhaps, an INI file, which does not require the use of the dictionary editor) and you could reasonably skip over this section. For most applications, however, particularly if they are business programs, you will actually begin development by defining your data files. That may sound a little strange at first, but when you think about it, it's only common sense to know what data you're working with before you attempt to design your presentation of that data.

Since CW lends itself to a rapid application development (RAD) approach, you don't need to fully define your data files before you start. You should have as much information in the dictionary as you know, as this will have a direct bearing on how much work the AppGen can do for you.

Depending on your situation, you may have only one Data Dictionary, or you may have many. If you are working on only one application, you will have one Data Dictionary. If you are working on many applications, and every one of these applications uses entirely different data files from the others, you will probably have as many Data Dictionaries as you have applications (although if you wanted to, you could place all the files into one large dictionary). The benefits of Data Dictionaries become particularly obvious when you have a number of applications that share the same file definitions. Since all these applications can use the same dictionary, you need to make changes to your file structures in only one place, and the change will take effect the next time you load any application using that dictionary.

> **NOTE**
>
> In older versions of Clarion, up to 2.x, data file definitions were stored inside each application. While this approach was satisfactory for developing single applications, it resulted in maintenance headaches when one file, shared by a large number of applications, changed. As a developer, it was your responsibility to ensure that all applications that shared the file definition had been updated.

CW Data Dictionaries actually contain several kinds of information. First, they hold your data file definitions. The dictionary editor lets you work with these definitions in a visual manner, adding fields and keys to complete the file definition. You do not need to worry about the details of how the file will be represented in source code, since the dictionary editor and AppGen will take care of that for you. The dictionary editor also lets you specify which file driver technology you will use for the data file. For the most part, CW's language statements that are used for data file processing do not change from one type of data file to the next. This means you can choose the type of file that best suits your needs, or you can easily use existing data files in various formats. For more information on database drivers, see Chapter 3, "Choosing Databases Wisely."

The dictionary editor is also a place to store some default rules about how the data will be treated. All fields have a picture token, which defines how they are displayed on screen and on reports. For example, the picture token @T4 indicates a time format of *hh:mm:ss*. You can indicate whether the field is to be uppercased, capitalized, or accepted as typed. You can set the typing mode to Insert, Overwrite, or as is, and you can specify alignment and indentation. You can even specify a Password attribute, which will display asterisks as you enter data, and the Read-only attribute, which will prevent users from changing the value in the field.

For each field in a data file, you can also specify Validity Checks. These include making the field required (it may not be zero or blank), verifying it is a numeric range, making it a check box or series of radio buttons, checking the field against a value in another file, and presenting the user with a list of available options in a drop-down list box.

NOTE

Most formatting and all validity check information is only for the benefit of the AppGen—it is not stored with the data file itself, and will not prevent someone else using another program from entering invalid data in the data file.

These are default settings only, and you can override them in the AppGen if you wish. In the interest of consistency and efficiency, however, it will pay you to work out what the correct picture tokens, entry options, and validity checks are so you don't have to modify them each time you place a field on a window.

Keys and Indexes

Once you have defined your fields, you can define keys and indexes. These are used to quickly retrieve data from files. In all but the smallest data files, it's far too time-consuming to read through a file record by record to find the information you want.

In CW, a key is updated whenever a record in the database changes. An index is updated only when the BUILD command is issued. Keys and indexes must be defined before the program runs. Dynamic indexes, on the other hand, can be created on-the-fly, but are accessible only to the program that creates them.

Relationships

You can also define relationships between data files. Now, to do this there must be some logical relationship between different files, and that presumes a reason for those relationships.

In most database applications there is the potential for duplication of information. For instance, let's say you're designing an address book application that has one file. The fields in the file contain name, street address, city, state/province, postal code, phone number, and so on. You've used Quick Start (which is discussed in Chapter 6, "Quick Start: The Two-Minute Application") so it only took you a few moments to create this application. You're filling in records and feeling pretty proud of yourself until you come to Uncle Henry and Aunt Marge, and you realize that they spend the summer in New York, the fall in Florida, the winter in the Bahamas, and the spring in San Diego. All of a sudden you're either going to have to put them in the database four times or add three more sets of address fields to the database.

You decide you don't want to add the fields because that would waste space on just about every record, so you go ahead and put them in four times. This works out just fine until Uncle Henry and Aunt Marge, in the throes of a dual midlife crisis, buy a couple Harleys and change their names to Rising Sun and Aurora Borealis. Since you've duplicated their names four times, you have to go back and change all four records. It would be a lot simpler if you could change the names just once and have it affect all the address records.

It's a principle of good database design that you should duplicate information as little as possible. In this example, what you really want to do is create one file for names and another for addresses and link them together. That way you have only one copy of the name information, and you can associate as many copies of the address information as you like. This is called a *many-to-one relationship.*

To accomplish this link, you'll associate a unique number with each name, and also add that number to each address record. Now you have an absolute minimum amount of duplicated information. The down side of this kind of arrangement is that you now have links between files which need to be maintained in order for the application to function properly.

The dictionary editor, in cooperation with the AppGen, can maintain these kinds of relationships for you. You define the keys that contain the linked fields, and then for each pair of files to be linked you specify which keys and which fields in the key are to be related. You also specify what actions are to be taken if you update or delete a "parent" record (in this example the parent would be a record in the names file).

> **NOTE**
>
> When defining links between files, you should, wherever possible, use fields that are not going to change. One good way of doing this is to have the AppGen create the code to assign sequential numbers to a link field on the parent record. You can do this in the dictionary editor by defining a key that has the link field as its only component and checking the Auto Number box on the Key Properties window. Since the field is automatically maintained, you do not need to (and in most cases should not) display it to the user at any time.

Maintaining links between fields is called *referential integrity,* or RI. In CW, although you define the rules in the dictionary editor, RI is maintained at the code level. The Application Generator writes code based on information in the Data Dictionary, and this code maintains the links. In a number of client/server systems, RI is also available in the database engine itself. This means that your code does not have to update the links between files, and in fact cannot override the

RI rules in the database engine. Engine-based RI has the advantage of enforcing the same rules for all users of the database, whatever the program accessing it tries to do. Code-based RI can perform the same job as engine-based RI, but also allows you a lower level of control over the database. You can, if you wish, override RI rules as needed.

CW actually lets you have it both ways, since some of its interchangeable file drivers can access client/server databases with engine-based RI.

As you can see, there is a lot of information that can go in the dictionary editor. You will use it not only to store files, but to maintain default information about how the fields in the files will be presented to the user, the keys and indexes that will be used to quickly locate data, and the links between related files. That's a lot to think about, and you're not even to the point where you're creating applications! But don't worry—you don't have to figure out all your data right away. CW is a true RAD system, and many developers find that their Data Dictionary evolves as much as their application over the course of development.

Now that you've had a taste of the dictionary editor, it's time to move on to where most of the action is—the Application Generator.

The Application Generator

In the simplest possible terms, the AppGen is a tool that greatly simplifies the task of programming by presenting you with a number of prompts, and generating CW code based on your responses and choices. In its most complex terms, the AppGen (shown in Figure 1.3) is a software-generating program running on your computer, to which you have the source code. In this section I'll discuss the AppGen in simple terms, but keep in mind that its real power lies in your ability to modify it to suit your own needs. As you'll see later, it really is an opportunity to clone your programming self.

One of the beauties of the AppGen is that you don't really need to know how it works to be productive. This is often considered to be a sign of mature technology. For instance, few of us really know how a computer works, yet this doesn't stop us from using them daily in productive ways. On the other hand, if you want to be as productive as you can be (and this is true even if you're a diehard hand coder) you will want to learn as much as you can about the Application Generator.

Let's start with some basics. First, whatever it means, the AppGen creates standard Clarion for Windows code. Any application you create with the AppGen can be duplicated, in hand code, by any programmer with more time and money than brains. There's nothing magical about the final result. The magic, if you wish to call it that, is the way the AppGen reduces the complexity of application development, and does away with the need for you, the programmer, to write repetitive code. This is done by means of a fully configurable set of templates, which are discussed shortly.

FIGURE 1.3.

The Application Generator.

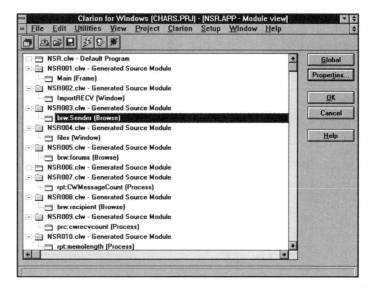

The Browse/Form Concept

Out of the box, the AppGen is geared toward (but by no means limited to) business applications. A typical business application deals with data files, hence the strong emphasis on the Data Dictionary. The AppGen also employs a particular paradigm for dealing with data files. As you navigate through a typical CW application you will encounter data files displayed in scrolling list boxes. You will normally use buttons labeled Add, Change, and Delete (or the keystrokes Ins, Shift+Enter, and Del) to update data file records. Updates will usually be done using a dialog box that appears when one of these buttons or keys is pressed, as shown in Figure 1.4.

Naturally, this is all under the control of the programmer, and you may see some quite unusual approaches to dealing with data files, but this approach is quite common and fairly intuitive. Other common types of procedures include the main menu, reports, and various dialog boxes that are not directly related to a data file, such as configuration or error message dialog boxes.

Another aspect of the AppGen's flexibility is the access it permits to the source code. If you wish, you can avoid looking at source code at all during the entire development process, but if you want to get under the hood and start tinkering, you can. The standard set of templates provide code embed points virtually anywhere you want.

In the event that simply adding a line or two of source code doesn't do the job, you also have the ability to create (or purchase) entirely new kinds of functionality for the AppGen, which is so configurable that adding a feature (such as user-definable control colors) can be as simple as copying a file to your template directory and clicking on a few buttons. (This can be done with template extensions—for more information see Chapter 20, "Creating Extension Templates.")

FIGURE 1.4.
An example of data file browse and update forms.

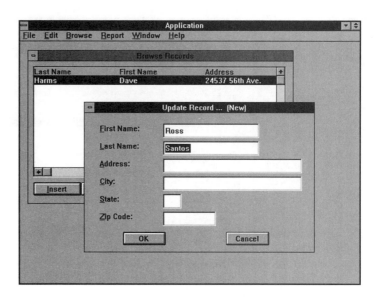

You can also use standard Windows dynamic link libraries (DLLs) and Visual Basic custom controls (VBXs) to add features such as graphing, spreadsheets, serial communications, and word processing. (DLLs and VBXs are covered in more detail in Chapter 26, "Using VBXs and Non-CW DLLs.")

To help you organize your application, the AppGen shows the application to you in outline or "tree" format. You can choose one of four views: Procedure view shows you a logical view of the calling hierarchy; Module view shows you a list of source modules with member procedures; Alphabetic view shows procedures only, in alphabetic order; and View by Template lists all templates used and the procedures that are based on them.

The AppGen also keeps track of all the source code modules it generates and knows how to make them into an EXE file. This information is called *project data*, and you'll learn a little more about it at the end of this chapter.

The Heart of the AppGen—The Template Language

All procedures created within the AppGen begin with a procedure template of one kind or another. A template is like a generic procedure with blanks for the specific information required for it to do some real work. All templates (and there are kinds other than procedure templates) begin life as readable source code, which is usually a combination of CW language statements and special template language statements. Yes, CW is two programming languages, and that's because just one won't do the job. The second language, the template language, is really a tool to write programs that create Clarion programs.

The template language, which is discussed in detail in Chapter 16, "Hand Code, Reuse, and the Application Generator," Chapter 17, "Creating Code Templates," Chapter 18, "Creating Procedure Templates," Chapter 19, "Creating Control Templates," and Chapter 20, has incredible potential for making you more productive and giving you increased control over code maintenance. Although you do not need to learn it to use CW, you will find it an invaluable addition to your programmer's toolbox if you make the effort.

The AppGen also makes use of some of CW's other standard tools. When you add some embedded source code to a procedure, you invoke the source editor. When you create a window or a report, you are invoking one of CW's resource formatters, which are visual design aids, and which are the subject of the next section.

The Source Code Editor and Resource Formatters

The source code editor is a programmer's editor with several special enhancements to support the CW environment. It is possible to create entire applications without using the source editor at all. It is more likely, however, that you will use it to edit source embed points. You may also write complete procedures and functions using the source code editor, and if you wish you can create your entire application here, although it will almost certainly take you far longer than if you use the AppGen.

There are times when it's appropriate to do a lot of coding in the editor. Small programs and utilities that do not do any standard AppGen-style file access (such as that be-all, end-all alarm clock program) are probably better choices for the source code editor. The development cycle is somewhat faster, since the AppGen imposes some overhead, as it must determine which of its source modules to generate. You may also be one of those programmers who does everything by hand out of sheer cussedness, in which case you may want to use CW in its "set of sharp knives" mode rather than in its "food processor" mode.

Configuring the CW Editor

The CW editor is user configurable. In your CW\BIN directory there is a file called CWEDT.INI, which contains a variety of settings by which you can tailor the editor to your particular way of working.

You can assign keyboard shortcuts for virtually all editing functions, from cursor navigation to Clipboard functions to menu options. If you get accustomed to your own twisted way of doing things, be sure to carry your CWEDT.INI file with you if you have to work on someone else's machine (but please, restore *their* INI file when you finish).

The CW editor also color-codes your source according to the values in the [color_map] and [color_values] sections. [color_map] contains the actual Windows color numbers for each of

32 different color groups, and [color_values] lists the color group to assign to the specified label or statement. If you wish, you can add to this list using the editor. To update the colors using the color dialog (which is rather more fun than figuring out colors by the numbers), choose Setup|Editor Options, and then press the Colors button. You will see the window presented in Figure 1.5.

FIGURE 1.5.

The Editor Color Settings window.

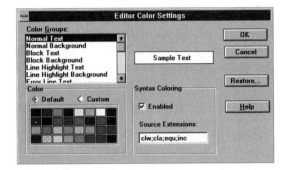

The source editor also contains two special functions—the Window Formatter and the Report Formatter.

The Window Formatter

Visual things are tough to design. Why? They aren't stored in the computer in the same way as they appear on the screen. Code statements are translated at runtime into graphic elements on the screen. If you had to write the code to actually display all those nice lines and chiseled buttons and create the entry controls and so on, you'd be wasting a lot of time.

Actually, in CW, writing the structures by hand isn't that difficult. A typical CW window structure is shown in Listing 1.1.

Listing 1.1. Source code for a window structure.

```
window          WINDOW('Search Parameters'),AT(45,26,198,102),GRAY
                   PROMPT('Forum:'),AT(13,8,,),USE(?g:SearchForum:Prompt)
                   ENTRY(@n_4),AT(69,8,24,10),USE(g:SearchForum),REQ
                   STRING(@s20),AT(97,8,,),USE(FRM:ForumName)
```

```
     CHECK('Case Sensitive Search'),AT(68,21,,),¦
        USE(g:CaseSensitiveSearch)
     PROMPT('Search String 1:'),AT(9,34,,),¦
        USE(?g:SearchString1:Prompt)
     ENTRY(@s20),AT(69,34,,10),USE(g:SearchString1),REQ
     PROMPT('Search String 2:'),AT(9,46,,),¦
        USE(?g:SearchString2:Prompt)
     ENTRY(@s20),AT(69,46,,10),USE(g:SearchString2)
     PROMPT('Search String 3:'),AT(9,58,,),¦
        USE(?g:SearchString3:Prompt)
     ENTRY(@s20),AT(69,58,,10),USE(g:SearchString3)
     BUTTON('Cancel'),AT(40,76,40,14),USE(?CancelButton)
     BUTTON('OK'),AT(120,76,40,14),USE(?OkButton),DEFAULT
   END
```

Figure 1.6 shows what this code translates into at runtime.

FIGURE 1.6 .

The window structure, as displayed at runtime.

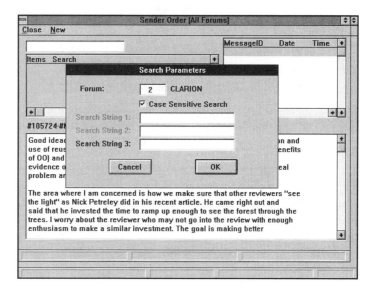

But why wait until it runs? If the program can figure out how to make it look at runtime, why can't the editor figure out how to make it look at design time? It can!

In fact, if you're in the AppGen you don't need to see the source code version at all. Whenever you want to look at the window, AppGen will show it to you in the formatter.

In the Window Formatter you can move controls, change properties, and generally configure the appearance and much of the behavior of your window. For more information on the individual kinds of controls that are built into CW, see Chapter 4, "Concepts You Should Know."

The Report Formatter

Reports, like windows, are difficult to create because they are also visual. So naturally there is a structure for reports and a Report Formatter. When you invoke the Report Formatter, you will see a window that looks like the one in Figure 1.7.

FIGURE 1.7.

The Report Formatter, in Band view.

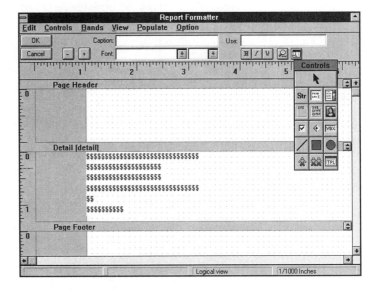

In its simplest form, each report consists of a page header, a pager footer, and one or more detail sections. Although this might suggest to you that you print a report in that order (header, detail lines, footer), in fact headers and footers are printed automatically whenever the page is printed, so you can actually wait until all of your detail lines have printed before putting information in the header or footer. This lets you do things such as put totals at the top of the page, if you wish.

If you're used to writing DOS reports where each line of the report gets fed to the printer in sequence, it may take you some time to get used to this page-oriented way of reporting. To assist you, the Report Formatter gives you two different views of the report. The one shown above is called the Band view, because it lets you see the logical "bands" of information that you will want to print. The other view is called the Page Layout view, shown in Figure 1.8, and it lets you see the report as it will come out of the printer. Both these views (and a Page Preview view) are available under the View menu. You will use Band view to help you group your information logically, and Page Layout view to ensure that the final appearance of the report is to your liking.

FIGURE 1.8.

The Report Formatter,
in Page Layout view.

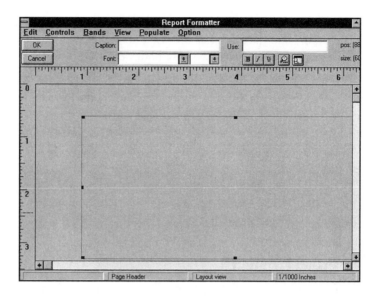

There are a number of similarities between the Report Formatter and the Window Formatter. The toolbars look much the same, with shortcut buttons and entry fields for quickly updating control attributes. There is also a floating toolbar for quick access to the various types of controls. You can place strings, fields, regions, check boxes, list boxes, even VBXs on reports the same way you place them on windows. Since you also have control over fonts and colors, you can make your reports just about as jazzy as you like.

As with the Window Formatter, the Report Formatter records your visual design in a structure. A simple report structure could look something like the following:

```
REP    REPORT,AT(1000,2500,6000,6000),THOUS
         HEADER,AT(1000,1000,6000,1000)
           STRING('My Report'),AT(2292,208,,),¦
             FONT('Arial Rounded MT Bold',28,0FFH,),USE(?String1)
         END
detail DETAIL
         END
         FOOTER,AT(1000,10000,6000,1000)
           STRING('Page No:'),AT(2292,313,,),USE(?String2)
           STRING(@n3),AT(2917,313,,),USE(ndx)
         END
         FORM,AT(1000,1000,6000,9000)
         END
       END
```

Like window structures, report structures are, for the most part, not intended to be edited directly. Once you become familiar with the code used to build reports, however, you may find it to your advantage to make certain kinds of changes. For instance, if you have a large number of currency fields in your report, and you change your mind about how you want to format those fields, it's much easier to change them by doing a simple search and replace than by loading the report into the formatter and going to each field individually. With both the source and the formatter, you have the best of both worlds.

Both resource formatters can be invoked within the source code editor, and are also called in AppGen whenever you select Window or Report on the Procedure Properties window. If you call the formatter from the editor, however, you will not have access to the templates and you will not be able to populate controls with fields from data files, since the editor on its own does not have any connection to the Data Dictionary or the template system.

You have seen how the AppGen and template language, together with the dictionary editor and the resource formatters, can enable you to create powerful applications in a minimum amount of time. There remains, however, another component of the environment without which it would be impossible to actually create a working program.

The Project System

All CW programs start off as one or more source modules, which are compiled into object code, which is linked with library code and made into a working Windows program. This business of making sure all the bits are there and that they all interconnect is the job of the Project System.

Although the Project System is a vital part of CW, it's entirely possible for you to create applications without ever being aware of its presence. If you work exclusively in AppGen, the project information is updated each time you create a new procedure, select a file that uses a new driver, or change the target of you application from an EXE to, say, a DLL. It's quite likely that this automatic operation of the Project System will serve you well, but, as with other features of CW, such as the resource formatters, sometimes it's to your advantage to know how to get under the hood.

Whenever you click on the Make, Debug, or Run icons, or choose the equivalent commands from the menu, you invoke the Project Manager. The project manager works on the basis of an application-specific project file, which contains a series of instructions specifying the process to use to make the destination file (EXE, LIB, or DLL). In the case of applications, this project file is embedded in the APP, so you won't be able to view it using an ASCII editor. For hand-coded applications, the project information is kept in a separate ASCII file, which usually has the same name as the main source module, but ends in .PRJ.

The project information embedded in an application might look something like Listing 1.2.

Listing 1.2. A sample of the project data embedded in an application file.

```
#noedit
#system win
#model clarion
#pragma debug(vid=>full)
```

```
#compile maprlgon.clw
#compile maprpptb.clw
#compile maprtime.clw
#compile maprlkup.clw
#compile maprmisc.clw
#compile maprattr.clw
#compile MAPRSTD.clw /define(GENERATED=>on)
#compile MAPRS001.clw /define(GENERATED=>on)
#compile MAPRS002.clw /define(GENERATED=>on)
#compile MAPRS003.clw /define(GENERATED=>on)
#compile MAPRS004.clw /define(GENERATED=>on)
#compile MAPRS005.clw /define(GENERATED=>on)
#compile MAPRS006.clw /define(GENERATED=>on)
#pragma link(CWc21.lib)
#pragma link(CWBTRV.lib)
#pragma link(mgstd.lib)
#link maprstd.dll
```

As you can see, much of the project information is instructions to compile various source modules (note that these will automatically be conditional compiles). Additionally, there will be instructions regarding the overall structure of the final program—how it will use memory, whether it will contain code to assist the Debugger in its job, and so on. At the bottom of the list you will see references to several libraries (the files ending in .LIB). Libraries are precompiled collections of code that may be required for the program's operation—in this case, several of the lines refer to the file driver libraries for Clarion and Btrieve data files.

As with Window and Report Formatters, it turns out that there is an easier way to view this information. CW provides a project editor that presents that textual information in a much friendlier manner. Figure 1.9 shows the project information from Listing 1.1, but as presented by the project editor.

FIGURE 1.9.

The project editor.

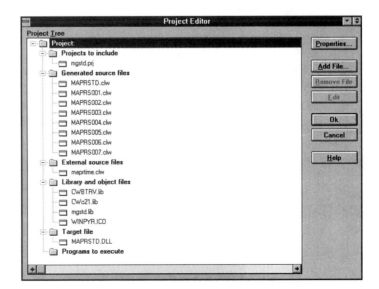

As you can see, the project editor is a somewhat friendlier way to view this information. It enables you to update the properties of the various components of the project. For instance, to prepare the program for debugging you will need to instruct the Project System to include certain debug information in the EXE. To do this in the project editor, you simply select Project, click on Properties, and choose, say, Full Debug. The result will be that the text `#pragma debug(vid=>full)` is inserted in your project. Of course, it's a little easier to click on a few buttons than to try to remember the syntax of that command.

The Redirection File

There is one other important aspect of the Project System that you should look at now: the Redirection File. In a typical development environment, the various files needed by the system are usually grouped by function. All the library code will usually be kept in one directory, the common source code in another, object code somewhere else, and so on. In order to keep track of both where these files are and where they should be placed, CW uses its redirection file, CW.RED. If you've installed CW on the C: drive, in the default directory, your CW.RED will probably look something like Listing 1.3.

Listing 1.3. The default CW.RED redirection file.

```
*.dbd = C:\CW\OBJ
*.dll = C:\CW\BIN
*.lib = C:\CW\OBJ;C:\CW\LIB
*.obj = C:\CW\OBJ;C:\CW\LIB
*.rsc = C:\CW\OBJ
*.tpl = C:\CW\TEMPLATE
*.tpw = C:\CW\TEMPLATE
*.trf = C:\CW\TEMPLATE
*.* = .; C:\CW\EXAMPLES;C:\CW\LIBSRC
QCKSTART.TXA = C:\CW\TEMPLATE
QCKSTART.TXD = C:\CW\TEMPLATE
```

Each line in the redirection file begins with a file spec, and is followed by one or more directories that will be searched, in sequence, for any files matching that file spec. If the file is to be created, it will be placed in the first directory specified for its matching file spec.

If you manually move your CW installation to a new directory, you will have to edit the redirection file to account for the new locations of CW-related files.

NOTE

For more information on the Project System, see Chapter 11, "From Here to EXE: The Project System."

Registries

Registries are places where CW keeps track of changing information. There's no such thing as a compiler registry or a linker registry, because in each case there is only one of these and it comes with CW when you buy it. On the other hand, some components of the development environment may change as you make your own modifications or purchase products from third-party suppliers.

Template Registry

Since the templates determine the behavior of the application generator, one of the easiest ways to change the way your applications look (assuming you use the AppGen) is to change the templates. If you buy or create a template, you make it available to the environment by placing it in the template registry, which is shown in Figure 1.10.

FIGURE 1.10.

The template registry, with the standard template set registered.

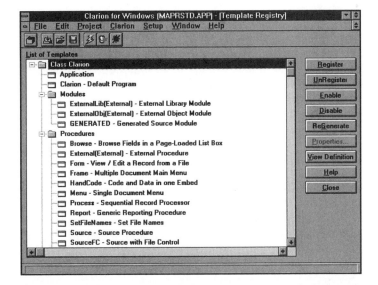

In fact, templates never get used by the AppGen as straight source. When you register a template, it is stored inside the registry, along with all other templates that have been previously registered. This is to ensure that a syntax check is made on the templates before they are used, and to provide faster access by the AppGen.

NOTE

The template registry is a TopSpeed-format file, which makes for much faster access than the ASCII files the templates are stored in.

> **TIP**
>
> If you inadvertently delete your templates, you can have the template registry regenerate them. You can also make changes to the templates inside the registry, and have those changes appear in the templates when they are regenerated.

VBX Registry

VBX is an abbreviation (of sorts) for Visual Basic custom control. VBXs are controls, in the same way that list boxes, prompts, buttons, text boxes, and the like are controls. In fact, there are a number of VBXs available that may be quite similar to standard CW controls. The really interesting VBXs, of course, are those that provide some unique functionality, such as spreadsheets, or word processing, or electronic mail. VBXs are an easy way to add such features to your CW program.

Support for VBXs is not only built into the Clarion language, it's part of the AppGen as well. In order for the AppGen to treat a VBX similarly to how it treats its own controls, it has to know which ones are available. It's up to you, the programmer, to give the AppGen that information by registering your VBXs.

Registration is a simple process—you choose Setup|VBX Custom Control Registry, and add your controls to the list. As each control is registered, CW will read the VBX and obtain information about its properties. The VBX is then available for use within the AppGen—you place it on windows (and reports) in much the same way that you place standard CW controls.

Generally, VBXs are not as tightly integrated into AppGen as are native controls. If you are defining a file in the dictionary, you can specify which type of control will be used to represent that data in AppGen. If you want to use a VBX to represent some data, you will need to do this in AppGen by placing the VBX on your window and then supplying some VBX property information, usually in the form of embedded source code.

> **TIP**
>
> It is possible to create control template "wrappers" for VBXs. Many VBXs have a large number of properties, some of which may take standard settings in CW, and some of which you may not need at all. Rather than repetitively specifying property information, you may find it convenient to use a control template with standard property information already preset, and the remaining information in template prompts. If you are not of a mind to write your own control templates, you should contact the VBX vendor. Third-party CW developers may also sell control templates for some of the more popular VBXs. Several such vendors are listed in the Appendix.

To be used with CW, VBXs must conform to what is known as the *Level 1 specification*. This is not as onerous as it might seem—CW uses the same interface to VBXs that C++ uses, so you have the same functionality available to you as all C++ programmers do. When purchasing VBXs, you should ask about C++ compatibility, since many VBX vendors are unfamiliar with the term "Level 1."

Database Registry

The registries, as you have seen, are places where CW keeps track of information crucial to the operation of the system, but that might change between releases. Database drivers also fall into this category.

To view the registry, select Setup|Database Driver Registry. As you can see in Figure 1.11, this is a simple list much like the VBX registry. The following drivers ship with CW version 1.0: ASCII, Basic (delimited ASCII), Btrieve, Clarion, Clipper, dBASE III, dBASE 4, DOS (binary), FoxPro, ODBC, and TopSpeed.

FIGURE 1.11.

The database driver registry.

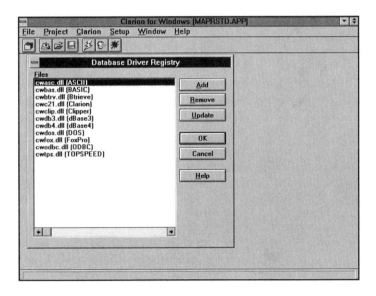

Before you can use a particular type of database, its driver must be in the registry. If it is not in the registry, it will not appear in the dictionary editor's drop-down list of drivers. Driver information is also used by the Project System to know what libraries to include so that your final EXE file contains all the code necessary to process your chosen file types.

TopSpeed sells drivers that do not ship with the base product. For instance, there is an AS/400 driver available, with several other SQL drivers in development (they quite possibly will be shipping by the time you read this).

There is a driver development kit available from TopSpeed, so if you wish to support your own file format using CW, you can do so. There may also be third-party developers providing drivers for other less-common formats. Contact TopSpeed for up-to-date information on file drivers.

The Formula Generator

The formula generator is a tool that assists you in writing CW language expressions and then stores those expressions by name for use throughout the application. For instance, if you have a file of personnel information that contains first and last name fields, and you frequently display this information in browse boxes as *last name, first name,* you may wish to define a formula so you don't have to write the code each time you want to accomplish this.

You can then have this formula automatically computed at specific times, such as each time a record is loaded into the browse box. The formula editor also includes an optional syntax checker, which can help ensure that your code is error free before you compile and run your application.

The Debugger

The Debugger is a separate program from the CW IDE, and it is a powerful tool for those times when you write that less-than-stellar code, or when you have to clean up after someone else. When you debug a program, CW invokes the Debugger first, and the Debugger then runs your program under its own control. The Debugger lets you step through your program a line at a time, if you wish. You can also set in you code *break points,* which are places where the Debugger halts program execution so you can examine the state of the program or its data. These break points can be conditional, if you like, and you can write expressions in the Debugger to determine what the condition will be.

You can also be selective about which parts of your program you wish to debug. In order for the Debugger to peer inside your code, you must include debug information at compile time, and this setting can be determined for the program as a whole, or for individual source modules. All you need to do is "flip the switch," and the Project System will automatically include the level of debug information you specify. The Debugger is covered in detail in Chapter 12, "Testing and Debugging."

Summary

CW is more than just a programming tool—it is a complete development environment with a wide range of tools covering just about every level of programming. It is built around an elegant and powerful programming language that produces compact, lightning-fast code. It has resource formatters that give you a visual way to design your windows and reports, without taking away the ability to work with those structures at the source level.

CW's Application Generator and revolutionary template language automate the most complex of programming tasks, again without taking away your ability to get down and dirty with the source, if that's your choice. CW also has a comprehensive Project System that allows you to easily manage large projects, and create EXEs, LIBs, and Windows DLLs. It gives you access to the huge VBX market, and through its database driver technology it gives you the ability to mix and match database files of various types within your application.

I believe that CW is the most complete, most flexible, and most powerful Windows development tool on the market at this time. I trust that the following chapters will bear this out.

2

Choosing a Development Style

Now that you've had an overview of the CW programming environment, you need to decide how to use it. While many application development systems provide a single method for creating Windows programs, CW offers you a wide spectrum of options. To help identify these options, this chapter begins with a discussion of the two ends of the spectrum: traditional programming using the CW language, and visual application design and development using the Application Generator (AppGen).

Traditional programming means working with the Clarion language directly. You write the code statements using the source editor, but you don't use the dictionary editor or AppGen. Every line of code (excluding any libraries you use) comes out of your own knowledge of programming in CW.

Programming exclusively with the AppGen does not *require* any knowledge of the Clarion programming language. Instead, you design your applications visually, and the AppGen creates the source code for you.

The following section shows the benefits and drawbacks of these two approaches, and the remainder of the chapter helps you define the particular blend that will best suit your development needs.

Option One: The Hand Code Style

Since time immemorial (well, at least since the introduction of Clarion 2.1), there have been two kinds of programmers in the world: those who use application generation tools and those who don't. The latter have traditionally been referred to, among Clarion aficionados, as *hand coders*. And it's fair to say that hand coders have enjoyed a certain reputation (if not always deserved) in the programming community as generally being more knowledgeable and more experienced than those who used application generation tools. After all, Clarion was originally just a hand coder's language.

Learning the language does have a certain appeal. Because you have full control over the code, your program can do anything the language is capable of. You have no restrictions, and you are not forced to live with anyone else's idea of how an application should look or behave (except, of course, the designer of the language itself).

If you're a hand coder, you're probably someone who likes to "get under the hood." You like to work out new ways of doing code. You like to feel the bits flowing from your fingertips. And as this section illustrates, CW lets you do all that. If you're not a hand coder, and the thought of reading source code makes your knees weak, relax. No one's going to force you to learn code. But please read on anyway—there are some tremendous benefits to be had from knowing how to hand code, and you may just see something that sparks your interest.

Hello, World

It's traditional for any discussion of a programming language to begin with a program that says to the world, in one way or another, "Hello." Don't ask me why. It's just one of those things that we all do, like not talking in elevators. Keeping with tradition, Listing 2.1 presents a CW version of the "Hello, World" program.

Listing 2.1. The CW "Hello, World" program.

```
PROGRAM

w_HelloWorld WINDOW('Hello, World')
     END

 CODE
 OPEN(w_HelloWorld)
 ACCEPT
 END
```

This is not going to be a lesson in using the Clarion language. That all happens in Chapter 14, "Hand-Crafted Code Defined." This chapter is about choosing a development strategy, and to that end you should have some idea of what CW source code looks like.

If you run Listing 2.1 (ignoring for the moment the steps required to do that), you will see the window shown in Figure 2.1.

FIGURE 2.1.

The CW "Hello, World" program in action.

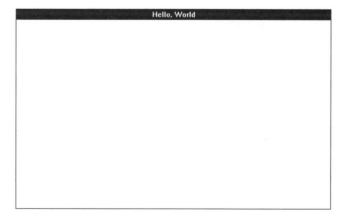

If you've programmed in other Windows languages, you may find Listing 2.1 somewhat deceptive. If you haven't programmed in Windows, you should know that you're looking at one of the most compact "Hello, World" programs on the planet. A comparable program in C can take over 50 lines of code and reads to the uninitiated like a treatise on quantum physics.

The thing that's deceptive is that size, in CW, is no indication of strength. The language is as expressive as it is compact. While it manages a lot of Windows' complexity for you, it does not prevent you from taking advantage of that complexity either, if you really want to. If you're currently a hand coder using a language other than CW, with CW you stand to become considerably more productive, simply because the tedious bits of Windows programming have already been taken care of for you.

Now, in practice, few programs are going to be only a couple lines long. For one thing, this is a pretty large and fairly ugly window to use just to display two words. It also doesn't have any obvious way of exiting the program, although you can get out by pressing the Esc key. A more appropriate version of the "Hello, World" program might look something like what is presented in Listing 2.2.

Listing 2.2. A more sophisticated "Hello, World" program.

```
PROGRAM

  include('equates.clw')

w_HelloWorld WINDOW('Hello, World'),AT(74,29,95,47),GRAY,DOUBLE,SYSTEM
       BUTTON('&Goodbye, World'),AT(13,17,,14),USE(?exit)
     END

 CODE
 OPEN(w_HelloWorld)
 ACCEPT
   CASE FIELD()
   OF ?exit
     CASE EVENT()
     OF EVENT:accepted
       break
     END
   END
 END
 RETURN
```

If you've done some Windows programming, you will start to notice some familiar elements in this listing, such as the use of attributes to determine the position and appearance of controls (in this case, a button). (Controls are discussed in detail in Chapter 4, "Concepts You Should Know.") There is also a mechanism called the ACCEPT loop to detect events (and this is also discussed in Chapter 4).

Even if you're not familiar with Windows programming, you can probably follow what's happening here. Near the top of the listing are several lines, the first of which begins with the label w_HelloWorld. These describe a window and its associated button control. There is a CODE statement, which marks the end of the data declarations and the beginning of program code. The next line opens the window, and the following code is a loop that terminates when the button is pressed. When the loop terminates, the program ends.

Real-World Coding

Again, although this is a more reasonable bit of code, it doesn't begin to approach the level of complexity of even a small application. A more typical scenario would show your source code split up over a number of modules (source code files), with one or more procedures (functions) per file. One of those procedures would contain a main menu, and the others might be used to display records from data files, update those records, generate reports, show graphical information, and so on. Listing 2.3 shows a source module containing an update procedure, which is used to add, change, or delete a record from a file. In this case it is called from a browse procedure, which displays a list of the records in the data file.

Listing 2.3. A source module containing a procedure for adding or updating data file records.

```
MEMBER('SAMPLE.clw')           ! This is a MEMBER module
UpdateProc PROCEDURE
LocalRequest           LONG,AUTO
OriginalRequest        LONG,AUTO
LocalResponse          LONG,AUTO
WindowOpened           LONG,AUTO
ForceRefresh           LONG,AUTO
ActionMessage          STRING(40),AUTO
RecordChanged          BYTE,AUTO
AppendedTitle          STRING(40),AUTO
SaveBuffer::NAM:Record STRING(SIZE(NAM:Record))
Label                  WINDOW('Update Record ...')¦
 ,AT(,,290,176),FONT('MS Sans Serif',8,,)¦
 ,CENTER,STATUS,SYSTEM,GRAY,MDI
PROMPT('&First Name:'),AT(14,16,,),¦
                       USE(?NAM:FirstName:Prompt)
                       ENTRY(@S20),AT(52,16,,),USE(NAM:FirstName)
                       PROMPT('&Last Name:'),AT(14,32,,),¦
                        USE(?NAM:LastName:Prompt)
                       ENTRY(@S20),AT(52,32,,),USE(NAM:LastName)
                       PROMPT('&Address:'),AT(14,48,,),¦
                        USE(?NAM:Address:Prompt)
                       ENTRY(@S30),AT(52,48,,),USE(NAM:Address)
                       PROMPT('&City:'),AT(14,64,,),USE(?NAM:City:Prompt)
                       ENTRY(@S30),AT(52,64,,),USE(NAM:City)
                       PROMPT('&State:'),AT(14,80,,),USE(?NAM:State:Prompt)
                       ENTRY(@S2),AT(52,80,,),USE(NAM:State)
                       PROMPT('&Home Phone:'),AT(14,96,,),¦
                        USE(?NAM:HomePhone:Prompt)
                       ENTRY(@S15),AT(52,96,,),USE(NAM:HomePhone)
                       PROMPT('&Work Phone:'),AT(14,112,,),¦
                        USE(?NAM:WorkPhone:Prompt)
                       ENTRY(@S15),AT(52,112,,),USE(NAM:WorkPhone)
                       STRING(@s40),AT(123,144,,),USE(ActionMessage),CENTER
                       BUTTON('OK'),AT(5,144,45,15),USE(?OK),DEFAULT
                       BUTTON('Cancel'),AT(59,144,45,15),USE(?Cancel)
                     END
  CODE
  LocalRequest = GlobalRequest
  OriginalRequest = GlobalRequest
```

continues

Listing 2.3. continued

```
LocalResponse = RequestCancelled
CLEAR(GlobalRequest)
CLEAR(GlobalResponse)
IF names::Used = 0
  CheckOpen(names,1)
END
names::Used += 1
OPEN(Label)
WindowOpened=True
INIRestoreWindow('UpdateProc')
CASE LocalRequest
OF InsertRecord
  ActionMessage = 'Record will be Added'
OF ChangeRecord
  ActionMessage = 'Record will be Changed'
OF DeleteRecord
  ActionMessage = 'Record will be Deleted'
END
SaveBuffer::NAM:Record = NAM:Record
CASE LocalRequest
OF ChangeRecord
OROF DeleteRecord
OF InsertRecord
  DO PrimeFields
  AppendedTitle = 'New'
END
ACCEPT
  CASE EVENT()
  OF Event:CloseWindow
    IF LocalResponse <> RequestCompleted
      RecordChanged = False
      IF LocalRequest = InsertRecord OR LocalRequest = ChangeRecord
        IF SaveBuffer::NAM:Record <> NAM:Record
          RecordChanged = True
        END
      END
      IF RecordChanged
        CASE StandardWarning(WRN:ConfirmCancel)
        OF Button:Yes
          SELECT(FIRSTFIELD())
          SELECT()
          CYCLE
        OF Button:No
        OF BUTTON:Cancel
          SELECT(FIRSTFIELD())
          CYCLE
        END
      END
    END
  OF Event:CloseDown
    IF LocalResponse <> RequestCompleted
      RecordChanged = False
      IF LocalRequest = InsertRecord OR LocalRequest = ChangeRecord
        IF SaveBuffer::NAM:Record <> NAM:Record
          RecordChanged = True
        END
      END
      IF RecordChanged
```

```
        CASE StandardWarning(WRN:ConfirmCancel)
        OF Button:Yes
          LocalResponse = RequestCompleted
          SELECT(FIRSTFIELD())
          SELECT()
          CYCLE
        OF Button:No
        OF BUTTON:Cancel
          SELECT(FIRSTFIELD())
          CYCLE
        END
      END
    END
  OF Event:OpenWindow
    DO RefreshWindow
    SELECT(FIRSTFIELD())
  OF Event:GainFocus
    ForceRefresh = True
    DO RefreshWindow
  ELSE
    IF EVENT() = Event:Completed
      CASE LocalRequest
      OF InsertRecord
        ADD(names)
        CASE ERRORCODE()
        OF NoError
          LocalResponse = RequestCompleted
          POST(Event:CloseWindow)
        ELSE
          IF StandardWarning(WRN:InsertError,ERROR())
            SELECT(FIRSTFIELD())
            CYCLE
          END
        END
      OF ChangeRecord
        LOOP
          LocalResponse = RequestCancelled
          IF RIUpdate:names(SaveBuffer::NAM:Record)
            CASE StandardWarning(WRN:UpdateError)
            OF Button:Yes
              CYCLE
            OF Button:No
              POST(Event:CloseWindow)
              BREAK
            OF Button:Cancel
              SELECT(FirstField())
              BREAK
            END
          ELSE
            LocalResponse = RequestCompleted
            POST(Event:CloseWindow)
          END
          BREAK
        END
      OF DeleteRecord
        LOOP
          LocalResponse = RequestCancelled
          IF RIDelete:names()
```

continues

Listing 2.3. continued

```
              CASE StandardWarning(WRN:DeleteError)
              OF Button:Yes
                CYCLE
              OF Button:No
                POST(Event:CloseWindow)
                BREAK
              OF Button:Cancel
                SELECT(FirstField())
                BREAK
              END
            ELSE
              LocalResponse = RequestCompleted
              POST(Event:CloseWindow)
            END
            BREAK
          END
        END
      END
    END
    CASE FIELD()
    OF ?ActionMessage
      CASE EVENT()
      OF Event:Accepted
        ForceRefresh = True
        DO RefreshWindow
        LocalRequest = OriginalRequest
      END
    OF ?OK
      CASE EVENT()
      OF Event:Accepted
        ForceRefresh = True
        DO RefreshWindow
        LocalRequest = OriginalRequest
        SELECT(FIRSTFIELD())
        SELECT()
      END
    OF ?Cancel
      CASE EVENT()
      OF Event:Accepted
        ForceRefresh = True
        DO RefreshWindow
        LocalRequest = OriginalRequest
        LocalResponse = RequestCancelled
        POST(Event:CloseWindow)
      END
    END
  END
  names::Used -= 1
  IF names::Used = 0 THEN CLOSE(names).
  IF LocalResponse
    GlobalResponse = LocalResponse
  ELSE
    GlobalResponse = RequestCancelled
  END
  IF WindowOpened
    INISaveWindow('UpdateProc')
    CLOSE(Label)
  END
```

```
  RETURN
!- - - - - - - - - - - - - - - - - - - - - - - - - - - - - - - - - - - - - - - - - - - - - - - - - - - - - - - - - - - -
RefreshWindow ROUTINE
  DISPLAY()
  ForceRefresh = False
!- - - - - - - - - - - - - - - - - - - - - - - - - - - - - - - - - - - - - - - - - - - - - - - - - - - - - - - - - - - -
PrimeFields ROUTINE
  NAM:Record = SaveBuffer::NAM:Record
```

At runtime, the window associated with this procedure looks like the one shown in Figure 2.2.

FIGURE 2.2.

The update procedure from Listing 2.3, at runtime.

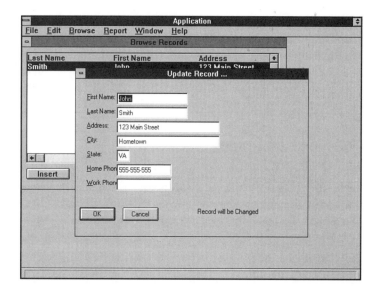

Much of the code in this procedure, as with many CW procedures, is taken up with responding to user actions such as pressing buttons or entering data. What you don't see is all of the code to handle standard Windows functionality, such as repainting the window if the user moves it, or setting a whole bunch of default values, or any of the myriad of tedious housekeeping tasks that Windows ordinarily imposes on the programmer. The CW runtime library, which is contained in the CWRUN10.DLL file that you ship with your application, handles all of this.

In a typical application, where a number of files need to be updated by the user, there might be a number of similar update procedures. As you add controls, and their associated code (such as entry validation or lookups on other files), the individual procedure will grow in size, but only incrementally—you'll simply have more procedures doing (probably) similar kinds of things.

Browse procedures, which display data file records in scrolling lists, can range from the very simple, where all the records that are to be displayed are loaded into a list box, to the complex, where only those records that can be displayed on the screen at any one time are actually loaded into the list box, and additional records are read from the disk (and discarded) as the user scrolls.

A browse of this type might take in the neighborhood of 300 to 500 lines (6 to 10 pages) of code to write, with about half of that being required for the actual paging of data from the data file.

There is, of course, no limit to the kinds of procedures you can create with CW, but the preceding example of browses and update forms is intended to give you some idea of the amount of code required to create this functionality.

Pros of Hand Coding

If you're a hand coder, the only thing standing between you and the ultimate Windows program is you. It will be as good a program as you can write. As long as you have the knowledge and the skill, you can create a program that fits your needs in the best way possible. You can be assured that you're writing the smallest, fastest possible version of the program. You can also walk around with a smug look on your face and call yourself a hand coder, and hopefully get lots of respect from other hand coders, if from no one else.

Cons of Hand Coding

Hand coding is not all peaches and cream, however. As long as you're working with a bunch of source files, you don't have any way of visually organizing your application (unless you use a third-party charting program or you pin 3×5 cards to your bulletin board). You will also need to maintain all your global data definitions (primarily data files) by hand, and you will have to establish your own procedures for enforcing referential integrity. (See Chapter 1, "Introduction to the Development Environment.")

Possibly the most serious problem with hand coding is code duplication. In just about any application there will be procedures and functions that are very much like each other, but not so much alike that one will serve a given purpose as well as the other. As a hand coder, you will end up duplicating some, if not much, of your code. In Listing 2.3, for instance, there is a considerable amount of code that stays the same, no matter which file is being updated or which controls are on the window. If you discover a bug in some common code, you will have to go to each instance of that code to apply the fix.

Code reuse (which is discussed in detail in Chapter 16, "Hand Code, Reuse, and the Application Generator") has long been an issue for programmers. It is not, however, a concern for users of the AppGen, since they have a code reuse solution built in.

Option Two: The AppGen Style

More developers use the AppGen than don't. It's a fact. And the reason they use it is because they can be phenomenally productive with it. It's become a bit of a joke among CW programmers that you can create an application and get it running while other Windows development environments are still loading, and there's some truth to that.

The AppGen is built around the notion of there being common elements in just about all kinds of programs. For instance, the example of hand code in the first part of this chapter describes an application that uses a number of update forms, and that much of the code for these forms is duplicated each time a form is created.

The AppGen knows about things such as database files, forms, browses, reports, menus, and so on. When you do application development using the AppGen, you decide how you want these various elements to appear and interrelate, and the AppGen goes about creating the required source code.

The AppGen, in its as-shipped configuration, lends itself to one particular approach to application development. Note the use of the term *as-shipped*. The AppGen is highly configurable, to the point where you could conceivably use it to generate code for virtually any type of program and in a wide variety of languages. As shipped, it is best suited to developing business and database applications. As the final section of this chapter explains, this is not a situation you need to worry about.

If you are a typical CW developer, you will spend at least some of your time developing applications that use data files. (This is probably getting to be a tired refrain by now, but you are not limited to this type of application. It is simply what CW comes preconfigured to do, and you can alter it to suit your purposes, often with very little effort.) To work with data files, you need to define the structure of those data files, and you do that in the Data Dictionary, as described in Chapter 1 and Chapter 3, "Choosing Databases Wisely." Having defined your data files, at least roughly (you can always go back and change them later), your next step will normally be to begin defining your application's procedures.

Many of the AppGen's standard procedure types and program elements are designed to work with data files. The Select Procedure Type window, which appears whenever you create a new procedure in the AppGen, lists some 10 different base procedure types. (See Figure 2.3.)

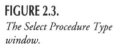

FIGURE 2.3.

The Select Procedure Type window.

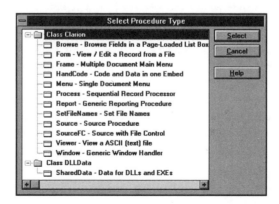

Of these procedure types, browse, form, report, and process are all designed to work with database files of one description or another (as discussed in Chapter 1, CW can access a wide variety of different database file formats). Browse procedures and form procedures, in fact, are often paired. The browse procedure, which is called from a menu item, will present a scrolling list of database records and will call an update form when the user wishes to add, change, or delete a record. Again, this is by no means the only way this kind of file maintenance can be accomplished, but it has been provided for in the standard configuration, and it is something of a tradition for Clarion application development tools.

Of the remaining procedure types, one (external) provides for the inclusion of library code (in the form of OBJs, LIBs, or DLLs), two (frame and menu) provide types of menus, another (source) allows for the inclusion of straight Clarion code, one (viewer) is a general-purpose ASCII file browser, and the last (window) is a generic window procedure.

In fact, almost every one of the procedure types is simply an enhanced generic window type, prepopulated with the appropriate window controls, such as buttons, list boxes, and so on. These procedure types have been placed in the system because they are frequently used in business and database applications, which is Clarion's traditional (though not only) market. There is nothing in CW to prevent it, at any time, from shipping with additional base procedure types such as serial communications, business graphics, or word processing.

Just about any procedure that you create with the AppGen will require a certain amount of information from you. It might be something fairly simple, such as the definition of several menu items and the procedures they call. You might also need to specify which file is to be used in that procedure, which fields from that file are to be displayed (and where), or what action is to be taken on records in that file. The vast majority of this information will be presented to you in the form of check boxes, pick lists (drop-down list boxes, usually), or dialog boxes of one sort or another (such as the font dialog box, which allows you to assign any font on your system to any text element in a CW program). When you have "filled in the blanks" to your satisfaction, you need only choose the Run command, and the AppGen will conditionally generate any needed code, then compile, link, and run the application. Depending on the nature of the changes, the speed of your hardware, and the size of the application, this may take only a few seconds or a few minutes.

Because the AppGen uses a number of well-tested, predefined components to build applications, most of the errors you encounter will not be coding errors, in the usual sense, but usage errors. You may place an inappropriate value somewhere on a dialog box, or choose an inappropriate control for the purpose you intend. Although there are many kinds of error-checking devices built into the AppGen, creating applications is by no means foolproof. The learning curve (to productivity, at any rate) for AppGen is considerably shallower than for the Clarion language itself, and far, far better than for a language such as C++.

Pros of Using the AppGen

Because the AppGen writes source code for you, it enables you to be productive almost immediately. Visual design tools help you not only create procedures but also see the relationships between procedures that call each other. With its default orientation toward the use of database files, CW is particularly well suited to creating business and other data file–related applications.

Cons of Using the AppGen

The AppGen is also no substitute for good program design. True, it will create some pretty stable source code for you, but it's still possible to put all that good stuff together in the wrong way. It will enable a good programmer to create good programs in a shorter period of time, and it will enable bad programmers to create bad programs, also in a shorter period of time.

The most serious criticism of the AppGen springs from its greatest benefit, however. Because it writes code for you, it may not write that code in exactly the way you want it to. Happily, there is a ready answer to that question (actually, the answers are many), and that is the subject of the final section of this chapter.

Choosing a Path

It is highly unlikely that you will choose to be either a pure hand coder or a pure AppGenner, although there are circumstances in which one or the other approach is quite appropriate.

Pure Hand Code

If you are writing very small programs, such as utilities, which have a limited number of procedures and almost no duplicated data, there are some real advantages to working entirely in the source editor. The AppGen, for all its benefits (and because of all its benefits) does impose some overhead. Each time you make a change to the application, the program module is ordinarily regenerated (though this is also configurable), meaning that even if nothing in your program module has changed, a certain amount of time will be lost. And if you're a meat-eating hand coder who sleeps on a bed of nails, you probably work right through your coffee breaks anyway.

Pure hand code is also very specific code. The AppGen is designed to handle a wide range of possibilities, which means that sometimes it generates code that, strictly speaking, it could probably do without. As this chapter shows, however, making assumptions about what the AppGen can and can't do is a fool's game, so it's probably best not to pursue that objection any further.

Pure AppGen

If your needs are quite simple, and CW in its standard configuration does all that you could ask or want, then there's absolutely no need to deal with hand code in any form. If you got along in Clarion 2.1 or Clarion for DOS 3.x without resorting to hand code, then you have every reason to expect that you can do the same in CW.

The AppGen and Source Embeds

If you've looked at the first two paths, pure hand code and pure AppGen, and you've realized that neither one is quite what you're looking for, then the next option you should consider is the use of source embed points.

One of the biggest complaints about the first version of Clarion that had an application design tool (Clarion 2.1 introduced Designer, which is discussed in Chapter 1) was its lack of extensibility. It was great to have a tool that wrote code for you, but more often than not the problem was that it didn't write enough code. Perhaps you wanted to add some interesting bit of functionality to a screen, but there was no way to plug in your own source code if you wanted to keep your application within the application design tool, anyway.

CW (and its predecessor, Clarion for DOS) solved this problem by providing for numerous source embed points throughout the application's procedures. This makes it possible for you to hang your snippets of code just about anywhere in any procedure you please. There are embed points when procedures start and when they end. Everything on a window that could get clicked on or tabbed to or have something entered in it has a set of embed points, one for each action that might take place. Processes have embed points, and there are places to put your own custom routines and your own data declarations. Figure 2.4 presents a partial list of the embed points in an update form from the Cookbook sample application that ships with CW version 1.

FIGURE 2.4.

A portion of the list of available embed points for the UpdateRecipe *procedure in* COOKBOOK.APP.

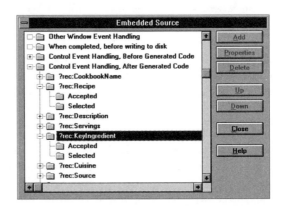

There are actually about 130 embed points available in that one procedure, which is why the embed list uses an outline control to display them. If you didn't have some way of organizing those embed points, it could get pretty difficult to find the one you want. (You can also get to many of the embeds through the window control they are connected to, which makes things a lot easier.)

Using embed points does presuppose a certain knowledge of the Clarion programming language. After all, you're going to be writing something in those embed points and it won't be Spanish (except possibly in comments, of course). It can also mean getting an understanding of what the generated code does.

If the embedded source you write is completely self-contained, (that is, it does not have any bearing on any other code in the procedure—some field validation code falls into this category), you don't really need to know what's going on elsewhere. On the other hand, there will probably come a time when you want to alter something in the existing procedure code, and then the scope of your source embeds widens.

In any case, the use of source embeds is a significant step up from exclusive AppGen use. You shouldn't let a minimal knowledge of the CW language stop you, but you should have a realistic appraisal of your abilities, and you should get as much assistance as you can.

If there is one serious drawback to using source embeds, it's that the source code can get hidden in your application, since the code itself is stored in the APP file along with all the rest of the application information. It's not a big issue if every one of your source embeds contains unique code, but if you've started cutting and pasting embeds, you're setting yourself up for some big trouble if ever you need to do a bug fix. You're going to have to track down every one of those duplicated source embeds. There is, of course, a way around this problem as well, which involves some relatively simple modifications to the AppGen, and I'll get to that shortly.

In general, the combination of the use of the AppGen and source embed points will serve you well if you use those embed points only occasionally. Once you get beyond occasional use, you're almost certainly going to benefit from some degree of tinkering with the AppGen itself.

Modified AppGen

You deserve fair warning. This section contains the Big Pitch. I firmly believe that the modified AppGen approach is what most CW developers should be using for most kinds of application development. That may sound a little intimidating. Modifying the AppGen to suit your own development style can be a complex task, but it can also be as easy as writing a few lines of code. Either way, if you want to get the job done, the AppGen can help you get it done more easily and quickly.

The Template Language—The AppGen's Intelligence

The key to modifying the AppGen to suit your needs is the template language. I'll go even further than that. The key to the AppGen is the template language. As mentioned in Chapter 1, templates are source files that determine the behavior and appearance of the AppGen.

More specifically, the relationship between the templates and the AppGen is much like the relationship between a source code interpreter such as BASIC and a BASIC program. When you run a (traditional) BASIC program, the source code is read by the interpreter and translated at that time into machine instructions, and your program runs. It is a cooperative effort between the interpreter and the BASIC program, but the vast majority of the information that actually determines how your program works is embodied in the BASIC source code. If you want to change your program, you change the source code, not the interpreter.

Similarly, the AppGen is an interpreter of the template language. If you don't like the way the AppGen does something, all you have to do is make a change to the template language (and go through one additional step of re-registering the template, as described in Chapter 17, "Creating Code Templates"), and the change will appear the next time you run the AppGen.

The template language is, in many ways, similar to the Clarion language. It contains parallels to statements such as IF...ELSE and CASE, it can read and write ASCII files, and it shows control declarations similar to those in CW. Listing 2.4 contains a template that is used to create a procedure that lets the user browse through an ASCII file, such as a report that has been printed to disk.

Listing 2.4. The ASCII file viewer procedure template (VIEW.TPW).

```
#PROCEDURE(View,'View a ASCII (text) file'),WINDOW
#INSERT(%FieldTemplateStandardButtonPrompt)
#INSERT(%FieldTemplateStandardMenuPrompt)
#INSERT(%FieldTemplateStandardEntryPrompt)
#INSERT(%FieldTemplateStandardCheckBoxPrompt)
#LOCALDATA
LocalRequest          LONG,AUTO
LocalResponse         LONG,AUTO
WindowOpened          LONG,AUTO
#ENDLOCALDATA
#CLASS('GeneralBefore','General, before lookups')
#CLASS('GeneralAfter','General, after lookups')
#PROMPT('&Parameters:', @s80), %Parameters
#PROMPT('Window Operation Mode:',DROP('Use WINDOW setting|Normal|MDI|Modal'))
➥,%WindowOperationMode
#ENABLE(%INIActive)
  #BOXED('INI File Settings')
    #PROMPT('Save Window Location',CHECK),%INISaveWindow,DEFAULT(1)
  #ENDBOXED
#ENDENABLE
#EMBED(%GatherSymbols,'Gather Template Symbols'),HIDE
#DECLARE(%HotControl),MULTI
#INSERT(%FileControlInitialize)
#IF(%Parameters)
%Procedure PROCEDURE%Parameters
#ELSE
%Procedure PROCEDURE
#ENDIF
#FOR(%LocalData)
%[20]LocalData %LocalDataStatement
#ENDFOR
#INSERT(%StandardWindowGeneration)
  CODE
  #EMBED(%ProcedureSetup,'Procedure Setup')
  LocalRequest = GlobalRequest
  LocalResponse = RequestCancelled
  CLEAR(GlobalRequest)
  CLEAR(GlobalResponse)
```

```
  #INSERT(%FileControlOpen)
  #INSERT(%StandardWindowOpening)
  #EMBED(%BeforeAccept,'Preparing to Process the Window')
  #MESSAGE('Accept Handling',3)
  ACCEPT
    CASE EVENT()
    #INSERT(%StandardWindowHandling)
     END
    CASE FIELD()
    #INSERT(%StandardControlHandling)
     END
  END
  #INSERT(%FileControlClose)
  #EMBED(%EndOfProcedure,'End of Procedure')
  IF LocalResponse
    GlobalResponse = LocalResponse
  ELSE
    GlobalResponse = RequestCancelled
  END
  RETURN
!-------------------------------------------------------------------
RefreshWindow ROUTINE
  #EMBED(%RefreshWindowBeforeLookup,'Refresh Window routine, before lookups')
  #INSERT(%StandardFormula,'GeneralBefore')
  #INSERT(%StandardSecondaryLookups)
  #INSERT(%StandardFormula,'GeneralAfter')
  #EMBED(%RefreshWindowAfterLookup,'Refresh Window routine, after lookups')
  DISPLAY()
!-------------------------------------------------------------------
#EMBED(%ProcedureRoutines,'Procedure Routines')
#INSERT(%FileControlUpdate)
#DEFAULT
NAME DefaultView
[COMMON]
DESCRIPTION 'View an ASCII file'
FROM Clarion View
[PROMPTS]
%WindowOperationMode STRING  ('Use WINDOW setting')
%INISaveWindow LONG  (1)
[ADDITION]
NAME Clarion ASCIIBox
[INSTANCE]
INSTANCE 1
PROCPROP
[PROMPTS]
%ASCIIFileDescription @S40  ('')
%ASCIIFile @S80  ('')
%ASCIIWarning LONG  (1)
[ADDITION]
NAME Clarion CloseButton
[INSTANCE]
INSTANCE 2
[WINDOW]
Label WINDOW('View an ASCII File'),AT(-1,1,340,200),SYSTEM,GRAY,MAX
     LIST,AT(5,5,330,170),FONT('FixedSys',9,,FONT:regular),
➥USE(?AsciiBox),HVSCROLL,FROM(Queue:ASCII), ¦
#SEQ(1),#ORIG(?AsciiBox)
```

continues

Listing 2.4. continued

```
      BUTTON('Close'),AT(150,180,,),USE(?Close),#SEQ(2),#ORIG(?Close)
      END

#ENDDEFAULT
```

As Listing 2.4 shows, a template is (in most cases) a mix of template language statements (which are prefixed with a # character) and Clarion language statements. Template code is there for one of two purposes: Either it will be used to present various windows and controls to you to collect information about the design of the program or it will be used to generate source code based on your input.

The Clarion language statements embedded in a template do not, generally speaking, come into play until code-generation time. (The exception is that you can use certain statements to process information collected from the programmer.) For instance, if you create a procedure based on the view template shown in Listing 2.4, you will see the Procedure Properties window shown in Figure 2.5.

FIGURE 2.5.

The Procedure Properties window for a procedure based on the view template.

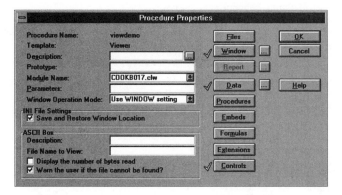

To create the procedure, all you really need to do is specify the name of the file to read and have AppGen create the code. If you specify C:\WINDOWS\WIN.INI as the file to read, your generated source code will look like that shown in Listing 2.5.

Listing 2.5. The source code generated by the AppGen for the ASCII file view procedure.

```
ViewFile PROCEDURE
LocalRequest          LONG,AUTO
OriginalRequest       LONG,AUTO
LocalResponse         LONG,AUTO
WindowOpened          LONG,AUTO
ForceRefresh          LONG,AUTO
ASC1:ProgressWindow   WINDOW('Loading ASCII File'),AT(,,151,79)¦
                      ,CENTER,TIMER(1),GRAY,DOUBLE,MODAL
STRING(''),AT(5,5,140,10),USE(?ASC1:UserString),CENTER
                   BOX,AT(20,20,110,20),USE(?ASC1:Box1),¦
                   COLOR(00H),FILL(0C0C0C0H)
```

```
                        BOX,AT(25,25,100,10),USE(?ASC1:ThermometerBack),¦
                         COLOR(00H)
                        BOX,AT(25,25,100,10),USE(?ASC1:Thermometer),¦
                         COLOR(00H),FILL(0FFH)
STRING(''),AT(20,45,110,10),USE(?ASC1:Progress),CENTER
                        BUTTON('Cancel'),AT(50,60,50,15),USE(?ASC1:Cancel)
                      END
Queue:ASCII             QUEUE
                  STRING(255)
            END
ASC1:FileName         STRING(80)
ASC1:CurrentFileName  STRING(80)
ASC1:FileSize         LONG
ASC1:BytesRead        LONG
ASC1:BytesPerCycle    LONG
ASC1:BytesThisCycle   LONG
ASC1:PercentProgress  BYTE
ASC1:ASCIIFile         FILE,PRE(ASC1),DRIVER('ASCII'),NAME(ASCIIFileName)
                      RECORD
STRING                   STRING(255)
                      END
                    END
ASC1:WholeWord        BYTE
ASC1:Matchcase        BYTE
ASC1:Direction        CSTRING(4)
ASC1:SearchString     CSTRING(80)
ASC1:CurrentPointer  LONG
ASC1:SearchWindow WINDOW('Searching Text...'),AT(43,25,267,60),¦
                        FONT('MS Sans Serif',8,,),GRAY,TOOLbox
PROMPT('Find What:'),AT(11,5,,),USE(?ASC1:TextPrompt)
                        ENTRY(@s20),AT(53,5,149,15),USE(ASC1:SearchString)
                        CHECK('Match &Whole Word Only'),AT(11,30,,),¦
                         USE(ASC1:WholeWord)
CHECK('Match &Case'),AT(11,44,,),USE(ASC1:MatchCase)
                        OPTION('Direction'),AT(111,28,81,26),¦
                         USE(ASC1:Direction),BOXED
                          RADIO('Up'),AT(117,39,,)
                          RADIO('Down'),AT(149,39,,)
                        END
                        BUTTON('Find Next'),AT(208,5,53,15),USE(?ASC1:Search)
                        BUTTON('Cancel'),AT(208,25,53,15),¦
                         USE(?ASC1:CancelSearch)
                      END
Label                 WINDOW('View an ASCII File'),AT(3,7,296,136),SYSTEM,GRAY,MAX
                 LIST,AT(5,5,285,110),FONT('FixedSys',9,,FONT:regular),USE(?AsciiBox),¦
                      HVSCROLL,FROM(Queue:ASCII)
BUTTON('Search'),AT(215,120,35,10),USE(?ASCIISearch)
                        BUTTON('Close'),AT(255,120,35,10),USE(?Close)
                        BUTTON('Print'),AT(175,120,35,10),USE(?ASCIIPrint)
                      END
  CODE
  LocalRequest = GlobalRequest
  OriginalRequest = GlobalRequest
  LocalResponse = RequestCancelled
  CLEAR(GlobalRequest)
  CLEAR(GlobalResponse)
  OPEN(Label)
  WindowOpened=True
```

continues

Listing 2.5. continued

```
INIRestoreWindow('test')
ACCEPT
  CASE EVENT()
  OF Event:OpenWindow
    DO RefreshWindow
    SELECT(FIRSTFIELD())
  OF Event:GainFocus
    ForceRefresh = True
    DO RefreshWindow
  END
  CASE FIELD()
  OF ?AsciiBox
    CASE EVENT()
    OF Event:Accepted
      ForceRefresh = True
      DO RefreshWindow
      LocalRequest = OriginalRequest
    END
  OF ?ASCIISearch
    CASE EVENT()
    OF Event:Accepted
      ForceRefresh = True
      DO RefreshWindow
      LocalRequest = OriginalRequest
      OPEN(ASC1:SearchWindow)
      ASC1:SearchWindow{Prop:ToolBox} = True
      ACCEPT
        CASE EVENT()
        OF Event:CloseWindow
          CLOSE(ASC1:SearchWindow)
        END
        CASE FIELD()
        OF ?ASC1:Search
          CASE EVENT()
          OF Event:Accepted
            IF ASC1:Direction = 'Down'
              STOP('Down')
            ELSE
              STOP('Up')
            END
          END
        OF ?ASC1:CancelSearch
          POST(Event:CloseWindow)
        END
      END
    END
  OF ?Close
    CASE EVENT()
    OF Event:Accepted
      ForceRefresh = True
      DO RefreshWindow
      LocalRequest = OriginalRequest
      LocalResponse = RequestCancelled
      POST(Event:CloseWindow)
    END
  OF ?ASCIIPrint
    CASE EVENT()
    OF Event:Accepted
```

```
            ForceRefresh = True
            DO RefreshWindow
            LocalRequest = OriginalRequest
          END
        END
      END
      FREE(Queue:ASCII)
      IF LocalResponse
        GlobalResponse = LocalResponse
      ELSE
        GlobalResponse = RequestCancelled
      END
      IF WindowOpened
        INISaveWindow('test')
        CLOSE(Label)
      END
      RETURN
    !------------------------------------------------------------------
    RefreshWindow ROUTINE
      ASC1:FileName = 'c:\windows\win.ini'
      IF ASC1:FileName <> ASC1:CurrentFileName
        ASCIIFileName = ASC1:FileName
        DO ASC1:FillQueue
        ASC1:CurrentFileName = ASC1:Filename
      END
      DISPLAY()
      ForceRefresh = False
    !------------------------------------------------------------------
    ASC1:FillQueue ROUTINE
      FREE(Queue:ASCII)
      IF NOT ASCIIFileName
        ?AsciiBox{Prop:Disable} = True
        EXIT
      ELSE
        ?AsciiBox{Prop:Disable} = False
      END
      OPEN(ASC1:ASCIIFile,10h)
      IF ERRORCODE()
        DISABLE(?AsciiBox)
        IF StandardWarning(WRN:FileLoadError,ASC1:FileName,ERROR())
          EXIT
        END
      END
      ASC1:FileSize = BYTES(ASC1:ASCIIFile)
      IF ASC1:FileSize < 1000
        ASC1:BytesPerCycle = ASC1:FileSize
      ELSIF ASC1:FileSize < 10000
        ASC1:BytesPerCycle = ASC1:FileSize / 4
      ELSE
        ASC1:BytesPerCycle = ASC1:FileSize / 100
      END
      OPEN(ASC1:ProgressWindow)
      ASC1:PercentProgress = 0
      ASC1:BytesRead = 0
      ?ASC1:Thermometer{Prop:Width} = 0
      ?ASC1:Progress{Prop:Text} = '0% Completed'
      ACCEPT
```

continues

Listing 2.5. continued

```
    CASE EVENT()
    OF Event:OpenWindow
      SET(ASC1:ASCIIFile)
    OF Event:Timer
      LOOP WHILE ASC1:BytesThisCycle < ASC1:BytesPerCycle
        NEXT(ASC1:ASCIIFile)
        IF ERRORCODE()
          LocalResponse = RequestCompleted
        END
        ASC1:BytesThisCycle += BYTES(ASC1:ASCIIFile)
        Queue:ASCII = ASC1:String
        ADD(Queue:ASCII)
      END
      IF LocalResponse = RequestCompleted
        LocalResponse = RequestCancelled
        POST(Event:CloseWindow)
      END
      ASC1:BytesRead += ASC1:BytesThisCycle
      ASC1:BytesthisCycle = 0
      IF ASC1:PercentProgress < 100
        ASC1:PercentProgress = (ASC1:BytesRead/ASC1:FileSize)*100
        IF ASC1:PercentProgress > 100
          ASC1:PercentProgress = 100
        END
        ?ASC1:Thermometer{Prop:Width} = ROUND(ASC1:PercentProgress,0)
        ?ASC1:Progress{Prop:Text} = FORMAT(ASC1:PercentProgress,@N3) ¦
          & '% Completed'
DISPLAY()
      END
    END
    CASE FIELD()
    OF ?ASC1:Cancel
      CASE EVENT()
      OF Event:Accepted
        IF StandardWarning(WRN:ConfirmCancelLoad,ASC1:FileName)=Button:OK
          POST(Event:CloseWindow)
        END
      END
    END
  END
  CLOSE(ASC1:ProgressWindow)
  CLOSE(ASC1:ASCIIFile)
```

There is, in fact, somewhat more code here than the view template alone can generate, but that is only because the controls that are part of the view template have their own related template code elsewhere in the system, and this is pulled in at code-generation time.

Simple Modifications

The view template in Listing 2.5 may look a little intimidating, and you might be thinking that if that's what you have to deal with when you start tinkering with the templates, you'd just as soon take up wrestling grizzly bears. And, unless you're either particularly brave or just lacking in judgment, you probably won't start by modifying whole procedure templates. You'll probably start with something much simpler: code templates.

In the same way that a procedure template enables you to avoid writing all the code that goes into a particular type of procedure, a code template typically lets you avoid writing the code that goes into a particular type of source embed. This is useful primarily if you find yourself repeating the same code in different places in your application. The creation of code templates is covered in detail in Chapter 17.

If you generally like to stay within the AppGen, but you find that you are frequently adding your own blocks of code to embed points, you owe it to yourself to investigate code templates. If you find that even this does not meet all your needs, you may be ready for a deeper knowledge of the template system.

Complex Modifications

You may have heard the statement that one day computers will be smart enough to write software. In a sense, this has come true in CW. Not only can the AppGen, by means of templates, write code for you, but because you have access to the templates, you can fundamentally change the AppGen to suit your own coding style.

If you get to the point of making more serious modifications than just creating code templates, you should make a serious commitment to learning the template language. Although it's not quite as extensive as the Clarion language, it will take some effort to understand. You will find a template language reference in the Clarion online help. Read it. Study the supplied templates. Wherever possible, create your own templates (either from scratch or by cutting and pasting from the existing templates). Avoid modifying the standard templates that shipped with CW, since any changes you make will have to be applied to the new standard templates whenever you obtain an upgrade.

If you do get serious about modifying the templates, Chapter 17, Chapter 18, "Creating Procedure Templates," Chapter 19, "Creating Control Templates," and Chapter 20, "Creating Extension Templates," will give you a head start. After you've had a look at control templates, you will be ready to move on to procedure and control templates and extension templates.

As with control templates, sometimes the smallest changes can have a huge impact. You do not need to completely rewrite the template system to accomplish most of what you need to do. The more you learn about the templates, the more you will come to appreciate their "plug and play" nature. You can create templates that stand entirely on their own or make use of template code in the standard template set.

Extreme Modifications

So you've looked at the existing templates, and you've decided that no matter how hard you try, you're just not going to make them suit your own purposes. Should you give up? Not a chance! The template language is all about flexibility, and if it can't be adapted to the way you program, then you don't program like anyone I've ever met. You may find it surprisingly easy to create a set of code templates that do exactly what you want, exactly the way you want to do it. In the same way that the Clarion language allows you to write just about any kind of program you choose, the template language allows you to create just about any type of AppGen you choose. Don't be afraid to blaze your own trail.

Summary

Traditionally, Clarion programming has been viewed as having two approaches: hand code and application generation. With the advent of the CW Application Generator, the line between these two approaches has not just blurred, it has disappeared completely. Not only can you integrate hand code into the AppGen, you can modify it to incorporate the kinds of functionality unique to your own work. Because the AppGen's intelligence is embodied in the templates, and you have access to those templates, you can even rebuild the AppGen so that it works exactly the way you do.

3

Choosing Databases Wisely

In today's technology arena there are many forms of data storage and retrieval available on the desktop, as well as throughout the enterprise (corporation): flat file systems, database management systems (DBMSs), relational database management systems (RDBMSs), Structured Query Language relational database management systems (SQL RDBMSs) and object-oriented database management systems (OODBMSs), to name just a few. Understanding the benefits, drawbacks, hazards, and usefulness of these technologies is essential for anyone doing serious database work.

Clarion for Windows, like its ancestors for DOS, focuses on solving business problems . Business applications utilize databases; therefore, Clarion for Windows focuses on a seamless interface for database access. To assist in solving these business problems, Clarion for Windows provides highly optimized database drivers in the form of DLLs, which have been developed using the TopSpeed database driver kit. If and when there is a situation in which a native database driver is unavailable to solve the problem at hand, Clarion for Windows provides a common Windows data access mechanism, known as open database connectivity (ODBC), for those database systems.

Clarion for Windows is a database-neutral language, which means that all data is handled in a generic way so that all data access is handled in a language-transparent manner. You do not need to understand the complexities of each file system, DBMS, RDBMS, or SQL database engine. Instead, you simply use the standard Clarion for Windows data access methods provided in the language itself. The database drivers provided with Clarion for Windows make all the proper translations and database-specific calls to retrieve, manipulate, and store data in these systems.

Some database systems use multiple physical files that together form a database, using record-oriented data access methods, and others use a single physical file with set-oriented processes, utilizing SQL. How do you know which is best?

When deploying applications that use databases, you must consider some principal differences between desktop databases and enterprisewide databases. For example, with desktop databases, you might be concerned with application referential integrity issues, file handles, and available PC memory requirements, whereas with enterprisewide databases you might be concerned with server-based referential integrity, server memory, and database-, table-, or row-level security issues.

Understanding your selected database technology and dealing correctly within the limits of it is essential to avoiding disaster. If you can't reliably manage your data, you and your clients are toast!

This chapter explains when to use a native database driver as opposed to a common access mechanism. It also covers the fundamental differences among the standard database technologies supported in Clarion for Windows, and will hopefully assist you in making the correct decision for your Windows applications.

Database Drivers

Database driver technology is nothing really new. As a matter of fact, most application development tools for Windows use some sort of database driver technology. A database driver is simply a dynamic link library (DLL) that contains the data access methods for a specific database technology.

Clarion for DOS saw the first use of these database drivers. The Clarion for DOS databases were initially targeted at the desktop using the Clarion, dBASE, FoxPro, Clipper, Paradox, and Btrieve database drivers, and then eventually targeted at the enterprise with the addition of the AS400 database driver.

If this technology is not new, why mention it at all? The new database drivers included in Clarion for Windows have been re-developed using the TopSpeed database driver kit technology, which provides a language-neutral access methodology, no matter what form the physical data may be in. This means that regardless of what database you have elected to use, all language syntax remains the same and common—there is no extra or special programming required. Also included in this technology is a standard translation architecture technology that provides a layer between the application code and the native database driver instruction code. What this means is that the database driver can receive a standard SQL statement or a Clarion for Windows record processing language statement and translate these statements into native database driver instructions. This benefits your applications because of the maximum performance that the native database drivers can provide without any manual or specialized optimizations.

For instance, if you have decided to use an SQL database engine and you perform a record-processing statement, it will be translated into standard SQL statements. The following:

```
KeyValue = Value
GET(File,Key)
```

translates into this:

```
SELECT * FROM File WHERE KeyValue = Value;
```

Both statements produce the same result, but the method in which the result is obtained is completely different.

Files Versus Databases/Tables

Depending on your background (and age), you most likely refer to databases as files. If you have been programming long, or if you have been programming recently in Windows, you most likely have come across the terms *database* and *table*. What's the difference?

Traditionally, desktop databases consisted of at least one primary physical data file, and possibly multiple files that included keys, indexes, memos, or binary data. There were exceptions of course, but for the most part, this was common practice. As desktop database technology has matured and the server-based RDBMSs and SQL RDBMSs have become dominant players, the physical makeup of the database has changed. Now, one physical file is used as a container for multiple files or tables, including the data, keys, indexes, memos, and binary data. The traditional file systems required multiple file handles and additional memory requirements utilizing precious system resources. The newer RDBMSs have reduced this requirement by implementing data access through one physical file.

By definition, a *database* is a collection of data. In Clarion for Windows, the term *dictionary* is used interchangeably for this definition. The dictionary performs the job of a container, embodying the component parts (files) within it. Therefore, when you are dealing with DBMSs such as Clarion or dBASE, the term database means a file. However, when you are dealing with SQL RDBMSs, the term database means the container and the term table means the file. All the same, whether you use a DBMS, RDBMS, or SQL RDBMS, the term dictionary is used in Clarion for Windows to indicate the entity that embodies the attributes or properties of the database.

Record and Field Versus Row and Column

In the transition from traditional file systems to the newer SQL RDBMS database systems, new terminology has emerged. In a Clarion or dBASE file, for example, a record is defined as the collection of fields that logically and physically make up the contents of the record. In an SQL RDBMS, a record is now called a *row* and a field is now called a *column*. Although the terms are different, the implementation is roughly the same.

Referential Integrity

Differences arise in functionality among database systems in the concepts of table-, row-, and column-level security and referential integrity enforcement. In a traditional DBMS, it is common to provide security access to the database itself. In contrast, most SQL RDBMSs enable the database administrator (keeper or shepherd of the data) to determine which users or groups of users can have access to the database and the tables within it. In some high-end database systems, the database administrator can also determine access to specific columns within a table of the database.

There are two distinct methods of referential integrity used among database vendors. Some provide no back-end (server-based) referential integrity solutions and require the application programmer to write and maintain his or her own rules, and others enforce referential integrity through the use of constraints and security access rights at the database server engine level. Both have their place, and most enterprise databases require the database server to enforce the data access rules to protect corporate resources.

Locking

In traditional databases, the level of locking (preventing two users from accessing the same information during a database transaction) is either by file or by record. In many SQL RDBMSs, there is a concept known as *lock granularity*, which means that there are database-, table-, page-, and row-level locking mechanisms available. A *database-level lock* locks an entire collection of tables. A *table-level lock* locks a specific database table. A *page-level lock* (a collection of rows that evenly fit into a contiguous block of disk space or memory that is defined by the RDBMS page size) locks a page of rows in a table, and a *row-level lock* will lock a specific record in a database table.

A page-level lock generally occurs when there are many requests for locks placed on closely related records within a table. A table-level lock occurs when there are many requests for locks placed on closely related pages within the table or a high percentage of the records are required to be locked for an operation or transaction. This process of locking is largely automatic, and each implementation may vary depending on the database vendor. The term for this process is *lock escalation*.

In some newer database engines, *column-level locking* is available. This is the capability to lock a specific column or field in a row or record in a table in a database. This can get more complicated as database internals are discussed, so I'll stop here on this subject.

> **TIP**
>
> If you use an SQL RDBMS, it is wise to thoroughly understand the various implications, limitations, or restrictions that locking levels can place within a database you use.

Transactions

Transactions are handled similarly between a traditional DBMS and an SQL RDBMS; that is, a log file is created and maintained until a successful COMMIT is issued or a ROLLBACK is encountered, or the database engine is stopped.

SQL RDBMSs provide pre- and post-images of the transactions within the server itself, some RDBMSs utilize a log file and some do not. How pre- and post-imaging and transaction logging are handled depends on the SQL RDBMS database server engine itself.

Good Database Design

As this section title indicates, you have much to consider when designing your databases. I would like to cover this area in detail, but in order to keep the focus more on Clarion for Windows, only the basics of designing databases are covered. Therefore, I will cover some basics that may aid you along the way.

The industry standard is to design databases using the relational model whenever possible. I say "whenever" because in some circumstances, it would be disadvantageous to require the overhead of the relational model when you can develop structures to handle specific cases directly. However, overall I think you will find that most programmers and database designers will opt for a form of the relational model in most instances.

The relational model is based on the concept of data uniqueness. That is, for every record in the database, there should be one unique way to identify a record. This unique access methodology is accomplished using a primary key. A *primary key* is generally a system-generated number that, in Clarion for Windows terms, is usually of a long data type. When you wish to access a record, the task is generally performed using the primary key value. Of course, because a primary key is a number, which may mean nothing at all to you or your users, you will generally define access keys or indexes to your data as required. When you reference a record in another record, the task is generally done by storing the primary key of the first record in the second record. This is known as a *foreign key*. When this relationship is established in some database systems, the term constraint is used. A *constraint* is the mechanism that prevents you from storing illegal data references in a record. This buys you peace of mind and data integrity. If you try to store a record without the proper data elements, the defined constraint will prevent the record from being stored.

An example may be in order at this point. Consider the following file definitions:

```
People              FILE,DRIVER('TOPSPEED'),RECLAIM,PRE(PEO),BINDABLE,¦
                    CREATE,THREAD
K_PeopleNo          KEY(PEO:PeopleNo),NOCASE,OPT,PRIMARY
K_StateNo           KEY(PEO:StateNo),DUP,NOCASE,OPT
K_CityNo            KEY(PEO:CityNo),DUP,NOCASE,OPT
K_ByName            KEY(PEO:NameLast,PEO:NameFirst,PEO:NameMI),DUP,¦
                    NOCASE,OPT
Record                RECORD
PeopleNo                LONG
NameLast                STRING(25)
NameFirst               STRING(20)
NameMI                  STRING(1)
Address                 STRING(40)
CityNo                  LONG
StateNo                 LONG
                      END
                    END

States              FILE,DRIVER('TOPSPEED'),RECLAIM,PRE(STA),BINDABLE,¦
                    CREATE,THREAD
K_StateNo           KEY(STA:StateNo),NOCASE,OPT,PRIMARY
K_ByStateId         KEY(STA:StateId),NOCASE,OPT
K_ByStateName       KEY(STA:StateName),NOCASE,OPT
Record                RECORD
StateNo                 LONG
StateId                 STRING(2)
```

```
StateName                      STRING(30)
                    END
              END
```

Notice that each file definition contains a primary key, indicated by the Primary attribute in the first key of each file definition. Notice also that in the People file definition, there is a StateNo field. This field relates to the StateNo field in the States file definition. You could store the two-character StateId in the People file—many do just that. However, in this case I have chosen to store the relational value of the StateNo instead. This strategy enables you to provide a pick list, in the form of a drop-down list box, which reads the values from the States file. When the user selects a record from the list, only the unique StateNo is stored on the People record, which ensures that the user can never input an invalid value for a StateId. The primary key in this case is STA:K_StateNo and the foreign key is PEO:K_StateNo.

This is the premise of the relational model. There are many forms to be learned, considered, and utilized (this is only one form, known as "first normal"). I therefore suggest that if you have not studied this theory, do so, because it will help your future database design efforts.

Native Drivers

Clarion for Windows ships with various native database drivers. All of these drivers can be used within your application at the same time if you desire. To better understand the use of the drivers I have put each one in one of three classifications: desktop, local area network (LAN), and wide area network (WAN). The next sections outline the classification of each driver and give you an idea of when or when not to use each one.

The Desktop (Local)

The *desktop* refers to a single-user, local-access database system. For this purpose, Clarion for Windows provides the following database drivers:

- ASCII: An ASCII file is a DOS file that commonly uses record delimiters in the form of carriage return/line feed characters. There are many uses for ASCII files. However, ASCII text generally is stored in an ASCII file.

- BASIC: A BASIC file is a comma-quoted delimited file that uses record delimiters in the form of carriage return/line feed characters. Other database systems (for which Clarion for Windows doesn't provide a native driver) can export to such a format, which can be used to import data into a native driver data format. You can also export your data in this format.

- DOS: The DOS file is a binary addressable file system. That means you can define any structure you want within this file and access it accordingly. This file system is useful for many simple storage systems in which keys or indexes are not required.

NOTE

The rest of the drivers in this section can be used in LAN- or WAN-based systems as well as in local desktop systems.

■ Btrieve: The Btrieve file system is a widely used commercial system that Clarion for Windows distributes for use on your machine only. The Btrieve file system uses low-level calls to access data and can be used to communicate with existing Btrieve databases. As noted in the manual with Clarion for Windows, there is a license limitation when you use Btrieve, and you must obtain the license directly from Btrieve Technologies, Inc., to distribute applications that utilize the Btrieve database system.

■ Clarion: The Clarion driver is a proprietary file format used by Clarion 2.1 (for DOS), Clarion for DOS, and Clarion for Windows. Clarion files utilize one primary file for the data and additional files for keys, indexes, and memos. For backward compatibility with existing Clarion 2.1 and Clarion for DOS applications, this format is suggested.

■ Clipper 5.0 Summer '87: The Clipper driver supports the Clipper 5.0 Summer of '87 file format data and indexes. This is a form of dBASE-compatible file structure. Use this driver when you are accessing externally created data in the Clipper format.

■ dBASE 3 and dBASE 4: The dBASE 3 and 4 drivers support the dBASE III and dBASE IV file systems. Many products have been developed using these files over the years. Even though these files are somewhat fragile (periodically after a crash you will need to rebuild the indexes), they are in widespread use—most likely they are the most widely used files in PC-based desktop systems today. Use these drivers when you are accessing externally created data in dBASE formats.

■ FoxPro: The FoxPro driver supports the FoxBase- and FoxPro-compatible file formats for data and indexes. This is a form of a dBASE-compatible file structure. Use this driver when you are accessing externally created data in the FoxPro or FoxBase format.

■ Paradox 3: The Paradox driver supports keyed and non-keyed Paradox file formats for data and indexes prior to release 4 of the Paradox file system. Many commercial systems take advantage of Paradox, and you can use this driver to access these data files.

■ TopSpeed: The TopSpeed driver is a new database file system created and released with Clarion for Windows. The TopSpeed driver supports keys, indexes, dynamic indexes, and multiple data and key files stored in a single DOS file. Because this is a new database system, we have yet to see the impact it will have on the desktop community. The TopSpeed driver is faster than the Clarion driver and performs remarkably well in batch processes such as appending records to a file and then rebuilding the keys. This file system is the core database system used in the Clarion for Windows product itself.

The LAN (Network)

The LAN, or network, refers to multiuser, network access database systems. For network databases, Clarion for Windows provides the database drivers described in the following sections.

- Btrieve: Of all the database drivers supplied with Clarion for Windows, the Btrieve file system has the best network-based database system. This is because Novell, Inc., formerly owned the Btrieve file system and built a network-based engine for Btrieve running on a network loadable module, or NLM. Because of this, a network server will perform the database access and send back only the data packets necessary to fulfill the request from the client (desktop PC system). Btrieve running on a network using the NLM technology is a candidate for client/server computing needs.

- ODBC: Open database connectivity, or ODBC, is a widely used option for accessing data across a network. ODBC is discussed in more detail in Chapter 24, "Using Open Database Connectivity." In a nutshell, ODBC is a common database access methodology created by Microsoft Corporation. It provides a layered data access approach with which your application communicates to retrieve, manipulate, and store data in available data sources. Your application will communicate with the ODBC driver, which will communicate to the actual data source driver requesting actions to be performed and passing data back and forth between the data source and the application.

NOTE

The rest of the drivers in this section are not all network aware and will pass large volumes of data across the network, thereby possibly slowing down data retrieval and overall network performance.

- Clarion
- Clipper 5.0 Summer '87
- dBASE 3 and dBASE 4
- FoxPro
- Paradox 3
- TopSpeed

The WAN (Enterprise)

The WAN, or enterprise, refers to multiuser and multicomputer corporate access database systems. This form of data access is generally known as client/server computing. For this purpose, Clarion for Windows provides the following database drivers:

■ ODBC: ODBC is often used to access WAN-based data that isn't supported natively across all hardware environments. For example, you could access data stored in a VAX RDB database engine natively when executing programs on a VAX or through ODBC when executing programs on a PC. See Chapter 24 for more detailed information on using ODBC in Clarion for Windows.

■ AS400: The AS400 driver is the first of many additional drivers that will appear in the near future to support corporate data access. The AS400 driver supports SQL and non-SQL-based AS400 database access.

■ Others: The future of corporate client/server computing with Clarion for Windows looks bright indeed. There are additional drivers under development at this time, including Gupta, ORACLE, and SyBase. Please contact TopSpeed Corporation about the availability of these or any others you feel are necessary.

Summary

Clarion for Windows is a software development tool that integrates tightly and easily with many database technologies. As you begin to investigate the various options that are available to you, I encourage you to take a long, hard look at the database technology you will ultimately choose for your program—this decision could make or break you.

4

Concepts You Should Know

Before you embrace any new development platform, I have found that you must first understand the rules, limitations, and benefits of doing so. This may be your first Windows programming experience or this may be another chapter in your ongoing Windows development effort. In either case, you will find that a basic knowledge of Windows terminology, along with a few key concepts, will equip you to get the most out of the rest of this book.

This chapter introduces you to the *window object*; gives you an overview of the window components, or *controls*, which are the building blocks of your program's user interface; and covers the essential role of *messages* and *events* in Windows programming.

What Is a Window?

In simple terms, a window is an area of the computer screen that is used to display a running program or a portion of a running program. Every Windows program that wishes to display information on the screen must have at least one window, but it may have more than one. In Windows, unlike in DOS, a window cannot have text directly displayed on it. Using a window control is the technique for doing this and is discussed in the section titled "Window Controls: An Overview" in this chapter. Windows can overlap or completely obscure each other, which means that they behave according to certain rules that the Windows environment sets out.

The Window Object

Throughout this book you will come across the term *object* in a number of different contexts. This term comes from object-oriented programming (OOP), and although CW is not an object-oriented language in the strictest sense of the term, it does have a certain object orientation about it.

An object is not nearly as magical as all the hype surrounding the term suggests. Simply put, it is a useful combination of code and data. If you really wanted to stretch the point, you could say that every computer program is an object, because it has both code and data. You could also say that all computer programs are really made up of a bunch of little tiny programs, all interacting with each other, and if you said that, you'd also be talking about objects.

One of the fundamental objects in Windows programming is, as you might expect, a window. It's an object because it's more than just a structure that appears on the screen as a rectangular area with some information in it: The window also contains a certain amount of code that is required to make the window operate correctly. The idea is that a basic window should have all the essential behavior that a window needs.

It seems to be human nature not to be satisfied with the basics, so in practice we almost never use a plain-Jane, basic window in a program. We use windows that are enhanced with additional objects, designed, and styled for particular purposes.

Window Styles

Clarion for Windows supports all major Windows 3.x window styles (discussed later in this chapter). It is important that you understand the major differences and subtle nuances of each style of window before building a Windows application.

There are two primary and distinct window-management schemes used in Windows programs: single-document interface (SDI) and the multiple-document interface (MDI). In both cases, the word "document" may be replaced by the word "window," which makes the following explanations easier to understand.

SDI

SDI limits the user to one active window (a single document), which must be responded to before the user can move to a different window. This is similar to the behavior of most DOS programs, which use multiple screens, only one of which can be active at any time. Using this scheme, you can force a specific course on the user.

MDI

MDI is the pre-eminent window-management scheme among today's Windows programs. MDI provides the ability to manage multiple documents within one application just as the Windows Program Manager maintains multiple applications itself. You can observe MDI in the Windows Program Manager and File Manager programs, which provide the capability to switch among many windows within each program as well as within Windows itself.

In an MDI application one window is determined to be the parent window or MDI frame. All other windows that are opened thereafter are known as children of the parent frame, or MDI children. This scheme allows you to open multiple document windows (MDI children) and switch between them.

A parent window can have many child windows, but not every child window has to be an MDI child. You can mix and match MDI child and dialog (application modal and system modal) windows as you chose.

MDI Business Applications

If you have used a Windows-based word processor at some time or another you have probably seen how you can open and maintain multiple documents within the word processor itself. This is a classic example of MDI. But aren't we talking about general-purpose applications here, not word processors? Can this window-management scheme apply to what you really want to do? It most certainly can! Consider a database or even the records in a database as documents. Each document could present a different view of the data that could be visible and accessible within the application, and all at the same time. Just a little imagination will take your application far!

NOTE

Since MDI is the preeminent standard in modern Windows programs, the following section focuses on the concept of MDI windows.

The Application Window (the MDI Frame)

As mentioned, all MDI applications must specify a parent window. This window is a backdrop for other windows within the program. It also has special functionality. For example, it might contain a menu and toolbar for the application. This window is known as the application window, MDI frame, or MDI parent window. It's also called some other things when it won't work right.

FIGURE 4.1.
An MDI frame.

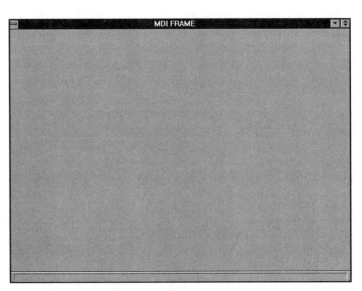

There are two basic components of the MDI frame window: The application window includes a title bar, menu, toolbar, resizing frame, system menu, minimize, maximize, and restore buttons, and a status bar; and the client area or workspace is the area where the MDI child windows reside.

The MDI frame has a close relationship with the MDI child windows within the application. It is directly accessible from the MDI child windows at any time. For instance, if you open an MDI child window you still have access to the parent window's main menu, even if the two windows appear to be quite separate.

The MDI frame and the child windows can communicate with each other. For example, if the MDI frame is instructed to close or terminate, it will inform all its MDI child windows that a close is in process, and the children will attempt to close. Upon successful closing of all the MDI child windows, the MDI frame will then close itself. Likewise, if the MDI frame is instructed to minimize or shrink down to an icon on the desktop, the MDI child windows will be minimized within the MDI frame's client area or workspace automatically.

> **NOTE**
>
> The MDI frame will manage all the MDI child windows during the life of the application program, and this behavior is largely automatic.

The MDI Child Window

An MDI child window is known as a "document" window (although it can be used for purposes other than processing documents). This window lives on and within the client area or workspace of the MDI frame or parent. As can be seen in Figure 4.2, the look of an MDI child is very similar to that of an MDI frame (since it inherits attributes from its parent the MDI frame). It contains a title bar, resizing frame, system menu, minimize, maximize, restore buttons, and possibly scroll bars (vertical and horizontal). Many MDI child windows may be open at any given time, and you can switch between them at will. The term for this kind of behavior is *modeless*, since it does not force on the user a particular mode of operation.

FIGURE 4.2.
An MDI child window.

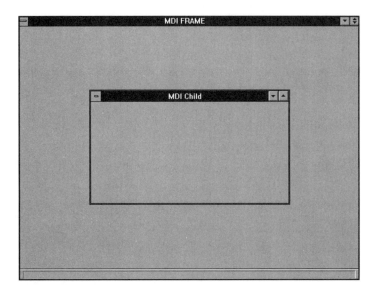

The MDI frame's menu and toolbar apply to each MDI child window and may look and respond differently for each MDI child window, as appropriate. For example, in one child window the Edit menu item may be visible while in another it is not. In the Clarion for Windows Window Formatter, you can logically define the menu and toolbar items that are appropriate for a given MDI child window. However, the menu affected is not that of the MDI child window, but rather is that of the MDI frame. This concept of varying menu and toolbar items is known as "menu merging" and is discussed in Chapter 29, "Multiple-Document Interface Versus Non–Multiple-Document Interface."

Since only one MDI child window may be active at any time, the active window is indicated by the highlight color of its title bar. Also, since an MDI child window resides within the confines of the MDI frame's client area or workspace, only the part of the window that lies inside the parent frame will show on screen. The rest of the window is still there, it's just not visible. When an MDI child is partially hidden in this way it is called a "clipped" window.

Dialog Windows

The term *window* usually refers to what is known as a standard-style window or a *dialog*-style window. Figure 4.3 presents a dialog window. A dialog window is a style that requires input or response before allowing the user to continue selecting another window within the application. A dialog window is considered application modal (that is, when opened, it requires response before the user may select another window in the application). The user can still switch to a different application.

In MDI applications, a side-effect of opening a dialog window is that the MDI frame's menu may not be selected until the dialog window is closed. Therefore, the user can proceed in only one direction at a time.

FIGURE 4.3.
A dialog window.

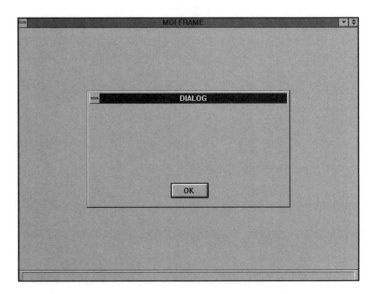

System Modal Windows

A *system modal* window is a dialog window with the Modal attribute, which prevents the user from accessing all other windows within the application, as well as any other running Windows program, until this window is closed. Extreme care should be taken when using this style of window because severe problems could occur. For instance, if the user is unable to exit a system modal window, whether because of a bug or because you have not provided an appropriate means of exit, the only recourse will be to reboot Windows.

Window Controls

Although the preceding text covers the many varieties of windows, all of these have so far been devoid of the kinds of functionality that make a program really useful. In short, they haven't had any way to display and update information on the window. Fortunately, this is not a particularly difficult task. Rather than rewriting each window from scratch to support features such as text display and data entry (the way you may have done in DOS), you populate the window with other objects, which are called *window controls*.

Some controls, such as buttons or text entry controls, are quite common and are found in virtually every Windows program. Others, such as spreadsheet or graphic controls, are found only in applications that require their special capabilities. The important point is that virtually anything that appears on a window is a control.

Accessing controls is generally done in one of two ways: using the Tab key or clicking on the control with the left mouse button. Whereas the mouse enables you to select controls in any sequence, the Tab key moves through controls in a predefined sequence. The standard Windows Tab order flows from left to right and top to bottom, and is known as the Z-order (for obvious reasons). In Clarion for Windows, you can determine the order of the window controls by using the SET ORDER command in the Window Formatter (which is discussed in Chapter 8, "Creating Procedures").

Two of the major benefits of graphical user interface platforms such as Windows are ease-of-use and reduced training cost. In order to attain these benefits you must follow a consistent interface design, which includes processing standards such as the Z-order. I recommend that you use the Z-order wherever it is practical to do so. Your users may not thank you if you do, but that's better than hearing from them when you don't.

Properties

In Windows, visual objects such as windows, window controls, and reports have properties or attributes that define their appearance and behavior. These properties are often preset, but may also be modified during program execution (runtime).

For example, say you have a window that has an entry control. If the user is adding records you might want this window control to receive input and be available to the user during this process. If the user is updating existing records, however, you might not want this window control to allow any input or even be selected by the user. This functionality can be managed through the use of the Disable property of the entry control. Properties are generally a switch that is either on or off (1 or 0, respectively), but they can be much more robust, as you will see later. If you set the value of the Disable property of the entry control to 1 this control will become dimmed and the user will not be allowed to change the value or even select the entry control at all.

Here's another example: You have a string control that you want to display "Hello" or "Goodbye," based on some criteria. In Windows, you would simply change the value of the Text property of the control to the actual text you desire to be displayed. You can also change the position of a control on the window, alter its font (if it uses text), set its color, decide whether it's visible, and determine a lot more. If you wanted to, you could make all your controls break into a frenzied, Technicolor dance at the press of a button. They would have killed for this stuff in the '60s.

Window Controls: An Overview

So what are these window controls and how are they used? In the Window Formatter, you can place controls by selecting the type of control you wish to use from the Controls toolbox. The Controls toolbox is shown in Figure 4.4.

FIGURE 4.4.
The Window Formatter Controls toolbox.

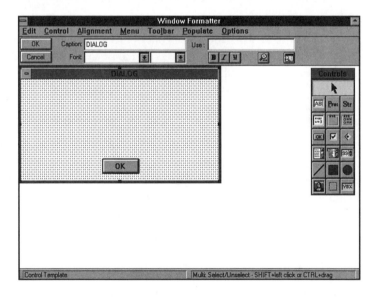

The Entry Control

You use an entry control the same way you might use a DOS entry field—for collecting user input. Figure 4.5 shows an entry control.

FIGURE 4.5.

An entry control.

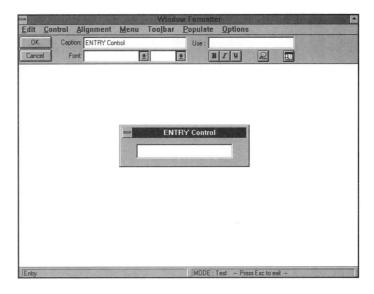

The Prompt Control

A prompt control is used to provide a keyboard-selectable control that is associated with another control such as an entry control. It typically has a hot letter in the prompt text, and if the
user presses this hot key, the control immediately following the prompt will be selected. Figure
4.6 shows a prompt control.

FIGURE 4.6.

A prompt control.

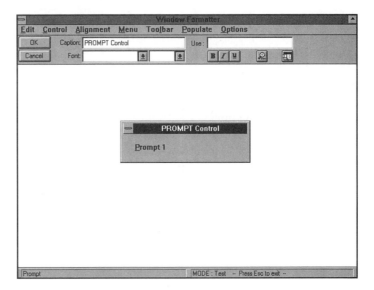

The String Control

As you may recall, in Windows you cannot place text directly on the window as you can in DOS. Instead, you use a string control. Figure 4.7 shows a string control.

FIGURE 4.7.

A string control.

The Text Control

A text control is similar to an entry control except that it allows multiple lines of input. It is not a word processor type of control and it may only use one font at any given time. Figure 4.8 shows a text control.

The Group Box Control

The group box control provides you with a visual means of separating data items on the window. For example, you might use one group box control to set apart the name and address of a person and use another group box control to set apart the phone numbers for the person. Figure 4.9 shows a group box control.

FIGURE 4.8.
A text control.

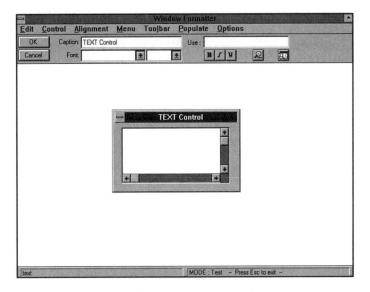

FIGURE 4.9.
A group box control.

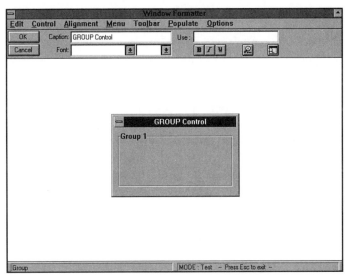

The Option Box Control

The option box control is similar to a group box control in that it is used to set apart data in a window. However, the only type of control it can contain is a radio button control. Figure 4.10 shows an option box control.

FIGURE 4.10.

An option box control with radio buttons.

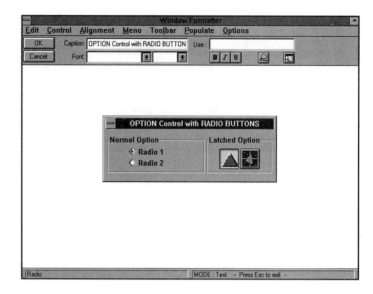

The Radio Button Control

Radio button controls are used for situations in which you wish to present the user with a number of options, only one of which may be selected. If an icon is used for the button, it will appear "latched" when the radio button is selected. Latched buttons are similar to the old-style push buttons used on car dashboard radios. Pushing a button in pops the previously pushed button out. This means that only one option button can be pushed in at a time.

The Button Control

A button control provides the user with the ability to initiate some process. It may contain text or a picture. By default, a button control is pushed once to perform a desired action. Figure 4.11 shows a button control.

NOTE

If you wish to have a button perform an action continuously while it is held down, you will need to turn on its IMM (immediate) attribute.

FIGURE 4.11.
A button control.

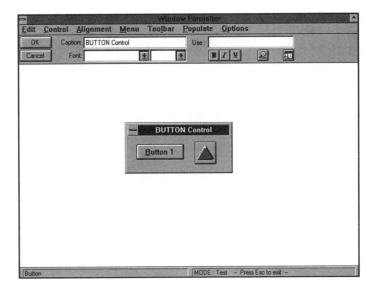

The Check Box Control

A check box control is used when the user needs to choose one of two states, such as on or off, yes or no, or true or false, selected or not selected. If an icon is used for the check box, the check box will appear to be a latched button when the box is checked. Figure 4.12 shows a check box control.

FIGURE 4.12.
A check box control.

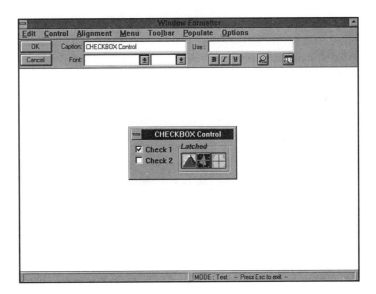

The List Box Control

A list box control is a very common and versatile object, which is used to scroll through data file records or items in a list. A list box control can be formatted with many different options, including fonts, size, orientation, underline, column separators, column resizability, an additional VCR-style positioning control, scroll bars, and much more. The list box is not a grid (spreadsheet) control but it can simulate many of the features of a grid control, using the edit-in-place options. Figure 4.13 shows a list box control.

FIGURE 4.13.

A list box control.

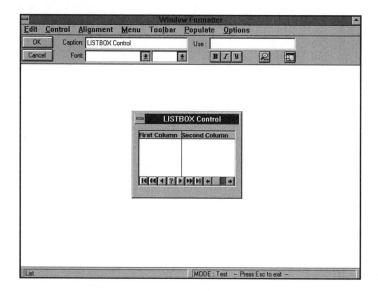

The Combo Box Control

A combo box control is a cross between an entry control and a list box control. You can either type in the value you wish the control to have or choose a preset value from the list box. The combo box control also supports an accelerator search. Figure 4.14 shows a combo box control.

> **NOTE**
>
> In an *accelerator search*, the user types one character, and the item in the list that's closest to that character is highlighted.

FIGURE 4.14.

A combo box control.

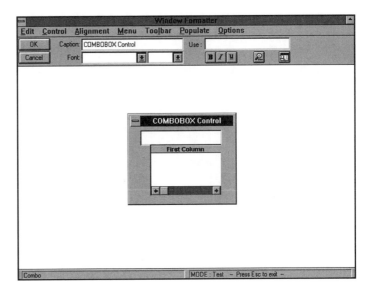

The Spin Control

A spin control is a form of entry control that permits the user to either type in a value or select from a range of values (or a number of preset values) by clicking on the spin arrows or using the cursor keys. It can be used for entry within a numeric range (for example, the user could use the mouse or cursor keys to step through numbers from 1 to 100), or to make a choice from a limited number of options (for example, move through a list of colors such as red, blue, and green). The purpose of the spin control is to provide a quick way to "spin" through the various allowable values for the control. Figure 4.15 shows a spin control.

FIGURE 4.15.

A spin control.

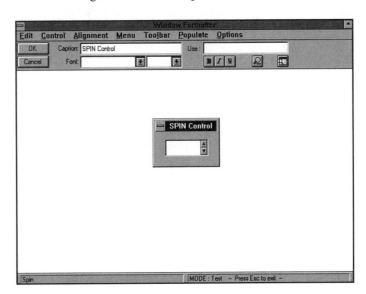

Line, Box, and Circle Controls

The line, box, and circle controls are basic graphic controls that you place on a window and use as desired. You have control over line, fill, color, size, and position. Figure 4.16 illustrates these controls.

FIGURE 4.16.

Line, box, and circle controls with various line styles and fills.

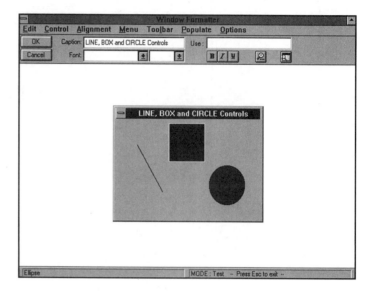

The Image Control

An image control displays a graphical image of one of the following formats: BMP, GIF, ICO, JPG, PCX, and WMF. This control may have both horizontal and vertical scroll bars for scrolling the image within the control. Figure 4.17 shows an image control.

The Region Control

A region control is a special type of control that designates an area of the window as active for sending and receiving Windows messages. For instance, you might use it to trap right mouse button clicks over a particular area of the window or to change the default cursor while the mouse is over that area. Regions may be visible or invisible. Figure 4.18 shows a visible region control.

FIGURE 4.17.
An image control displaying a BMP file.

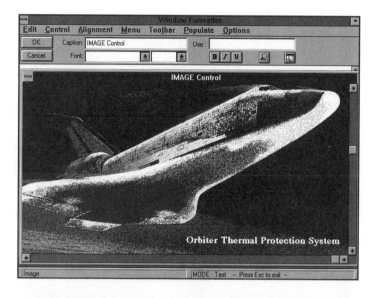

FIGURE 4.18.
A visible region control.

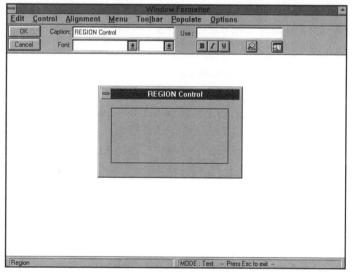

The VBX Control

A VBX control is a special external control of the type designed to be used with Microsoft Visual Basic. VBXs are available for a wide variety of purposes, ranging from all those provided by standard Clarion for Windows controls to special functions such as communications and word processing. Figure 4.19 shows a VBX control from Microsoft. VBXs are covered in more detail in Chapter 26, "Using VBXs and Non-CW DLLs."

FIGURE 4.19.

Microhelp's 3D Calendar VBX.

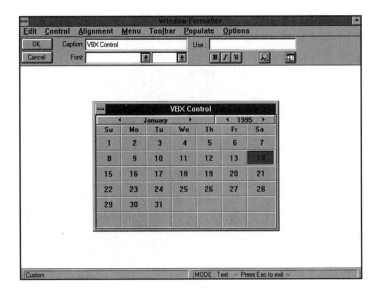

Clarion for Windows can use VBXs that conform to the level 1.0 VBX specification (that is, they can be used with the Visual C++ programming language).

If you have successfully registered the VBX in the Clarion for Windows environment, it will appear on the list presented when you select this control from the Controls toolbox.

WARNING

Although VBXs are an easy way to quickly enhance your applications, they do not perform as well as standard Clarion for Windows controls, so use them wisely.

Responding to the User

So far this chapter has dealt with windows and window controls that give the windows their most obvious functionality. The interesting thing about all these windows and window controls is that they are somewhat loosely connected. That doesn't mean that your buttons are about to fall off your monitor—it means that they all tend to be available for use at just about any time. You have undoubtedly noticed that in most Windows programs you can switch away from the program at just about any time, or change windows within the program at the click of a mouse, or skip to a particular entry on a form just by pressing a hot key.

In DOS programs, on the other hand, the user's path through the program is under tight programmatic control. Users are not usually toggling between two separate parts of the program at will or jumping around the screen in generally unforeseen ways. It is quite possible (and very traditional) to take the user through a particular series of entry fields in a particular order, and the user's only options other than stepping through each field may be to save all entries before completing the form, or to abort the process.

Windows flexibility is part and parcel of its object orientation. If each control (and window) is designed to be more or less self-sufficient, then in theory there is nothing to stop the user from choosing which control to interact with at any given time. But this flexibility also raises an important question: How do I control where the user goes?

In a nutshell, you don't control, you respond. Your job as a Windows programmer is not to restrict the user to a particular path through the program, but to respond to the user's choices. DOS controls, Windows responds.

Messages and Events

It's pretty difficult to respond to something when you don't have the faintest idea what the request is. Windows has the same problem, so every time the user does something (and not just then) Windows generates one or more messages that describe what has happened. The thing that happened is called an *event*. Much of what you will need to know about Windows programming is wrapped up in those two little words: messages and events. So that's it. You can close the book now and get back to work.

Well, there is a little more to it than that. Knowing that there are events that trigger messages is one thing. Realizing the extent of the messaging that happens under Windows is quite another. It's bedlam behind the screen, and this is one of the reasons (probably the main reason) that before Clarion for Windows, serious Windows programming in C or C++, for example, was something you did only if you had to, or you really, really wanted to. It helped to be a rocket scientist.

Compared to a DOS program, a typical Windows program has a vast number of things that can happen during its execution. Consider a DOS entry form. The form opens with the cursor in a field, the user fills in the field and presses Enter, the cursor moves to the next field. In a Windows program, the window opens and the first enabled control in the Z-order is selected. Is the program ready for data entry? No way. Windows is busy giving the Print Manager a couple of cycles to feed that word processing document you started a couple of minutes ago off to the printer, and then it's time for the copy of CLOCK.EXE you have running to update its display, and then you bumped the mouse as you went for the keyboard and that set off a torrent of mouse movement messages, and your program is busy trying to figure out if it ought to be telling Windows to change the mouse cursor depending on which control it's now sitting over and....

You get the idea. It should be pretty obvious by now that procedural or linear coding just won't do. You have to set up some sort of queue that all the messages can funnel into, and then it's up to Windows to see that each program gets all potentially relevant messages, and it's up to each program to decide what to do when such a message arrives.

Messages can signal either that something has happened or that something ought to be done. These messages are not conversational in the sense of "Hello" or "Good-bye." Rather, they are numeric representations or constants constituting some programmatic communiqué. For example, the following represent specific window events, and are taken from the standard Clarion for Windows library file EQUATES.CLW:

```
EVENT:CloseWindow    EQUATE (201H)
EVENT:CloseDown      EQUATE (202H)
EVENT:OpenWindow     EQUATE (203H)
```

As you can see, by using the EVENT:CloseWindow, EVENT:CloseDown, and EVENT:OpenWindow constants (which are far more readable than numbers) your program will receive the related hexadecimal values for these constants and your code will respond correspondingly.

Clarion for Windows' EQUATES.CLW file is comparable in function to the C (or C++) language's WINDOWS.H definition file. It is quite different in size, however. There are hundreds of Windows messages, all listed in WINDOWS.H, and only somewhere around 50 listed in EQUATES.CLW. Why the difference? Primarily, it's because for most programming you shouldn't have to deal with a lot of the low-level messages.

When programming in C or C++, you develop programs to use the Windows API and Window structures directly. This means that you have a lot of control and flexibility. It also means that you have a lot of responsibility and risk—risk that is just not necessary to take for each development task.

Clarion for Windows has removed this programming risk by developing a library manager that every Clarion for Windows program relies on. This library manager resides in CWRUN.DLL, which is loaded at runtime. The library manager understands and responds to standard Windows messages in such a way that you as a developer are concerned with only a few messages, and primarily, only those messages that can affect your application execution. Does this limit you? No, it liberates you! Of course, if you wish, you can always use the Windows API to work at a deeper level.

Simply put, whereas C and C++ programmers can spend a lot of time writing superfluous event logic and responses, Clarion for Windows programmers spend time much more efficiently, enhancing the application's functionality to meet end-user demands. The result is more productivity and profit for you and your customers.

The *EVENT* Loop

In every Windows program there is a main EVENT loop that controls and directs all the other event loops and related processes. An event loop is defined as a process wherein messages are fetched and sent from and to Windows relative to the executing process in which communication with Windows or another executing process or program is possible. It can get pretty complicated at times. The following pseudocode illustrates a typical main event loop in a C (not Clarion for Windows) program:

```
LONG Callback(UINT msg, WPARAM wParam, LPARAM lParam)
{
   switch (msg)
   {
      case WM_PALETTECHANGED:
            /* Someone has changed the windows pallette you need to act */
            /* CW HANDLES THIS AUTOMATICALLY */
      case WM_QUERYNEWPALETTE:
            /* You are recieving focus, do you want to change the pallette */
            /* CW HANDLES THIS AUTOMATICALLY */
      case WM_CREATE:
            /* Your first pass around the callback (the window is being created) */
            You get an open window which is fairly similar
      break;
      case WM_INITMENU:
         /* Your user is heading for the menus, now is a real good
➥time to set them up */
            /* CW HANDLES THIS AUTOMATICALLY */
            break;
      case WM_LBUTTONUP:
          /* The user has released the left button */
          /* CW HANDLES THIS AUTOMATICALLY */
      case WM_NCACTIVATE:
          /* Your frame needs activating or not */
          /* CW HANDLES THIS AUTOMATICALLY */
      case WM_NCPAINT:
      case WM_SETTEXT:
          /* Repaint your frame */
          /* CW HANDLES THIS AUTOMATICALLY */
          break;
      case WM_SETFOCUS:
          /* You are getting focus */
          You get something similar
      case WM_WINDOWPOSCHANGING:
          /* Your window is on the move, you have to track it noting
            zorders etc */
          /* CW HANDLES THIS AUTOMATICALLY */
      case WM_MDIACTIVATE:
          /* Swapping the active MDI child, have to keep sibilings
            under control here */
          /* CW HANDLES THIS AUTOMATICALLY */
      case WM_CHILDACTIVATE:
          /* One of your children is being activated. This can include
          one of your controls (which are windows) */
          /* CW HANDLES THIS AUTOMATICALLY */
      case WM_ACTIVATEAPP:
          /* The active window is swapping between apps */
          /* CW HANDLES THIS AUTOMATICALLY */
      case WM_ACTIVATE:
          /* When a window becomes active or inactive. This is not
           -quite- the same as who has focus */
          /* CW HANDLES THIS AUTOMATICALLY */
      case WM_PAINT:
      /* Ok, someone has messed up the screen, time to redraw yourself.*/
       /* CW HANDLES THIS AUTOMATICALLY */
      case WM_COMMAND:
          /* Someone is sending you a command such as a keypress, or a
          menu selection */
```

```
      This is a kind of catch-all for windows. For CW it gets
      translated into alrts, or simple accepted messages.
  case WM_ERASEBKGND:
     /*You are about to be moved, please get off the screen */
     /* CW HANDLES THIS AUTOMATICALLY */
  case WM_CHAR:
     /* SOmeone press a key ! */
     /* CW HANDLES THIS AUTOMATICALLY */
  case WM_CLOSE:
     /* Get lost */
     /* CW HANDLES THIS AUTOMATICALLY  but you do get a number
      of different close-down messages.*/
  }
DefWindowProc(msg,wparam,lparam)
}
```

Clarion for Windows handles the tedious bits automatically, so you don't have to. It uses a library manager called CWRUN10.DLL, which provides the main event loop processes (fetching and sending messages) for all Clarion for Windows programs. Subsequent event loops are handled in Clarion for Windows code by a construct known as the ACCEPT loop.

The *ACCEPT* Loop

In Clarion for Windows programs, messages are sent and received within an ACCEPT loop, which obtains those messages from the library manager. What happens is the library manager determines which messages are generally important for an application program to receive and those messages are passed on to the ACCEPT loop process of the application. However, your program may send messages that are not of a general nature via the Windows API, when necessary.

An ACCEPT loop is a construct similar to that of a Windows EVENT loop, but with the main purpose of taming the Windows messaging noise so that you can be more productive, writing application-oriented code instead of low-level Windows management code.

How the *ACCEPT* Loop Works

The ACCEPT loop is a very simple construct to use, yet it is highly sophisticated and optimized for programmer productivity and program performance. Messages in Clarion for Windows are read via the EVENT() function and are sent via the POST() function. These two functions provide the mechanisms required for communicating in a Clarion for Windows program. Messages are placed in the Windows message queue in FIFO (first in first out) order, therefore these messages will be processed in the correct order by the library manager and accordingly processed in the correct order by your ACCEPT loop.

The following is an example of the ACCEPT loop, assuming that you have a window and at least one control on the window:

```
ACCEPT
  CASE EVENT()
  OF EVENT:OpenWindow
```

```
OF EVENT:OpenFailed
OF EVENT:CloseDown
OF EVENT:CloseWindow
OF EVENT:Iconize
OF EVENT:Iconized
OF EVENT:Maximize
OF EVENT:Maximized
OF EVENT:Restore
OF EVENT:Restored
OF EVENT:Move
OF EVENT:Moved
OF EVENT:Size
OF EVENT:Sized
OF EVENT:GainFocus
OF EVENT:LoseFocus
OF EVENT:Completed
END
CASE FIELD()
OF ?Button
  CASE EVENT()
  OF EVENT:Selected
  OF EVENT:Accepted
  OF EVENT:Drop
  END
END
END
```

The *ACCEPT* Statement

The ACCEPT statement is the top of a loop that is closed by the last END statement shown. This loop is the controlling mechanism for all Clarion for Windows programs that use a window. For all intents and purposes, each time the loop cycles (goes back around) the library manager takes over and determines whether there are messages waiting for this process to read, and if so they are passed on to this process.

The *EVENT()* Function

The EVENT() function is invoked when there are waiting messages. The EVENT() function is used in a CASE statement, which is similar to a SWITCH statement in the C programming language. What this does is check the value returned by the EVENT() function in the order specified in the CASE statement. If there is a match, the corresponding code in the OF condition of the CASE statement is processed, otherwise the next OF condition is checked, and so on. If there are no matching conditions, nothing happens and program control flows to the CASE FIELD() statement.

At this point I would like to digress and discuss some general Windows programming considerations. First, there are different classifications of messages or events. Some events apply to the window, whereas others apply to the controls on the window. It is standard Windows programming practice to check for window messages first and then to check for window control messages. I call the first process *global window event processing* and the latter *window control event processing*. This is done in order to ensure that global window events are processed before any window control events. Since some window events can override or even bypass other events, it is important to process these events first. Just such a case is the EVENT:CloseDown, which will automatically stop the ACCEPT loop. You will want to make sure to process this event before processing any control specific events that might slow down the closing of the window.

I have listed in the OF condition of the CASE EVENT() function lines most of the standard global window events you might need to be concerned about. I encourage you to study these events and how they affect your application in the Clarion for Windows language reference manual or online help.

The *FIELD()* Function

The FIELD() function is invoked for checking which window control the user is positioned on when an event or message occurs. For example, say the user is positioned on a button and an EVENT:Accepted is read from the Windows message queue. The global CASE EVENT() is ignored, and the CASE FIELD() function is invoked. First the control to receive the message is determined by the OF condition of this CASE statement, and then the subsequent EVENT() function is invoked to determine which event was posted to this control. In the case of a button control, an EVENT:Accepted means that the user pushed the button. Any code you desire to execute when this condition occurs would be placed beneath the OF EVENT:Accepted line of the CASE FIELD() and OF ?Button line.

What happens when there are neither global window events nor control events, but something happens to cause the event loop to cycle? In this case, the library manager will take control at the top of the ACCEPT loop and check the Windows message queue for waiting messages again and the whole process will start over again.

The ACCEPT loop is a simple and elegant way to deal with the barrage of messages that continue to flow during the life of your program. The ACCEPT loop is small, efficient, and easy to comprehend, unlike its cousin the C/C++ event loop.

Summary

In this chapter you have seen some of the basic concepts at work in the wonderful world of Windows programming. If you've come from DOS programming, this must seem like an alien planet. Instead of screens you have windows, instead of fields you have controls, and instead of some simple program logic you have a complex system of events and messages.

Programming for Windows really does involve a shift in your worldview. If you're coming to Clarion for Windows from another Windows development platform, you may already have made the shift. If not, hopefully this chapter has given you some fundamental concepts that will serve you well as you make the transition. Chapter 5, "Unlearning DOS: Old Habits Die Hard," expands on this theme and explains some of the practical ways the Windows programming paradigm will affect your program design.

5

Unlearning DOS: Old Habits Die Hard

Whether you have limited or extensive programming experience in DOS, you probably have formed a programming mind-set that, whether you realize it or not, makes certain assumptions based on features that are part of the DOS operating system, but not necessarily part of Windows. For example, you may be accustomed to dealing with a screen of 25 rows and 80 columns; you may rely on the use of terminate-and-stay-resident (TSR) programs; or it may be your practice to access hardware directly to give your programs a performance boost. You may use any of a number of other programming techniques that become problematic or simply obsolete when you begin programming for Windows. The simple fact is that you cannot program in Windows the way you program in DOS.

By nature, DOS is a static environment and it does not support a standard programming interface other than low-level service interrupt access. Windows, on the other hand, is dynamic and removes many of the limitations imposed by the DOS screen I/O architecture. It forces the programmer to work at a higher level of abstraction from the machine and provides a complete programming application programming interface (API). Actually, Windows has many APIs, depending on what you need to accomplish. This makes for a robust and rich application development platform.

In DOS, a simple application may have some screen fields and specific keystrokes that determine an action to perform. The same Windows program has objects that provide access to their attributes by way of mechanisms known as properties. User actions are determined by messaging via events instead of via simple keystrokes. Most if not everything you see on a Windows screen is modifiable at runtime. DOS programs in most cases cannot be changed this way—they are static. Generally, in Windows, if you can see an object, it can be queried for the current value of its attributes and in most cases, these attributes can be modified to fit your program's needs.

To help you better understand how DOS and Windows differ, this chapter covers the user interface (UI) differences between DOS and Windows programs and the impact those differences have on the way you program.

Interface Conventions

Most DOS development platforms don't force any structure or standard on the developer, and as a result many DOS programs don't follow any standard at all. There are some development environments, such as Clarion for DOS (CDD), which guide the developer into a common user access (CUA) interface; CUA was the first interface standard that many developers encountered.

Although programs written in CDD by default use a CUA interface design model, it is possible to override this model and do just about whatever you desire. For all intents and purposes, most DOS programs employ an unstructured user interface that leads to end-user confusion.

Windows uses a modified CUA interface standard. I say *modified* because in some respects, such as menuing, Windows has replaced the rigid CUA standard with a specific design that Microsoft deemed more consistent and easier to use.

The idea behind using a common interface standard is to ease the learning and training curve that new users must undergo from application to application, so that they are more familiar, comfortable, and productive. Windows, while using these standards extensively, does not force you to rigidly stay within these standards, which again means that it is up to you, the programmer, to ensure that the standard is adhered to. Thankfully, Clarion for Windows aids you in attaining this goal by using a standard Windows CUA menuing system that can use standard Windows *actions* such as Cut, Copy, and Paste, among many others. In addition, through the definition, integration, and use of the dictionary and AppGen templates, you can define your default application frame and every default window's attributes for your project, which will help you to ensure that these standards are upheld in your applications. Remember, whatever you can do to give your users a common and familiar way of doing something, the more chance your application has of being widely accepted and successful. Clarion for Windows makes it easy to achieve interface consistency in your applications.

Enter and Esc Versus Tab and Shift+Tab

In DOS programs, the de facto standard is to use the Enter key to complete an entry field after entering some data. In Windows, the job of the Enter key is done with the Tab key. A Tab keystroke will move focus (the control that is waiting for input) from one control to another in the Z-order. (See Chapter 4, "Concepts You Should Know" for more details on the Z-order.)

WARNING

If you are coming from a DOS background, you will most likely be tempted to replace the Tab key default behavior with the Enter key. Although this would make your Windows programs work similarly to your DOS programs, you would be violating the standard Windows interface convention for control completion. Even though using the Enter key may cut down your new users' learning curve (if they are coming from DOS), it will surely confuse those who already know Windows and those who use other Windows programs. Remember, consistency engenders productivity and acceptance.

In DOS you may have used the Esc key to back up a field. In Windows, Shift+Tab (normally called a back tab) is used to back up from the current control to a previous control in the Z-order.

In Windows the Enter key is used to signal completion of the form and the Esc key is used to signal the cancellation and exit of a form.

Standard Keys

In Windows, there are standard keys that perform consistent operations across programs (or at least they should). The F1 key is one of these keys and is used to invoke *content* help. Content help is generally the base help window for the application. The Shift+F1 key combination is used to invoke context-sensitive help for the window or control. *Context-sensitive help* is a window that displays specific help for the currently selected item. Windows provides a help engine for all programs (WINHELP.EXE), which Clarion for Windows communicates with through the use of the HLP attribute on the window or control objects.

In DOS, you may have used function keys (F1 through F12) to invoke a process. In Windows you could do the same, but in most instances a button is the preferred method. This is done primarily for ease of use. In DOS the user would need to remember that F7 might mean to print a report. In Windows, a button labeled Print might be used in place of the function key, making this functionality more explicit and obvious to the user.

In DOS menus, you may have used a hot letter (highlighted a different color) to inform the user which key to press to invoke an action. In Windows, hot letters are shown by an underscore and are called *accelerator keys*. They are used on menus as are function keys. In many cases, function keys in a Windows program are used in combination with the Ctrl or Alt key. For example, in Windows you have a menu with an item called Exit. This is the standard menu item name that is used to exit a program. To add the hot letter, in the text of the menu item you would place an & (ampersand) to denote that the following letter is the hot letter for this item. In the case of the Exit menu item, the letter *x* is the generally accepted standard hot letter for this item. So, the text for the item would be E&xit. In addition, the Alt+F4 key combination is used as a standard keystroke to exit an application, and it could be included on the menu as well.

An interesting aspect to menus in Clarion for Windows is the STD attribute on the menu item. When used, this automatically invokes the associated functionality when the item is selected. The available standard attributes are listed in the Equates.clw file in the \CW\LIBSRC directory. In Listing 5.1, look at the STD attribute on the Exit item. I have used STD(STD:Close) to indicate that when the Exit menu item is selected (clicked on), the application should automatically attempt to exit. I say "attempt to exit" only because it is possible to stop this action from actually taking place.

Listing 5.1. The Exit Example program.

```
ExitExam    PROGRAM

            INCLUDE('Equates.Clw')

            MAP
            END

wMdiFrame APPLICATION('Exit Example'),AT(0,0,317,172),Center,    ¦
          MSG('Developing Applications in Clarion for Windows'), ¦
```

```
STATUS,SYSTEM,MAXIMIZE,RESIZE
            MENUBAR
              MENU('&File')
                ITEM('E&xit'),STD(STD:Close)
              END
            END
          END

  CODE
    OPEN(wMdiFrame)
    ACCEPT
      CASE EVENT()
      END
      CASE FIELD()
      END
    END
    CLOSE(wMdiFrame)
```

As you can see, there is no code inserted to support the exiting of the application, yet if you were to run this program, you would see that the program in fact will exit automatically when the Exit menu item is selected.

Screen Versus Window

What you used to call a screen in DOS is now referred to, in Windows, as (you guessed it) a window. As mentioned earlier, one of the primary differences between DOS and Windows programming is that in DOS you can place text wherever you desire on the screen, using either a screen variable or by simply displaying text at a given screen coordinate. In Windows, you will place a control on the window. This control communicates with the window and Windows itself through messaging.

DOS screens can have text placed at explicit coordinates in the screen structure. These coordinates can normally range from 1 to 80 columns by 1 to 25 rows. Control positioning in Windows offers a finer level of accuracy—using pixels instead of rows and columns. You can also change the control's position at runtime, and Windows will automatically move it and redraw the window in the control's old and new locations (in CW, that is).

For example, a title on a DOS screen might utilize a variable. To center this title variable in a DOS screen would take some effort. You would need to determine the actual length of the title (the text in the variable, less the spaces) and the actual width of the screen (the maximum number of columns), determine an algorithm to center the string within the variable itself, and of course write the code to finally display the title on the screen. All this just to center the title on the screen.

In Windows, by contrast, you define a window's title attribute via a string literal, not a variable. This attribute contains the logic to automatically center the title on the window for you, thus eliminating the need to center the title manually. It sounds simple, doesn't it? It is! But why use a literal instead of a variable? Does this mean that you are limited to only the initial value of this string literal as the title? No, you can change this value through property settings. Consider the following window structure:

```
wMdiFrame APPLICATION('Title Example'),AT(0,0,317,172),Center,  ¦
          MSG('Developing Applications in Clarion for Windows'),  ¦
STATUS,SYSTEM,MAXIMIZE,RESIZE
```

In this window structure, the string literal `Title Example` is the default title for the window. To change this you would simply insert the following code in the `CODE` section of your program anyplace after the `OPEN(wMdiFrame)` statement:

```
wMdiFrame {PROP:TEXT} = 'My Window'
```

This statement changes the value in the Text property of the window to My Window. It even centers it automatically for you!

Although setting a property may seem like a bit more work than simply setting a variable, it accomplishes much more. The fact that the Title attribute already understands and provides for centering the Text property of the Title attribute clearly illustrates the benefits of object-oriented programming and the reduction of code required to accomplish similar tasks in the much more complex world of Windows. You will need to get used to this method of changing properties if you want to take full advantage of Windows' capabilities.

Field Versus Control Editing

You might recall that in DOS when data was input into an entry field, you could trap the completion key stroke that signaled that the user had input data and it was ready for validation. You might have performed the validation at that point or later on in the program or maybe not at all. In any case, you relied on a particular sequence of events happening to instruct the program to take some action. For instance, say your program uses a Social Security Number field that's a required field. To move from field to field, the user presses the Enter key, and when that happens you might need to validate that the user actually input some data into this field. If the field is blank or invalid, you might display an error message and then reselect the field for the user.

In Windows, the concept of control editing at first appears similar to DOS's field editing, yet it is very different in practice, and for the most part it is far more intuitive.

There are essentially three control editing events (messages) you need to learn and understand. Two of these are control-level events and the other is a window-level or control-independent event. An event, as you might recall from Chapter 4, is a message that is an instruction to perform an action. The following events are used for control editing:

■ `EVENT:Selected` is a control-level event that is generated by Clarion for Windows when you move from control to control by using either the Tab key or the mouse. This event informs your program that the control that is receiving this particular event is going to be selected (it will become the active control).

- ■ EVENT:Accepted is a control-level event that is generated by Clarion for Windows when the user has input data into the control and presses either a completion key assigned to the control or the Tab key, or selects another control with the mouse.

- ■ EVENT:Completed is a window-level event that is generated by Clarion for Windows upon successful editing of all controls after the PROP:AcceptAll property has been issued for the window. That needs some explanation. Given that you have a window with OK and Cancel buttons as well as some entry controls, you may assume that if the user presses the OK button, all edits must be performed on the controls to ensure that data is both valid and, when required, present. When the user presses the OK button, you can force this situation by setting the Window property PROP:AcceptAll to 1 or TRUE. This action informs the ACCEPT loop that an Auto-Accept mode has been set which will post an EVENT:Accepted to each control on the form, forcing any control edits to take place automatically for your program. There are no EVENT:Selected events generated—instead, EVENT:Accepted events are generated.

The beauty in this logic is that there are no external flags or variables required in order to inform the ACCEPT loop that it has to process an EVENT:Accepted on each control. Better yet, when the Auto-Accept mode has successfully completed, the ACCEPT loop will set the current event to EVENT:Completed for you automatically so you can break out of the loop and exit the window.

The following are the equate definitions (constants) for the events just described. They are found in the \cw\libsrc\equates.clw file:

```
EVENT:Selected      EQUATE (101H)  !Control Level
EVENT:Accepted      EQUATE (01H)   !Control Level
EVENT:Completed     EQUATE (225H)  !Window Level (Control independent)
```

In addition to the previous events, there are two properties that concern control editing:

- ■ PROP:AcceptAll, as mentioned, informs the ACCEPT loop that an EVENT:Accepted should be automatically generated for every control on the window, thus invoking control-editing logic for each control.

- ■ PROP:Touched can be used to determine whether a control edit should even be invoked at all. PROP:Touched will be set to 1 or TRUE whenever the user has input or changed the value contained in the control.

The following are the equate definitions (constants) for the events just discussed. They are found in the \cw\libsrc\equates.clw file:

```
PROP:AcceptAll      EQUATE(7C9AH)  ! 0 = off, else on
PROP:Touched        EQUATE(7C9BH)  ! 0 = off, else on
```

Listing 5.2 is a simple example of a basic ACCEPT loop that includes control-editing code.

Listing 5.2. A simple example of control editing.

```
OPEN(w_ControlEditExample)
ACCEPT
  CASE EVENT()
  OF EVENT:CloseDown
     BREAK
  OF EVENT:CloseWindow
     BREAK
  OF EVENT:Completed
     POST(EVENT:CloseWindow)
  END
  CASE FIELD()
  OF ?Entry1
    CASE EVENT()
    OF EVENT:Selected
    OF EVENT:Accepted
       IF ?Entry1{PROP:Touched} = TRUE
!        do some control editing here
       END
    END
  OF ?OkButton
    CASE EVENT()
    OF EVENT:Selected
    OF EVENT:Accepted
       w_ControlEditExample{PROP:AcceptAll} = TRUE
    END
  END
END
CLOSE(w_ControlEditExample)
```

Looking at Listing 5.2, you can see that for the window and each control there is a CASE EVENT() check processed. The EVENT() function retrieves any waiting messages for the window or control, respectively. Within the EVENT:Accepted event, you can see that if the value has been input or changed, control editing should be performed (based on PROP:Touched = TRUE). Assuming that you have the Req (required) attribute on the control, it must pass through the control-validation logic. But what if you want to display your own error message for this situation. In that case you will add a little more to the validation condition like this:

```
IF ?Entry1{PROP:Touched} = TRUE
!  do some control editing here
ELSIF ?Entry1{PROP:TEXT} = ''
!  do some required control editing here
END
```

Note that the dictionary allows you to set the Req (required) attribute of a field in a file, which is (through AppGen) translated to a required property on the window control. However, for ultimate control over the data-entry process and if you have special data entry requirements (such as displaying a message to the user that informs him of the exact problem), you may want to resort to something of this nature. In any event, control editing is simple to implement, straightforward to use, and robust enough for almost any data-entry problem you might encounter.

Menus Versus Menus, Toolbars, and Toolboxes

A menu is an object that allows you to provide a drop-down list of available options to the user. In DOS there are many styles from which to choose. In Windows, there is only one—the Windows CUA menu control. A Windows menu contains a menu bar (the horizontal menu option line) and drop-down, cascading menus.

The Windows CUA menu provides you with *menus* and *items*. A menu is an option that can act as a container for additional options, which are known as items. An item is a subcomponent of a menu. You can nest menus within menus—these are called submenus. It is standard practice to associate at least a hot letter to each menu and item. You denote this by using an ampersand (&) in the option name. When the menu structure encounters an &, it will place an underscore on the letter following the &. If the hot letter is associated with a horizontal menu option, you will use the Alt key and the hot letter together to invoke the option. If the hot letter is on an item or submenu on a drop-down list, you will simply press that letter to invoke it. Additionally, you can associate a key combination to invoke the option. This is generally done by using the Ctrl key and the hot letter together. In some cases, such as Exit, an Alt key and a hot letter combination is used.

Menus are set up topically (that is, by the area of functionality). For instance, the Edit menu (a standard Windows menu) represents editing functions that can be used in your program. There are four main topical areas that all Windows programs should contain: File, Edit, Window, and Help. File and Edit are usually the first two menus on the menu bar, and Window and Help are usually the last two. Application-specific menus appear between these two sets.

Table 5.1 contains a table of standard topical Windows menu option names, the hot letter, and the associated key combinations.

Table 5.1. Standard topical Windows menu option names.

Menu/Item Name	Hot Letter	Key Combination
&File	F	
&New	N	Ctrl+N
&Open	O	Ctrl+O
&Close	C	
&Save	S	Ctrl+S
&Print	P	Ctrl+P
E&xit	X	Alt+F4
&Edit	E	
&Undo	U	Ctrl+Z
Cu&t	T	Ctrl+X

continues

Table 5.1. continued

Menu/Item Name	Hot Letter	Key Combination
&Copy	C	Ctrl+C
&Paste	P	Ctrl+V
C&lear	L	Delete
&Window	W	
&Tile	T	
&Cascade	C	
&Arrange Icons	A	
&Help	H	
&Contents	C	
&Search for Help On…	S	
&How to Use Help	H	
&About	A	

Menus, Toolbars, and Toolboxes

The multiple-document interface (MDI) frame is usually given a menu. This menu is the base menu for the application and will always be available to the user when MDI child windows are opened. In addition, an MDI child can define a menu that is merged onto (combined with) the MDI frame menu when it is opened. This merging then makes the new menu context specific. When the MDI child window is closed, the child's menu is removed and the menu will return to its previous state.

In a non-MDI menu scheme, each window can have a menu. There is no merging of menus since each window is independent from the others (they are non-MDI windows). Therefore, you could have two windows open, each with their own menu structures.

In many Windows programs, you will notice an area just beneath the menu bar that usually contains buttons with little graphics on them. This is known as a toolbar and is a placeholder for controls that appears under the menu bar and can have any number of controls placed on it. A toolbar is generally used for providing access that's quicker than selecting a menu item, and is generally made up of buttons that use graphical representations of their functionality. This representation is done by the use of an icon (ICO file) on a button control. You are not limited to using only buttons—any standard control can reside on the toolbar. For example, you might have a button with a drawing of a door on it that says EXIT. This button would contain the STD(STD:Close) attribute so that whenever the user presses it, the application will exit back to Windows. This button would correlate to the Exit item on your menu.

Toolbars, just like menus and items, can be *context aware,* which means that they can change when merged with the toolbar of an MDI child. In other words, the toolbar responds to MDI in the same way a menu or item does.

Listing 5.3 illustrates a simple program that includes a menu and toolbar.

Listing 5.3. The Menu Example program.

```
MenuEx                 PROGRAM

                       INCLUDE('EQUATES.CLW')
                       INCLUDE('ERRORS.CLW')
                       INCLUDE('KEYCODES.CLW')

                       MAP
                         Main()
                       END

wMdiFrame APPLICATION('Menu Example'),AT(0,0,317,190),Center, ¦
          SYSTEM,MAX,MAXIMIZE,RESIZE
MENUBAR
        MENU('&File')
          ITEM('E&xit        Alt+F4'),KEY(AltF4),STD(STD:Close)
        END
      END
      TOOLBAR,AT(0,0,317,16)
        BUTTON('Exit'),AT(2,2,,),KEY(AltF4),USE(?ExitButton),¦
        ICON('WINPYR.ICO')
END
      END            Window & Pyramid

 CODE
 Main()

Main                   PROCEDURE
 CODE
 OPEN(wMdiFrame)
 ACCEPT
   CASE EVENT()
   OF EVENT:CloseDown
     BREAK
   END
   CASE FIELD()
   OF ?ExitButton
     CASE EVENT()
     OF EVENT:Accepted
       POST(EVENT:CloseDown)
     END
   END
 END
 CLOSE(wMdiFrame)
 RETURN
```

In some Windows programs, you might have noticed a floating window that has buttons on it, and that always resides on top of the other windows that you open. This type of window is known as a toolbox and is defined by the Toolbox window attribute. A toolbox is similar to a toolbar, but is always visible and is the top-most window on the client workspace of the MDI frame.

Note that recently toolbars have been given the capability to become toolboxes, often known as *dockable toolbars*. In CW, there is no standard control that provides a dockable toolbar, but a Visual Basic Control (VBX) can be used for this purpose.

The main purpose of a toolbox is to provide a place to hold controls that generally provide common tools to perform common tasks among multiple windows. For example, you could have a Save button represented as an icon of a disk on the toolbox window. This toolbox would always be visible and on top of every window in your application. The button might be enabled (available for selection) only when a certain condition exists, such as changing or adding a record, otherwise it might be disabled (not available for selection).

Pick Lists Versus Drop-Down List Boxes

There are many occasions when you might need to select a value for a given entry control from a list of values in another file. In DOS, this was typically performed by using a pick list, a menu, or a browse screen. In Windows, these techniques can be used as well, but there is another alternative—the combo box.

A combo box is a list-style control that provides a few special features to support this selection-style activity. A combo box is really composed of two controls: an entry control and a list control. The entry control portion is where the user will input the selection value and it is also where the result of the selection from the list portion of the control will be displayed. The list control portion is where the possible values for selection are displayed. The user typically has three options: to type in a value; to press the down arrow, which "drops" the list portion of the control so the user may select a value; and to type in a value and press the down arrow, which causes the list control portion to search for the closest matching value in the list.

The combo box control is generally used when there are a limited number of values to choose from (a few hundred or so) or when the choices are static. The reason for this involve concurrency of data (a value on a list could be changed or deleted from the time it was originally read into the list), memory, and performance. The smaller the list, the faster the combo box will respond to the user's search request.

In many cases, you can limit the amount of data in a combo box since the data allowed for a given entry control is generally limited to a subset of a file. For example, you may want to keep your static choices in a file in case these values change over time. In this case, you would read data from a file into a queue and assign the queue to the combo box. Specifically, using a combo box for something like gender or religion might work well as there are a limited number of entries possible. However, something like ZIP code might prove to be too large for your purposes and better suited to a browse or pick list.

A variation on the idea of the combo box is to use a list box with a Drop attribute. This functions much the same way, except the user is not able to type in new values—entries must be chosen from the list box. Both list boxes and combo boxes with the Drop attribute may be referred to as drop-down list boxes.

Colors, Fonts, and the Creative Mind

Some technologists insist that programming is a science. Others say it is an art. I contend that it is a balance of both of these disciplines.

In many DOS-based programs, colors are used to denote functionality or give an indication of a condition to the user. In most DOS programs, fonts are not a large consideration at all, except for those that are graphically based and utilize font technology as well. The problem is that on a DOS text screen, the most obvious option you have to distinguish one item from another is color, maybe sometimes a font, and you are most likely accustomed to using this technique. In Windows, the problem is completely different. There are many choices—maybe too many.

One major problem in early Windows programs was color and font abuse. That is, many different colors were used with various font families, sizes, and orientation on a single window, which gave Windows a really strange persona in its infancy. A friend of mine asked me to come see his first Windows program that he had written in Visual Basic. The window background was bright cyan, the prompts were BIG and blue (some prompts used colons and others didn't), and the entry controls were black on white. The window included some text strings that were in some shade of red and also in an italic font. It also had buttons that were green, yellow, and red (indicating OK, cancel, and abort, respectively).

Now, all this seemed intuitive and logical to the programmer (he was a musician, of course), but I found myself reeling for the closest toilet bowl. After composing myself, I gave him my honest—and brutal—opinion. This single incident has forever affected the way I approach window design.

> **TIP**
>
> It is easy to fall into design pitfalls as you move into the world of Windows programming. To avoid them, you should always attempt to keep your programs as simple as possible until you are comfortable with Windows and Clarion for Windows. Use the KISS (keep it simple, stupid) principle.

Thankfully, programming environments soon supported the 3D (three-dimensional, or gray) look, which helped programmers avoid going overboard on colors. However, fonts are still a big issue. It seems that since color has been replaced with gray, programmers have found their creative outlet in the use of fonts—many fonts. Both colors and fonts are traps awaiting the new graphical user interface (GUI) programmer, and many get caught.

Take a moment to think about the commercial Windows software you use every day. What does it look like? I suppose that most of it has a consistent look and feel, with few colors and few font families, type sizes, and orientation. There must be a reason, right? Yes, it is because it looks better and it's far easier to understand what's going on without all the confusing and distracting colors and fonts. It may seem a bit boring to some, but the fact remains that mixing too many colors and too many fonts makes for a busy and unintuitive interface.

Windows has default colors and fonts assigned when you install it. Some users will customize these settings, which can greatly affect the look and intuitive nature of the colors you chose for your system, based on your default window colors and fonts. In DOS you used colors simply because there was a lack of graphical controls and it made complete sense to do so. In Windows, you have many other options and alternatives, such as check boxes, spin buttons, and so on. Using a gray or 3D background is safe (and in vogue and politically correct at this time) and provides a consistent backdrop for your programs.

Using an application-centric, uniform color and font scheme (for example using magenta for group boxes with an MS Sans Serif 10-point font, using dark blue for prompts with an MS Sans Serif 9-point font, and using black for entry controls with an MS Sans Serif 8-point font) provides a unique and friendly interface for your users. Whatever you do, remember, just as the user can control the way the application itself works, the user can also adjust the system settings, which can have adverse effects on the look and operation of your programs. Moreover, since programming is a creative effort of sorts, I suggest that you make your application unique in functionality, performance, and benefit to the user, instead of through colors, fonts, and graphics.

Summary

There are some similarities between DOS and Windows programs, and there are some very striking differences. First, leave behind your preconceptions of what a program is and does, how it works, and how it communicates with the underlying operating system. Second, understand the principles of the new operating system you are developing for—in this case "responding" versus "controlling." And finally, you must explore, learn, read, and comprehend the numerous choices available to you as a developer. Learn what works for your users. Your goal is not to use every option, but to provide an effective user interface that increases productivity and solves the business problem at hand.

II

Developing with the
Application Generator

6

Quick Start: The Two-Minute Application

The title of this chapter is somewhat misleading—the fact is that it's quite possible to create an application in Clarion for Windows (CW) in well under two minutes, depending on how speedy a typist you are, how fast your computer is, and how complex an application you ask Quick Start to design.

Quick Start is a utility that creates database applications, and in that sense it represents a fairly narrow kind of functionality within the realm of possible CW applications. The good news is that any application you create with Quick Start can be enhanced in any way you choose. Even if you have no intention of writing database applications, a Quick Start application will give you a clear idea of how to create a multiwindow (and fully multiple-document interface, or MDI) application, whatever you choose to use the windows for.

Quick Start is also by no means the only way to begin developing applications. If you're already comfortable with the concepts of data dictionaries and the Application Generator, you may want to skip this chapter entirely. If not, read on.

The Two-Minute Application

To create your two-minute application you should be at the CW main menu. Get your egg timer ready. Choose File|New|Application, and CW will ask you if you want to use Quick Start, as shown in Figure 6.1.

FIGURE 6.1.

Whenever you create a new application you have the option of using Quick Start.

Answer Yes to load Quick Start. The Quick Start dialog window appears, as shown in Figure 6.2. This is where you will fill out all the information needed for Quick Start to create a fully functional application for you. At the very minimum, this will be seven entries.

Notice that as you move from entry to entry on the Quick Start window, the help text at the bottom changes to apply specifically to that entry. The entries are the following:

■ Application Name. This is the name you will assign to your application. It must be a valid DOS filename, and may include the drive and path. If the drive and path are omitted, the default directory is assumed. If you want to look up a directory (or even an application you want to replace with your Quick Start application) you can click on the button with the ellipsis (…) immediately to the right of the Application Name entry box. That will bring up a standard file dialog box.

FIGURE 6.2.

The Quick Start dialog window.

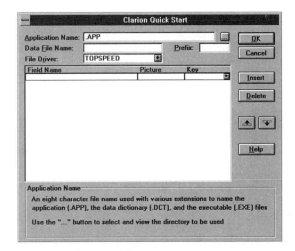

■ *Data File Name.* This entry is for the label that will be assigned to your data file. Quick Start, as mentioned earlier, creates database applications, and database applications require data files that are separate from the application itself. The filename you are specifying here is not the actual physical filename but the label that the program will use to refer to the file in source code. The physical filename will be taken from the first eight characters of the name you specify. The extension will be the default value for the type of data file created. If you'd like to use a filename other than the label you've specified, you can change that later. See Chapter 7, "Defining Your Data," for more information.

■ *Prefix.* A prefix is a one- to three-character string that helps to uniquely identify a field in a file. For instance, in an application that uses more than one file (although Quick Start creates applications with only a single data file, you can easily add more files yourself) you might have several files with a field called Customer. Unfortunately, the compiler will not allow two fields (or any two variables) in one application to share the same name, since it wouldn't know which one was being referred to. The solution is to use a file prefix. If your Customer file has a prefix of CUS:, and your Invoice file has the prefix INV:, the two fields will be known as CUS:CUSTOMER and INV:CUSTOMER, and the compiler will be happy. It is customary to use the first three characters of the filename as the prefix, although you can use any characters you like, provided that they are valid for Clarion labels.

■ *File Driver.* This allows you to choose the type of file to create. As discussed in Chapter 1, "Introduction to the Development Environment," and Chapter 3, "Choosing Databases Wisely," CW uses a database driver technology that allows you to access a wide range of database file types. The drivers that ship with CW 1.0 include ASCII, BASIC, Btrieve, DOS (binary), Clarion, Clipper, dBASE3, dBASE4, FoxPro, ODBC (which allows access to many other file formats and SQL databases), and TopSpeed. For purposes of this exercise, you can use any that appear in the list. The TopSpeed driver is an excellent choice if you're not sure which one to use. You may also notice that not all the file formats listed here appear in the drop-down list box. Only those file formats that support keyed access appear in the list.

■ *Field Name.* In order to create the data file, you specify the names of the various fields you want stored. As Chapter 7 shows, CW applications (through the use of the Data Dictionary) keep track of not only the names of the fields but their default appearance as prompts on windows and reports. A label that is suitable for a field definition is probably not suitable for a prompt, since labels do not allow the use of spaces. Where the label might be CUS:Firstname, you would probably want the prompt on an update form to appear as First Name:. If you follow the convention of capitalizing the different words in your label, Quick Start will automatically separate them when it creates the prompt data. For instance, if you want CUS:Firstname to appear as First Name: on windows, specify it as CUS:FirstName.

TIP

Quick Start automatically creates a data dictionary for your Quick Start application. Data dictionaries contain a wealth of options for prompts, file relationships, field validations, and more. As with the AppGen, Quick Start's treatment of Data Dictionary issues is fairly simplistic.

■ *Picture.* All fields in a file must have a picture token that determines how the value in that field will be formatted. The two examples in the help text at the bottom of the window show you how to do strings and numbers. You can also use any of the date picture tokens that are valid for CW. For instance, to create a date field with the format *mm*/*dd*/*yy*, you would use the picture token D1. To create a time field with a format of *hh*:*mm*:*ss*, use the picture token T4. For more on picture tokens, see your CW Language Reference or look in the online help under Picture Tokens.

The variable type is automaticaly assigned to the field based on the picture you choose. For instance, the picture S30 will automatically result in a string field, whereas a picture of D1 will result in a long field. Also, while the CW language requires you place an @ character before a picture, Quick Start will do this for you automatically.

■ *Key.* A key determines in what order you can get at the information in the file. Although you can read file information in the order in which it was placed in the file, Quick Start requires you to have at least one field keyed. Keys can be unique, or they can allow duplicate entries. If you want a key on last names, for instance, the key ought to allow duplicates. A key on customer number, on the other hand, should probably be unique.

Quick Start's approach to keys is a very simple one—it allows you only one field per key. In fact, the Data Dictionary allows you to build any key structure permitted by the file driver you are using. Quick Start's purpose is not to give you full access to all of CW's features, but to get you on the fast track. You can enhance your application once it has been created.

Start Your Timer

Well, maybe starting your timer isn't such a good idea, if this is your first crack at creating an application using Quick Start. You will, after all, require some time to refer to this text. After you've gone through the process once or twice, however, you will probably be able to get an application up and running in less than two minutes.

The nature of the data fields in this example isn't particularly important, so if you want to digress a little, that's OK. If you want your example to exactly parallel this discussion, however, fill out the Quick Start window as shown in Figure 6.3.

FIGURE 6.3.

A sample Quick Start application.

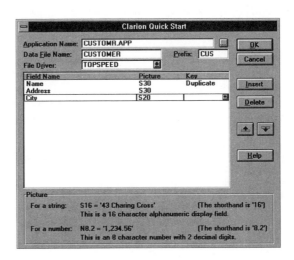

Once you've filled out all the entries, click on OK or press Enter. Confirm that you want to create the application, and Quick Start will take a moment to build an application file and a matching Data Dictionary. It will then drop you into the AppGen and into a tree display of the procedures in your application, as shown in Figure 6.4.

FIGURE 6.4.

The application created by Quick Start.

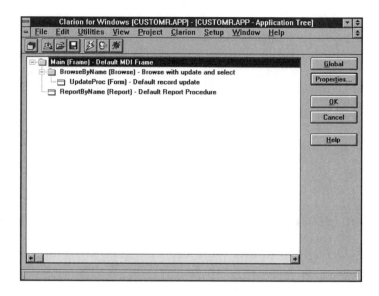

If you've followed the example, you'll see a main menu or frame procedure called Main, a browse procedure called BrowseByName, an update form called UpdateProc, and a report procedure called ReportByName. These four procedures were all created from the information you specified in Quick Start. If you had specified additional keys on some of the fields, there would have been additional browse and report procedures created for each key, allowing you to view and report on your data in the order you choose.

Creating an EXE file out of this application is child's play. In fact, if you have a child handy, you may want to have him/her take the next step. Select Project|Run from the main menu, or click on the run icon, which is the roadrunner-style cloud of dust just to the right of the lightning bolt. You will see a message box describing the code generation going on, and once that is complete the Make window will appear, as shown in Figure 6.5.

FIGURE 6.5.

The application created by Quick Start being compiled in the Make window.

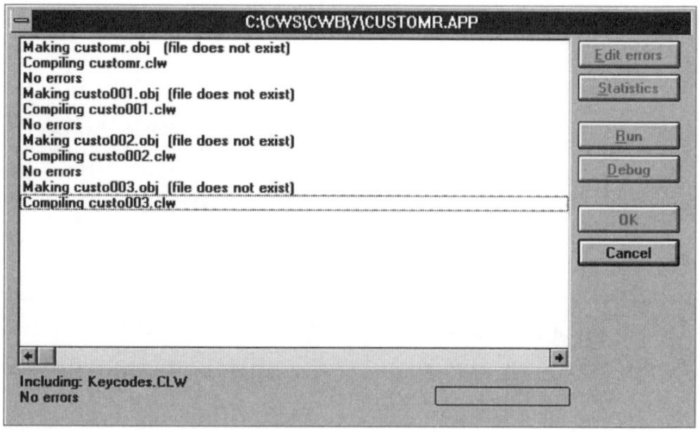

The Make window gives you the status of the compile and link process. (See Chapter 11, "From Here to EXE: The Project System.") If any errors occur, a message will be posted here. Once the compile and link processes have finished, your EXE is complete, and it will be automatically run, as shown in Figure 6.6.

FIGURE 6.6.

The application in action.

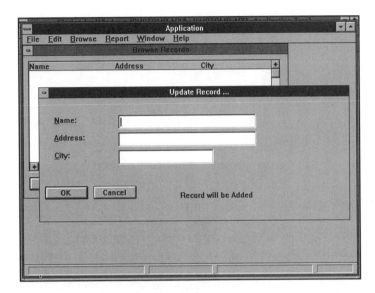

NOTE

If you want only to make the EXE, and not actually run it, choose Project|Make or click on the lightning-bolt icon.

Quick Start creates multiple-document interface (MDI) applications. There's a lot more on MDI in Chapter 29, "Multiple-Document Interface Versus Non–Multiple-Document Interface," but here's a practical demonstration. Choose Browse|Browse by Name from your application's main menu. Right now there isn't any data in the browse procedure's list box, so click on Insert and add a few records. Then, without closing the Browse by Name procedure (but after closing the update form), select Browse|Browse by Name again. A second copy of the browse procedure will appear, and if you experiment a little you will find that you can switch between the two browses at will.

NOTE

You may want to use the Window|Cascade command to arrange multiple procedures within the frame's client area.

You can open up to 64 copies of the same procedure, depending on the available resources in your system. You can also open a number of different procedures at the same time. You also use standard MDI features, such as those found under the Window menu, to organize these procedures on the screen. All of this is ludicrously easy to accomplish in CW.

Exit your application and return to the AppGen main window. Along the right side of the application tree are several buttons; the important one, for the following discussion, is the Properties button.

Procedure Properties

Select the Main procedure and click on Properties to get the Procedure Properties window, as shown in Figure 6.7.

FIGURE 6.7.

The Main Procedure Properties window.

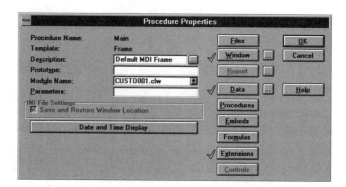

The Procedure Properties window is both a place to enter some basic information about the procedure (which Quick Start has already done for you) and a gateway to the visual design tools. Click on the Window button to bring up the Window Formatter for that procedure, as shown in Figure 6.8.

The Window Formatter is really a special tool that takes the source code that describes your window and translates it into what it will look like when the program runs. It allows you to make changes to the window, and then when you exit the formatter and save your changes, it writes them back into source code. This is a true two-way process, and Clarion has had it since the beginning. You can make your changes either in the source code or in the formatter, although most people use the formatter because it's much easier for most things.

FIGURE 6.8.

The Window Formatter displaying the application's main menu.

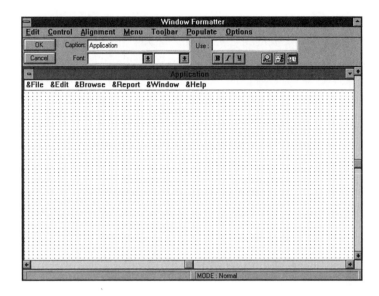

The Property Menu

Click somewhere in the middle of the application so that handles appear on the application window. Then click on the right mouse button to pop up the Properties menu, as shown in Figure 6.9.

FIGURE 6.9.

The Properties menu.

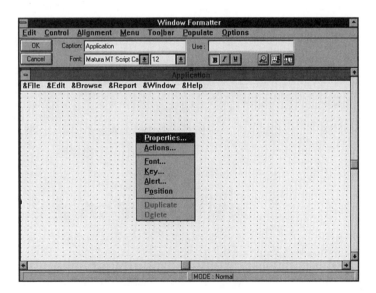

You'll use this pop-up Properties menu a lot. Although you can reach all the items on this menu through standard menu choices, you'll probably find this a convenient way to change the characteristics of the various controls that you will place on windows.

From the Properties menu choose the top item, Properties. Another window appears that lets you set some characteristics of the application window. Find the Title: entry at the top of the window and change it to Chapter 6 Example. Click on OK to return to the Window Formatter, then click OK again to return to the Procedure Properties window, and click OK once more to get to the application tree window. Click on the Run icon. When the application comes up, it will have the title Chapter 6 Example in the title bar. The title is only one of the application properties you can change.

Many features that in some languages have to be explicitly coded are simply attributes in CW. For instance, on the application window's Properties window, there are check boxes for things such as the system menu box, scroll bars, and the maximize button. There are also drop-down list boxes for choosing the frame (border) type, and for the initial size (default, maximized, or iconized) of the window. You can specify a default cursor shape for the application frame, and which icon to use if the window is minimized. These features and others do not cause any additional lines of code to be generated—they simply add corresponding attributes to the window structure.

Calling Procedures

There is another feature of the Window Formatter that makes it easy to create and maintain menus. Choose Menu|Menu Editor, or double-click anywhere in the menu bar. The menu editor will appear, as shown in Figure 6.10.

FIGURE 6.10.

The menu editor.

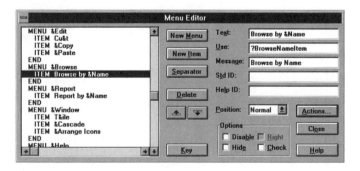

Find the menu item called Browse by &Name and make sure it is selected. On the right-hand side of the menu editor is one special button labeled Actions, which is what you use most (but not all) of the time to associate a procedure or action with a menu item. Click here, and you will get a Prompts window for the selected menu item, as shown in Figure 6.11.

FIGURE 6.11.

The Prompts window for the Browse by &Name menu option.

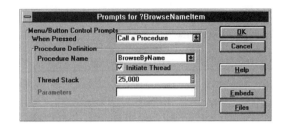

This window is the same one you'll see if you select Actions for a button—it's designed to make it easy for you to call a procedure or embed code at the menu item or button. For procedure calls, all required code will be generated for you—you only need to specify the procedure to run and optionally whether you want it to run on its own thread.

> **NOTE**
>
> For more information on threading and MDI, see Chapter 28, "Multithreading and Thread Management," and Chapter 29.

Select Cancel to return to the menu editor, and choose the T&ile item under the &Window menu. This is a slightly different case than the menu option that calls the browse procedure. Notice the contents of the Std ID: entry. There are certain kinds of standard functionality that you can associate with a menu item. These include tiling and cascading MDI windows, calling the Printer Setup dialog box, cutting and pasting Clipboard text, and so on. A complete list of STD values can be found in \CW\LIBSRC\EQUATES.CLW. Menu items with STD attributes do not normally have any other actions specified (via the Actions button).

> **TIP**
>
> A Quick Start application comes set up with most of the standard menu items in place, including STD:Exit, which should always be used in MDI application frames as the means of terminating the program. This ensures that any MDI children will be properly notified of the program shutting down and will have an opportunity to execute their own shut-down code. Even if you create your applications from scratch, you may want to import a Quick Start menu procedure to lay some of the groundwork.

Creating menus and calling procedures from them is covered in more detail in Chapter 8, "Creating Procedures."

Exit the Window Formatter and have another look at the Procedure Properties window (as shown in Figure 6.7). Notice that the Window and Data buttons have checkmarks beside them—they indicate that the buttons lead to some existing data. You've seen what's behind the Window button—now click on the Data button. You'll see a list of variables local to this procedure, and if you click on Insert or Properties you'll see the Field Edit Properties window. This is where you declare data that you want to be available only to this procedure. Most templates will place some data in this list, and you should avoid making any changes to that data or your procedure may not compile or function properly. You may, however, add whatever data you like.

The Browse Procedure Properties Window

Exit back to the application tree, and select the BrowseByName procedure. Click on the Properties button. You will see a Procedure Properties window much like the one for the Main procedure. One significant difference is that the Files button has a checkmark next to it, indicating that at least one data file has been selected for the procedure. Since you have only one file defined in your application, it's a safe guess that it's the NAMES file.

Additionally, there are a number of new buttons and drop-down list boxes, check boxes, and what-not in the lower-left quadrant of the window. These additional controls all pertain to the browse procedure's functionality and allow you to do things such as determine a subset of the files to display, choose a style of locator to use when searching for a record, and specify fields from the file that are to be displayed separately from the list box (*hot fields*) as the user scrolls through the file.

As with the Frame Procedure Properties window, the Browse Procedure Properties window has a Window button, which takes you to the Window Formatter. The only procedure types that do not have active Window buttons are External, Process, Report, and Source. Take a moment to view the procedure's window. This is somewhat different from the main menu's window. It does not have a menu (although it could), but it does contain a number of button controls and a list box control. You can not only change the appearance of these controls, but you can alter their behavior. (Modifying control behavior is discussed in more detail in Chapter 8.) Exit the Window Formatter by pressing OK or Cancel so that you return to the Procedure Properties window.

Ranges and Filters

One of the most important features of the browse procedure is the Range and Filter button. This is what you use to determine which subset (if any) of the records in the data file you wish to display. If you want to display all the records in the file, you don't need to go in here at all, but if you do you'll see the window shown in Figure 6.12.

FIGURE 6.12.

*The Range and Filter
dialog box.*

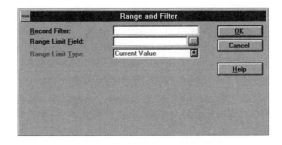

The Record Filter entry is free-form—you can enter a valid Clarion expression of up to 255 characters in length. You can also specify a formula that you have created with the formula editor. A valid, although somewhat impractical, record filter for the demonstration application would be UPPER(NAM:Name[1:1])='A', which would limit the displayed records to those beginning with A. You can type any expression here, and as long as it evaluates to a non-zero value, the record will be accepted for display.

Record filters are not a good choice as the primary method of getting chosen records to display when you have a lot of data to look through. The alternative to record filters is a range limit.

Range limits, unlike filters, are based on keys. The key is a file sort order that is maintained along with the data file itself, either in the same physical file or in a file with the same name as the data file and a separate extension. You can have multiple keys per file (in most file systems), but the browse procedure requires that you specify one key as the one to be used to display records. If you have multiple keys on a file because you want to view it in different sort orders, you will ordinarily have one browse procedure for each key, unless you are using a third-party template that allows you to switch between keys within a single browse procedure.

The trick with browse boxes and keys is to make the best possible use of the key when you want to display a subset of records, and that's where range limits come into play. A range limit is always based on at least one field in the key, and the AppGen restricts you to choosing only key fields. If you click on the ellipsis button next to the Range Limit Field entry, you will get a Select Component From Key pick list.

Ordinarily, you will choose the first element in the key for a range limit. This is because keys are sorted in the order in which the fields appear. For instance, if the file used by this application has a Last Name field and a First Name field, and a key with the first element being the Last Name field and the second element being the First Name field, then records in that key would be sorted in Last Name, First Name order. If you wanted to view only the Dents, you could tell the AppGen to restrict the range to Dents, and that wouldn't be a problem because all the Dents would be adjacent to one another in the key.

If you wanted to view all the Arthurs, however, you'd have a problem, because unless all the Arthurs happen to be Arthur Dents, you'd have no way of getting only the records you wanted. The solution to this kind of problem is to create a key suitable to the task at hand, and that usually means having the range field as the first field in the key. There are special circumstances in which you might want to use a range on a field other than the first one, but if you do this you always have to account for the values in the key fields above it.

Range limits are frequently used when information in one file is related to another file. For instance, if your old friend Arthur Dent is a customer of yours, you may wish to display only the invoices with his customer number, out of all the invoices that are in the invoice file. Range limits are discussed in more detail in Chapter 9, "Refining Procedures: Code and Control Templates."

Return to the Procedure Properties window (you do not need to specify any filters or ranges at this time, as this is just an informational tour) and take note of an entry in the lower-left corner called Update Procedure. This entry field lets you specify the procedure that will be called when the user wishes to add, modify, or delete a record in the browse box. If you decide that you do not want an update procedure, all you have to do is highlight the text in this entry and delete it.

Although browse procedures may seem complicated (and can become so), they are for the most part quite straightforward. You have a window that displays records from a data file in a list box, you have buttons that allow the user to update those records, you have an update procedure for changing the data, and you can specify ranges and filters for the data to display.

The Form Procedure Properties Window

Exit back to the application tree and select the UpdateProc procedure. Click on the Properties button to see the window shown in Figure 6.13.

FIGURE 6.13.

The Form Procedure Properties window.

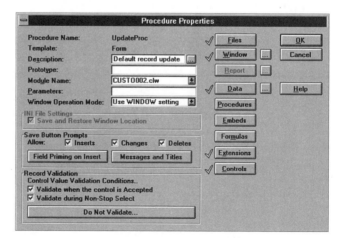

By now the Procedure Properties window should be starting to look familiar. A lot of the buttons and prompts are the same as for frame and browse procedures.

> **TIP**
>
> You may want to take a look at the procedure's window and go exploring with the right mouse button, which brings up the Properties menu for each of the controls. Don't worry about messing something up—after all, it only took you a couple minutes to create this application.

Most of the Procedure Properties window differences again are in the lower-left quadrant. There are check boxes to determine under what circumstances the form may be called (you might want a particular form to allow inserts and changes, but not deletes), and the buttons Field Priming on Insert and Messages and Titles.

The Field Priming on Insert button allows you to specify initial values for fields when a new record is added. If you have a customer list, you might also have some source code that you use to create new customer numbers following some special format. Field priming will let you select the customer ID field and enter an expression or function name to return the new customer ID. This feature is in effect only for adding new records.

The Messages and Titles button lets you alter the default messages that are displayed when the user adds, updates, or deletes a record. You can also decide where you want that message to appear, if at all.

Form procedures, like browse procedures, are not necessarily that complicated. There is a window that displays fields from the file and buttons to cancel or update the record, and there are some options that determine how information is displayed on that window. There is no need to use any kind of range limit or filter, since update procedures are typically called from browse procedures, and the user will have selected the data file record. All the update procedure needs to know is which file it's supposed to update.

The Report Procedure Properties Window

As far as properties go, reports are something of a hybrid between browses and forms. They have ranges and filters, but the actual placement of fields on a report is more like that in creating a form, since a report is often much like series of forms, one for each data file record. Figure 6.14 shows the Report Procedure Properties window.

The Window button is grayed out (there is a default progress-indicator window, but it is not available from within the AppGen) and the Report button is active. Click on it to use the Report Formatter.

FIGURE 6.14.

The Report Procedure Properties window.

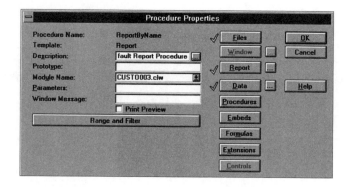

As discussed in Chapter 1, the Report Formatter gives you both a logical (band) view and a layout view. You use band view to place controls on the report, which may be string controls referencing fields on a data file, graphic images, or even controls such as radio buttons and list boxes. The report in this sample application is an indication only of how easy it is to create reports, not how jazzy they can be.

Summary

The four procedure types demonstrated in this Quick Start application have common use in database and business applications. You may use them (you will almost certainly use the frame type) or you may go another route, and many routes are possible. For most applications, however, the first step is defining the data. Quick Start takes this approach—you create a data file structure, and based on that, Quick Start builds an application.

Your own application development will probably also need to begin with some level of data definition, and that is the subject of Chapter 7.

7

Defining Your Data

As Chapter 6, "Quick Start: The Two-Minute Application," shows, most application development begins with defining data. If you're going to create procedures that use data files, you better figure out what those files are going to look like. Although you don't have to define all your files right away, or even define them in their final form, the more you know about your data files, and therefore about your data, the easier the development process will be.

The Quick Start application you created in Chapter 6 was about as simple as database applications get: one data file, one browse procedure, one update procedure, and one report. Real-world applications are usually considerably more complex and involve more than one set of data. The problem any designer of a business/database system faces is how to best store, and then represent, this data.

There are really two facets to this problem. One is the database design—the breakdown of data into separate files or tables, and the relationships between those files. The other facet is the application development process—whether the design will be specified before coding begins, or whether it will evolve over the development of the application.

A Database Design Primer

First, a disclaimer: This book is not about database design. It is about programming in Clarion for Windows. The more you know about database design, however, the better CW programming will go for you.

CW is designed for relational database programming, a concept that was first published by Dr. E.F. Codd in 1970. Dr. Codd's paper accomplished two things: It set a standard for database design that has spurred vendors worldwide to create better database products, and it generated enough heat over what really is and isn't a relational database to suggest an alternate explanation for global warming. The following discussion is *not* intended to aggravate this problem.

A typical relational database will contain related groupings of information. In an invoicing program, there would be customer information, invoice header information, and invoice detail information. Invoicing programs are common enough that few people redesign them from the ground up—you know that you will have multiple invoices per customer, so you keep track of invoices separately from customers to avoid duplication. (For a discussion of duplicated data in databases, see Chapter 1, "Introduction to the Development Environment.") You use a customer number as the link between customer information, and you use an invoice number as the link between invoices (or invoice headers) and invoice detail, since you will also have multiple invoice detail items per invoice.

As long as you write only invoicing programs, life is going to be pretty easy for you, because there are established ways of doing these things that work well. The tricky bit happens when you're asked to develop an application where you don't have anybody else's design to fall back on. That's where the more you know about data modeling, the better you'll be able to solve the problem.

A Plausible Example

Imagine that you have been commissioned to write software for a flea circus. Alphonse, the owner of the circus, wishes to keep track of his fleas, the tricks they perform, and the dogs they reside on when not performing. You look through your back issues of the *Clarion Tech Journal*, but unfortunately you are unable to locate any helpful articles. You will have to think this one out for yourself.

Begin your design with an overview of the data you will be dealing with and the kind of information your user is going to require from the system. You learn from Alphonse that there are approximately 50 fleas in the circus and they live on 4 dogs. Each flea can perform only 1 of 15 standard "feats of skill and daring," as Alphonse likes to say. Fleas frequently change dogs, and since they get bored easily, they also frequently change their acts.

File Relationships

Even with small databases, diagramming the relationships between the different data groups can be helpful. In large database systems, it quickly becomes essential. Figure 7.1 shows one way to diagram these relationships.

FIGURE 7.1.

A simplified entity-relationship diagram.

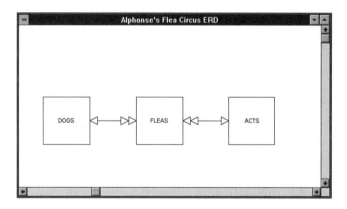

The *entity-relationship*, or *ER*, diagram in Figure 7.1 shows the three groupings of data in the flea circus application. There is one file for fleas, one for dogs, and one for acts. There are more fleas than dogs, and there can be any number of fleas per dog, which means that there is a *many-to-one* relationship between fleas and dogs. The diagram shows this with a double arrow pointing to the many side, and a single arrow pointing to the one side. Similarly, there are more fleas than acts, and a number of fleas can be in the same act, so there is a *one-to-many* relationship between acts and fleas. One-to-many and many-to-one relationships are really exactly the same thing, only seen from opposite sides of the relationship.

As you design your database, you need to keep in mind how the user will interact with the information. As an application grows beyond a few data files, your options for organizing the data also increase.

Fortunately, Alphonse's needs are not that complex. He would like to be able to maintain a list of fleas, their acts, and their dogs, and he would also like to easily view the cast for any given act and the population of any given dog. The structure diagrammed in Figure 7.1 meets all of these requirements.

Linking Data Files

There is one more point that bears discussion. In order for files to be related, they need to share at least one common field. It's good practice to make this field something the user is unlikely to change. To link dogs and fleas, for instance, you could use the dog's name as the link field. You would keep Bowser's name and vital statistics in the DOGS file, and have a field in the FLEAS file containing the name Bowser. In this way you could easily collect a list of all of Bowser's resident fleas. The problem is that names have a tendency to change. They may have been misspelled, or Alphonse may be one of those people who forgets names and makes up new ones to suit the purpose at hand. If you simply change Bowser's name, then all the related FLEAS records suddenly point to a no-longer-extant dog.

The dictionary editor and the AppGen actually handle this kind of situation quite gracefully. You can define a relationship between the two files, so that any time you update Bowser's name, all the related FLEAS records will also be updated. Although this is an improvement, and may suit your needs, the safer approach is to use a code or an automatically generated number as the link.

Maintaining correct links between related data files is called *relational integrity*, or *RI*. In some database systems, RI is handled at the engine level. When you make a change to the DOGS file in such a system, the related FLEAS records are automatically updated, provided that the appropriate rules have been defined. You may, in fact, work with such a database using one of CW's installable database drivers. If your database does not support that functionality, you can have the AppGen write the code to do it for you.

The effort you make in designing your data files and their relationships can repay you many times over when it comes time to do some coding, but don't worry about it too much, particularly if you're new to CW. This development system is quite forgiving, and you can make substantial changes to your application as you go.

Defining Data Files

Once you've decided what your data files will be, you're ready to store their definitions in the Data Dictionary. Again, the dictionary editor is not required if you're strictly hand coding, although it's difficult to imagine even hand coders not being intrigued by some of its features.

From the main menu, choose File|New|Dictionary. The dictionary editor main window appears. On the left is a list of the currently defined files. On the right is a list of the relationships that have been defined for that file, and on a new dictionary both lists are quite naturally empty.

Click on the Add File button. You will be asked if you want to use Quick Load. Chapter 6 discusses Quick Start, and Quick Load is a subset of that feature. It lets you quickly design a file layout with just a few different data types and simple keys. In fact, it's identical in appearance to the Quick Start window, except that it doesn't create an application for you.

Since you've already encountered Quick Load as part of Quick Start, answer No. After all, sometimes you just have to do an honest day's work. The New File Properties window will appear.

Essential File Properties

Only three fields here are essential to creating a file: name, prefix, and file driver. Everything else is informational or alters some aspect of the file itself.

The name entry is *not* where you specify the name of the physical data file (you can do that in the Full Pathname entry), but where you define a label by which the application makes reference to the file. This is necessary partially because you may wish to use the same file definition to open different files at different times, such as when the user changes data directories. The program needs a consistent label.

Often this label will be the same as the name of the file, such as a label Address for a file called ADDRESS.DAT. File labels (or *names*, as the dictionary editor calls them) follow standard rules for Clarion labels: They must begin with a letter or underscore character, and they may contain only letters, numerals, underscores, and colons.

The prefix of the file defaults to the first three letters of the file label, and will be prepended to the fields in the file. For example, if the FLEAS file has the prefix FLE:, the AGE field will be referenced in code as FLE:AGE.

The purpose of the prefix is to help differentiate fields in one file from like-named fields in another file. Although file prefixes are not required in the Clarion language, the AppGen generates code based on the assumption that you have defined them, and if you leave this field blank you will get numerous errors in your generated code from labels that begin with a colon, which is not a valid first character in a label.

The third essential field is the file driver. The concept of file drivers is discussed in Chapter 1, and the differences between different file drivers are discussed in Chapter 3, "Choosing Databases Wisely." For purposes of this exercise, the TopSpeed driver will do just fine.

Optional File Properties

Technically, the description entry is optional, but you should always fill it out, if not for your own benefit, then for the benefit of someone who may need to maintain your application in the future.

The Options entry is a way to communicate information directly to the driver when it is loaded. For instance, if you are using the Btrieve driver to maintain compatibility with Clarion 2.1 Btrieve files (using the Btrieve LEM), you will need to insert the text /MEMO=SINGLE in Options to place the memo field in a separate file. You do not need to place quotation marks around the text, because the dictionary editor will do this for you.

TIP

You can also communicate with the file driver using the SEND function at runtime. For instance, the Paradox driver allows you to specify international sort sequences using a set of internal tables. To specify the Norwegian/Danish sort sequence, you could either use the Options entry /SORTORDER=NORDAN or the command SEND(*file*, 'SORTORDER=NORDAN').

The Owner Name entry typically contains a password, if there is one, for the file. The ODBC driver is a special case—it also uses the Owner entry to determine where to look for the data file. (For more information on ODBC, see Chapter 24, "Using Open Database Connectivity.") You will also (usually) have to set the Encrypt attribute to On.

The Create attribute ensures that the code required by the driver to create the file is linked in. If you don't need it, leave it off, as it reduces your code size and complexity somewhat. You will need it for this exercise.

Encrypt, as mentioned, is used in conjunction with the password specified in the Owner entry to give your data security. The Reclaim attribute specifies that new records are to be placed in the spaces left by old records, which makes file storage more efficient but may prevent you from undeleting records.

The Bindable attribute makes all the fields in the file available for runtime evaluation. You might use this attribute if you want users to be able to build runtime expressions using the fields, and most of the fields in the file will be used. (You can also set the Bindable attribute for individual fields in the file.) There is quite a lot of overhead associated with binding variables, so do it only as needed.

The Threaded attribute causes a separate copy, or instance, of the file's buffer to be created each time the file is opened on a new thread, as when you start multiple copies of an MDI browse procedure. In this way, you can navigate the same file in two separate browse procedures, and the browse procedures will behave exactly as if they were in completely separate programs. This is the approach all Quick Start applications use, and it greatly simplifies the problems associated with opening the same file across multiple threads.

Ensure that you have filled out the file properties as shown in Figure 7.2, then click on OK.

FIGURE 7.2.

The File Properties window, filled out for the FLEAS file.

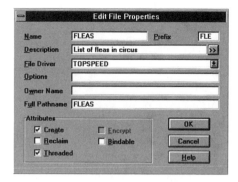

Fields

The next step is to add fields to the file definition. From the dictionary main menu, click on Fields/Keys to bring up the Field/Key Definition window. Click on Insert to add a field. The New Field Properties window will appear, as shown in Figure 7.3.

NOTE

If Insert is grayed out on the Field/Key Definition window, click on the left, or Field, list box—the update buttons do dual duty between fields and keys.

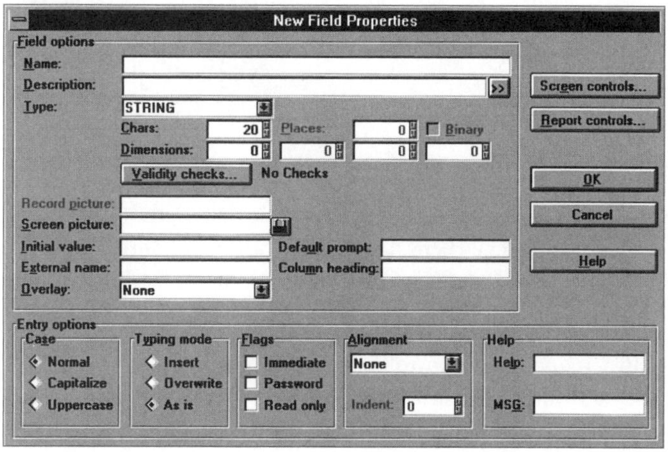

FIGURE 7.3.

The New Field Properties window.

There are a lot of options to consider here. They can be loosely grouped into four categories: declaration, validation, control type, and behavior.

Field Declarations

The field's declaration is simply the name or label, and the data type and size. These are the essential bits of information without which you cannot have a field. New fields default to a string type, and the additional data types available depend on the driver you use.

Field Validation

The field's validation options determine whether the contents of the field will be checked against some criteria. These include requiring a field to be filled in with some value, restricting numeric fields to a range of numbers or a true/false condition, validating the field against a related file, or choosing from a predefined list of options.

Field Control Type

The Data Dictionary lets you specify the type of control that will be used when you place a field on a form. Make sure you have specified a label for your field (such as FleaName), and click on the Screen Controls button to see the Edit Screen Controls window, as shown in Figure 7.4.

FIGURE 7.4.
The Edit Screen Controls
window for a string field.

The first thing to notice is that a default control has already been defined. You absolutely do not have to go to this level to create suitable field definitions, but if you don't care for the defaults, you can change them here. Select different control types from the list, and watch the screen control data change in the Screen Controls list box. In many cases, there are actually two controls defined: the prompt that will appear with the control and the control itself.

You can set any of the control properties right in the dictionary editor. Select a control type that uses a prompt, then select the prompt in the Screen Controls list and click on Properties. You will see the same property information that appears if you select this prompt after it has been placed on a window. The advantage of setting this information here, of course, is that you have to do it only once, and the settings you choose will be the default for that control.

The kinds of controls that appear in the control list are dependent on whether you have any validity checking turned on. Return to the Field Properties window and select Validity Checks. Select Must Be In List, and in the entry type A¦B¦C¦D¦E. Click on OK, then click on Screen Controls again. This time the Check control is gone (there is more than one option now, and a Check control is always true or false) and it has been replaced by List Box, Drop List, and Option controls. Select Drop List, and then select the second line in the Screen Controls list box (which defines the drop list) and click on Properties. These are the same properties you would see in the Window Formatter after you place the control. Again, the big advantage to setting this information here is that you have to do it only once, no matter how many different windows the control appears on. This approach also ensures consistency across windows and applications that share the dictionary.

Field Behavior

The last category of attributes is those that affect field behavior. They are grouped at the bottom of the Field Properties window, and allow you to specify capitalization or case, typing mode (avoid messing with this unless you have good reason to—it can confuse users to suddenly be in overwrite mode when they thought they were in insert mode), and whether the field immediately completes (triggers an accept event) when the user has typed enough characters to fill the field. You can also specify whether a field is a password and should have asterisks displayed instead of the actual characters typed, and you can make a field read-only. Read-only fields can still be selected with the cursor, and even have their contents copied (for example, to the Windows Clipboard), but they do not allow the user to make changes.

Two entries deserve special mention. The Help entry allows you to assign a standard Windows help ID or context string. (See Chapter 10, "Assigning and Building Your Help Files.") The MSG entry lets you specify a short message that will display in the window's status bar (assuming that it has one) when the user has selected the field. You should use both these fields as much as possible, even when the purpose of a particular field is perfectly clear to you, because it might not be clear to your user.

Using Table 7.1, define the fields for the FLEAS file.

Table 7.1. Fields in the FLEAS file.

Field Name	Declaration and Picture	Validation	Control Type	Behavior
Flea	STRING @20	Cannot be 0 or blank	Entry	Uppercase
Birthday	Long @D1	Cannot be 0 or blank	Spin Box	Default
EmployeeID	STRING @KF###K	Cannot be 0 or blank	Entry (using key-in template)	Default
DogCode	STRING @s6	No checks	Entry	Uppercase
ActCode	STRING @s6	No checks	Entry	Uppercase

There are some subtleties to the dictionary editor. Notice that the EmployeeID field has an unusual picture, called a key-in template, which accommodates Alphonse's scheme for employee numbers. He uses a leading *F* to indicate flea, followed by a three-digit number.

While you could just key in the picture to the Picture entry the way it's shown, there is a tool that makes the whole process a little easier. Click on Screen Controls. Select the Entry line in the Screen Controls list and click on Properties to get the Entry Properties window. The top entry in this window is the picture, and to the right of that is one of those ellipsis (…) buttons that indicates more to come. Click on it, and you will get the Edit Picture String window, as shown in Figure 7.5. That's about as deep into the bowels of the dictionary editor as you're ever likely to get, but if you're editing key-in templates, it's worth the trip.

FIGURE 7.5.

The Edit Picture String window.

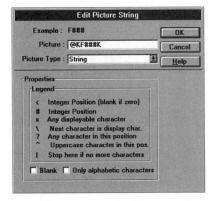

From the legend that displays when Key-in Template is selected as the picture type, you can see that this picture will force the entry of a field with a leading *F* (for flea, naturally), followed by three numbers.

TIP

Any of the field options you specify in the dictionary can be overridden in the AppGen. You should pay particular attention to control types. When you place fields on a window in the AppGen, you can do it with the Populate option, which is quick and easy and reaps all the benefits of your work in the dictionary editor, or by creating the controls and then attaching the field to the control, which is somewhat more work. If you want to use a control other than the one specified in the dictionary, you will have to use the latter approach.

Defining Keys

After you've defined your fields, the next step is to create suitable keys. Two things usually determine the kinds of keys you require: viewing/reporting data and file relationships. Alphonse would like to view his fleas in alphabetical order, and also in order of the acts they perform. Create the first key by clicking in the Keys list box on the right side of the Field/Key Definition window. Insert a new key, and fill out the Edit Key Properties window as shown in Figure 7.6.

FIGURE 7.6.

The Edit Key Properties window.

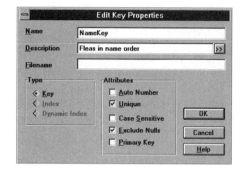

As soon as you accept the Key property information, you will be asked to select a key component. Choose FLE:FleaName and click OK. The window reappears to allow you to select another component. Click Cancel. The window disappears and is replaced by the New Key Properties window, so that you can add a second key. (As with adding fields, the dictionary editor is designed to speed up lengthy data entry by assuming that you wish to continue adding whatever kind of item you have just added.) Use the name ActCodeKey and the description List of Fleas in Order of Act performed, and make sure Unique is *not* selected, but Exclude Nulls *is* selected. There may be more than one flea for any given act, and if the key is unique it will not permit this.

After selecting FLE:ActCode as the field for ActCodeKey and clicking OK, click Cancel. Add a third key called DogCodeKey, which will be required for the link to the DOGS file. It should be non-unique and have the DogCode field as its only component.

After you've added the DogCode field, click Cancel to stop adding fields to the key, and Cancel again when the New Key Properties window appears.

That's all there is to the FLEAS file. You'll need to create two more files before proceeding to the next step.

The DOGS file lists all the dogs the fleas live on. Create the fields as shown in Table 7.2.

Table 7.2. Fields in the DOGS file.

Field Name	Declaration and Picture	Validation	Control Type	Behavior
DogCode	`STRING` `@s6`	Cannot be 0 or blank	Entry	Uppercase
DogName	`STRING` `@s30`	Cannot be 0 or blank	Entry	Uppercase
EmployeeID	`STRING` `KD###K`	Cannot be 0 or blank	Entry (using key-in template)	Default

Create one key called DogCodeKey. Give it the Unique and Exclude Nulls attributes, and use the field DOG:DogCode as the single component.

The ACTS file lists all the acts the different fleas might perform. Create the fields shown in Table 7.3.

Table 7.3. Fields in the ACTS file.

Field Name	Declaration and Picture	Validation	Control Type	Behavior
ActCode	`STRING` `@s6`	Cannot be 0 or blank	Entry	Uppercase
ActName	`STRING` `@s30`	Cannot be 0 or blank	Entry	Uppercase
ActDesc	`MEMO` `4000 Chars`	No checks	Text with horizontal and vertical scroll bars	Default

Create one key called ActCodeKey. Give it the Unique and Exclude Nulls attributes, and use the field ACT:ActCode as the single component.

Defining Relationships

In order to define relationships, you logically need more than one file. (To be more precise, you need more than one logical file—CW supports aliases, which let you reference a file under another name. Press the Help button while on the dictionary main window for more on aliases.)

Begin by creating the link between the FLEAS file and the DOGS file. Select the FLEAS file from the dictionary editor main window and click on Add Relation. The Edit Relationship Properties window appears, as shown in Figure 7.7.

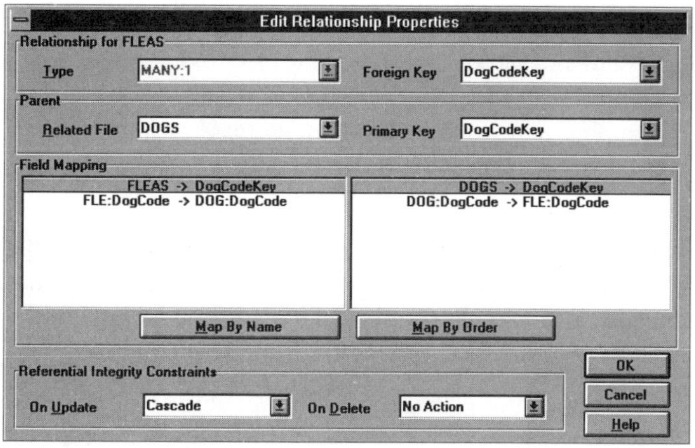

Figure 7.7.
The Edit Relationship
Properties window showing
the link between FLEAS
and DOGS.

NOTE

If you have any difficulty with the following section, and your data does not appear to match this data, refer to FLEACIRC.DCT in the CHAP8 directory of the sample disk.

The FLEAS/DOGS relationship is a many-to-one relationship—many fleas to one dog (as if you needed to be told that). Set the type to MANY:1, and the foreign key to DogCodeKey. Set the related file to DOGS, and the primary key to DogCodeKey. Then click on Map By Name to assign the fields, or double-click on each field separately to map manually.

You've established the relationship between files. That's enough for the AppGen to use if you ask it to verify a field against a related file, or if you want to display a field from a related file in a list box, or the like. You can also use this window to set up rules about how the data links are to be enforced.

Referential Integrity Constraints

If you select referential integrity constraints of one form or another, the AppGen will automatically write code corresponding to those constraints and execute it as appropriate. As an example, set the On Update constraint to Cascade and the On Delete constraint to Clear.

Constraints work from the perspective of the primary key. In this example, the primary key (the "one" side of many-to-one) is on the DOGS file. That means that if you change the DOG:DogCode field on update, the AppGen will execute code to find all the FLEAS records with the old DogCode in the FLE:DogCode field, and update them to the new value. If you delete a DOGS record, the delete constraint of Clear will tell AppGen to execute code to blank the FLE:DogCode field for all related records. If you chose Delete as the delete constraint, all related FLEAS records for that DOGS record would be deleted. The remaining option, Restrict, would not allow you to update or delete the DOG:DogCode field if any related records existed.

If you return to the dictionary editor main window and select the DOGS file, you will see that a relationship also shows for DOGS and FLEAS. It is in fact the same relationship, and the only thing that has changed is the display. The DOGS file is shown above the FLEAS file, and the relationship is many-to-one, not one-to-many.

You will need to create one more relationship, this time between the ACTS file and the FLEAS file: a one-to-many relationship based on the ActCode field. Select the ACTS file, click on Add Relation, and select ActCodeKey as the primary key. The related file is FLEAS, and the foreign key is ActCodeKey. Again, you can use Map By Name to assign the relationship. The referential integrity constraints are On Update: Cascade and On Delete: Clear.

You have now defined the basic files needed for Alphonse's Flea Circus Information System. In the next chapter, you'll begin creating procedures based on these definitions.

The Dictionary and Rapid Application Development

Although there are many benefits to traditional, Data Dictionary-driven application design, you won't necessarily have that luxury. Increasingly, developers are turning to rapid application development, or RAD, where a software design may evolve (some would say mutate) quite rapidly.

The Data Dictionary is at least as well suited to RAD development as to traditional methods. You do not need to define all your fields ahead of time—you can add new ones from within the AppGen (although if you want to define new files or relationships, you will have to exit the AppGen and open the dictionary editor). You can also change field names, and the next time you load an application that uses that dictionary, the changes will ripple through the application. You can add new files and create relationships without disturbing any of your previous work.

Summary

For applications that access data files, you will ordinarily begin developing your application by creating the Data Dictionary. You may have some idea of what your program will look like, but you're asking for trouble if you don't have a clear concept of how your data is structured before you start in with the Application Generator.

You should do as much design as you can before you start so you don't waste your time, but if you have to make changes on-the-fly, you can. Your dictionary will almost certainly evolve significantly as you build new functionality into your application.

8

Creating Procedures

Although this chapter discusses creating the procedures that make up a working program, it does so from the perspective of a business application, based on a Data Dictionary. You're probably getting tired of hearing this by now, but you don't really need a Data Dictionary to create applications in Clarion for Windows (CW). The kinds of procedures that are discussed here are perhaps typical, but in no way cover the full range of what is possible.

That's it for the disclaimers—on to application design! The first order of business is to create the application that will contain all of these wonderful procedures.

Creating an Application

From the CW main menu, choose File|New|Application. You will be asked if you want to use Quick Start. You do not. (Quick Start is discussed in Chapter 6, "Quick Start: The Two-Minute Application.") The Application Properties window appears. Fill it out as shown in Figure 8.1 in preparation for building the Flea Circus application you started in Chapter 7, "Defining Your Data."

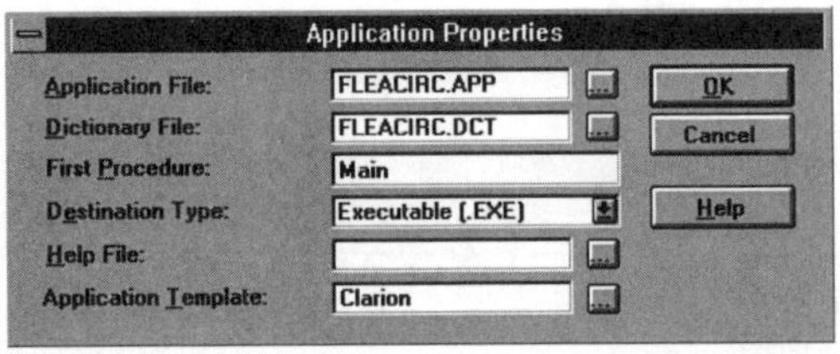

FIGURE 8.1.

The Application Properties window for FLEACIRC.APP.

The dictionary is the one you created in Chapter 7. If you did not do that exercise, you can copy the dictionary from the \Chap8 directory on the disk that's included with this book.

If you have the dictionary on your hard drive and you get an error message saying that the dictionary could not be found, press the ellipsis button to the right of the Dictionary entry to get a File dialog box that helps you locate the dictionary.

After you fill out the application properties and click on OK, the Application Tree window appears. The only procedure in the tree will be Main, and it is labeled (ToDo), which indicates that it needs to be created. (If, in the course of running one of your programs, you call a ToDo procedure, you will simply see a message to the effect that the procedure has not yet been defined.)

Since the Main procedure is already highlighted, click on the Properties button (or choose Edit|Properties). The Select Procedure Type list appears. Choose Frame, because you will be creating a main menu for an MDI application. (For more on the Procedure Type list, see Chapter 2, "Choosing a Development Style.") The Procedure Properties window appears for the Main procedure, as shown in Figure 8.2. Procedure properties, along with the general process of compiling, linking, and running an application, are covered in a general way in Chapter 6, and in more detail in this chapter. If you feel you are getting lost, you might want to take a look through Chapter 6 to familiarize yourself with the territory again.

FIGURE 8.2.

The Procedure Properties window for the Main *procedure.*

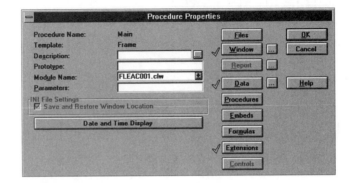

If you are at the Procedure Properties window in Figure 8.2, you're two mouse clicks away from a working application. It won't do much, mind you, but give it a go anyway. Click on OK, then click on the Run icon, which is the cloud of dust between the lightning bolt (Make) icon and the forbidden bug (Debugger) icon. The AppGen will generate the code, the compiler will compile, the linker will link, and your application will appear in all its muted glory, as in Figure 8.3.

FIGURE 8.3.

The Main *procedure in action (so to speak).*

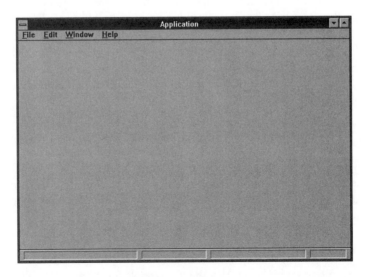

Only three menu choices in your fledgling application will accomplish anything. Selecting Help|How to use Help will bring up the standard Windows help file on the subject of (what else) help, File|Print Setup will invoke a standard Windows printer dialog, and File|Exit will terminate the program. All three are accomplished through the use of STD attributes on menu choices, as discussed in Chapter 6.

Modifying the Main Menu

Naturally, you're going to want to add your own procedures to this menu, and maybe lose some of the stuff that's there (but probably not). Exit the application and return to the CW environment. Bring up the Procedure Properties window for Main and click on Window. Load the menu editor (Menu|Menu Editor) and place the cursor at the end of the Edit menu, as shown in Figure 8.4.

FIGURE 8.4.

The Main *procedure's menu, as viewed in the menu editor.*

Select New Menu to insert a menu after the Edit menu and before the Window menu. As you do, the Text and Use entries will be populated with some default values. Text will contain Menu&5, and Use will contain ?Menu5. You definitely want to change the Text entry to something more descriptive, because this is what will appear on your menu. Make it C&ircus. The ampersand (&) indicates which letter will be the hot key for this menu, and I is a good choice because it isn't already used on the menu bar and won't interfere with the hot keys on a typical MDI browse procedure.

Use Variables

Whether you change the Use entry is really up to you. Use variables, one of which you are declaring in the Use entry, are a handy way to refer to a particular menu item in source code. All menu items (and controls) must have sequence numbers corresponding to the order in which they appear on the window, in order for the program to run. Rather than forcing you to assign and maintain those numbers, the Clarion compiler does it for you. All you have to do is supply a unique use variable, which is a standard CW label with a question mark (?) at the beginning.

The important bit here is that the use variable must be unique. That's why, as you create new menus and menu items, the menu editor assigns use variables such as ?Menu5. That's all fine, but if you ever want to refer to that menu item in a source code embed point, for instance, you have to remember the use variable. It may not be readily apparent that ?Menu5 corresponds to the Circus menu option, but it will be apparent that ?Circus does. If you're never going to tinker with the source code, it doesn't matter. It's all a question of readability.

The Message entry, on the other hand, is quite important. Get into the habit of placing message attributes on everything—whatever you type here (this is a straight text entry) will appear on the status bar at the bottom of the window (assuming that there is a status bar) whenever that menu item is highlighted. The message attribute is also available for all other controls such as buttons and entry controls.

> **TIP**
>
> It's standard practice in Windows applications to have a File menu on the left (which, among other things, will contain the program Exit command), followed by an Edit menu (if used), followed by application-specific menus, followed by the Window menu (if this is an MDI app), with the Help menu appearing last on the menu bar.

Calling Procedures from a Menu

Add three new items to the Circus menu by placing the cursor on the MENU C&ircus line and clicking Insert three times. Select the first item and change its Text entry to &Fleas and its Use entry to ?Fleas. Now click on the Actions button. The Prompts for ?Fleas window appears, as shown in Figure 8.5. Choose Call a Procedure from the When Pressed drop-down list box.

FIGURE 8.5.

The Prompts for ?Fleas window, with Call a Procedure selected from the When Pressed drop-down list.

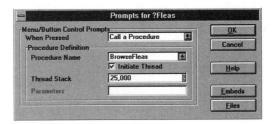

There is only one entry here that is really required: the procedure name. You can either type one in directly or pick from the list of existing procedures. Because the one you want to call does not exist, you will have to type it in. Call it BrowseFleas. For this particular procedure, also check the Initiate Thread box. The Thread Stack entry will become enabled, and you can leave it at its default value of 25,000.

Threaded and Nonthreaded Procedures

So what is a thread and why would you want to initiate one? The detailed answer to that is in Chapter 28, "Multithreading and Thread Management," and Chapter 29, "Multiple-Document

Interface Versus Non–Multiple-Document Interface." The short answer has to do with the ability to view multiple windows at once, a common feature of Windows applications and the standard approach in Quick Start applications.

If you call a procedure the way you would call it in a DOS program, you will get DOS-like behavior. If you have two items on a menu, you can call one or the other, but you cannot call them both and switch between them at will. In Windows programs, however, switching between windows (and therefore usually between procedures) is quite common.

The Clarion language uses the START( ) function to run a procedure on its own *thread* of execution. A thread is really much like a program; in fact, every program is composed of at least one thread, and DOS programs are usually only one thread. The whole idea of threads is that you can switch between them, often by clicking on a particular thread's window. Only one thread can be active at a time, however, so this is not multitasking, where multiple procedures run concurrently.

As a rule of thumb, it's safe to have procedures that simply view data files on their own threads (provided that the file has the Thread attribute—see Chapter 7), but it's not a good idea to do this with procedures that update data.

With all the entries filled in, your Prompts for ?Fleas window should look the way it does in Figure 8.5.

Click on OK to save your changes. Select the second item in your Circus menu. Set the Text entry to &Dogs and the Use entry to ?Dogs. Click on Actions and add a procedure called BrowseDogs. Check the Initiate Thread box and save your changes.

Select the third item in your Circus menu. Set the Text entry to &Acts and the Use entry to ?Acts. Click on Actions and add a procedure called BrowseActs. Check the Initiate Thread box and save your changes.

Close the Menu Formatter, click on OK for the Window Formatter, and click on the Procedure Properties window OK button. Your application tree should now look like the one in Figure 8.6.

Select the BrowseFleas procedure and click on Properties. The Procedure Types window appears, and you need to decide what kind of procedure to create. In this case, you will choose the Browse type. Browse procedures are typically used to view records from a file, and they often call a form procedure to update records in the file.

The Browse/Form Concept

The concept of a browse and a form is, of course, only one take on application development. The software world is full of word processors, spreadsheets, communications programs, database programs, games, and so on, and many of these don't use browse and form procedures.

FIGURE 8.6.

*The application tree
with ToDo stubs for the
procedure calls in the
main menu.*

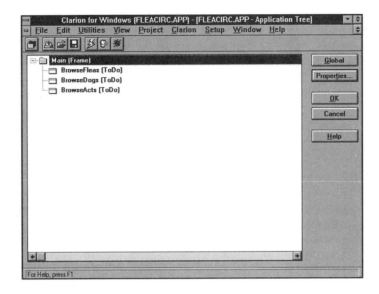

Each category of application seems to have its own metaphor for doing work. Although CW is a general-purpose language suited to many kinds of applications, its ancestry is database programming, and one of the places that this shows is in the browse and form. If you don't like it, don't worry. There are other ways of doing these things.

A browse procedure (called a table procedure in earlier versions of Clarion) is a window that contains a list box showing records in a database file. Because there will often be more records than can display on the window at any time, the list box normally allows scrolling up and down through the list.

NOTE

You will also see the term *browse box* used, which refers to the list box *and* the associated code required to browse the file. A list box is a window control, and a browse box is a list box with a bunch of Clarion code added to it.

The form is a window that displays one or more of the fields in the record and allows you to set or change those values when adding or updating a record. It can also be used to display the fields and ask for confirmation when deleting. It is usually activated from the browse by the user clicking on the appropriate button (typically labeled Add, Change, or Delete) or pressing the appropriate hot key (respectively Alt+I, Alt+C, and Alt+D). None of these conventions is written in stone—as the programmer, you have complete control over the ultimate result.

Creating a Browse Procedure

At a minimum, there are two things you need to do to make a working browse procedure. You need to specify which file to use, and you need to place one or more fields from that file in a list box. Additionally, in most cases you would want to specify the name of the update procedure.

Choosing a File

To tell the browse procedure which file to use, click on the Files button. The File Schematic Definition window appears, as shown in Figure 8.7.

FIGURE 8.7.

The File Schematic Definition window for a browse procedure, with no file yet selected.

The important thing here is the item labeled ToDo, under File-Browsing List Box, which is a reference to the list box control already placed on the window by the template. Make sure the ToDo line is selected, and then click on Insert. Select FLEAS from the Insert Files list that appears. The File Schematic Definition window should now look like the window shown in Figure 8.8.

The AppGen has automatically assumed that you want to view records in the order of the first key in the file definition. It so happens you do, but if you wanted to change that you could click on the Key button and get a list of available keys.

Populating the List Box

Click on OK to return to the Procedure Properties window, then click on Window to bring up the window formatter. To bring up the Property menu for the list box, make sure it is selected, and then press the right mouse button, or choose Edit|Properties. The List Properties window appears, as shown in Figure 8.9.

FIGURE 8.8.

The File Schematic Definition window for a browse procedure, with the FLEAS file selected and FLE:NameKey as the key.

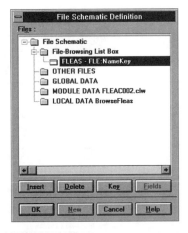

FIGURE 8.9.

The List Properties window.

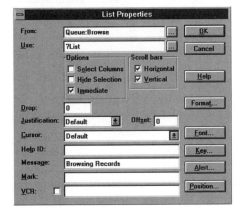

There's nothing you need to change here, with the possible exception of checking on the VCR attribute, which will place a VCR-style navigation control on the list box.

On the right side of the window, about halfway down, is the Format button. Select it to bring up the List Box Formatter window, as shown in Figure 8.10.

Because there are no fields in the list box yet, the only buttons that are active are Populate, Help, Cancel, and OK. This is the base window for list box populating activities—after you have added fields, you will also update their properties. Choose Populate to bring up the Select Field window, as shown in Figure 8.11.

Choose FLE:FleaName from the right side of the Select Field window by highlighting the field and clicking on Select. (If that field is not visible, be sure that the highlight on the left side of the window is on the FLEAS—FLE:NameKey line.)

FIGURE 8.10.
The List Box Formatter window.

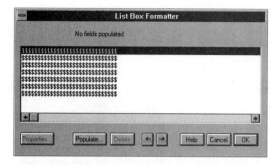

FIGURE 8.11.
The Select Field window.

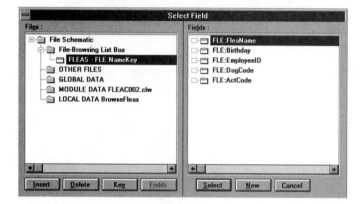

This window actually has a number of functions. The left side of the window specifies the particular group of data that you will work with, including any files used by the procedure, and any global, module, or local data. You can add existing files to the schematic, and even add new fields to those files. You can also create new global, module, and local data.

After you've selected the field with which to populate the list box, you will see one more window, which lets you specify list field properties. (See Figure 8.12.)

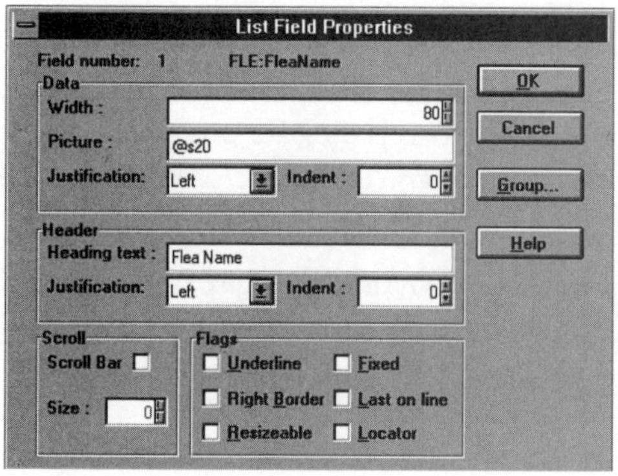

FIGURE 8.12.
The List Field Properties window.

This is where most of the action is when you're working with list boxes. Although this window appears when you select a field, you can also bring it up any time from the List Box Formatter window (shown in Figure 8.10).

You can accept all of the defaults if you're just in a rush to get some fields on the list box. On the other hand, you might want to make some change to the heading text, or to the width of the field (although you can also do this interactively in the list box formatter). Note that field widths are in dialog units (DLUs), not characters. As a rule of thumb, allow four DLUs in width for each character. (A DLU is actually one-fourth of the width of the average system font character, so if your system uses a larger or smaller font you may want to change the width accordingly.)

For particularly long text fields you might want to consider using a scroll bar just on that field, rather than taking up most of the list box with information most users don't need. The scroll size will always be greater than the field width, and will normally correspond to the length of the field to scroll. This number is also in DLUs, so if you wanted to scroll an 80-character field and show only 30 characters on the list box, the field width would be 120 and the scroll width would be 320.

Special Effects

There are also a number of flags that make it particularly easy to add special effects. The Underline flag will make the text in that field underlined, the Right Border flag will place a border on the right edge of the field, and the Resize flag will allow users to grab that border with the mouse and dynamically resize the columns in the list box (although these changes will not be saved unless you write the code to save them).

The Fixed flag freezes a column in its position in the list box, so if you have a horizontal scroll bar on the list box (which is separate from any scroll bars on individual fields) the field will not scroll off the list box. The Last on line flag indicates that the following field should appear directly below this field, allowing you to create multiline list boxes.

The Locator flag indicates that the field in that column is to be used as an entry locator. This is actually unnecessary for creating entry locators in the AppGen in version 1.0, and you can safely ignore it.

TIP

To create an entry locator, where you type in the value you want the browse to locate and it finds the nearest match, you will need to do two things. First, place the field that is also the sort key for the browse, on the form as an entry control (using Populate). Second, on the Procedure Properties window change the locator type to Entry.

Accept the defaults for the FLE:FleaName field to return to the list box formatter. This field should now appear in the list box. Go through the populate procedure four more times until all five fields in the FLEAS file are in the list box. There is one special case—the FLE:EmployeeID field, with the picture @KF###K. Since the leading *F* is stored in the data field, you should not attempt to reformat the string when displaying it. Replace the key-in pattern with a picture of @S4. (You will also need to do this when you populate the DOG:EmployeeID field on the update form for the DOGS file.)

From the list box formatter, you can use the mouse to adjust the column widths. If you place the mouse cursor between two columns it will turn into a double arrow, and if you click and drag you can move the columns farther apart or closer together as desired. You may also choose to adjust spacing by means of the Indent settings on the Field Properties window. To change these or any other field property settings, select the field to modify and click on Properties.

When you are satisfied that all the fields are as you want them, click on OK to return to the Window Formatter. Click on OK again to return to the Procedure Properties window.

You've selected the file to use and you've populated the fields. Because you'll also need to add any records that will be in the file, you should also specify an update procedure. There is an entry for just this purpose in the lower-left corner of the window. Enter the procedure name UpdateFleas. Click OK to return to the application tree window.

Creating a Form

You should now have an UpdateFleas ToDo procedure in the tree. Select it and click on Properties. Select a procedure type of form.

The requirements for forms are much like those for browse procedures: Choose a file, and populate the window with fields. The process is slightly different: When you choose a file, you do not need to specify a key, because the only processing going on is adding, updating, or deleting a record chosen by another procedure (usually, but not necessarily, a browse procedure).

To populate the form with fields, load the Window Formatter, and either choose Populate|Multiple Fields or click on the two-person icon at the bottom of the Toolbox. The Select Fields window appears. If you have not already selected a file, and the entry under Update Record on Disk is a ToDo procedure, as shown in Figure 8.13, you can do so now. Highlight the ToDo line, click on Insert (or double-click on the ToDo procedure), and choose the FLEAS file from the list. You will see the list of fields on the right side of the window.

Placing Fields

To place a field on the window, select it from the list. You are returned to the Window Formatter, and the cursor is a crosshair with a Populate icon. You will be placing both the prompt and the entry field at the same time, so click to the left of the window, near the top. Because you chose Populate Multiple, you are immediately returned to the Select Field window to choose another field to place. Go through all five fields in this way, and when you've reached the last one click on Cancel in the Select Field window.

Don't worry too much about exact placement as you populate—the Window Formatter provides two tools to help you get everything nicely lined up: the grid and the Alignment menu.

Using the Grid

To set the grid, choose Options|Grid Settings. As with field lengths in the list box, and most measurements in CW, the grid settings are in DLUs. Experiment to find the settings that work best for the look and feel you are trying to achieve.

> **TIP**
>
> You may find that you have somewhat less real estate on the screen than you were used to with DOS, as Windows controls tend to take more space. A reasonable minimum is to use a grid vertical spacing of 12 (or a divisor of 12) DLUs and a standard control height of 10 DLUs. This will give you a 1 DLU buffer between controls (vertically), and your text will still look reasonably comfortable inside those 10-DLU entry fields (provided you are using standard fonts).

Using Alignment Options

The Alignment menu allows you to modify the size and placement of groups of controls, one of which will always be the reference or *anchor*. To select more than one control, either hold the Ctrl key and click and drag a selection box around the controls, or hold the Shift key and select the controls you want one by one. The last control selected is always the anchor control—it has red rather than blue handles, and any alignment action you take under the Alignment menu will use it as the reference. If you want to left-align the prompts, for instance, make sure that the prompt control you want to use as a reference has the red handles.

> **TIP**
>
> If it's your practice to right-align prompts, you might want to consider switching to left alignment. Prompt length is dependent on the font in use, and the prompt text (which is an issue if you create international versions of your programs). Left-aligned prompts are much easier to maintain than right-aligned prompts, because you only need to allow enough space for any likely prompt length.

Setting the Tab Order

In standard Windows programs, the user can use the Tab key to move from field to field. The tab order is not necessarily the same as the physical order of controls on the window. In fact, the default tab order will be the same order as the order in which you populated your controls, and if you haven't started with the topmost control, or if you've juggled the controls after populating them, you should update the order. Choose Edit|SetOrder. The Ordering Type window appears, as shown in Figure 8.13.

FIGURE 8.13.

The Ordering Type window.

If you choose Automatic Horizontally, the tab order will move left to right, row by row. If you choose Automatic Vertically, the tab order will move top to bottom, left to right. If you choose Manual, you can set the tab order yourself. Whichever of these methods you choose will be presented with a tab view of the window, with each control showing a colored number box indicating the control's place in the sequence. (See Figure 8.14.)

FIGURE 8.14.

A window with tab order showing on the controls.

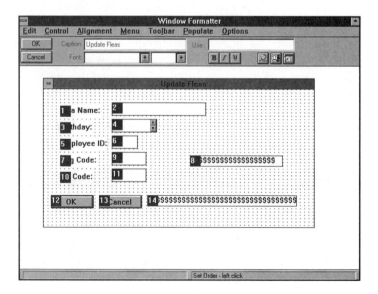

To override the tab order as shown, regardless of whether you have selected an Automatic or Manual mode, click on the controls in the tab sequence you want. Click on the first control (whether or not it is already tab sequence 1), then the second, and so on. As you move through the controls, the current control's number is shown in red, so you can keep track of where you are. Subsequent controls are renumbered as necessary. When you're done renumbering (and you don't have to go all the way to the end), just click away from the controls and the tab sequence markers will disappear.

Control Properties

By now you should be getting reasonably familiar with control properties. If you faithfully entered the Data Dictionary information as described in Chapter 7, then all should have been carried through to the AppGen as expected. You can, however, override any of those settings if you wish. The one thing that's a little tricky to change is the control type—to do that, you would have to delete the existing control and add a new one of the desired type from the toolbox, then fill in its Use entry with the appropriate field name. You would also need to specify any additional properties as required, and create a suitable prompt for the control.

Entry Patterns

Entry controls can use pictures that apply formatting to the values they hold. Dates and times are common examples. Ordinarily, formatting is applied only after the field has been completed. You can instruct the window to format such fields at entry time by selecting the window, bringing up the Property window, and checking the Entry Patterns checkbox.

Property Shortcuts

You've probably noticed a number of entry controls in the Window Formatter's toolbar. These allow you to quickly specify the caption (or picture) and use variable, font, and size for whichever control is currently selected. You don't actually need to bring up the Properties window to make these changes. If the window is selected, you can update the window title in the Caption entry.

File Relationships and Field Lookups

Before proceeding with the next section, you should create browse/form procedures for the two remaining files, ACTS and DOGS. The process will be much the same: You can populate the browse procedures and the forms with all the fields from each file. Call the update forms UpdateActs and UpdateDogs. Remember to change the display picture for the DOG:EmployeeID field on the BrowseDogs list box from @KD###K to @s4, as discussed in the earlier section on creating the `BrowseFleas` procedure.

Once you have all your procedures in place, your application tree window should look like the one shown in Figure 8.15.

FIGURE 8.15.

The application tree window showing FLEACIRC.APP with the browse and form procedures created.

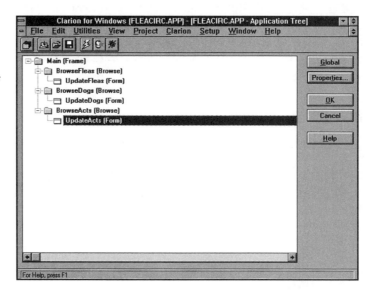

Make and run the application (click on the Run icon, or choose Project|Run from the main menu). Fill in at least two dog records and two flea records. Since this is an MDI app (the browse procedures are threaded), you can have more than one browse procedure onscreen at one time, as shown in Figure 8.16.

FIGURE 8.16.

The FLEACIRC application with Dogs and Acts browse procedures showing.

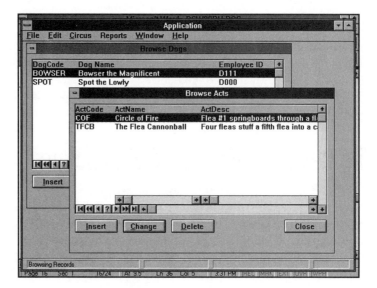

You might recall that the FLEAS file contains fields for the dog ID and the act ID. While Alphonse may know his fleas and dogs quite well, his memory isn't what it used to be and he would appreciate being able to verify these entries. Return to the `UpdateFleas` Window Formatter, and select the FLE:DogCode control. Click on the right mouse button to bring up the Property menu and choose Actions. The Prompts for ?FLE:DogCode window appears, as shown in Figure 8.17.

FIGURE 8.17.

The Prompts for ?FLE:DogCode window.

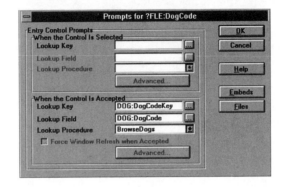

You will be adding the lookup code after the entry control is accepted. (If you add the lookup code when the entry control is selected, it will execute before you have a chance to enter a value.) Click on the ellipsis button to the right of the entry to bring up the Select Key window, as shown in Figure 8.18.

FIGURE 8.18.

The Select Key window with the DOGS file shown as related to the FLEAS file.

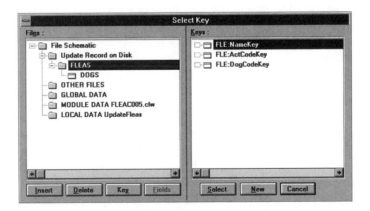

At this point, neither the DOGS file nor any of its keys appear in the window, so it won't look quite like Figure 8.18. There are two ways to add the DOGS file—under the FLEAS file or under OTHER FILES.

Both options ensure that the file is opened when the procedure begins, if it isn't already open. Both options also make it possible for you to do a lookup on the DOGS file, and neither option has any effect on referential integrity. If you add the DOGS file under FLEAS (which you do by selecting the FLEAS file and clicking on Insert), every time the `RefreshWindow` routine is called, the DOGS record, which is related to the FLEAS record, will be located. That's useful if, for instance, you want to display the dog's name along with its code. Placing the DOGS file under OTHER will not get you the automatic lookup.

NOTE

If the file on which you wish to look up the field does not have a relationship to the current file defined in the Data Dictionary, you will not be able to insert it under the current file, and you will have to place it under OTHER.

This same kind of association is also useful in browse procedures, as you'll see shortly. In the meantime, make sure your Select Key window looks like Figure 8.18, and select DOG:DogCodeKey from the key list.

The Lookup Field entry on the Prompts for ?FLE:DogCode window should be DOG:DogCode, and you can pick the BrowseDogs procedure from the procedure list by activating the drop-down list box. Save your changes and return to the Window Formatter.

Display Lookup Fields

Now that you've established an automatic lookup of the DOGS file, using the `DOG:DogName` field as a display string is quite simple. Place a string field on the Window Formatter where you want the dog's name to appear. On the string's property window, check the Variable String box, then select the DOGS file and the DOG:DogName field from the Select Field window that appears. If you make a wrong choice, you can bring this window up again by clicking on the ellipsis box to the right of the Use entry on the string's Property window.

Save your changes, and compile and run your application. On the FLEAS update form, type in a dog's code. If you get it right, the program will display the dog's name beside the code. If you get it wrong, the procedure you named as a lookup procedure (in this case, also the procedure you use to update the DOGS file) pops up so you can select the appropriate record.

Approaches to Field Validation

This kind of lookup is only one of the approaches you can take to validating fields. It has the advantage of being easy to accomplish, but it also has some drawbacks. Unless you write some extra code, you don't know where the validation list will pop up, and it might not be anywhere near the field you're editing. It's also somewhat DOS-like in appearance—after all, most Windows programs use things like drop-down lists or combo boxes when you have a multiple-choice field. Alternate approaches to field validation are discussed in Chapter 9, "Refining Procedures: Code and Control Templates."

Browse Lookup Fields

In the BrowseFleas procedure you currently display the flea's dog and act codes. You can quite easily look up the dog and act names from those files, if you wish. Go to the BrowseFlea window, select the list box, and bring up the List Box Formatter. Delete the FLE:DogCode field, and click on Populate. In the Select Field window, add the DOGS file under the FLEAS file, and select DOG:DogName. Do the same for the ACTS file and the ACT:ActName field, making sure you add the ACTS file under FLEAS, not under DOGS (which it won't let you do anyway).

Compile and run the program. In the BrowseFleas procedure, you should now see the full dog and act names in the browse procedure.

Reports and Processes

Along with browse procedures and forms, reports are a common element in most business applications. Following the procedure you learned at the beginning of this chapter for calling procedures from the main menu, add a new menu called Reports to the main procedure's menu bar. Under that new menu place an item with the name &Flea List and the use variable ?FleaList. It should call a procedure named FleaList, which should *not* be threaded.

If you've correctly added the procedure call to the main menu, a ToDo procedure stub will appear in the menu tree for FleaList. Select it, click on Properties, and choose Report. The Report Properties window appears, and it looks much like the other Procedure Properties windows you've seen. Click on Files and add FLEAS as the primary file, with DOGS and ACTS under it. Your File Schematic window should look like the window shown in Figure 8.19.

FIGURE 8.19.

The File Schematic window for the FleaList report, showing the FLEAS file as the primary file and DOGS and ACTS as related files.

Save your changes to the File Schematic window, and from the Procedure Properties window select Report to load the Report Formatter. When you first see the report, you will be looking at it in Band view, which is also where you will do most of your work. This view shows you the logical parts of the report, rather than the actual way the data will appear on the page. For a discussion of the different report views, see Chapter 1, "Introduction to the Development Environment."

Page-Oriented Reporting

The report engine in Clarion for Windows is substantially different from that of earlier DOS versions of Clarion. Instead of feeding information line-by-line to a printer, it composes one page at a time. It's still possible to do reports much the same way you're used to doing them in DOS, but it's not necessary.

For instance, you no longer need to have your total fields at the bottom of the page. They can be anywhere at all on the page, because the page never goes to the printer until it's completely ready. The report engine is page oriented, not entire-report oriented, however, so you can't have a report total on page 1 (unless you have a one-page report).

Most reports have at least three logical parts. The header, which traditionally goes at the top of the page, often contains the report title, date and time of printing, and any other data that uniquely identifies the report. Click on the Str button on the toolbox and place a text string in the header. Change the text to `Alphonse's Fleas`, and make it a suitably large font. To center it on the form, make the string control as wide as the report and change its Alignment property to Centered.

The footer, which traditionally goes at the bottom of the page, may hold page numbers and total fields. To place a page number on the footer, again place a string field, but in the string's Properties window change the total type from <None> to Page No, as shown in Figure 8.20.

FIGURE 8.20.

Changing a string control's property to Page No.

Printing Report Detail Bands

The detail section is what traditionally makes up the meat of the report. In its simplest form, it contains all the information you want printed for each selected record in the primary file.

Your detail band should take up only as much space as you want each record to take up on the report.

Use the Populate Multiple feature (either choose it from the menu or click on the two-person icon in the toolbox) to place fields FLE:FleaName, FLE:Birthday, FLE:EmployeeID, DOG:DogName, and ACT:ActName in the detail band, as shown in Figure 8.21. To select fields from the different files, make sure the appropriate file is highlighted on the left side of the Select Field window. Because you have placed both the ACTS and DOGS files in the file schematic under the FLEAS field, their related records will automatically be looked up each time you print a record from the FLEAS file.

FIGURE 8.21.

The FLEAS report populated with fields from FLEAS, DOGS, and ACTS (showing properties for DOG:DogName).

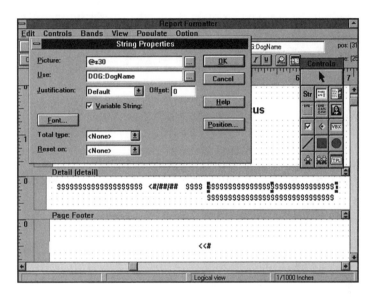

You will probably also want to add some column headings to the report. There are two ways to do this. If you have your header at the top of the page, you can put your column headings there. A better approach, however, is to use another feature of the Report Formatter—the page form.

Using the Page Form

The page form is like a background to your report. Anything you want to appear on every page should go here. To get to the page form from Band view, scroll down the report—it appears right after the footer. It may take some fiddling to get the controls lined up the way you want, but you can make the job easier by playing with the grid size and paying close attention to the ruler.

The Future of Reports

Reporting in Clarion for Windows 1.0 is still a little on the sketchy side, although the feature list is expected to be considerably more robust by version 1.1. If reporting is your primary requirement, and you have version 1.0, you might need to get down to the hand-code level to accomplish your goals. You might also want to consider using a file driver for which other report writers are available.

TIP

Although CW's report-writing capabilities are due for significant upgrading, you may still want to consider using a file driver (such as Btrieve) that is supported by third-party report writers, particularly if your clients are already using one of these tools.

Summary

Chapter 6 shows the fastest possible way to create an application in CW. Chapter 7 and this chapter take the discussion to a deeper level, showing how you can create the same kinds of procedures Quick Start did, but in a way that suits your own needs and is appropriate to a more complex multifile data model. Chapter 9 concentrates on some of the individual building blocks that make up AppGen procedures and shows you how you can use these building blocks to create your own style of program.

9

Refining Procedures: Code and Control Templates

In Chapter 8, "Creating Procedures," you learned about the standard procedure templates, including the frame, browse, and form templates. Creating procedures using these templates is a lot like creating procedures in earlier versions of Clarion, where the procedure's functionality is closely tied to the procedure template. In Clarion for Windows, this is no longer necessarily true.

For the most part, what the procedure does depends far more on what controls are populated on that window than on what template you used in the beginning. And the most basic procedure template you can begin with, one that makes the fewest assumptions about what it should look like or do, is the window procedure template.

The Window Procedure Template

The window procedure template is the base template type for menus, forms, browse procedures, and frames. By that I mean you can duplicate any of these procedures simply by starting with a basic window template and adding the required controls. In fact, when the new template technology debuted in CW, there was some discussion about whether it was even necessary to have any other base procedure types. It quickly became clear, however, that providing some semi-customized starting points would save a lot of confusion among DOS Clarion users, and would also speed up the development process somewhat.

The downside of this decision is that it isn't immediately obvious how radically different CW's approach to templates is from that of its predecessors. The functionality that used to be embodied in the procedure template has now been moved to the control that requires that functionality. For instance, a browse procedure requires a certain amount of code to scroll data records in the correct order and with the correct filter. But what happens if you want to place two list boxes on the same window? You can't, without rewriting the template (which is what some third-party template vendors did with Clarion for DOS).

In CW, just as you can associate a control with a procedure, you can associate source code with the control. The mechanism that makes this possible is called a control template. *Control templates* are essentially blocks of template code wrapped around one or more controls. You populate them the same way you populate entry controls, buttons, fields from a file, list boxes, or any other control. The difference is that you're not just adding the control; you're also adding all the support code it requires. (The actual template language statements used to create code templates are discussed in more detail in Chapter 19, "Creating Control Templates.")

If it's possible to create just about any procedure using a basic window procedure template and a bunch of control templates, you may have to do some rethinking about how you approach program design. There is a strong element of object orientation here, albeit with a more structured framework than you usually find in object-oriented languages. As the rest of this chapter shows, you now have buttons that can close procedures, list boxes that populate themselves, other buttons that know how to call update procedures for list boxes, and so on.

You may find that you still create most of your procedures from the templates such as browse, form, or report. Even if you do, you can make good use of control templates. After all, you can populate just about any kind of control template on a form or browse window just as easily as you can populate controls on a generic window.

Creative *BrowseBox*ing

One of the most useful control templates is the BrowseBox template. The BrowseBox template is made up of a list box that you place on the window, some event-handling code snippets, and a set of routines that accomplish the scrolling and paging of data from a file. You don't see the code—it gets generated for you automatically, although you can go to the generated source code and see the changes that a just-added control template has brought about. The template will also add a number of embed points to your Embeds list.

TIP

One highly effective way to learn what various code templates do is to add them one at a time to your procedure, generate the code, and then compare that code to a previously generated version of that procedure saved under another name. You will need a difference, or diff, program to show you the changes—one that I use often, and which is available on CompuServe, is a copyrighted, free program called VCOMP. If you use version-control software, you probably already have a difference program.

This template is particularly useful because, as I implied earlier, you can have multiple browse boxes on a window. How easy is this to do? Easy. Very easy.

In the previous chapter you began developing an application for Alphonse, king of the Flea Circus Circuit. In this exercise, you'll create a window with a list of dogs on one side and a list of fleas on the other. The list of fleas will show only those that are resident on the currently highlighted dog, so as you change dogs, the list of fleas is updated.

NOTE

You can find a completed FLEACIRC.APP in the CHAP9\ directory on the source code disk that accompanies this book.

Open your FLEACIRC.APP again. Add a new item to the main menu, under the Circus menu, and call it Fleas &on Dogs, as shown in Figure 9.1.

FIGURE 9.1.

Adding a new menu item to the main menu.

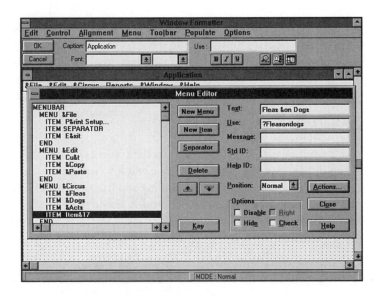

Click Actions in the menu editor, and fill out the Prompts window as shown in Figure 9.2.

FIGURE 9.2.

Adding the procedure call to FleasOnDogs *to the menu item.*

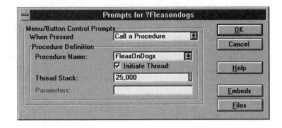

Return to the application tree. You should now see a ToDo stub for the FleasOnDogs procedure. Highlight it, click Properties to bring up the Select Procedure Type window, and choose the Window—Generic Window Handler procedure type. This is the base window template.

The Procedure Properties window, shown in Figure 9.3, is much like those you have already seen, only a little less crowded. This is because it doesn't have any default controls whose settings appear on the Procedure Properties window.

Click the Window button to bring up the Window Formatter. When you do, you'll be presented with a list of available window types, as shown in Figure 9.4.

This list will appear only the first time you click the button. This list is taken directly from the DEFAULTS.CLW file in your CW\LIBSRC directory, so if you'd like to add a few choices of your own to the list, that's where you do it.

FIGURE 9.3.

The Generic Window Handler Procedure Properties window.

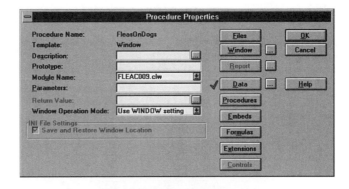

FIGURE 9.4.

Choosing a new window type.

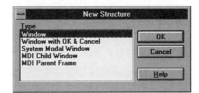

TIP

Of the five windows shown, four are window structures and the last is an application structure. The attributes of the first four can all be changed in the Window Formatter—you can make a system modal window into an MDI child window, into an ordinary window, or into one with a couple buttons on it. What you can't do in the formatter is change a window to an application (although you can do this if you edit the window structure directly using the ellipsis button).

Choose Window (with no buttons). In the Window Formatter, bring up the Properties window for the window and make sure MDI Child is checked and the 3D Look check box is also on. You want this procedure to have that same spiffy gray background as the rest of your windows, right? Also make sure that Entry Patterns is checked.

Next, either choose Populate|Control Template from the menu or click the TPL icon in the Toolbox. The Select Control Template window appears. Choose BrowseBox—File-Browsing List Box, and when the selection window disappears and you get your crosshair cursor, choose the upper-left location for the browse box and click. As you do, the List Box Formatter window appears (shown in Figure 9.5) and you should start to feel you're in familiar waters.

FIGURE 9.5.

The List Box Formatter window, which appears after a list box template is populated onto the form.

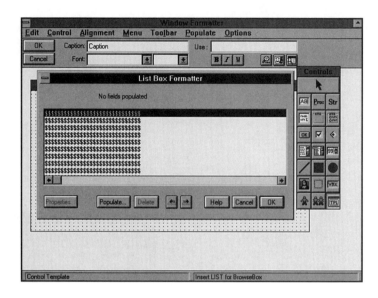

Click the Populate button, and the Select Field window shown in Figure 9.6 pops up, showing you a browse box in the schematic and asking you to fill in the file from which it's supposed to read records.

FIGURE 9.6.

The File Schematic window showing the newly placed browse box that needs a file attached.

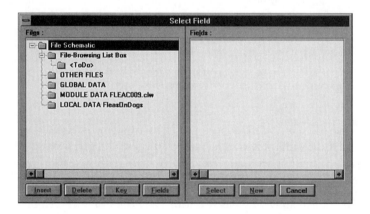

For this first browse box, you'll need to populate some fields from the DOGS file. You can follow the same process you used in Chapter 8, except that you don't need to worry about an update procedure (at least not yet). Remember to change the display picture for the DOG:EmployeeID field on the BrowseDogs browse box from @KD###K to @s4, in the manner discussed in Chapter 8 in the section on creating the `BrowseFleas` procedure.

Adding a Second Browse Box

Now add a second browse box to the same window by again clicking the TPL icon on the Toolbox. From the Select Control Template window, choose BrowseBox. Place it to the right of the existing browse box, and the Format List Box window appears. Click Populate. This time the Select Field window, shown in Figure 9.7, looks a little different than it did in Figure 9.6.

FIGURE 9.7.

The File Schematic window showing two browse boxes, with the second one still to be filled out.

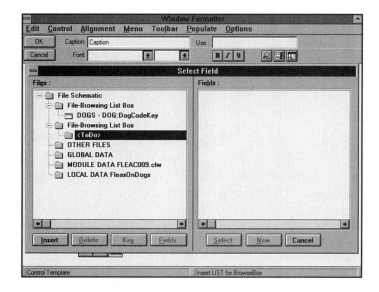

Select the second File-Browsing List Box <ToDo> entry and click Insert to again bring up the list of files. Choose FLEAS, then click Key to select the DogCodeKey. This is important, because you will later use this key to set the link between the browse boxes.

Populate this browse box the same way you populated the DOGS browse box, but be sure you have the FLEAS file selected when you choose the fields to populate. Again, change the picture on the EmployeeID field to @S4.

You should now have a window that looks something like what's shown in Figure 9.8.

The next step is to establish a relationship between the two browse boxes. In this case, you'll always want to display the entire list of dogs, so you won't need to do anything with that browse box. You will need to tell the second browse box that it's supposed to show only those records that are related to the dog currently selected in the first browse box.

FIGURE 9.8.

The FleasOnDogs *procedure with both browse boxes in place.*

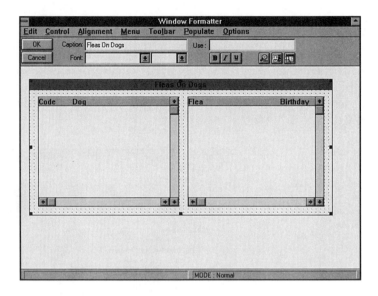

Double-click the Flea browse box to bring up the Actions window, and click Range and Filter. The Range and Filter window, shown in Figure 9.9, appears.

FIGURE 9.9.

The Range and Filter window for the Flea browse box.

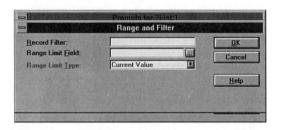

Click the ellipsis button to the right of the Range Limit field. This will bring up a window that shows you a list of key elements you can use to limit the range of records shown. If you previously selected DogCodeKey when you added the file to the browse box, you should see only the field FLE:DogCode listed. Select it. (If you see another field listed, you will have to go back to the File Schematic and change the key used by this browse box. That is easily done from the Files button on the Procedure Properties window.)

Now change the range limit type from Current Value to Related File. A prompt for the name of the related file will appear in the window. You can use the ellipsis button to the right of the entry to bring up a list of files. Choose DOGS. Your window should now look like that shown in Figure 9.10.

FIGURE 9.10.

The Range and Filter window for the Flea browse box with the fields filled in.

The reason this code is going to work is because you have defined a relationship in the Data Dictionary between the FLE:DogCode field in the FLEAS file and the DOG:DogCode field in the DOGS file. The AppGen will use that information to ensure that records in the Flea browse box will be appropriately limited.

TIP

Although file relationships are a useful way of arranging related list boxes, they are by no means a requirement. You can also link the Flea browse box by making the range limit type a Single Value, and specifying the DOG:DogCode field as the field in which to hold that value. To ensure that the DOG:DogCode field contains a value corresponding to the currently selected record, add the DOG:DogCode field to the Hot Fields list for the Dog browse box.

There's one other thing this procedure needs: a Cancel button. You could just place an ordinary button on the window using the Toolbox, change its text to Cancel, and write some code to exit the procedure, or you could grab a control template to do the job. You're a quick learner, so naturally you'll do the latter.

Give yourself enough room in the lower-right corner of the window to place a button, and click the TPL icon. Choose CloseButton—Close the Window from the list. That's all there is to it!

Save your changes and run the program. When you choose Fleas On Dogs from the Circus menu, you should see your procedure with a list of dogs in the left browse box, and a list of only those fleas that reside on the currently selected dog on the right. Click the Close button to exit the procedure.

The *BrowseSelectButton* and *BrowseUpdateButtons* Templates

So far you're just using this procedure to display values. What if you want to update either of these browse boxes? Once again, click the TPL button to populate another template, this time to update the browse box.

You may have noticed that after you placed the first browse box, several control templates appeared in the list that weren't there before. These are the `BrowseSelectButton` and `BrowseUpdateButtons` templates, and they didn't appear in the list before because they have an attribute that restricts them from appearing until a template of the type `BrowseBox` has been populated on the window.

Choose BrowseUpdateButtons from the list. The Select Parent window, shown in Figure 9.11, appears because you have two browse box controls on the window, and the AppGen needs to know to which of the two it should attach the buttons. Select Browse on DOGS, and click just below the lower-left corner of the Dog browse box. There are three buttons to this template, and the AppGen places them in succession. (When a template has multiple controls, it is up to the template writer whether they are placed automatically or whether the user places each one individually. In this case, it's automatic.)

FIGURE 9.11.

The Select Parent window appears when a child control template has more than one possible parent.

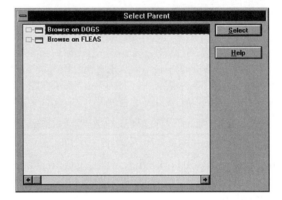

Click any one of the buttons (it doesn't matter which one) to get the Prompts window. Here you can specify the name of the update procedure from the list of existing procedures. Type or select `UpdateDogs`. You may have to use the cursor keys to scroll down, because in version 1.0 there is no scroll bar on the procedure list. Changing the `Update` procedure on one button also changes it on all other buttons in that set.

Now add the `BrowseUpdateButtons` template to the second browse box. This time you won't be asked which parent to attach the buttons to, because there is only one left that does not already have the update buttons. Set the update procedure for these buttons to `UpdateFleas`.

Save your changes and run the application. You should now be able to update FLEAS and DOGS from the `FleasOnDogs` procedure.

Do-It-Yourself Updates: The *SaveButton* Template

The SaveButton template is more than a little deceptive. All you place on the window is one tiny button. What you get in your procedure is about 150 lines of source code that effectively transform your window procedure into a form procedure.

There are a few differences between the SaveButton template and the form procedure: on a SaveButton, the prompts associated with the template are only visible from the button itself, whereas on a form they are also visible on the Procedure Properties window. Forms also have a default ValidateRecord extension loaded (see Chapter 20, "Creating Extension Templates," for more on extension templates) with prompts visible on the Procedure Properties window. Add one of these ValidateRecord extension templates to your window-based procedure, and you'll have the same functionality as the form has.

The other difference between a form and a window with a SaveButton on it is you can't delete the SaveButton on a form, but you can on a window.

DDLB Validations: The *FileDrop* Template

One of the big changes in program design between DOS and Windows is the way file lookups are handled. In DOS you often call a procedure when you want to validate an entry, but Windows provides drop-down list boxes (DDLBs) for this sort of thing. CW also provides a DDLB control template to make it easy to add this kind of functionality to your program.

Go back to the UpdateFleas procedure in the FLEACIRC application. On that form, as you'll remember, there is a field called FLE:DogCode, which is validated against the DOGS file. Delete that field so that you can replace it with a DDLB that contains dog codes from the DOGS file. (When you do this, the prompt will also disappear; that's normal behavior, and just means you'll have to manually add it again later.)

Populate the FileDrop--File Loaded Drop Box template using the same process you've used to populate other templates onto the window. Once you've positioned the drop box where the entry field used to be, double-click the control. This will bring up the Prompts window.

This template can be a little trickier to use than some of the others. The first step, from the Prompts window, is to click on Files to bring up the File Schematic window. You'll see an entry for the File-Loaded drop box. Specify a file and key for the drop box. Click OK. Back at the Prompts window, click the ellipsis button next to the Field to Fill button. That will bring up a list of fields in the file. Choose the DOG:DogCode field. Click OK.

Now you need to make sure that the use variable is correctly set to the field you want. This will be the field into which DOG:DogCode is to be loaded: FLE:DogCode. Bring up the List Properties window for the control, and verify that the use variable is FLE:DogCode. If it isn't, click the ellipsis button next to the entry to bring up the File Schematic window, and select the field. Your List Properties window should look like the one shown in Figure 9.12.

FIGURE 9.12.

The List Properties window for the FileDrop *control template, as used to look up FLE:DogCode in the DOGS file.*

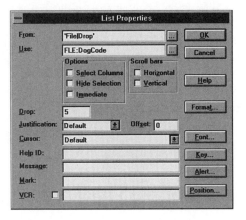

This is where it starts to get really tricky. There is a bug in CW 1.0; sometimes the use variable on control templates does not get saved. You should exit the window after changing the use variable, then go back in and check it again. If you find that the FileDrop control template is not working properly, the use variable is the first thing to check.

One more word of caution: The FileDrop template is suited only to files where you don't need to do any filtering or range checking on the file, and where the number of records is quite small. We have included an enhanced FileDrop-style template on the code disk that accompanies this book. It answers most of these limitations, and is discussed in Chapter 17, "Creating Code Templates." Unfortunately, this template suffers from the same problem of use variables not being saved, so you should take the same precautions.

Getting Out: The *Close* and *CancelButton* Templates

You've already used the CloseButton template in the BrowseBox example. The CancelButton template is identical in function, except that it sports the text Cancel instead of Close. Both can be used to exit any procedure. In addition to posting a CloseDown event (which is the template-friendly way to exit an AppGen procedure), these templates also set the LocalResponse variable to RequestCancelled, another template-friendly action which helps ensure that your window procedure dovetails with other standard procedure templates that may be used to build the calling procedure.

Viewing Text Files: The *ASCIIBox* Template

The ASCIIBox template is a fun little thing. It makes it easy to add to any window the capability to browse ASCII files. In your FLEACIRC application (or any application, for that matter), create a new procedure based on the Window template. Populate an ASCIIBox template onto that window, and double-click it to bring up the Prompts window. Fill it out as shown in Figure 9.13. Note that the local variable LOC:FileName (which you'll create shortly) has a ! prepended to it to indicate that it is a variable and not a literal filename.

FIGURE 9.13.

The Prompts window for the ASCIIBox *control template.*

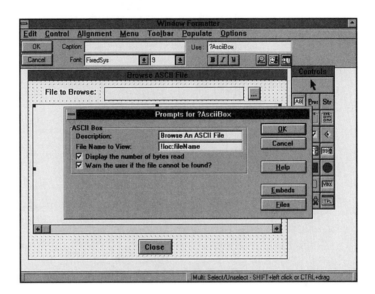

Next, populate a local variable onto the window. Use the same populate method you use to place entry fields from a file; that is, click the icon with the figure of a man, or choose Populate|Field from the main menu. Make sure Local Data is selected on the resulting Select Field window, then click New and add the LOC:FileName field you specified earlier on the ASCIIBox Prompts window. Declare it as a string of 80 places. Click OK (you can accept defaults for everything else).

You should now have an entry field with LOC:FileName as the use variable placed on the window. To the right of this, populate a DOSFileLookup control template, using the method you have learned in this chapter for populating control templates. This template is a button that invokes the standard Windows File dialog box to let you choose which file to view.

On the Prompts window for the DOSFileLookup control template, set the DOS Filename Variable field to LOC:FileName. For now, everything else can stay at default values for this control. Click OK.

You may want to add a prompt to the left of the entry control (just click the Pro: icon and change the text on the resulting prompt to something suitable), and after you've done this your window should look something like the one shown in Figure 9.14. Don't forget to add that `CloseButton` template!

FIGURE 9.14.

A window procedure populated with the `ASCIIBox` *and* `DOSFileLookup` *control templates.*

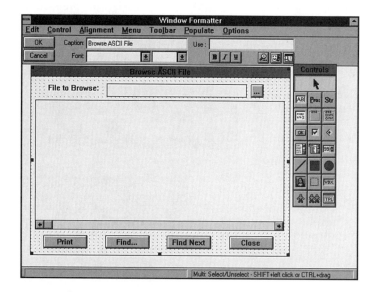

If everything works as planned, you will have a procedure that lets you pick the file to view, and then displays it in a list box. If you wish, you can add some extra functionality to this procedure.

The *ASCIISearchButton* and *ASCIIPrintButton* Templates

These two templates give you a quick way to add print and search capabilities to the `ASCIIBox` template. Neither of these templates have any prompts be filled out—just drop them in and go.

Summary

Although Clarion for Windows provides a number of default procedure types that do the kinds of things Clarion programmers have come to expect of an Application Generator, the underlying technology is radically different from that of the DOS versions. Procedure logic is no longer dependent on the procedure, but comes packaged with controls through the use of control templates.

The base template type for most procedures is the window. By populating a window with the appropriate control templates, you can turn it into a browse, a form, a text file viewer, or just about anything else you (or, to be practical, third-party template vendors) can imagine. You can also use whatever combination of control templates suits your needs to enhance the appearance and function of procedures based on other template types.

Clarion for Windows has brought plug-and-play to application development in a new and powerful way, and the more you think about development in terms of control types rather than procedure types, the better you'll be able to use that power.

10

Assigning and Building Your Help Files

Context-sensitive help, in Clarion for Windows, is much like the rest of the Windows development world—that is, you must use an external program to create and maintain the help system. For many Clarion "old timers" this may seem like a step backward, because in previous versions of Clarion for DOS there was always an integrated help system included with the development environment. Why has TopSpeed (formerly Clarion Software) elected not to include an integrated help management system? Primarily because there are many third-party products already available that have been developed specifically for this task. These tools range from shareware word processor add-on products to complete help authoring systems.

Windows users expect that a language will support the standard Windows help file format, not create and manage it. Clarion for Windows is following the industry standard, focusing on the most important aspect of the product: application development. You see a difference between Clarion for Windows and other development platforms in the ease of integration of the standard Windows help files into your application.

This chapter covers the details of using the standard Windows help system, and it helps you make the right decisions when reviewing and selecting your help authoring tools.

The Windows Help System

Windows includes the standard Windows help engine known as WINHELP.EXE. This engine is distributed with every copy of Windows and is used by every program that provides a help file. Standard Windows help files are designated by the extension .HLP. If you look in the \cw\bin directory, you will notice there are various help files that are used by the Clarion for Windows integrated development environment (IDE).

A standard Windows help file can include many different components, including topics, context strings, images, hot spots, hypergraphics, hypertext links, macros, extended links including sound and other help files, nonscrolling regions, and so on. It is entirely up to you what components you include. The Microsoft Windows Software Development Kit (SDK) provides a detailed discussion of each of these help concepts.

Generally, in Windows you define the help file for your program, and once it is invoked (through various methods that are discussed later in this chapter) the Windows help engine takes over until the user exits the Windows help system. There is nothing modal about the help system; your program can continue to run while the help engine is running the help file for your program. This makes it possible to have both the help system and the program running alongside each other.

The process of creating help files is a lot like creating executable programs. You start with some source files, and you create a project file to tell the help compiler what it needs to do. There are two different help compilers that you can obtain through various methods, such as purchasing the SDK or buying a Windows development platform or a Windows help add-on product. Both of these compilers, HCP.EXE and HC31.EXE, are DOS-based products developed by Microsoft Corporation. Both provide the same functionality, with the former being a protected-mode version.

To build a help file, you will first create a project file, then you will create the help text using a word processor or Windows help editor (whatever you use, it must be capable of saving text in a rich text format (an RTF file). Then you add the appropriate macros, if any, and compile the components to a new help file. It's not quite that simple, but you get the idea.

There is one more important tool: SHED.EXE. This is the Windows hot spot editor, which allows you to place *hot spots* or regions on an image and link the appropriate help to that hot spot. As a result, you provide the user with the ability to click on an area of the image and get the appropriate related help information, enhancing the visual aspects of your help file.

TIP

Help can be one of the most important aspects of your program. You should take some time to review the help files of the other Windows programs that you use, learning what you like and dislike, before you attempt to create a help file—it will save you a lot of effort and time in the long run. A help file, just like a program, must be a planned exercise.

Setting Up Help in Your Application

Clarion for Windows makes integrating your Windows help file quite easy. First, you will need to identify the help file to the program. For example, if you had a help file called CWBOOK.HLP you would identify it with the following code:

```
HELP('CWBOOK')
```

If you are using the AppGen, you will specify this file in the Application Properties window, and the AppGen will write the code for you.

This form of the HELP() function nominates the help file to your program. When your program executes and the user invokes the help system, it will attempt to locate the CWBOOK.HLP file in the current working directory of your program or in the \WINDOWS directory. If your help file could not be found, the Windows WINHELP.EXE program will execute and display an error message stating that the help file could not be found. If it is found, a help window will appear on top of your running program.

There are various uses of the HELP() function:

```
HELP('CWBOOK')
HELP('CWBOOK','KeyWord')
HELP('CWBOOK',' ~ContextString')
HELP(,'KeyWord')
HELP(,'~ContextString')
```

To understand what each of these statements does, you will need to clearly understand the difference between a keyword and a context string. A *keyword* is a word, phrase, or code that is stored as a key field for help topics and is used in the standard Windows help search function. In other words, a keyword provides a means of quickly finding related topics within the Windows help system—by keyword searching. A *context string* is a unique identifier for a help topic. So the keyword is used for searching and relating help topics, and the context string is used to identify and locate a unique help topic.

The first option, HELP('CWBOOK'), which has already been covered, only nominates or sets the target help file for the program to use. The second option, HELP('CWBOOK','KeyWord'), attempts to locate the actual help keyword specified in the second parameter. I say *attempt* because if there are multiple instances of the 'KeyWord', instead of a help window being displayed, the Help Search window will appear for the user to select the specific instance of the related help information from a list of options. The third option, HELP('CWBOOK','~ContextString'), searches the help file for the specified context string in the second parameter. It is assumed that a context string is a unique help topic. The fourth and fifth options are identical to the second and third options, except that the help file that has already been nominated to the program will be used. This is because the first parameter has been omitted.

The HLP Attribute

Using the HELP() function is one of two ways to provide help file access in your program. The other method is to use the HLP attribute on an application window (MDI frame), a window, or a control. The HLP attribute can consist of either a 'KeyWord' or a '~ContextString', and it assumes that you have already nominated a help file using the HELP() function.

If you have specified the HLP attribute on an application window (MDI frame window), this will become the default help location for your program. That is, whenever help is invoked and there is no specific help keyword or context string specified for an active window or control, the default help window will be used. If you have added the HLP attribute on another window and you are on that window, the help engine will attempt to locate the specified keyword or context string for the window or control. Listing 10.1 illustrates a basic help concept.

Listing 10.1. Help1.EXE—An example of a basic help file.

```
HELP1                         PROGRAM

                  INCLUDE('Equates.CLW')
```

```
                    INCLUDE('Keycodes.CLW')
                    INCLUDE('Errors.CLW')

                    MAP
                      MainMenu()
                      MdiChild()
                      AboutHelp1()
                    END

wMdiFrame APPLICATION('help Example 1'),AT(1,1,309,163),CENTER,¦
          ICON('WINPYR.ICO'),STATUS,SYSTEM,MAX,                 ¦
MAXIMIZE,RESIZE,HLP('Mainhelp')
        MENUBAR
          MENU('&File'),MSG('File menu')
            ITEM('&Mdi Child'),USE(?MdiChild), ¦
            MSG('Open a new MDI Child window')
ITEM('Item'),SEPARATOR
              ITEM('E&xit'),MSG('Exit help Example 1'),STD(STD:CLOSE)
          END
          MENU('&help'),LAST,MSG('help')
            ITEM('&Contents'),MSG('help Contents'),STD(STD:help)
            ITEM('&Search for help On...'),MSG('Search for help On...'),¦
            STD(STD:helpSearch)
ITEM('&How to Use help'),MSG('How to use help'),STD(STD:helpOnhelp)
            ITEM('Item'),SEPARATOR
            ITEM('&About'),USE(?AboutHelp1),MSG('About help Example 1')
          END
        END
      END


  CODE
  MainMenu()


MainMenu                 PROCEDURE

  CODE

  HELP('Help1')
  OPEN(wMdiFrame)
  ACCEPT
    CASE EVENT()
    OF EVENT:CLOSEDOWN
      BREAK
    END
    CASE FIELD()
    OF ?MdiChild
      CASE EVENT()
      OF EVENT:ACCEPTED
        ThreadNo# = START(MdiChild)
      END
    OF ?AboutHelp1
      CASE EVENT()
      OF EVENT:ACCEPTED
        AboutHelp1()
      END
    END
  END
```

continues

Listing 10.1. continued

```
CLOSE(wMdiFrame)
RETURN


MDIChild                    PROCEDURE

wMdiChild WINDOW('MDI Child'),AT(1,1,130,47),SYSTEM,¦
        GRAY,MAX,RESIZE,MDI,HLP('MDICHILD')
ENTRY(@s20),AT(35,6,,),HLP('~Name'),USE(?Name),CAP
      PROMPT('Name'),AT(7,8,26,10), ¦
        FONT('MS Sans Serif',10,0800000H,FONT:bold),USE(?Prompt1),RIGHT
BUTTON('&Ok'),AT(50,26,,),FONT('MS Sans Serif',8,,FONT:bold),¦
      USE(?OkButton),STD(STD:Close),DEFAULT
    END

CODE
OPEN(wMdiChild)
ACCEPT
  CASE EVENT()
  OF EVENT:CloseDown
    BREAK
  END
END
CLOSE(wMdiChild)
RETURN
AboutHelp1                  PROCEDURE

wAboutHelp1 WINDOW('About help 1'),AT(28,42,260,80),SYSTEM,GRAY,DOUBLE
      STRING('help Example 1—Developing Applications in CW'),¦
      AT(2,6,256,15),FONT('Times New Roman',18,0800000H,FONT:bold), ¦
USE(?String1),CENTER
      STRING('By Ross A. Santos and Dave Harms'),AT(2,34,256,10),¦
      FONT('Arial',10,080H,FONT:bold),USE(?String2), ¦
CENTER
      BUTTON('&Ok'),AT(112,60,,),USE(?OkButton),STD(STD:Close),DEFAULT
    END


CODE
OPEN(wAboutHelp1)
ACCEPT
  CASE EVENT()
  OF EVENT:CloseDown
    BREAK
  END
END
CLOSE(wAboutHelp1)
RETURN
```

In Listing 10.1, take a look at the MDI frame window in the MainMenu() procedure. Notice that the HLP('Mainhelp') attribute has been added to the application window. This will become the default help window for your program. In the same procedure, under the CODE statement, you will see the nomination of the help file in the HELP('Help1') statement. This is where you specify what help file will be used in the program. If you run this program and press F1 while on the application window, you will invoke the Windows help engine and the default help window will appear. If you select the option MDI Child from the File menu, an MDI child window will appear. Pressing F1 on this window will bring up the help context string for the control labeled ?Name. This is because by default you are positioned on the ?Name control when the window opens, and it has a context string assigned.

If you press Tab once, you will be positioned on the OK button. Pressing F1 at this point will display the window's help window, since the OK button does not have any HLP attribute defined and the window does.

Included the program in Listing 10.1 are the standard Help menu options that you can use in your programs. Notice that all of these options with the exception of the About help 1 menu item use the STD attribute. Clarion for Windows uses this attribute for invoking standard Windows behavior. For example, the menu item Contents uses the STD:help equate. When you choose this item, the runtime library invokes WINHELP.EXE and displays the default program help window (Mainhelp). Selecting the menu item Search For help On... invokes the WINHELP.EXE using the STD:helpSearch equate and displays the standard Windows Help Search dialog box, which lists all the available topics in your help file. Selecting the menu item How To Use Help invokes WINHELP.EXE using the STD:helpOnhelp equate and loads the standard Windows help (which is a part of Windows, not your program).

Listing 10.2 is the project file Help1.HPJ used in the creation of the Help1.HLP file.

Listing 10.2. Help1.HPJ—The Help1.Hlp help project file.

```
[OPTIONS]
TITLE=Help1
COMPRESS=false
WARNING=3
REPORT=ON
COPYRIGHT=WYSI-help 1.25    124070488 © DDTEC

[FILES]
Help1.rtf

[MAP]
#include <Help1.h>
```

A full explanation of what this project file does is beyond the scope of this book—if you want detailed information, you should refer to the documentation that comes with the Microsoft help compiler. The key point, for the purpose of this discussion, is the [FILES] section. Notice that the Help1.RTF file was used as the source for the help text. The help compiler requires that your text be in a rich text format, which is a mark-up style format that contains hidden characters that denote fonts, spacing, style, and so on. An RTF file was used because it is a somewhat portable format that most word processors will read and write, thereby making the creation of a help text file more affordable if you already have one of these word processors.

Listing 10.3 is the include file that is used by the project system to determine the help windows to be generated and linked into the final Help1.HLP help file.

Listing 10.3. Help1.H—The Help1 include file.

```
#define MAINHELP   1
#define NAME       2
#define MDICHILD   3
```

Listing 10.4 is the Help1.RTF file used in the creation of the Help1.Hlp file.

Listing 10.4. Help1.RTF—The Help1 help text file format.

```
{\rtf1\ansi
\deff0{\fonttbl{\f0\fmodern Courier;}{\f1\froman Times New Roman;}
{\f2\fswiss System;}{\f3\froman Times New Roman;}{\f4\fswiss Arial;}
{\f5\fswiss Arial;}{\f6\fswiss Arial;}{\f7\fswiss Arial;}}
{\colortbl;\red0\green0\blue0;\red0\green0\blue255;\red0\green0\blue128;
\red255\green0\blue0;}
{\stylesheet{\fs20 \snext0 Normal;}{\s245 \fs20 \sbasedon0\snext245
texte de note;}}
\ftnbj \sectd \linex576\endnhere
\pard\plain\fs20
{\fs16\up6 #{\footnote \pard\plain \s245 \fs20 {\fs16\up6 #} MAINHELP}}
{\fs16\up6 ${\footnote \pard\plain \s245 \fs20 {\fs16\up6 $} Mainhelp}}
{\fs16\up6 K{\footnote \pard\plain \s245 \fs20 {\fs16\up6 K} Mainhelp}}
{\b\f1\fs29\cf3 Welcome to }
{\b\f1\fs29\cf4 MAIN HELP}
{\b\f1\fs29\cf3  for the HELP EXAMPLE 1\'2e}
\par

\par

{\f2\fs25\cf1 We hope that you have enjoyed the book so far and that
you are getting the most out of it as you continue reading\'2e}
\par

\par

\par

\par \page
\pard\plain\fs20
{\fs16\up6 #{\footnote \pard\plain \s245 \fs20 {\fs16\up6 #} NAME}}
{\fs16\up6 ${\footnote \pard\plain \s245 \fs20 {\fs16\up6 $} Name}}
{\fs16\up6 K{\footnote \pard\plain \s245 \fs20 {\fs16\up6 K} Name}}
{\b\f3\fs34\cf3 NAME}
\par

\par

{\b\f5\fs20\cf1 This is the name of the person you wish to search for\
'2c simply type if any portion of a person\'27s name and press }
{\b\f5\fs20\cf3 OK}
```

```
{\b\f5\fs20\cf1  to continue\'2e}
\par

\par \page
\pard\plain\fs20
{\fs16\up6 #{\footnote \pard\plain \s245 \fs20 {\fs16\up6 #} MDICHILD}}
{\fs16\up6 ${\footnote \pard\plain \s245 \fs20 {\fs16\up6 $} MDICHILD}}
{\fs16\up6 K{\footnote \pard\plain \s245 \fs20 {\fs16\up6 K} MDICHILD}}
{\b\f3\fs34\cf3 MDI CHILD}
\par

\par

{\f2\fs25\cf1 This is the }
{\i\f7\fs29\cf4 MDI CHILD}
{\f2\fs25\cf1  window in the HELP1\'2eEXE example program\'2e}
\par

\par

\par \page
}
```

As you can see, this is a very strange-looking file format. It is included so you can get a feel for what is happening "under the covers." The help compiler will read this file definition and re-construct the help topic, fonts, position, spacing, and colors into a standard Windows help file format for you. This may seem a bit daunting at first, but later in this chapter you'll explore the various methods of getting this process done quickly and easily without having to understand an RTF file or the details of the "hidden text" values of the help file format.

The F1 Key

In Windows there is a hard and fast convention for invoking help from the keyboard—the F1 key. Accordingly, in Clarion for Windows, the F1 key is reserved for invoking the Windows help engine from your program. The following rules apply when you press the F1 key:

- When there is an HLP attribute defined for the application window (MDI Frame) and it is the only help defined in the program, the program will always display this help window.
- An HLP attribute on a window when there is no HLP attribute on a selected control will override the default application window's help window and will display the window's help window.
- An HLP attribute on a control will override an HLP attribute on a window if the control is selected and will display the control's help window.
- When there is no HLP attribute on a window and no control on a window, the default application window's help will be displayed.

As you can see, there is a clear hierarchy—the lowest level in the help chain is used when all other levels fail the test.

Another Use of Help Files (an Infobase)

You may have seen products that include additional help files as *infobases,* or information storage and retrieval tools. You can use a standard help file for this purpose. For example, help systems ordinarily deal with how software functions. If you sell a point-of-sale product to several different types of clients, you might provide each of them with a Windows help infobase tailored to each client type.

You don't even need to write any code to use a standard Windows help file. This is because Windows understands what a help file is and what to do with it. For example, go to Program Manager, select the File menu, then the Run option, and type \cw\bin\CWHELP.HLP. The result is that the Clarion for Windows help is now executing.

There are all sorts of things WINHELP.EXE can be used for, and since it contains hypertext searching, it is a wonderful tool for those odd sorts of things you need to do from time to time.

Different Tool Approaches

I bet you are wondering how to build these help text files I keep referring to. Well, there are plenty of options. There are essentially three approaches.

The first is to manually create the help file using a word processor that can read and write RTF files. This approach is by far the least desirable, but it is still practical. You will need to purchase either the Windows SDK or the Microsoft Help Compiler package, which includes a small manual that explains the process. Basically you place in the document hidden text that will be used to inform the compiler what sort of help component the text represents. You will also need to create and manage your help project file. All in all, this is the hard way, and I don't recommend it.

The second approach is to use a macro-based help-generation system. In this widely used approach macros will prompt you for information, allow you to specify criteria about the type of links you want to create, and interact with your specific word processor, allowing you to create the text and import graphics for the help file. You also use macros to create and maintain your project system and execute the help-generation process using one of the previously mentioned compilers.

There is a wealth of this sort of tool on the market—from freeware to shareware to complete commercial systems. The downside is that most of these tools are fairly slow due to the use of macros and the level of interaction with your word processor. The hardware and memory you have available can be the determining factor as to whether the system is usable.

The third approach is to use an integrated help system. These are not as common as macro-based tools, but they generally do more work for the money, and some, such as WYSI-HELP (see the appendix at the back of the book for more information on this product), make creation and maintenance of help systems a breeze. The benefit of this approach is that all the tools you typically need are included in the package: a word processor, online help and tutorials, automated topic-linking features, integration of graphics, sound, other help files, integrated project management tools such as those for setting the colors and nonscrolling regions of your help file, use of style sheets or templates to aid in keeping your help files consistent in look and feel, spell checking, browse sequence editing, screen capture and image management tools, help file generation, and much more. This type of help-authoring tool is the most robust, the easiest to use, and the fastest way to get your Windows help project completed. I'm sure you know which approach I suggest you use.

Using Resource-Editing Tools

Depending on which approach you take, there is always room for more tools to help you get the job done faster and more professionally. Many of you may already have some time-saving tools and not even realize it. For example, most Windows C/C++ compilers come with resource-editing tools. These tools generally provide you with the ability to create BMP or ICO files as well as many other things. Many include sophisticated image capture and editing tools, as well. I mention this because Windows help files should be as graphical as possible, providing the easiest means of communicating your subject matter to the reader. Most of these tools come cheap these days and include other tools that you may find of value. If you do have other Windows development tools, take a peek at them and see what you can use to make those Windows help files as snazzy and professional as possible—your users will thank you for it.

Summary

Clarion for Windows provides a simple and easy integration of Windows help into your Windows programs. Although you will need to use some third-party tools to actually create and maintain your help files, you will find that implementing help in your Clarion for Windows programs is an easy and rewarding task. When creating your help files, take the time to plan and contemplate just how using Windows help in your program will benefit your users the most—they'll love you for it!

11

From Here to EXE:
The Project System

Windows programs are usually quite complex entities, made up not just of source code, but of a number of other types of files, as well. These include icons, bitmaps, compiled libraries, and cursors.

It's the project system's job to keep track of all the little bits that make up your program, and to know if, when, and how to fit them all together whenever you issue the Run or Make command from the main menu. It's not a particularly easy task to do efficiently. For instance, when you make a change to a module in an application that contains 50 modules, you don't want to have to recompile every module just make sure that your change is compiled. Similarly, if you make a change to global data, you probably do want to recompile all modules, because any one of them could be affected by the change to global data.

These are the kinds of issues the project system deals with. However, much of its complexity is hidden from you, the programmer. In fact, it's entirely possible to build an application using the AppGen and never even know that there is such a thing as the project system, because the AppGen manages much of this information for you. In that case, the closest you will come to the project manager might be choosing Run from the Project menu.

There will probably come a time, however, when you will want to make a change to the project information, perhaps to enable debugging or to tailor your application to a particular platform. At that time, you will want to know about another option on the Project menu: Edit Project.

The Application as Project

There is some potentially confusing terminology surrounding the project system, partly because of the way the AppGen handles project information. In a traditional source code (non-AppGen) programming environment, project information is kept in a separate text file. This is still true of hand-coding in CW—when you create a program in the editor, you need to create a new project as well, and this will be stored in a file that usually has the same name as your main source module, but with the extension .PRJ.

When CW's designers created the AppGen, they had to choose between maintaining this same approach or concealing the project information inside the APP file. They chose the latter approach because this greatly reduced the risk of developers, particularly those new to CW, accidentally losing the project information if the application were moved to a new drive or directory.

The result of all of this is that the term *project* now applies both to the original idea of a text PRJ file and to application (APP) files. If you choose Project|Set Current Project from the main menu, you will be presented with a file dialog box of, by default, APP files. The idea is that you determine what EXE, DLL, or LIB you will create by choosing a project file; but in most cases choosing a project file will automatically mean choosing an application as well, because project information is embedded in each application file.

> **NOTE**
>
> If the Project|Set Current Project option is grayed out, it is because an application is active. Close the application and try again.

Project Options

The Project menu contains a number of options that let you set the current project, edit the project settings, and use the project data to generate, compile, debug, and run your application.

Set Current Project

Selecting a project (which usually means selecting an application, as described previously) also means selecting a working directory. The first time you run CW, the working directory will be whatever you have specified for CW in the Windows Program Manager. After you load your first application or project, the working directory will remain set to the directory in which that APP or PRJ file resides. When you restart CW, it will restore the project and the working directory from your previous session.

> **TIP**
>
> In order to set a different working directory, you really need to set a project from that directory as the current project. If you need to work for a time in a directory other than the one your application is in, select File|New and Project, fill in arbitrary data for the project file (because you will never compile it anyway) and save it in the directory to which you want to switch.

Edit Current Project

Locate a CW application (any one will do) and open it (choosing Clarion|Load Application will bring up a list of your most recently used applications). Choose Project|Edit Current Project. The Project Editor window appears. It should look something like what is presented in Figure 11.1 (you may want to maximize the window to see as much of the project as possible).

The majority of the window is taken up with the project tree, which is a graphical representation of the different groups of information contained in the project. Along the right side of the window are several buttons.

FIGURE 11.1.

A typical application's project information viewed with the project editor.

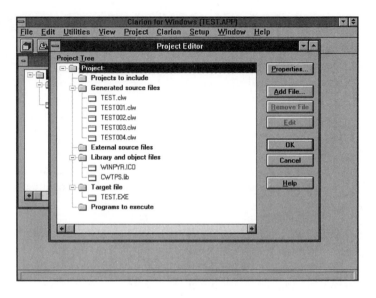

The Properties button has varying functions, depending on which item in the project tree is selected, but as its name suggests, it enables you to change various properties, or attributes, of project items.

The Add File and Remove File buttons are used to add or remove the various types of files that can make up a project. In general, you will not delete any files from a project unless you first added them, and you won't be needing to manually add any files to a project until you start mucking around with source code. So if you're just working with the AppGen, chances are you don't need to worry about these buttons at all.

Project Properties (Global Options)

At the top of the tree is the project itself. If you select it and click the Properties button, you will see the Global Options window, which looks like what is presented in Figure 11.2.

FIGURE 11.2.

The project editor's Global Options window.

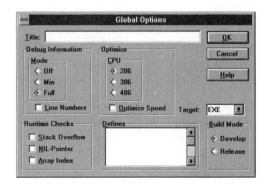

Debug Information

Although you might be one of the world's most meticulous programmers, there will probably come a time when you need to run the debugger. Before you do so, you need to ensure that the information the debugger requires has been included in your program, and that's what this option is for.

If Debug is set to Off, you can still run the debugger. However, because there is no debug information in the EXE for it to read, the debugger will behave just as if you have not selected any source files for it to debug.

The Min setting enables the debugger to be used, but local variables cannot be traced.

The Full setting causes full debug information to be placed in the program. You will probably use this setting most often when debugging.

These settings are also displayed on the Compile Options window for each module, which enables you to override debug settings on a module-by-module basis.

The Line Numbers check box will add line numbers to your EXE or library so that you can use third-party debuggers. If you need to use this, you probably already know how.

Optimize Settings

You can build *chip-specific* versions of your CW programs that take advantage of special instructions in the different Intel chips that support the Windows operating system. CW programs are upwardly compatible. If you make a program for the 286 chip (the default setting), it will run on a 386. A program optimized for a 386 will not run on a 286, but will work fine on a 486, and 486-specific programs require a 486 or better. It is usually not a good idea to use chip-specific versions of programs if your programs have wide (that is, commercial or shareware) distribution, because you will probably get a number of complaints from people who can't run your 486-specific software on their 386 box.

CW programs are normally optimized for size. However, if speed is your primary consideration, you should check the Speed option under Optimize. This may result in a slightly larger, but quicker, EXE.

Target

The Target setting determines which kind of output you will get: an EXE, which is a standard Windows program; a LIB, or library of compiled functions that can be linked into another program; or a dynamic link library (DLL) which, instead of being linked into a program when the program is created, is only linked in when the program is run. DLLs and LIBs are discussed in more detail later in this chapter.

Runtime Checks

The CW compiler is able to do several different types of code validation that can help trap errors in your code that would otherwise go unnoticed. Ideally, you should check on all the following options while you are developing, but once you are certain (or at least highly confident) that the program is working as it should, these options should be checked off. This is because, like debug code, they add to the size and detract from the speed of your program.

Stack Overflow checking ensures that your program does not run out of stack space while it is running. This is not exactly a common problem, but it can occur if you have particularly memory-hungry procedures or have otherwise reduced the amount of stack space available. This is one of those settings that you shouldn't worry about much if you don't know what it means.

Nil-Pointer checking is also not particularly germane to most CW programming, because CW uses references rather than pointers. It may be an issue if you are doing mixed-language programming, particularly using C or C++.

If by now you thought that nothing in this section applied to you, you might want to think again. Array Index checking is something that applies to anyone who uses an array anywhere in a CW program. When you specify an array (a *dimensioned variable,* in CW parlance), the program can warn you if you use a subscript that is out of range. Reading an out-of-range subscript might just get you garbage, but writing one can affect programs currently running, with potentially disastrous results.

Defines

Defines are an advanced feature of the project system that are primarily useful to people who do a significant amount of hand coding. These are conditional compile symbols that you insert at appropriate locations in your code. You set the value of the symbol here, in the project editor, and when the source code is compiled, any code that lies inside conditional compile symbols is either included or excluded based on the value of the symbol. You might, for instance, have a define for the type of file driver to use for your data files, which would let you create two different versions of your program simply by changing the value of the define.

If you are using CW's AppGen, you will probably find that much of what you would use a define for can be more easily accomplished through the use of customized templates. The template language is quite well-suited to conditional compilation.

Build Mode

The Build Mode radio buttons are a quick way to switch off all possible runtime checks and debug settings. As long as at least one debug or runtime check is turned on, the build mode will be set to Develop. When you select Release, you will get a dialog window that asks if you want to reset all runtime and debug settings. If you answer yes, these will all be turned off, and your target file (EXE, LIB, or DLL) will be as compact as possible.

> **TIP**
>
> You should always use release mode for your final product. Although you may think that including debug code will make your program more stable, in fact the opposite is true. Having debug code in your program increases its complexity, and something that works correctly in build mode may not work nearly as well when it is laced with additional instructions that are there for the benefit of the debugger, not your program.

Source Code Properties (Compile Options)

If you select any source file (external or generated) and click Properties, you will see the Compile Options window, which is the same as the Global Options window except that it lacks the Build Mode and Target settings.

You will probably use this window to override global debug or runtime check settings. For instance, if you are working on a large application in build mode (all debug settings are off) and you want to debug one procedure that is giving you some trouble, you could turn on debug information for the program, which would necessitate a complete recompile. It would be wiser to turn on debug information for the source module to which the procedure belongs. When you go to debug that procedure, the project system will detect that the debug pragma has been added, and it will recompile only that one module.

Target File Properties (Link Options)

If you select the target file (your EXE, LIB, or DLL), you will see the Link Options dialog window (see Figure 11.3). These options fall into the category of "If you need to use them, you probably know something about them already," so if your eyes are starting to glaze over, feel free to skip to the next section.

FIGURE 11.3.
The Link Options dialog window.

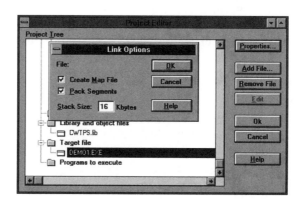

A *map file* is a text file that contains information about the program's segment sizes, public symbols, and so on. You might need to use the Create Map File option, in conjunction with the debugger Line Numbers option, if you wish to use a third-party debugger. By default, the map file is created.

The Pack Segments option tells the linker to pack program segments together. The default setting for Windows programs is to Not Pack Segments.

The Stack Size field enables you to override the default stack size, which is 32KB. You might need to do this if you get Out of Stack Space error messages while running your program, but it's not very likely.

New Project

Although the term "project" might, at times, refer to an application (because applications contain project data), this particular menu item refers strictly to PRJ files. You do not use it to create applications. You use it to create separate project files that apply (usually) to hand-coded applications.

If you select this menu item, you will see the dialog window presented in Figure 11.4.

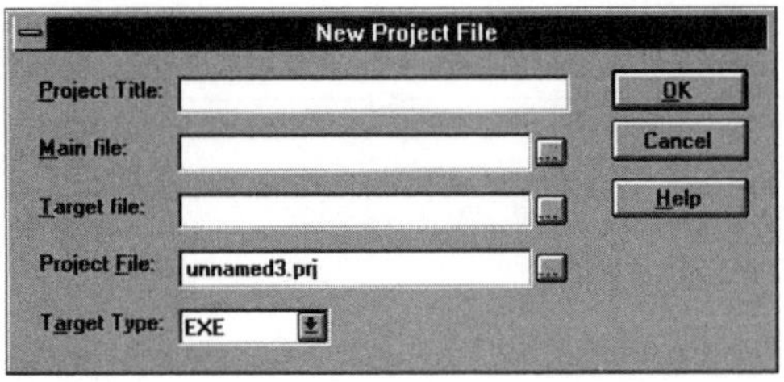

FIGURE 11.4.

The New Project File dialog box.

The project title is a text field that is for your reference only. You should make it reasonably descriptive of the application that will be created. The Main file is the source module that contains the program statement, the program map, and the global data declarations. There is a button with an ellipsis next to the field. If you click it, you will get a File dialog box that will enable you to pick the source file to use as the main file.

The Target file is the name of the program, library, or dynamic link library to be created. You can type the name in, or, if the file already exists, you can pick it by clicking the button to the right of the entry field. Note that if you change the target type, using the drop-down list box at the bottom of the dialog window, the extension will automatically be adjusted for you. For more on target files, see the section "EXEs, LIBs, and DLLs," later in this chapter.

You will also need to specify the name of the project file you are creating. Ordinarily, you will make this the same as the name of the main source file, since the name of the project file is used as the default for the name of the main source module.

After you have saved this information, you can edit the project file, as described previously. Because you will most likely be creating project files only if you are not working in the AppGen, you will need to select Project|Edit Current Project to specify all the source files, libraries, and other components that make up your project.

TIP

Although PRJ files are ordinarily used for hand-coded projects, you can also use them with applications created with the AppGen. If your PRJ file contains all the relevant information, and you have generated the source code for the application, you can set the PRJ file (instead of the APP file) as the project and Make or Run as you usually would. Probably the easiest way to make a text PRJ copy of the project information embedded in the APP is to open the APP using NOTEPAD.EXE, and copy the project data to a text file with the extension PRJ. Do not save the application with Notepad or you will corrupt it.

Make

When you choose Make from the project menu (or press the Make icon), the project system determines everything that has to be done with your application to turn it into an EXE in the shortest possible time. This is known, appropriately enough, as the *make* process. If you are using the Application Generator, doing a Make will even trigger the generation of source code for any procedures that have changed since the last Make. It will compile any altered source code into new OBJ files, and invoke the linker to combine these OBJ files into the target file.

While Make is running, you will see the Make window, which looks something like what is presented in Figure 11.5.

FIGURE 11.5.

The Make window, after a program has been compiled and linked into an EXE.

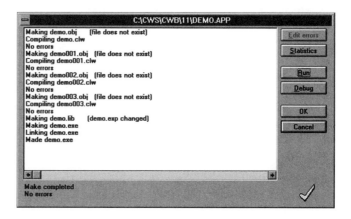

If the compiler or linker encountered any errors during the Make process, these will be shown in the Make window, and clicking the Edit Errors button will take you to the first error. If no errors were encountered, the Edit Errors button will be disabled. If warnings were encountered, indicating that something happened that the compiler or linker wasn't happy with, but was prepared to let go, you have the option of editing the errors or continuing with the process, which would probably involve running the program.

Pressing the Statistics button displays information about the Make, including the source code compiled, the resulting object code, the size of code and data (in bytes) for each component, and the date and time of the last Make.

Assuming that the Make has completed without error, both the Run and Debug buttons will be enabled. If you select Run, your program (assuming it is an EXE) will be loaded (if it isn't an EXE, you'll get an error message saying that the program could not be loaded). If you select Debug, the debugger will be loaded, and it will then run your program. If you wish to use the debugger, you will need to ensure that debug information has been included for the source modules you want to debug.

Run

The Project|Run menu item accomplishes exactly the same function as the Project|Make item. It also automatically runs the program following a successful Make.

This is the command you will probably use the most as you develop your application. If you are using the AppGen, you will probably find it convenient to test your application by pressing Ctrl+R (the Run shortcut key) when you are at the Application Tree window.

Debug

The Project|Debug menu item accomplishes exactly the same function as the Project|Make item, plus it automatically runs the debugger following a successful Make. The debugger then loads your program. Please ensure that you have turned on debug information for those modules you wish to debug.

Make Statistics

This menu item calls the Make Statistics window, which gives you information about the last Make process.

EXEs, LIBs, and DLLs

By now you should be familiar with the three kinds of target files you can create with CW: EXEs, or executable (normal) programs; LIBs, or libraries of precompiled code that can be incorporated into EXEs; and DLLs, a special form of library that can be shared by multiple EXEs at runtime.

All of this discussion of targets begs the question of what is required to make a program in the first place. After all, if the source code contains the instructions for the computer, why does it need to be made into another form to be useful? In fact, source code, which you and I can read, is practically useless to computers. For one thing, it's far too verbose.

The process of creating an EXE goes something like this: The compiler reads the source file and applies a set of tests to check for language or syntax errors. If the source code passes all the tests, the compiler produces a file that is much smaller than the original source code. Computers deal with much more compact symbols than people do, because they have more literal memories. A good example of this is in your \LIBSRC directory, in the EQUATES.CLW file. The following is a sample:

```
EVENT:Accepted       EQUATE (01H)
EVENT:NewSelection   EQUATE (02H)
EVENT:ScrollUp       EQUATE (03H)
EVENT:ScrollDown     EQUATE (04H)
```

These are EQUATE statements, which simply state that for the benefit of the programmer, the compiler will recognize the phrase EVENT:Accepted to mean the same thing as the hex number 1. Now, if you wanted to be on a little more even terms with the compiler, you wouldn't use the phrase EVENT:Accepted in your code. You'd just put the number 01H in your code. And if that was the only event you had to be concerned with, it might not be a problem. Because there are over 50 common events that you might be concerned with, you generally find it easier to reference them by descriptive words and phrases. The compiler, however, will never waste space by storing an entire 14-byte phrase such as EVENT:Accepted when 1 byte (or less) will do as well.

When the compiler has checked the source file and given it a clean bill of health, it creates a compact OBJ file.

You might wonder why the compiler doesn't turn the source file into an EXE (or DLL or LIB) immediately. If all programs were made up of single source files, this might be a practical solution. It is more usual, however, to have programs that are made up of multiple source modules, and it's much more efficient to deal with them in those units. If you're currently working on a source file in a program that has 10 source files, you don't want to have to create OBJ code for the other 9 each time you make a change.

Another reason for compiling code into an intermediate form is so you can link that code into another EXE without having to distribute the source code. As you'll see later, most people take an additional step of making this code into a procedure library, but it is quite proper to do it with OBJ code as well, and it is certainly preferable to making multiple copies of source code.

The compiler's job, as described previously, is to check source files for errors and create compact, generally temporary files that can be linked together to make a working program. This job falls to a program called the *linker*. In some systems, the linker is a separate EXE. In CW, it's all part of the project system, and you never actually call it by itself. The linker is automatically invoked after the compiler has completed successfully.

Executable Programs

The most common type of target file is the *executable* program, or EXE. This is the only type of target that can be run on its own, although many EXEs also incorporate code from other compiled sources, such as LIBs and DLLs.

Libraries

A file ending in LIB is really just a collection of OBJ files. If you have only one OBJ file to worry about, you might want to leave it as-is. Most programmers, however, who find themselves sharing OBJ code between applications usually share quite a lot of it, and if it's kept in OBJ files it doesn't take long to clutter up the directory. It also makes maintenance more of a headache.

The solution is to combine the OBJ files into a single file with the extension .LIB. This is particularly useful in workgroup situations in which multiple programmers need access to common procedures. The LIB files will typically contain code that has been thoroughly debugged and which is not likely to change in the immediate future.

You might have developed the habit, particularly if you have programmed in Clarion 2.1 or earlier, of sharing actual source code between programs. I would like to discourage you from that practice (except when it is done using the templates, as described in Chapter 17, "Creating Code Templates," Chapter 18, "Creating Procedure Templates," Chapter 19, "Creating Control Templates," Chapter 20, "Creating Extension Templates," and Chapter 21, "The AppGen: The Ultimate Hand Coding Tool"). It is (almost) always preferable to distribute precompiled code (OBJ, LIB, or DLL) rather than uncompiled code. For one thing, uncompiled code needs to be compiled again and again, and that's a waste of resources. In workgroup situations, the more copies of the uncompiled code there are around, the more likely it is that one of your programmers will alter a copy to suit the needs of a particular situation, and then you no longer have truly common code. This defeats the purpose of sharing the code in the first place.

> **TIP**
>
> If you're a 2.1 programmer, you will have noticed that you can no longer have empty MEMBER() statements in your procedures. Those procedures are prime candidates to be put into LIBs or DLLs.

Dynamic Link Libraries

Dynamic link libraries are a special kind of library. In the usual scheme of things, for a program to make use of a library, the library must be linked into the program. This means that a copy of the OBJ code that is inside the library becomes part of the target file.

A dynamic link library is not linked into the target file at link time; it's linked in at runtime. Take a moment to digest that. Let's say you have a library that contains a standard login security procedure. If you put that procedure in a LIB file, and then include that LIB in the project for an application, the final EXE will contain the OBJ code that is embodied in the LIB file. The end result will be just the same as if you had placed the source code for that procedure inside the application. The advantage to you, the programmer, is that you didn't have to mess with any source code. You've just plugged one software component (a login procedure) into an application. You also don't need to distribute anything extra with the application, since the LIB code is linked in.

If you put that same procedure in a DLL, something quite different happens. All that will go in the application (and this is actually optional) is a small bit of code (contained in a LIB file) that tells the application that the library exists and that it contains such and such procedures. The actual login procedure is not contained in the EXE, but in that separate DLL file.

When the EXE runs, it loads the DLL into memory (either initially or when the login procedure is called). At that point, and not before, the DLL effectively becomes part of the program, in the same way that code would be part of the program had it been linked in earlier as an OBJ or LIB file.

Okay, I can hear you saying What's the big deal? So far it seems that all we've done is create an extra file that you need to track. The first benefit is that multiple EXEs can use the same DLL. You will already be using this approach with CWRUN10.DLL. If you haven't already created more than one CW program, you soon will. If it weren't for CWRUN10.DLL, each EXE would have to have all the code in CWRUN10.DLL linked into it, which would mean an extra half-megabyte of disk space used for each EXE.

Because DLLs link at runtime and not at link time, you can integrate a changed DLL into an EXE without having to recompile the EXE. If the actual interface to the procedure has not changed, you may only have to ship a modified DLL.

Summary

The project system is a powerful tool that supervises the creation of EXEs, LIBs, and DLLs. Because it is so tightly integrated into the CW environment, you may not even realize you are using it, but it's always there, and it's available to you through the project editor. As your use of CW becomes more sophisticated, you will discover that the project system is a far more extensive tool than this chapter has time to show.

12

Testing and Debugging

The TopSpeed Debugger is a truly remarkable tool. It is fully Windows hosted, which means you run it from Windows as you would any other Windows program (some debuggers require you to load components before Windows runs). You can use the Debugger to step through your source code a line or procedure at a time, you can set various break points (fixed or conditional), watch variables change as the program executes, and change those variables. You can even launch the Debugger after your program starts and use it to find out what's going wrong.

Notice that I called it the TopSpeed Debugger, not the Clarion Debugger. That's because it's designed to work with all the TopSpeed Windows languages, not just Clarion. It does sport some special enhancements to make it particularly effective when running Clarion code, however.

Preparing Your Application

Before you can use the Debugger, you need to make sure your program has been compiled with the necessary switches turned on. For any debugger to work effectively, it needs information that the program itself does not require. If you kept all this information in the program at all times, you'd end up with an EXE that was larger and slower than necessary.

Debug settings are stored with the project data. Whether you're hand coding or using the AppGen, when your project or application is loaded you can choose Project|Edit Current Project to get the project editor, then choose the Project line (at the top of the window) and click on Properties for the application or project's debug settings. This process is discussed in more detail in Chapter 11, "From Here to EXE: The Project System."

It's important to note that you can turn debug information on for individual modules (if you have one procedure per module, that means you can effectively turn it on for individual procedures), as well as for the entire application.

Calling the Debugger

Ordinarily, you start the Debugger by choosing Project|Debug from the main menu. This invokes the standard code generation and compile/link cycles, and if the program is successfully created, tells the Debugger to load that program. The first window you'll see when you run the Debugger is shown in Figure 12.1. It asks you which source files to include in the debug session.

If you have only a few source modules, or if you're not sure what part of the code you need to debug, choose Select All.

FIGURE 12.1.

The Sources to include in session window.

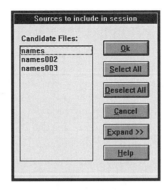

TIP

If you don't see any files in the source list, it's probably because you've compiled your program without any debug information. The Debugger looks in the directory specified in your CW.RED file for DBD, or Debugger data, files and displays only module source files that have corresponding DBD files. A second potential cause is that your source files are in a directory other than the current directory. This sometimes happens when you start the Debugger on a running program. You can get around this by loading a redirection file that points to your source code, using the File|Load Redirection menu option in the Debugger.

After you choose which files to load, you'll be at the Debugger main menu, as shown in Figure 12.2.

FIGURE 12.2.

The Debugger main menu.

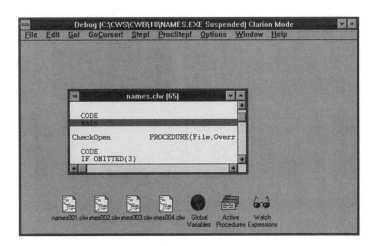

The Debugger is a full MDI application, which means that you can switch between any of the various windows that present information about your program. These windows are discussed in the following sections.

Source Windows

These windows, one for each module included in the debug session, contain your procedures' source code. Code that is not used is marked in red, although in version 1.0 you have to be a little careful about interpreting this, because some structures that are used are marked in red (windows, for example), as are code statements, maps, and procedure declarations. Variables that are never used do show in red, and if you have an entire procedure in red it indicates that the procedure itself is never called.

TIP

CW employs Smart Linking, which strips out unused code so there's no penalty to your EXE, but you may want to use the color coding in the Debugger as an aid to removing deadwood from your source.

Global Variables

The Global Variables window (with the globe icon) contains a list of all global variables used in your program. When you first open the window it will look something like the one shown in Figure 12.3.

FIGURE 12.3.

The Global Variables window with trees collapsed.

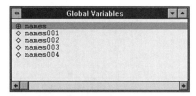

The symbol to the left of the variable indicates its status. If it's a ⊕ character, that means there's more below. Click the ⊕ to expand the display. A ○ character indicates that the variable has been expanded, and a ◇ indicates that no further expansion is possible because this is the lowest level. Figure 12.4 shows a partially expanded global variable list.

FIGURE 12.4.

A partially expanded list of global variables.

Some global variables show up as special types on this list. Record structures are marked by `"RECORD"` to the right of the variable name, and strings are shown as the first and last characters of the string. This also tells you how many characters are in the string.

String Display Options

For both global variables and local variables (which are discussed in the section "Local Variables") you can change the characters to display. Simply double-click the variable, and the Change Element dialog box appears, as shown in Figure 12.5. If you select Change Element Range, you will have the option of specifying which array elements will be displayed on the variables list.

FIGURE 12.5.

The Change Element dialog box.

If you simply want to display the entire string, a better option is to place it in the Watch Expression window.

Watch Expression

You access the Watch Expression window via the cool sunglasses icon. Double-click this icon to display the Watch Expression window, or choose Window|Watch Expressions.

To get a variable into the Watch Expression window, you can double-click the variable in the local or global variable list, or you can double-click a line in the Watch Expression window to bring up the watch expression editor, as shown in Figure 12.6.

FIGURE 12.6.

The watch expression editor.

In addition to displaying variables here, you can evaluate expressions. For a full list of operators that can be used in these expressions, which include standard math, bitwise, logical, and indirection operators, click the Help button.

Local Variables

The display window for local variables, called the Active Procedures window, is much like the one for global variables. If you bring it up and it doesn't have variables for the procedure you want to view, it is because that procedure is not currently active. Once a procedure is terminated, all of its nonstatic memory is deallocated, so there's no way to examine any local variables, because they no longer exist.

Library State

No, this isn't the way you left your books lying around, it's a peek into the internals of Clarion for Windows. To view it, choose Window|Library State. Among the interesting tidbits of information shown here are the following:

- The identifying number and field equate of the control currently selected or accepted.
- The current field (control)—this is the same value as the one returned by FOCUS().
- The current field—this is the same value as the one returned by FIELD().
- The number and field equate of the first and last fields in the currently open structure. Menu items are numbered negatively, starting with –1, and all other controls are numbered positively.
- The current event number (and its standard CW name).
- ERRORCODE and KEYCODE(), if any.
- The mouse coordinates.
- The thread number—this is the same value as returned by START().

Library state information can be particularly helpful when you're stepping through code and you want to keep an overview of which control is being processed at a given time.

Windows Messages

If you're a casual programmer, you probably won't find yourself here very often, if at all. As discussed in Chapter 4, "Concepts You Should Know," Windows revolves around the concept of events and messages. Everything that happens is an event, and events trigger messages that require responses from Windows or the programs running under Windows. To get a real appreciation for what CW does for you, browse through the list once in a while. If CW didn't handle all those messages for you, you'd have to do much of it yourself, in code.

If you're an advanced programmer you can use this window much as you would a spy program. Once you know which messages are being generated for a particular situation, you'll be able to design your code to intercept and respond to those messages. This is not, however, something for the faint of heart, and it's well beyond the scope of this book.

Machine Registers

Another feature for the bit-twiddler in our midst is the Machine Registers window, also available under the Window menu. You'll most likely want to use this with Options|Disassembly On, which gives you an assembly-level look into some of the cleanest executing code you're likely to see. Again, this isn't exactly beginner-level stuff, and it's totally unnecessary for just about all development, but if you need it, the power's all there.

Stepping Through Code

Most of your debugging will involve stepping through code in one way or another. When the Debugger first loads a program, it doesn't begin executing it right away. Instead, it waits for you to exercise one of three options:

- ■ You can choose GO! from the main menu, in which case the program will run until it encounters a break point (I'll discuss break points in a moment).

- ■ You can choose Step! from the main menu, which will take you through your code one excruciating line at a time.

- ■ You can choose ProcStep! from the main menu, which will take you through your code a line at a time, but will treat any procedure calls as a single line of code, which is somewhat less excruciating.

The biggest problem you're likely to face in debugging your code is avoiding all the endless stepping through code that doesn't have anything to do with your bug. Wouldn't it be nice if you could just tell the Debugger to stop at a particular place under particular circumstances? You can, and the thing that makes it possible is called a break point.

Setting Break Points

A *break point* is an instruction to the Debugger to stop the program and enable you to examine its current state and, if you wish, take control. There are three ways to set break points, and all require you to first select the source line where you want the break to occur: You can press the space bar, you can double-click the source line, or you can choose Edit|Break Points from the Debugger main menu.

When you do this, you will be asked which of five different kinds of break points you want to set.

Always is an unconditional break point. Whenever the Debugger comes across this line in the code, it will halt the program and display the Debugger windows.

Watch Expression #0 is a conditional break point. You specify the watch expression number from the Watch window that is to trigger the break. If you have simply placed a variable in the Watch Expression window, then this will act just like an unconditional break point. To make it conditional, you need to evaluate an expression. For instance, if you want to break the program whenever you insert a record, go to the Active Procedures window, find the update procedure (you will need to have called it first), double-click the LOCALREQUEST variable to copy it to the Watch window, and then in the Watch window modify the entry so it reads as follows:

```
names002.UPDATEPROC.LOCALREQUEST = 1
```

Your module and procedure names will probably vary; the main thing is to add the = 1 to the end of the watch. Next, in the UPDATEPROC procedure set a break point just after the LOCALREQUEST variable is updated. Select GO! from the Debugger main menu, and the next time you insert a record using that procedure the Debugger will see the break point. And, because logical operators such as AND and OR are valid in break points, you can set up whatever conditions are necessary for you to stop the program only when it suits you.

The last three types of break points all have to do with Windows messages. You can select break points that occur whenever a particular message occurs, whenever one of a group of messages occurs, or whenever a message that is not part of a message group occurs. The standard message groups are Window, Mouse, Key, System, Init, Clip, DDE, and non-Client. You also can build up to four custom message groups.

For most Clarion programming, you won't use the message break points. They are primarily intended for use with other TopSpeed languages that do not have Clarion's runtime library to manage Windows messaging.

Editing Variables

Editing variables at runtime is straightforward. Just highlight the variable you want to change (in either the Global Variables window or the Active Procedures window) and press F2, or choose Edit|Edit from the main menu.

You need to be somewhat careful about doing this. Ideally, if you need to change a value, you should change only one variable. The more variables you change, the more difficult it will be to track down which change caused or fixed a problem.

The Control Panel

Under the Options menu is a check box for the control panel. When it's selected, the control panel appears, as shown in Figure 12.7.

FIGURE 12.7.
*The Debugger control
panel, as it appears while
you're stepping through a
program.*

The control panel is a Debugger window that always stays on top of your Windows programs (more usefully, it stays on top of the program you are debugging). It has six buttons, which among them have five functions.

Clicking the Debug button will bring the Debugger to the top.

The Go button gives up control of the debuggee (until a break point is reached or the program ends). It corresponds to the GO! item on the main menu.

The Step button executes a single line of code, and corresponds to the Step! item on the main menu. The current line is shown in the space just below the windows.

The ProcStep button is like the Step button, except it executes procedure calls as if they were single lines of code. It corresponds to the ProcStep! item on the main menu.

The minimize and maximize buttons above the other buttons affect the Debugger, not the control panel. You use them to hide and unhide the Debugger. You may need to first click the minimize button, then the maximize button to make the Debugger the top window.

Debugging a Running Program

When you choose Debug from the Project menu, CW loads both the Debugger and the debugee. If your program begins to exhibit a problem and you haven't loaded the Debugger, you can still do so. Just run it from the Program Manager, or choose Debug from the CW menu. The Debugger will find your program executing, and ask you if you want to debug the running program. Answer Yes. At that point, you are in the same situation as if you'd loaded a program in the Debugger and selected GO!. You'll need to set a break point in the code before you can get control of the program with the Debugger.

The CLWDB.INI File

The Debugger maintains an INI file in the Windows directory. It's called CLWDB.INI, and it is used to store the configuration settings you choose in Debugger Options, as well as the size and position of whichever windows were open when the Debugger terminated. You probably won't ever need to edit it directly.

The CLWDB.LOG File

The CLWDB.INI file serves all Debugger sessions, and each session also creates a CLWDB.LOG file in the current directory. A sample is shown in Listing 12.1.

Listing 12.1. A sample CLWDB.LOG file.

```
handle count0020
0000,0000,0000,0000
mnameCWTPS
mnameCWRUN10
mnameCWRUN10
__Win87EmInfo0000
fpstatesize01CD
Version 0600
SizeSaveArea 01CD
WinDataSeg 11D7
WinCodeSeg 117F
Have80x87 0001
collect info CWRUN10.dll
CWRUN10.dll does not contain TS debug information
collect info C:\CWS\TEST\CWTEST.EXE
collect info CWTPS.dll
CWTPS.dll does not contain TS debug information
load_selectd_dbds start
cwtes001.dbd
cwtes002.dbd
cwtes003.dbd
cwtest.dbd
load_selectd_dbds end
```

```
build_globals
debugger task 466F
debuggee task 470F
transfering watch cwtest.NMA:RECORD.NMA:NAME
(debug_mode=single_step_proc) AND (r.sp<proc_sp)
(debug_mode=single_step_proc) AND (r.sp<proc_sp)
(debug_mode=single_step_proc) AND (r.sp<proc_sp)
(debug_mode=single_step_proc) AND (r.sp<proc_sp)
(debug_mode=single_step_proc) AND (r.sp<proc_sp)
debug_mode=single_step_proc) AND (r.sp<proc_sp)
seg_free 0001
```

There are a lot of little tidbits here. The Windows data and code segment addresses are listed, as is the result of a test for the 80×87 math coprocessor chip. As the two DLLs used by this program (the standard runtime library and the TopSpeed file driver) are loaded, the log file notes that they do not contain any debug information. It then shows which DBD (debugger data) files were loaded. Everything after the Debugger and debuggee task numbers is a log of activity during the session.

Hard, Soft, and Clarion Soft Modes

You can run the Debugger in one of three modes. In hard mode (where both soft mode and Clarion soft mode are unchecked on the Options menu) the desktop is not redrawn. If you want to see what your program looks like, you have to switch over to it. In soft mode, the desktop is redrawn by the Debugger. Clarion soft mode is an enhancement to soft mode that uses the Clarion runtime library to process messages, which hopefully mimics the program's non-debugged behavior more accurately.

Unless you have a specific reason to do otherwise, you should probably use Clarion soft mode. If you're avoiding it because you don't like the flickering of the window, you might want to set up your desktop so that the Debugger and the debuggee are side by side. You can use the Position Debuggee option under the Window menu to make the debuggee as large as possible without obscuring the Debugger.

Summary

Whether you just need to check out a misplaced bit of code or set extensive break points in pursuit of some obscure bug, the fully Windows-hosted TopSpeed Debugger can accommodate you. You can examine and change variables, monitor critical runtime values including currently selected and accepted controls, or watch the disassembled code scroll by.

You can even load the Debugger after your program has started, for true "debugging on demand." Once you've become familiar with the Debugger, you'll wonder how you ever got along without it.

13

Distributing Your Application

You've finished your application, and now you're ready to distribute it to an eagerly waiting public, right? Well, if this is the first thought you've given to how you're going to distribute it, you're probably not ready.

This chapter is not just about the mechanics of distributing applications, but about the requirements for making your installations work. To that end there is really only one warning to heed: Every installation of a Windows program, in whatever language it's written, is a disaster waiting to happen.

That may sound a little harsh, but if you take a worst-case-scenario approach, you'll make your clients' lives easier and save yourself a bundle in tech support costs.

Program and Data Directories

The time to think about where your program and its data will be stored is when you're designing the application. Will you use variables for filenames? If you don't, and you haven't explicitly coded a path for the files, your program will attempt to open files in the current directory. That's fine as long as the current directory your program sees is the one in which your data files exist, and for simple programs that's sufficient. It doesn't take much to cause trouble, though.

Say that you allow the user to use the standard File dialog box to do something such as pick a graphic to display. If you must change directories to find the file, the current directory changes. If all the files are already open, this isn't a problem. If you are closing unused files, however, you may find that the next time the user opens a file the program attempts to locate it in the new current directory. If your program creates nonexistent files (another design decision), you suddenly have two or more sets of data. The client calls you and wants to know why information she entered yesterday is now missing, and from which school did you say you got your computer science degree?

By now you're probably getting the idea that it's safest to explicitly set filenames, and you're probably right. It's also a little tricky.

Under no circumstances should you hard code a pathname for a file. I realize some programmers disagree with this position, but if you want to distribute your application to more than a handful of people, you're just asking for trouble. You might think it's a safe bet that C:\WHIZBANG is a unique enough name for a directory, until you find out that half your clients already have a WHIZBANG program they bought from your competitor, and the other half want to install your program on a network drive, not drive C.

Having been beaten into submission on the subject, you decide to use variables for filenames. Now you need to work out how to tell your program where to find those files. The usual way to do this is with an INI file.

In the past, Windows programs used the WIN.INI file for this kind of information, but that practice is now discouraged because of file bloat. If you like, you can use the WIN.INI file to point to your own INI file. Some of these options are discussed in more detail in Chapter 27, "Using Initialization Files."

Whatever approach you take, you need to collect the appropriate information—which will probably include the program directory and the data directory—from your user at installation time. Your installation program must then update the INI file (or other data file) with the correct path for the data files, and the program itself needs to read this information before it attempts to open any data files. (Installation software is discussed later in this chapter.) The time to experiment with INI files and using variables for filenames is during the early stages of development, not a week before you ship.

Interface Design Considerations

Vitally important is the video resolution your program requires. If you do all your design work in 1024×768 on your 25-inch monitor, and your clients all have standard VGA, there's a good chance they'll only be able to see about 40 percent of your wonderful program. Even if you tell all of your customers that they need high-resolution monitors, you better put some kind of check in your code to make sure all the necessary conditions are there before the program runs. Never assume the customer has read the manual, the readme file, the installation program help screens, or any of the other documentation you have so lovingly prepared. Don't even assume that the user has the minimum requirements to run the program.

> ### TIP
>
> To determine the maximum amount of displayable space on whatever monitor the program is running, open a window maximized and check its width and height using the property syntax. Because CW windows do not actually appear until an `ACCEPT()` or `DISPLAY()` statement is encountered, you can do this in a few lines of code with nothing at all appearing on the screen. Although this value is dependent on the system font, it works as a rule of thumb for determining resolution. Standard VGA will get you a screen of something like 329×219 DLUs, a resolution of 800×600 gets you approximately 409×279 DLUs, and a resolution of 1024×768 will be about 521×363 DLUs. You can also use the Windows API function `GetSystemMetrics()` to obtain information on the video mode.

The Ship List

You've worked out all your issues regarding window designs and data file locations. You're ready to start making install disks, so you need a ship list that shows all the files your system requires. The AppGen creates such a list, called appnam.SHP, each time it generates code. You'll find this list in your working directory.

The generated ship list will tell you what files you need, but it should not be used as an absolute guide. It will show the following:

- All file-driver dynamic link libraries (DLLs) used by the application.
- All VBXs used by the application and visible to the template system.
- All LIBs used by the application and visible to the template system. Because the LIBs themselves are linked into the application, these should be used as indicators that a DLL by the same name is also required. It's up to you to know if the LIB is a stand-alone LIB or has a corresponding DLL.

It will not show the following:

- DLLs that are referenced in included files in the global map.
- VBXs that are referenced in included source code.
- Any files required by any DLL that is required by this application. You will have to build a ship list for any related DLLs and add those items to the master ship list.
- Icons or images that are not linked into the application.

As you can see, you're probably going to have to do some detective work when it comes time to work out which files to ship.

The Project System: Another Option

There is another way to get ship list information, and if you're hand coding it's the only way. The application's project data (a PRJ file if you're hand coding; otherwise this is embedded in the APP) contains a list of all LIBs used, and you can use that as a guide to which DLLs are required. This approach is also less complete because it won't tell you about any VBXs, or even that you need the CWVBX.DLL (which has no corresponding LIB).

Putting It All Together

In addition to the ship list of files that make up the executable program, you may or may not have data files (depending on whether your application creates default files the first time it is run). You will probably want to ship a help file (creating Windows help files is discussed in Chapter 10, "Assigning and Building Your Help Files"). If your program uses any other files that are not linked into the EXE (or DLLs), you'll need to ship them, too.

It's always a good idea to do a test install on a computer that either does not have CW installed or on which you've removed the CW directory from the path. If you use your development system for this test, you should also remove the directory your VBXs are on from the path. If you use \WINDOWS or \WINDOWS\SYSTEM for this, you're probably better off just verifying your VBX list from the generated ship list. Do your install to a new directory where there's no possibility of the program taking advantage of any existing files.

If your install goes well, it's time to give your install disks to a few hardy souls for testing.

Shared DLLs

Windows DLLs (of which VBXs are a type) bring wonderful code-sharing benefits. They also bring some major headaches. Because all CW programs use at least one DLL in common (CWRUN10.DLL), it makes sense, if you have multiple CW programs, to keep just one copy of it on your system.

This brings up the issue of where to install the DLLs, including CWRUN10. The potential problem is having different versions of the same DLL spread around a user's system. This is mostly a problem with non-CW DLLs and VBXs.

One option that avoids the mess is to install everything in the program's directory.

- Pros: Everything is kept in one place, and you have control over what gets replaced when you do upgrades.
- Cons: Users with multiple CW programs (and there is no reason to assume they won't have any other CW programs on their system) will be keeping multiple copies of the standard DLLs. That's wasted space.

A second option is to install the standard DLLs in the Windows directory.

- Pros: Minimizes disk space used.
- Cons: There is the potential of name collisions between different versions of DLLs and VBXs.

Whether you're talking about your own DLLs or third-party products, you face the problem of making sure users are working with the correct versions. Not all vendors of DLLs and VBXs use numbering schemes (and perhaps you don't either on your own DLLs). This means that while your program uses version 3 of WHAZOO.VBX, revision 3.11037B, shortly after your client installs your program he installs someone else's that also uses WHAZOO.VBX, but it's only revision 3.11037A, which doesn't have a critical bug fix that your program happens to need. Your program blows up, and so does your client.

> **TIP**
>
> If you want to be really thorough, consider searching the user's hard disk(s) for copies of the DLLs and VBXs that you're about to install. If you find copies that are not identical to yours, give the user the option of replacing them. But be nice; make backups of any files you do replace, possibly by replacing the last character of the file extension with a tilde (~) or another seldom-used character.

You might find it simplest to install the CW standard DLLs in a common directory and your third-party DLLs in your own directory. That way, if the client wants to economize on space, you're not responsible for problems that arise when programs use different versions of the same file.

The Standard CW DLLs

Table 13.1 shows the standard Clarion for Windows DLLs that you may need to distribute with your application.

Table 13.1. Standard Clarion for Windows DLLs.

DLL	Approximate Size	Description
CWRUN.DLL	560KB	You always distribute this DLL with your applications. It contains standard window- and message-handling code that is used by all applications. This is the only DLL that will not appear in your project file as a corresponding LIB.
CWASC.DLL	13KB	The ASCII file driver. You would typically use this driver to read and write nondelimited text files.
CWBAS.DLL	16KB	The BASIC file driver, used for reading or writing various kinds of delimited ASCII files.
CWBTRV.DLL	43KB	The Btrieve file driver. (Note that although you can distribute this DLL, you may not distribute the Btrieve client engine DLLs without a client engine license from Btrieve Technologies.)
CWC21.DLL	54KB	The Clarion 2.1 file driver DLL. Compatible with Clarion Professional Developer and Clarion Database Developer.

DLL	Approximate Size	Description
CWCLIP.DLL	112KB	The Clipper file driver DLL.
CWDB3.DLL	111KB	The dBase III file driver DLL.
CWDB4.DLL	152KB	The dBase IV file driver DLL.
CWDOS.DLL	12KB	The DOS file driver DLL. This is used to read or write binary DOS files.
CWFOX.DLL	133KB	The FoxPro file driver DLL.
CWODBC.DLL	26KB	The ODBC file driver DLL.
CWPDX3.DLL	135KB	The Paradox 3 file driver DLL.
CWVBX.DLL	239KB	The VBX interface DLL. There is no corresponding LIB for this DLL.

Install Disk Programs

It's standard practice in the software industry to ship Windows software with an install program. These programs typically do the following:

- Provide the user with the ability to change the default installation directory
- Display help or promotional information during the install process
- Create a Program Manager object for each EXE that is installed
- Optionally create a Program Manager group for the EXE(s)
- Display a README-style file with any late-breaking information, after the installation process is complete
- Allow the user to abort the install at any time

There are a great many installation programs available. Quite a few are shareware, and you can find them on larger bulletin boards and information services such as CompuServe. There are commercial products, as well. The point is, you need something. Some of your clients may be sophisticated enough to create their own directories, copy files, and make new Program Manager objects, but even those who can won't understand why they have to.

Roll-Your-Own Installs

You can certainly write your own installation program using Clarion for Windows. In fact, you can write just about any kind of utility program in CW. Whether you choose to do this depends on whether you have the time and resources and whether the products on the market (of which there are many) meet your needs.

Upgrades and DLLs

After you've shipped the first version of your product, and the world is beating a path to your door, throwing roses at your feet, and generally being very nice to you, your thoughts will inevitably turn to upgrades.

If you're shipping a simple product that uses only the standard CW DLLs and nothing else, your only concern is whether you are using a later version of CW than your clients. If you are, you'll almost certainly have to send a complete install set. This is because the old CWRUN10.DLL will have been replaced by CWRUN11.DLL or CWRUN20.DLL, or something of that ilk, and the file driver DLLs will also probably be newer.

If your version of CW has not changed, you can probably ship just the EXE (plus any software needed to convert your customers' data files).

Upgrading Your Own DLLs

If you're developing large systems, it's quite likely you've started creating your own DLLs, as discussed in Chapter 32, "Sharing Code: Creating Clarion DLLs."

The existence, size, and number of these DLLs is entirely up to you, and you might want to build them in such a way that frequently upgraded code is contained in only one or two of them. With some restrictions, you can then upgrade your customers just by shipping the required DLL or DLLs. These restrictions are also discussed in Chapter 32.

The standard CW DLLs will also be specific to the particular version of CW you are running. This means that if you upgrade your system and create new EXEs and/or custom DLLs, you will probably also have to ship new standard DLLs as well.

Summary

Distributing applications built into Clarion for Windows is marginally more complex than distributing the same applications in DOS, primarily thanks to DLLs that can contain code shared by multiple EXEs or DLLs. You need to understand which of the standard CW DLLs you need to ship. You also need to make sure that you include all required DLLs of your own creation, any image and icon files not linked into your application, and any data files that will not be created by the user.

Distributing applications to users also has consequences for your application design. You need to be prepared for users with different video resolutions than what you use, and you must anticipate installations on different hard drives and in different directories. The better you anticipate the way users will install and use your application, the lower your support costs will be.

You should consider it a requirement to include an install program for distributing Windows applications. You can create your own in Clarion for Windows if you want. On the other hand, there are plenty of good, inexpensive install programs out there. Find one you like, and use it.

III

Hand Coding in
Clarion for Windows

14

Hand-Crafted Code: A Language Primer

Hand-crafted coding, what most people call "traditional programming," is a skill that can be developed incrementally in Clarion for Windows thanks to the Application Generator (AppGen) and the template system. Using the AppGen, you can for the most part avoid manually programming anything of substance as long as you stick to the functionality provided in the standard templates. The AppGen shields you from writing source code by presenting options to you from window to window, and then the AppGen actually builds your code based on your responses to these options. This process is known as abstraction. *Abstraction* is a term used to identify the highest-level (easiest) process by which a goal can be met appropriately for the task at hand. This generally means that by using abstraction, you have moved the high-water mark for accomplishing something to a higher level, where less and less work must be physically done in order to gain the same result. To that end, the AppGen is changing programming as we know it.

What about those times when the standard templates just cannot provide the necessary functionality to meet your needs? In that case, you could always purchase a third-party vendor template (if one exists for the functionality you desire), or you could roll up your sleeves and do some traditional programming. In either case, sooner or later you will need to write some code. Therefore, if you don't know how to develop programs by hand in Clarion for Windows, this chapter is for you. If you understand the basics of developing programs by hand, you might want to skip this chapter and read Chapter 15, "Hand-Crafted Code: Principles and Approaches," instead.

This chapter is designed to quickly provide you with some basic concepts and related information so that you can begin writing Clarion for Windows programs with the language, or write embedded code, or extend the templates as needed.

Rationale for Choosing to Hand Code

In various situations, you will find yourself with a problem that just cannot, and possibly should not, be addressed by the templates alone. This might be because the problem you are solving is of a specific, non-generic nature. Or maybe you just need to insert some embedded code. In either case, knowing the language and understanding the basic concepts of writing programs in Clarion for Windows will greatly enhance your ability to reach any goals you may have.

In the past, the term "hand coders" was used in Clarion circles to denote those who did not use the code-generation tools provided with various Clarion products. Hand coders by nature wrote programs from scratch, using only the language as a tool.

A hand coder was therefore known as a craftsman; one who refined code to run as tightly as possible, making the best use of available resources (such as memory, disk, cache) with the goal of building reusable code and avoiding the "code bloat" caused by generic code-generation tools. To this end, a hand-coded application would generally yield higher performance and produce a smaller footprint than would similar code-generated programs.

The primary drawback to hand coding is the amount of time it takes to develop programs. To solve this problem, hand coders have developed complete (core) libraries containing functions and procedures that can be used from project to project. This has traditionally given the hand coder one great advantage over those who used the code-generation systems: Because there was no reworking or regeneration of code, the hand coder would simply add the (core) library functions and procedures to his or her project and take full advantage of code reusability.

This has all changed due to the Clarion for Windows template technology. The line between hand coders and AppGen users has blurred greatly, leaving only a few remaining hand coders who still insist on using traditional programming approaches. But what the traditional hand coder has missed in this transition to the AppGen is that a hand coder can still reuse his or her code in the template system by using an old, familiar approach. He or she can include the same functions and procedures as an external library or DLL in a project, but use the AppGen to design and build the majority of the program, reducing the time it takes to deliver the application to market.

So, is hand code dead? Heavens no! It is a more strategic resource today than in the history of programming.

The following are several reasons a person might want to hand code:

- There is no template available for the desired functionality
- To create templates
- It can be more efficient (resource usage) and promotes code reusability, thus reducing code bloat and overall resource requirements
- There are fewer programming maintenance activities when code is highly reusable
- You need to solve a specific problem in a specific way that templates cannot address
- You like to and want to write code without using templates

Program Basics: A Language Primer

At the heart of generated code is the same concept hand coders have relied on for years: program basics.

The very first thing you will need to have is a project file (refer to Chapter 11, "From Here to EXE: The Project System," for information on creating a new project file). The next thing you must have is a source file. By definition, all source code has the extension .CLW and contains ASCII text. You can name your source file with another extension, but I recommend that you use .CLW to keep with the standards used by Clarion for Windows programmers. Now it's time to create a source file. Do this by selecting File|New at the Clarion for Windows main menu, then select Clarion Source from the New dialog box and click on OK. This will present you with a blank editor window. To name your source file at this point, select File|Save, which presents the Save UNNAMED.CLW as File dialog box. Simply type in the name of your source file and press OK. Now that you have a source file, you can get right to work.

Every Program Has a Beginning and an End

A program is identified by the keyword PROGRAM. This statement alone identifies a program to the Clarion for Windows compiler as the beginning of the program. A PROGRAM statement may or may not use a label to identify itself. A label is an identifier (placeholder) that you'll often use in your programs to identify and reference other program components.

The following are the two rules about column one in your source code:

■ Labels must always appear in column one of your source code. Labels are nonexecutable code.

■ Executable code statements may never be placed in column one of your source code.

For example, for a program called TEST.EXE the PROGRAM statement could look like either of these lines:

```
TEST            PROGRAM

                PROGRAM
```

A MAP statement is used to enable the Clarion for Windows compiler to identify each component of the program. A MAP statement simply identifies modules, functions, and procedures (more on these in just a moment) that are used in a program. The MAP statement has a beginning and an end. The beginning is identified by the keyword MAP and the end of the MAP statement is terminated by a corresponding END statement.

A MAP statement in the TEST.EXE program that included the procedures MAIN() and FIRSTPROC() might look like the following:

```
MAP
  MAIN()
  FIRSTPROC()
END
```

The MAP statement follows a PROGRAM statement and precedes a CODE statement. The CODE statement identifies the beginning of executable code statements and is considered to be an executable statement itself. Therefore, by definition, it cannot be in column one of your source code. Your executable code area ends when either a RETURN statement is encountered, there are no more executable statements in the source file, or another procedure or function is encountered.

So far your source code for the TEST.EXE program might look like the following:

```
TEST                    PROGRAM

                INCLUDE('EQUATES.CLW')
```

```
              MAP
              END

CODE
STOP(TEST)
RETURN
```

I also included a file known as EQUATES.CLW, which contains the standard equates (constants) used in Clarion for Windows programs. EQUATES.CLW is located in the \CW\LIBSRC directory. By including this file, you may use standard constants in your program, such as `ICON:EXCLAMATION`, which will place an exclamation point in the Clarion for Windows `MESSAGE()` dialog box window. You will see an example of a `MESSAGE()` dialog box window later in this chapter.

TIP

If you wish to use the built-in functions in Clarion for Windows (and you most certainly do), you must supply at least an empty `MAP` statement such as the following:

```
MAP
END
```

Of course, this program would do nothing except compile and link to an executable that would execute and terminate. This is the smallest form of a program; it includes all built-in library functions and procedures. The built-in library functions and procedures are core libraries in Clarion for Windows and are prototyped in the builtins.clw file in the \CW\LIBSRC directory. These functions and procedures are physically located in CWRUN10.DLL and are exported so you can use them in your programs as necessary. For example, if you use the `MESSAGE()` dialog box window to display a warning, error, or message to the user, you are using a function that is a Clarion for Windows core library function.

MODULEs

The Clarion for Windows language uses modules to identify source functions and procedures that are not included in the program source code. A `MODULE` is specified in the `MAP` statement. A `MODULE` may contain one or more functions or procedures, and generally uses the name of the source file in which these functions or procedures are found. For example, say you have a source file called Test1.CLW that contains the `TestProc()` procedure. The `MODULE` statement used in the `MAP` might look like the following:

```
MAP
  MODULE('Test1')
    TestProc()
  END
END
```

As you can see, you may identify the MODULE by using the name of the source file that contains the procedure. This is useful for tracking which physical source file the procedures or functions are in. In addition to include the module in the MAP statement, in your project you would include the external source file called Test1.CLW. This way the compiler can resolve the reference to the procedure contained in this MODULE.

Adding this MODULE to the previous example of the TEST program, the program source file might look like the following:

```
TEST                    PROGRAM

                        INCLUDE('EQUATES.CLW')

                        MAP
                         MODULE('Test1')
                           TestProc()
                         END
                        END
         CODE
         RETURN
```

A MODULE can contain data (see the section "Data and Code"). If data is declared in the MODULE, it is global (accessible) to all procedures, functions, and routines in the MODULE.

Members

In order to enable the compiler to find and include the external source file that contains procedures or functions in your program, you must use a MEMBER statement.

In the source file called Test1.CLW, you will need to include a MEMBER statement. This statement identifies the MODULE source file with the program source file. The MEMBER statement is used prior to any data definitions, procedures, or functions in the MODULE and might look like the following:

```
                        MEMBER('TEST')
!Data definitions

!Procedures/Functions
```

I added two comment lines after the MEMBER statement—comments are identified by the exclamation point (!).I added these lines to illustrate the importance of the MEMBER statement preceding any data and code definitions, and how to create a comment as well.

Procedures, Functions, and Routines

Clarion for Windows provides three distinct types of executable code: procedures, functions, and routines.

A procedure is a process that is an isolated execution unit that may contain data and code. You can define a procedure that utilizes parameters (passing values to the procedure) in the procedure statement or none at all. In the previous `TestProc()` example, this procedure does not utilize the passing of parameters. You execute a procedure by simply placing the following line in your executable code section in a program, a procedure, a function, or a routine.

In the TEST program example, I will add a procedure called `MAIN()` to the program source file. The result would look like the following:

```
TEST                    PROGRAM

                        INCLUDE('EQUATES.CLW')

                        MAP
                         Main()
                         MODULE('Test1')
                           TestProc()
                         END
                        END
 CODE
 Main()
 RETURN


!========================================================================
Main                    PROCEDURE
!========================================================================
!Data Section

!Code Section
 CODE
 TestProc()
 RETURN


                        MEMBER('TEST')
!========================================================================
TestProc                PROCEDURE
!========================================================================

!Data Section

!Code Section
 CODE
 MESSAGE('This is My String','TestProc Procedure',ICON:EXCLAMATION)
 RETURN
```

As you can see, the line following the `CODE` statement is `Main()`, which will call the `TestProc()` procedure. The `TestProc()` procedure is defined in another source file and is identified by the `MEMBER('TEST')` statement. If the `TestProc()` procedure had utilized the passing of parameters—say, for instance, a `STRING`—it might look like this:

```
TEST                    PROGRAM

                        INCLUDE('EQUATES.CLW')

                        MAP
```

```
                        Main()
                        MODULE('Test1')
                          TestProc(STRING)
                        END
                        END
  CODE
  Main()
  RETURN


!==============================================================================
Main                    PROCEDURE
!==============================================================================

!Data Section

!Code Section
 CODE
 TestProc('This is My String')
 RETURN


                        MEMBER('TEST')
!==============================================================================
TestProc                PROCEDURE(SomeString)
!==============================================================================

!Data Section

!Code Section
 CODE
 MESSAGE(SomeString,'TestProc Procedure',ICON:EXCLAMATION)
 RETURN
```

Notice the change made to the TestProc() prototype, which is now TestProc(STRING), and the change made to the TestProc() procedure line, which is now PROCEDURE(SomeString). The prototype of the procedure TestProc() determines the type of data that will be passed—in this case it is a string. The TestProc() procedure definition defines the variable being passed into the procedure, which is a string, and in this case is called SomeString. You are not limited to passing in only one value; you may pass in as many values as you need.

A function is identical to a procedure, except that it will return a value to the calling procedure, function or routine. You may call a function using a variable to receive the value returned by the function, or as a parameter of another procedure or function call, or you may call it as you would call a procedure. If you call the function as if it were a procedure, you will receive a warning when you compile, informing you that you have called a function as a procedure. You can disregard this warning and eliminate it altogether by using a variable to receive the function's return value.

In the TEST program example, I will add a function called TestFunc() to the program source file:

```
TEST                    PROGRAM

                        INCLUDE('EQUATES.CLW')
```

```
                        MAP
                         Main()
                         MODULE('Test1')
                           TestProc(STRING)
                           TestFunc(),STRING
                         END
                        END
 CODE
 Main()
 RETURN


!=========================================================================
Main                    PROCEDURE
!=========================================================================

!Data Section

!Code Section
 CODE
 TestProc(TestFunc())
 RETURN


                        MEMBER('TEST')
!=========================================================================
TestProc                PROCEDURE(SomeString)
!=========================================================================

!Data Section

!Code Section
 CODE
 MESSAGE(SomeString,'TestProc Procedure',ICON:EXCLAMATION)
 RETURN


!=========================================================================
TestFunc                FUNCTION
!=========================================================================

!Data Section

!Code Section
 CODE
 RETURN('This is My String')
```

Notice the addition of the TestFunc(),STRING to the prototype statement in the MAP. This informs the program that a function called TestFunc() will return a value of a string. Now notice the change made to the MAIN() procedure: TestProc(TestFunc()). In this case a procedure that utilizes a string parameter calls a function, which returns a string that is used as the value for its string parameter. The TestFunc() function is first called and returns a string, then the TestProc() procedure is executed using as its parameter the value returned by the TestFunc() function.

The following lines illustrate the three methods of calling a function:

```
VariableName = TestFunc()
```

```
TestProc(TestFunc())

TestFunc()
```

To create a procedure or function, you simply use a label, and on the same line use the keyword procedure or function and any passing parameters. If multiple procedures or functions are used within the same source file, you can explicitly denote the end of a procedure or function by using a RETURN keyword at the end of the procedure or function, or implicitly by the using another procedure or function. If you plan on using structured programming practices, there should be only one RETURN statement per procedure or function, and that should appear at the end of the procedure's or function's code.

As you can see, this provides an extremely versatile model for developing your code the way you want.

Routines are similar to subroutines in other languages. That is, a routine is a unit of execution that resides in another isolated unit of execution (procedure or function). A routine cannot have parameters, nor can it return any values; it is simply a named executable unit that can be executed only by the DO statement in the related procedure or function where it resides. As the following example illustrates, I have moved the MESSAGE() function into a routine called ShowMessage in the TestProc() procedure.

```
TEST                    PROGRAM
                        INCLUDE('EQUATES.CLW')

                        MAP
                         Main()
                         MODULE('Test1')
                           TestProc(STRING)
                           TestFunc(),STRING
                         END
                        END
 CODE
 Main()
 RETURN


!=============================================================================
Main                    PROCEDURE
!=============================================================================

!Data Section

!Code Section
 CODE
 TestProc(TestFunc())
 RETURN


                        MEMBER('TEST')
!=============================================================================
TestProc                PROCEDURE(SomeString)
!=============================================================================
```

```
!Data Section

!Code Section
 CODE
 DO ShowMessage
 RETURN

ShowMessage             ROUTINE
 MESSAGE(SomeString,'TestProc Procedure',ICON:EXCLAMATION)
 EXIT


!==============================================================================
TestFunc                FUNCTION
!==============================================================================

!Data Section

!Code Section
 CODE
 RETURN('This is My String')
```

Notice that there is no prototype for a routine. This is because a routine is local to the procedure or function in which it is defined. There is no CODE statement for the routine either—a simple label with a ROUTINE keyword will identify the routine.

To create a routine, you simply append a label—in this case ShowMessage—and on the same line use the keyword ROUTINE to identify the code that follows as a routine. If multiple routines are used, you can explicitly denote the end of a routine by using the EXIT keyword, or implicitly by using another ROUTINE. If you plan on using structured programming practices, there should be only one EXIT statement per routine and that should appear at the end of the routine's code.

Data and Code

In Clarion for Windows, every program contains a data section and a code section. Likewise, each module, function, and procedure has a data and code section.

A data section contains declarations for the data (files, queues, variables, and groups). The data section should appear before any window, report, or code sections. By following this guideline, you will define data before it could possibly be used by another component within your program. All declarations start in column one with a label by which to reference the data item.

For example, say you have one variable and one group declared for use in your program. The declaration might look like the following:

```
ThisIsAVariable         LONG

ThisIsAGroup            GROUP
StringVariable            STRING(20)
LongVariable              LONG
                        END
```

A code section contains executable code. The code section is preceded by the keyword CODE, which can appear in any column except column one. Additionally, no executable code statements can appear in column one.

Variables

Clarion for Windows, like any other true programming language, provides various types of variables (which hold places for data) that should address all business-related programming situations.

Soon I will explain the various variable types, but first I should mention the implicit variable category. An *implicit variable* is a variable that can be used without declaration—the type of the variable is determined by the use of a special character appended to the name of the variable. Although use of an implicit variable is convenient, this category of variable is a slow performer and can be dangerous to use. Why dangerous? As you recall, there is a data section in each program, module, function, and procedure. This data section aids you in locating the variables declared in your program. Because an implicit variable can be used at any time, you may miss these in your program while editing or debugging. This makes life hard when you are chasing down a bug, to say the least. I recommend that you avoid using implicit variables if possible. Implicit variables are defined as follows:

- VariableName": The double quote implies a string variable, which is 32 bytes long.
- VariableName#: The pound sign implies a long variable.
- VariableName$: The dollar sign implies a real variable.

When you define data in a data section, you have a large range of choices from which to choose. The following list illustrates the types of variables available in Clarion for Windows:

- BFLOAT4: 4-byte, signed floating point, signed numeric single-precision format
- BFLOAT8: 8-byte, signed floating point, signed numeric double-precision format
- BYTE: 1-byte, unsigned integer
- CSTRING: Variable character string that is null terminated (ASCII zero)
- DATE: 4-byte date that matches the Btrieve record manager's DATE type
- DECIMAL: Variable-length, signed numeric, packed decimal
- LONG: 4-byte, signed integer, using the Intel 8086 long integer format
- PDECIMAL: Variable-length, signed numeric, packed decimal used in Btrieve and IBM/EBCDIC
- PSTRING: Character string with a leading length byte
- REAL: 8-byte, signed numeric, floating point using the Intel 8087, long real double-precision format
- SHORT: 2-byte, signed integer, using the Intel 8086 word integer format

- SREAL: 4-byte, signed numeric, floating point using the Intel 8087 short real single-precision format
- STRING: Fixed-length character string
- TIME: 4-byte, time, that matches the Btrieve record manager's time type
- ULONG: 4-byte, unsigned integer using the Intel 8086 long integer format
- USHORT: 2-byte, unsigned integer using the Intel 8086 word format

In addition to these variable types, there are two other types of variables: group and reference variables.

A GROUP is a structure similar to the structures used in a C program. A GROUP may contain various variable definitions. The following is a GROUP called MyGroup that includes one of each type of variable listed in the variables section:

```
MyGroup         GROUP,PRE(MG)
MyBFloat4         BFLOAT4
MyBFloat8         BFLOAT8
MyByte            BYTE
MyCString         CSTRING(21)   !String of 20 characters
MyDate            DATE
MyDecimal         DECIMAL(5,1)
MyLong            LONG
MyPDecimal        PDECIMAL(5,1)
MyPString         PSTRING(21)   !String of 20 characters
MyReal            REAL
MyShort           SHORT
MySReal           SREAL
MyString          STRING(20)    !String of 20 characters
MyTime            TIME
MyULong           ULONG
MyUShort          USHORT
                END
```

Notice that a PRE(MG) attribute was used on the GROUP structure. This enables you to refer to each variable in a GROUP by prepending the prefix MG and a colon to the variable name within the GROUP. This practice enables the compiler to determine the difference between, say, a variable called MyString and MG:MyString. The first would be a reference to a variable, the second would be a reference to the group's variable MyString.

You will find group structures extremely useful as you move into more detailed hand-coded work. Some examples of using GROUPs are discussed in Chapter 15.

The last variable type to consider is a *reference* variable. A *reference* variable contains a reference (memory address) to another data declaration or structure. You declare a *reference* variable by prepending an ampersand (&) to the variable type.

Reference variables may be used on the following variables and structures: BFLOAT4, BFLOAT8, BYTE, CSTRING, DECIMAL, FILE, GROUP, LONG, PSTRING, QUEUE, REAL, SHORT, SREAL, STRING, ULONG, USHORT, VIEW, and WINDOW.

To define a reference variable for a Window you might use the following:

```
rMDIFrame    &WINDOW
```

What this essentially does is create a variable called `rMDIFrame`, which is the same type as the window structure. To assign a window called FrameWindow to this variable you would use something like the following:

```
rMDIFrame    &WINDOW

!The FrameWindow Structure goes here

 CODE
 rMDIFrame      &=FrameWindow
```

What this does is save the memory location of the window pointed to by the label FrameWindow in the `rMDIFrame` *reference* variable. Now any operation that can be performed on the window structure FrameWindow may be referenced by the `rMDIFrame` *reference* variable. For instance, to open the window FrameWindow, instead of typing `OPEN(FrameWindow)`, you would type `OPEN(rMDIFrame)`. So where is this sort of thing useful? What if you wanted to change the text of the second width in the MDI frame's status bar? If you created a global *reference* variable called `rMdiFrame`, from any place in your application you could set the values of the status bar `TEXT` property by using property syntax such as the following:

```
rMdiFrame {PROP:StatusText,2} = FORMAT(TODAY(),@D2)
```

As you can see, this is a powerful mechanism when you use it judiciously.

There are various attributes that can be used on the definition of a variable, which can affect the behavior and properties of a variable. These include the following:

- Dim: The variable is dimensioned, an array.
- Over: The variable shares a memory location with another variable.
- Name: The variable may be exported.
- External: The variable is defined and is allocated memory in an external library.
- Static: The variable is allocated on the program heap, not on the program stack.
- Thread: The variable will receive a new instance (fresh copy) in each new thread you have started.
- Auto: The variable has no initial value and no memory is allocated for it in the program until it is used.

Of all of these, the most misunderstood is the Auto attribute. In use, it means that no automatic initialization is used, which means that you are responsible for setting the initial value for the variable, otherwise it will contain garbage (whatever is in memory at that particular time when your code is executed). The Auto attribute is extremely useful for gaining speed and compactness in and of your program. Why? You are required to initialize the variable manually in your code, the library code used to initialize a variable of a specific type is not brought into the compile sequence. Therefore, for each variable defined as Auto, you have informed the compiler to omit the library initialization code, which reduces the time it takes to execute during initialization. It also reduces the size of the resultant code. The following is an example of how to do this:

```
MyLong    LONG   , AUTO
MyString  STRING , AUTO

 CODE
 MyLong   = 0
 MyString = ''
```

It is reasonable to code for this usage because of its advantages. You must remember that it is your responsibility to initialize any variables with an Auto attribute before using them in your code.

Files

Clarion for Windows provides a record-oriented structure for storing data. The term *file* is used to declare such a structure. For each file structure, an internal record buffer is created that manages the data stored in the current file's record structure. Record buffers may be threaded or persistent, depending on the definition in the file structure. For more information on threaded record buffers, refer to Chapter 28, "Multithreading and Thread Management." A file structure might look like the following:

```
MyFile  FILE, DRIVER('TopSpeed'), CREATE, RECLAIM, OWNER('RAS'), |
        ENCRYPT('RAS'), NAME('MyFile'), |
        PRE(MF), BINDABLE, THREAD
K_Number KEY(+MF:MyNumber)
I_String INDEX(+MF:MyString)
D_Index  INDEX()
RECORD   RECORD
MyNumber  LONG
MyString  STRING(20)
        END
      END
```

A file requires a label, which appears in the first column of your source code. This is the name used by your program when referring to the structure—a file label is sort of the logical name of the file.

A record structure is defined by the keyword RECORD and ends with a corresponding END statement. Any fields contained between the RECORD and END statements are considered part of the record structure.

The File attribute defines the structure as a file. The Driver attribute identifies which database management file system you are using. The Create attribute enables the file to be created at runtime. The Reclaim attribute reclaims space held by deleted records. The Owner attribute identifies a user name associated with the file. This attribute is used differently in ODBC-compliant databases (to review the use of this attribute with ODBC, refer to Chapter 24, "Using

Open Database Connectivity"). The Encrypt attribute provides a string to password protect, or encrypt, the file. The Name attribute is used to specify the physical name and location of the file (a variable may be used, as well). The Pre attribute identifies a prefix that is used to uniquely identify fields within the file. The Bindable attribute is used to make all fields in the record structure of the file available in dynamic expressions such as BIND and EVALUATE statements. Finally, the Thread attribute specifies that the file's record buffer is threaded.

The following are the attributes of a file structure:

- File: Defines the structure as a file.
- Driver: Identifies which database management file system you are using.
- Create: Allows the file to be created at runtime.
- Reclaim: Reclaims space held by deleted records.
- Owner: Identifies a user name associated with the file. This attribute is used differently in ODBC-compliant databases (to review the use of this attribute with ODBC, refer to Chapter 24).
- Encrypt: Provides a string to password protect or encrypt the file.
- Name: Used to specify the physical name and location of the file (a variable may be used as well).
- Pre: Identifies a prefix that is used to uniquely identify fields with the file.
- Bindable: Used to make all fields in the record structure of the file available in dynamic expressions such as BIND and EVALUATE statements.
- Thread: Specifies that the file's record buffer is threaded.

A file can contain keys, indexes, and a dynamic index, all of which are driver dependent. A key or index definition consists of a field or fields (components) within the record structure, each optionally preceded by either a plus (+) or minus (–) sign (indicating the collating sequence of the component) and separated by commas.

A key is an index that is updated each time the data is updated; therefore, a key is always kept up-to-date. You do not have to do anything special to maintain a key. In the file structure example, the K_Number consists of an ascending key based on the MF:MyNumber field.

An index and a dynamic index require that you issue a BUILD() statement to bring the index into sync with the data. In other words, an index is only valid as long as no additions, deletions, or updates have been made to any component contained in the INDEX statement. In the previous example the I_String INDEX will be rebuilt using the BUILD(MF:I_String) statement.

A dynamic index is a bit different from either a key or an index in that the components are defined in your program code rather than in the file structure. For example, say you wanted to create the D_INDEX consisting of an ascending MF:MyString and MF:MyNumber. The following statement would do just that:

```
BUILD(MF:D_INDEX,'+MF:MyString,+MF:MyNumber')
```

When you issue a BUILD() statement in your code on a normal index the file state must be closed, locked, or opened—not shared. In other words, you must have exclusive control of the file. When you issue a BUILD() statement in your code on a dynamic index you do not need exclusive control, but the file must be open or shared for you to be able to issue the BUILD() statement.

Queues

Queues are available in Clarion for Windows as a complement to files and variables. A queue is a doubly linked list (which resides only in memory) that appears to be similar to a group definition; yet it has functions similar to that of a file. The following is an example of a queue definition:

```
MyQueue      QUEUE,PRE(MQ)
MyLong         LONG
MyString       STRING(20)
             END
```

A queue requires a label that appears in the first column of your source code. This is the name that you will use in your code when referring to the queue structure. Notice that I used a Pre attribute; this works the same way as it does for a file. A queue may be threaded; that is, each new thread started will receive a fresh copy of the queue and queue buffer. Other attributes might be useful to you—you can learn about them in the CW language reference manual.

The key thing about a queue is that it is not simply a data definition that has one instance of data; rather, it is more like a file in which you store records. You can insert, update, and delete queue records. You can also insert queue records in sorted order or sort them after you have added the records to a queue.

To add queue records in sequential order you would use the ADD(MyQueue) form. To add queue records in sorted order you would use the ADD(MyQueue,MQ:MyString) form. Note that adding in the second form will take longer to perform than in the first form. If you wanted to build a queue in sorted order as quickly as possible, you would use the first form for adding records and then use SORT() on the queue.

TIP

When defining a queue, place your largest or least-used string field as the last field. A queue will clip the last field to the actual length used by the field when the field is a string. This increases the performance you will get from a queue.

For example, if you had a STRING(20) that would most likely only have a value about 25 percent of the time, this would be a great candidate for the last field in a queue.

One last note on queues: If you define a queue and want to clear the value of the queue record buffer, you can do so using the statement CLEAR(MyQueue). If you wish to discard the queue altogether, issue the statement FREE(MyQueue).

You will find queues used heavily in Clarion for Windows because they provide a quick and manageable way to store and use a subset of data. For instance, the standard browse template uses a page-loaded queue to display data in a list box control.

Operators

When you use a file, queue, or variable you will need to perform operations and assignments. To assign a value to a variable, for instance, you would write the following:

```
VariableName = SomeValue
```

where the VariableName will receive the value to the right of the equal sign. Clarion for Windows provides plus (+), minus (-), multiply (*), divide (/), exponentiation (^), and modulo (%) operators. To expand on the preceding example you might write the following:

```
VariableName = VariableName + SomeValue
```

In some languages you are required to use this sort of syntax. However, there is another way: Clarion for Windows provides a shorthand method for assigning values to the original value of a variable. This is done by using one of the following operators: +=, -=, *=, /=, ^=, and %=. To illustrate how to use this type of operator, I will modify the previous example so that it reads as follows:

```
VariableName += SomeValue
```

If the VariableName variable was a long variable and held the value of 4, and the SomeValue variable was a long variable and held the value of 10, the result of the VariableName variable after the operation was completed would be 14.

Data Scoping

Clarion for Windows provides various levels of data scoping (the visibility, life, and death of a variable), as any good programming language should do. Traditionally, most high-level programming languages provided global and private variables. Clarion for Windows goes well beyond simply global and private definitions of data. The following are the kinds of data in Clarion for Windows:

■ Static: Defined and allocated on your program's heap and not released back to Windows until your program is stopped. This is known as persistent data.

■ Dynamic: Defined and allocated on your program's stack and released back to Windows as a procedure or function is exited. This is known as transient data.

■ Global: Defined after the PROGRAM statement and before the first code section in the PROGRAM module. *Global data* means that any files, queues, groups, or variables defined as global will be available at any time and any place (they are always visible) within your program. This is convenient, but it's wasteful. As a programmer you understand when variables need to be available. If you find that you have no need for a variable except in one procedure or function, then this variable should not be declared as global data. Global data is defined as static.

■ Module: Defined after the MEMBER() statement and before any procedures or functions are declared. Module data is visible to all procedures and functions contained in a given module. Module data is defined as static.

■ Local: Defined after a procedure or function statement and before the code section in that procedure or function. *Local data* means that any files, queues, groups, or variables defined as such will be available (limited visibility locally) only for the lifetime of the procedure or function that defined it. Local data is defined as dynamic unless it is overridden by the Static attribute.

Window and Report Structures

The Window and Report structures are maintained by the Window Formatter and the Report Formatter, respectively. A Window or Report structure should follow the data section and precede the code section.

A Window structure is the definition used to declare and define a window in Clarion for Windows. Although a Window structure is defined as a specific type of window and various fonts, controls, and properties, all of these may be dynamically modified at runtime.

The following illustrates a basic Window structure with OK and Cancel buttons (this is a dialog window):

```
window WINDOW('Caption'),AT(,,185,92)
      BUTTON('OK'),AT(144,10,35,14),USE(?OkButton),DEFAULT
      BUTTON('Cancel'),AT(144,28,36,14),USE(?CancelButton)
    END
```

When you're defining a Window structure exclusively (not with a Report structure), the general rule is to define one window per procedure or function. Of course, you could conceivably have many windows defined in any given procedure or function.

A Report structure is the definition used to declare and define a report in Clarion for Windows. The Report structure can be modified at runtime, just as the Window structure can.

The following illustrates a basic report structure with portrait orientation:

```
report REPORT,AT(48,96,288,336),PRE(RPT)
      HEADER,AT(48,48,288,48)
      END
detail DETAIL
```

```
        END
        FOOTER,AT(48,432,288,48)
        END
        FORM,AT(48,48,288,432)
        END
    END
```

When you're defining a Report structure, you generally have one report and possibly one or more Window structures defined per procedure or function, depending on what you are attempting to accomplish.

Use Variables

Before moving on to the last topic of discussion in this chapter, it is important to note a special Clarion for Windows construct that is found in both the window and report structures: use variables. A use variable is an attribute available on each control that binds data directly from a file, queue, or variable. When you insert a data element into the use variable attribute, the data item will be automatically associated with the control. This means that when the control displays, the associated use variable's data will display, and when you update the value in the control, the associated use variable's data will be updated, as well. The following illustrates the use of all three types of entities utilized as use variables:

```
ENTRY(@S15),AT(40,10,50,8),FONT('MS Sans Serif',8,,FONT:regular),¦
  MSG('Unique Code'),USE(MAS:Code), LEFT,REQ,OVR,UPR
```

This entry control uses a field called Code from a file called MASTER, hence the USE(MAS:Code) assignment.

```
ENTRY(@S15),AT(40,10,50,8),FONT('MS Sans Serif',8,,FONT:regular),¦
  MSG('Unique Code'),USE(MQ:Code), LEFT,REQ,OVR,UPR
```

This entry control uses a field called Code from a queue called MYQUE, hence the USE(MQ:Code) assignment.

```
ENTRY(@S15),AT(40,10,50,8),FONT('MS Sans Serif',8,,FONT:regular),¦
  MSG('Unique Code'),USE(Code), LEFT,REQ,OVR,UPR
```

This entry control uses a variable called Code, hence the USE(Code) assignment.

There is a special type of use variable that is known as a dummy field variable. A *dummy field variable* is simply a placeholder that you can use for reference or into which you can place data, as desired. A dummy field variable is available only as long as the window is open; once the window is closed, the dummy field variable and its contents are destroyed. To specify a dummy field variable in the Use attribute, you precede the name of the variable with a question mark (?). The following illustrates how this might be done:

```
BUTTON('&Save'),AT(230,4,28,10),FONT('MS Sans Serif',8,,FONT:bold),¦
  MSG('Confirm action'),USE(?Save)
```

This button control uses a dummy field variable for trapping the EVENT:Accepted of the button. Hence the USE(?Save) assignment.

In all of the preceding cases, you may set or get the properties of these controls by using the following syntax:

```
To Set the Property:
?UseVariableName {PROP:SomeProperty} = SomeValue

To Get the Property
SomeValue = ?UseVariableName {PROP:SomeProperty}
```

The question mark (?) is used in your code to denote that a window control is being referenced instead of a file, queue, or variable. For example, if you are addressing the MQ:Code control, you would use ?MQ:Code instead of just the MQ:Code identifier.

When you check for control-specific events on a window, use the CASE FIELD() statement. For the OF condition of this statement, always use the use variable, as follows:

```
CASE FIELD()
OF ?MAS:Code
  CASE EVENT()
  OF EVENT:Accepted
  END
OF ?MQ:Code
  CASE EVENT()
  OF EVENT:Accepted
  END
OF ?Code
  CASE EVENT()
  OF EVENT:Accepted
  END
END
```

Notice the question mark (?) again. This denotes that you are interested in the control referenced by the use variable and not in the variable itself.

The *ACCEPT* Loop

In Windows, as with almost every other user interface, the main programming construct is a loop to control the presentation of data and response of the user.

Clarion for Windows has made your life as a Windows programmer simple, yet Clarion for Windows has not limited you; rather, you have been liberated. There is no preconceived notion of how you should or can write the user interface logic of your program. However, there are some standards you should use, and there is an extremely good reason for them. They help you avoid writing obsolete code that will be difficult to change as your program grows beyond its original design, as is almost always the case. If you are hand coding, this is extremely important—doing it right the first time will help keep you from doing it over the second time.

With this in mind, the last topic of this chapter is the Clarion for Windows ACCEPT loop process—the key ingredient in writing Clarion for Windows programs.

What exactly is the Clarion for Windows ACCEPT loop? To explain this, it is better to ask What isn't the Clarion for Windows ACCEPT loop? I say this because you may have programmed in another language that has no notion of this concept at all, or maybe you programmed in C or C++, which utilize the standard Windows EVENT loop as the core for your program logic (which you must maintain).

In either case, what the Clarion for Windows ACCEPT loop is not is the standard Windows EVENT loop. The Windows EVENT loop logic, events, and messaging structures are all managed by the Clarion core libraries, so you don't have to manage them—this certainly relieves you of a heavy burden. The Clarion for Windows ACCEPT loop is like a child of the core libraries' Windows EVENT loop, which enables those core libraries to communicate with your programs in an intelligent manner. When I say intelligent, I mean that the core libraries send certain events (messages) to your ACCEPT loops while keeping other events out, performing subservient tasks for you, so you don't have to. For example, in Clarion for Windows you don't have to worry about all those messages that are sent to and fro in the standard EVENT loop for redrawing or repainting a window. This is all taken care of for you. Only those messages that really apply to most applications are passed along to your ACCEPT loops for your program to manage. This amounts to a huge reduction in work that is required to write fast and efficient Windows programs.

The ACCEPT loop must have a window defined. This is because Windows sends messages to handles (more specifically, to a window or control handle). A *handle* is an identifier that Windows uses to uniquely address a visual object. Therefore, because only those pertinent messages that either affect the window itself, or a control placed on the window, will be passed into the ACCEPT loop. You must have first defined a window so you can receive messages in the ACCEPT loop.

The following example is used for the remainder of this chapter. Please take a look at it before reading on:

```
1                       PROGRAM

2                       INCLUDE('EQUATES.CLW')

3                       MAP
4                        Main()
5                       END


6 CODE
7 Main()
8 RETURN

9 Main               PROCEDURE
10 DialogWindow WINDOW('ACCEPT LOOP'),AT(,,95,41),|
   FONT('Arial',10,,FONT:regular),CENTER,STATUS,SYSTEM,GRAY, DOUBLE

     BUTTON('E&xit'),AT(30,12,35,14),FONT('Arial',10,,FONT:bold),|
     USE(?ExitButton),MSG('Press the Exit Button to Quit'),DEFAULT
   END
```

```
11 CODE
12 OPEN(DialogWindow)
13 ACCEPT
14   CASE EVENT()
15   OF EVENT:CloseDown
16     BREAK
17   END
18   CASE FIELD()
19   OF ?ExitButton
20     CASE EVENT()
21     OF EVENT:Accepted
22       POST(EVENT:CloseDown)
23     END
24   END
25 END
26 CLOSE(DialogWindow)
27 RETURN
```

As you can see, I have given each line a number for reference in this discussion. I will use these numbers from here on when I refer to a particular statement line.

This example program simply displays a dialog window that contains a button control for exiting the window. I have annotated each line here:

1. This is your PROGRAM statement, which is required in order to define a source file as a PROGRAM module.

2. This is an INCLUDE statement that includes (in lines) your standard EQUATES.CLW file during the compilation process.

3. This is the beginning of your program MAP statement.

4. This is the definition (prototype) for the only procedure in this program, the Main() procedure.

5. This is the end of your MAP statement, which began in line 3.

6. This is the beginning of your CODE section for this program.

7. This is the call of the procedure Main().

8. This is the final RETURN statement for the program, signifying program termination. This statement is not required but was added for clarity.

9. This the Main() procedure definition statement.

10. This is the DialogWindow window structure definition used in the Main() procedure. This is the window that will be used for the ACCEPT loop in this procedure.

11. This is the beginning of your CODE section for the Main() procedure.

12. The OPEN(DialogWindow) statement opens the window but does not display it. The display of the window actually occurs when either a DISPLAY() statement is used or the ACCEPT loop is entered the first time. This has a wonderful side effect. You may manipulate the properties of any or all controls on the window, as well as any properties of the window itself before the user has a chance to see what has been done. For example, say you want a control to appear conditionally. You could have the control

defined but hidden unless the condition is present. This condition could be checked after the OPEN(DialogWindow) statement and before a DISPLAY() or the ACCEPT loop is entered, making the transition appear seamless to the end user. When the window is opened, an EVENT:OpenWindow is posted, which is a window (control-independent) event.

13. This is the top of the ACCEPT loop.

14. The CASE EVENT() statement is first checked to see if there are any pending messages for the window (control-independent events). When the core libraries pass events to the ACCEPT loop, this is the construct to read these messages.

15. The OF EVENT:CloseDown condition is checked because this is the message I am most concerned with in this example, although there could be many others included here as well. An EVENT:CloseDown is sent to the ACCEPT loop whenever a double-click is detected on the System Control Box menu (found in the upper-left corner of the window) or by a user-posted event. This event tells your ACCEPT loop that the user is closing down this window.

16. When the EVENT:CloseDown is present, a BREAK statement is used to stop the ACCEPT loop immediately. At this point, control drops out of the ACCEPT loop and resumes on line 26.

17. This is the end of the window (control-independent) event-checking process that began on line 14.

18. The CASE FIELD() statement is used to determine which control has current input focus. This is the beginning of control-checking logic.

19. The code following the OF ?ExitButton condition is only executed when the current control is the ?ExitButton.

20. The CASE EVENT() statement is used to check for control-specific events and is similar to that used in line 14, except that it is specific for a control. This is the beginning of the control event–checking logic.

21. The OF EVENT:Accepted condition is an event that is generated whenever you have changed a value of a edit control and tabbed to another control or have completed the control by using a defined completion keystroke or mouse press. In this case, a single click of the mouse on the Enter button (because the button is defined with the Default attribute), or use of the Alt+X keystroke combination, will complete this control and generate an EVENT:Accepted event for the control that has input focus.

22. The POST(EVENT:CloseDown) statement issues a close down message to the window, effectively producing a break of the ACCEPT loop. Posting a message is the Windows way of doing things. In this case it works beautifully because using the exit button is synonymous with double-clicking the System Control Box menu, which produces the same result by posting only an EVENT to the window, using only one exit point for your ACCEPT loop—clean and simple.

23. This is the end of the control event logic that began on line 18.
24. This is the end of the control-checking logic that began on line 20.
25. This is the bottom of the `ACCEPT` loop that began on line 13.
26. The `CLOSE(DialogWindow)` statement closes the window.
27. The `RETURN` statement ends the `Main()` procedure.

As you can see, the `ACCEPT` loop is the key component of the Clarion for Windows GUI language. By mastering this concept, you have prepared yourself to master the remainder of the language.

Summary

This chapter has only touched the surface of the power available to you in the Clarion for Windows GUI language. To further enhance this discussion, I suggest that you read the Clarion for Windows language reference manual and then take some time to explore each of the topics discussed in this chapter. The next chapter explores some advanced topics to aid you in your quest to learn the language and become an expert in Clarion for Windows.

15

Hand-Crafted Code: Principles and Approaches

In Chapter 14, "Hand-Crafted Code: A Language Primer," you were introduced to some basics of the Clarion for Windows language. This chapter introduces you to some advanced topics you may need to use in the programs you create. However, as in the previous chapter, I can touch on only a few advanced topics due to space limitations. This chapter assumes you understand the basics of the Clarion for Windows language, the ACCEPT loop, and how to code a simple Clarion for Windows program by hand (without using the AppGen).

Managing Required Controls

There are circumstances in application development in which you need to manage whether an input value is required. Sometimes managing a required control is simple; other times it can be a bit more complex, such as when a control requires a value based on the presence of another condition.

The Example Program

In the sample program in Listing 15.1, two different styles of required controls are discussed. The first is an entry control that is required only when the OK button is pressed, not when the Cancel button is pressed. This example uses the Req attribute (discussed later) on the entry control and is found in the procedure called Form1(). The second style of control is an entry control that is required only when an associated check box control has been checked, and only when the OK button is pressed, not when the Cancel button is pressed. This example is found in the procedure called Form2(). There are other examples hidden in this program that are discussed here as well.

Listing 15.1. REQTEST.EXE: The required controls sample program.

```
REQTEST                 PROGRAM
INCLUDE('EQUATES.CLW')

                        INCLUDE('KEYCODES.CLW')

NIL                     EQUATE('')
THIS                    EQUATE(0)
ZERO                    EQUATE(0)

AppClosing              BYTE      ,AUTO
Junk                    STRING(10),AUTO
Ndx                     BYTE      ,AUTO

TQ                      QUEUE,PRE(TQ)
ThreadId                   LONG
ThreadName                 STRING(20)
                        END

                        MAP
                          Main()
                          Form1()
```

```
                              Form2()
                          END

CODE
Main()
RETURN


!===========================================================================
Main                        PROCEDURE
!===========================================================================

MdiFrame APPLICATION('REQUIRED Controls Example'),AT(0,0,317,208),¦
        FONT('System',10,,FONT:bold),CENTER, ¦
        MSG('Welcome to REQUIRED Controls Example'),STATUS,SYSTEM,MAX,RESIZE
      MENUBAR
        MENU('&File'),USE(?Menu1)
          ITEM('Form&1'),USE(?Form1),MSG('Start Form 1')
          ITEM('Form&2'),USE(?Form2),MSG('Start Form 2')
          ITEM('Item&3'),USE(?Item3),SEPARATOR
          ITEM('E&xit'),USE(?Exit),MSG('Exit Example')
        END
      END
    END

CODE
AppClosing    = ZERO
Junk          = NIL
Ndx           = ZERO
OPEN(MdiFrame)
SELECT(FIRSTFIELD())
DISPLAY()
ACCEPT
  CASE EVENT()
  OF EVENT:CloseWindow
    AppClosing = TRUE
    POST(EVENT:Accepted,?Exit,1)
    CYCLE
  OF EVENT:CloseDown
    IF ~RECORDS(TQ)
      BREAK
    ELSE
      CYCLE
    END
  END
  CASE FIELD()
  OF ?Form1
    CASE EVENT()
    OF EVENT:Accepted
      CLEAR(TQ)
      TQ:ThreadName = 'FORM1'
      GET(TQ,TQ:ThreadName)
      IF ERRORCODE()
        Junk = START(Form1)
      ELSE
        POST(EVENT:Restore,,TQ:ThreadId)
      END
    END
  OF ?Form2
```

continues

Listing 15.1. continued

```
      CASE EVENT()
      OF EVENT:Accepted
        CLEAR(TQ)
        TQ:ThreadName = 'FORM2'
        GET(TQ,TQ:ThreadName)
        IF ERRORCODE()
          Junk = START(Form2)
        ELSE
          POST(EVENT:Restore,,TQ:ThreadId)
        END
      END
    OF ?Exit
      CASE EVENT()
      OF EVENT:Accepted
        AppClosing = TRUE
        Ndx = ZERO
        LOOP Ndx = 1 TO RECORDS(TQ)
          GET(TQ,Ndx)
          IF ~ERRORCODE()
            POST(EVENT:CloseWindow,,TQ:ThreadId)
          END
        END
        POST(EVENT:CloseDown)
      END
    END
  END
  CLOSE(MdiFrame)
  RETURN


!================================================================================
Form1                    PROCEDURE
!================================================================================

wForm1 WINDOW('Form 1 (Required Controls)'),AT(,,185,41),|
       FONT('Arial',10,,FONT:regular),CENTER,STATUS, |
       SYSTEM,GRAY,RESIZE,MDI
       PROMPT('&Name'),AT(5,4,,),FONT('Arial',8,0800000H,FONT:bold),|
       USE(?Prompt1),RIGHT
       ENTRY(@s40),AT(30,4,149,10),FONT('Arial',8,,FONT:regular),|
       MSG('Name is required'),USE(?Name),LEFT, |
           REQ,OVR,CAP
       PROMPT('&Phone'),AT(2,16,,),FONT('Arial',8,0800000H,FONT:bold),|
       USE(?PhonePrompt),RIGHT
       ENTRY(@p(###)###-####p),AT(30,16,62,10),FONT('Arial',8,,FONT:regular),|
       MSG('Phone is optional'),USE(?Phone),LEFT,OVR
       BUTTON('&Ok'),AT(112,24,,),FONT('Arial',8,,FONT:bold),|
       MSG('Validate before exiting this form'), |
           USE(?OkButton),DEFAULT
       BUTTON('&Cancel'),AT(146,24,32,13),FONT('Arial',8,,FONT:bold),|
       MSG('Exit this form'),USE(?CancelButton)
       END

  CODE
  OPEN(wForm1)
  DISPLAY()
  SELECT(FIRSTFIELD())
  ACCEPT
```

```
  CASE EVENT()
  OF EVENT:OpenWindow
    CLEAR(TQ)
    TQ:ThreadId   = THIS{PROP:Thread}
    TQ:ThreadName = 'FORM1'
    ADD(TQ,TQ:ThreadName)
    IF ERRORCODE()
      Junk = MESSAGE('ThreadQueue Error: ' & |
                      CLIP(ERROR())        , |
                      THIS{PROP:Text}      , |
                      ICON:Exclamation       )
      BREAK
    END
  OF   EVENT:CloseWindow
    POST(EVENT:Accepted,?CancelButton)
    CYCLE
  OF EVENT:CloseDown
    BREAK
  OF EVENT:Completed
    POST(EVENT:CloseDown)
  OF EVENT:Restore
    THIS{PROP:Active} = TRUE
    POST(EVENT:Resume)
  END
  CASE FIELD()
  OF ?OkButton
    CASE EVENT()
    OF EVENT:Accepted
      IF INCOMPLETE()
        Junk = MESSAGE('The "' & |
                        (INCOMPLETE()-1){PROP:Text} & |
                        '" Control<13,10> '        & |
                        'is required to continue...', |
                        THIS{PROP:Text}              , |
                        ICON:Exclamation               )
        AppClosing = FALSE
        SELECT(INCOMPLETE())
        CYCLE
      END
      THIS{PROP:AcceptAll} = TRUE
    END
  OF ?CancelButton
    CASE EVENT()
    OF EVENT:Accepted
      POST(EVENT:CloseDown)
    END
  END
END
CLOSE(wForm1)
CLEAR(TQ)
TQ:ThreadName = 'FORM1'
GET(TQ,TQ:ThreadName)
IF ~ERRORCODE()
  DELETE(TQ)
ELSE
  Junk = MESSAGE('ThreadQueue Error: ' & |
                  CLIP(ERROR())        , |
                  THIS{PROP:Text}      , |
```

continues

Listing 15.1. continued

```
                 ICON:Exclamation         )
    END
    IF AppClosing THEN POST(EVENT:CloseDown,,1).
    RETURN


!===============================================================================
Form2                      PROCEDURE
!===============================================================================
Check1                     BYTE      ,AUTO
Entry1                     STRING(50),AUTO

wForm2 WINDOW('Form 2 (Dependent Required Controls)'),AT(,,280,33),¦
       FONT('Arial',10,,FONT:regular),CENTER, ¦
         STATUS,SYSTEM,GRAY,RESIZE,MDI
       CHECK,AT(2,2,133,10),FONT('Arial',8,,FONT:bold),¦
       MSG('Check if true'),USE(Check1),LEFT
       ENTRY(@s50),AT(137,2,139,10),FONT('Arial',8,,FONT:regular),¦
       MSG('Enter how good you are...'),USE(Entry1), ¦
          LEFT(1)
       BUTTON('&Ok'),AT(210,16,,),FONT('Arial',8,,FONT:bold),¦
       MSG('Validate before exiting this form'), ¦
          USE(?OkButton),DEFAULT
       BUTTON('&Cancel'),AT(245,16,32,13),FONT('Arial',8,,FONT:bold),¦
       MSG('Exit this form'),USE(?CancelButton)
     END

  CODE
  Check1 = ZERO
  Entry1 = NIL
  OPEN(wForm2)
  ?Check1{PROP:Text}    = '&Do You Like To Program?'
  SELECT(FIRSTFIELD())
  DISPLAY()
  ACCEPT
    CASE EVENT()
    OF EVENT:OpenWindow
      CLEAR(TQ)
      TQ:ThreadId   = THREAD()
      TQ:ThreadName = 'FORM2'
      ADD(TQ,TQ:ThreadName)
      IF ERRORCODE()
        Junk = MESSAGE('ThreadQueue Error: ' & ¦
                       CLIP(ERROR())         , ¦
                       THIS{PROP:Text}       , ¦
                       ICON:Exclamation       )
      BREAK
      END
    OF EVENT:CloseWindow
      POST(EVENT:Accepted,?OkButton)
      CYCLE
    OF EVENT:CloseDown
      BREAK
    OF EVENT:Completed
      POST(EVENT:CloseDown)
    OF EVENT:Restore
      THIS{PROP:Active} = TRUE
      POST(EVENT:Resume)
```

```
      END
    CASE FIELD()
    OF ?Check1
      CASE EVENT()
      OF EVENT:Accepted
        IF Check1 = TRUE
          ?Entry1 {PROP:Req} = TRUE
        ELSE
          Entry1 = NIL
          ?Entry1 {PROP:Req} = FALSE
        END
        DISPLAY(?Entry1)
      END
    OF ?Entry1
      CASE EVENT()
      OF EVENT:Accepted
        IF Entry1 <> NIL AND Check1 = FALSE
          Check1 = TRUE
          DISPLAY(?Check1)
        END
      END
    OF ?OkButton
      CASE EVENT()
      OF EVENT:Accepted
        IF INCOMPLETE()
          Junk = MESSAGE('The "'                    & |
                          (INCOMPLETE()-1){PROP:Text} & |
                          '" Control <13,10> '       & |
                          'is required to continue...', |
                          THIS{PROP:Text}            , |
                          ICON:Exclamation           )
          AppClosing = FALSE
          SELECT(INCOMPLETE())
        END
        THIS{PROP:AcceptAll} = TRUE
        CYCLE
      END
    OF ?CancelButton
      CASE EVENT()
      OF EVENT:Accepted
        POST(EVENT:CloseDown)
      END
    END
  END
CLOSE(wForm2)
CLEAR(TQ)
TQ:ThreadName = 'FORM2'
GET(TQ,TQ:ThreadName)
IF ~ERRORCODE()
  DELETE(TQ)
ELSE
  Junk = MESSAGE('ThreadQueue Error: ' & |
                  CLIP(ERROR())         , |
                  THIS{PROP:Text}       , |
                  ICON:Exclamation      )
END
IF AppClosing THEN POST(EVENT:CloseDown,,1).
RETURN
```

The Global Data Section

Notice that in the program's data section (that is, the global data section), I have defined a few equates and variables, which need some clarification.

The equates NIL (an empty string), THIS (used for referring to the current window in property syntax), and ZERO (the number zero) are used in place of literals in the code. This makes things easier to read and modify in case you ever need to search and replace values. Imagine how difficult it would be—and how easy it would be to cause errors—if you blindly searched and replaced based on the literal zero (0).

The variable AppClosing is a flag that informs the MDI child to post a message to the MDI frame, informing the MDI frame that it is OK to close down. The variable Junk is used to collect garbage data from function calls that will never be used in the program logic. This practice prevents warning messages during compilation when you have called a function as a procedure.

The variable Ndx is used as a counter for processing the TQ (thread queue). Notice that I used the Auto attribute on these global variables, which are initialized in the Main() procedure. For more information on the Auto attribute, please see Chapter 14. Finally, the TQ is a queue that contains data for a very limited thread-management scheme used in this example. Both the Form1() and Form2() procedures are started from the Main() procedure. For information on the START() function, see Chapter 28, "Multithreading and Thread Management." There can be only one instance of each MDI child window in Form1() and Form2() procedures (more on thread management later).

A Standard Required Control

In the Form1() procedure, there are two ENTRY controls. The first is identified by the use variable ?Name, which has the Req attribute present. The second control is identified by the use variable ?Phone, which is an optional control and does not require an input value.

First, take a look at the window (control-independent) events that are checked by the CASE EVENT() statement following the start of the ACCEPT loop.

The Clarion for Windows library posts the EVENT:CloseWindow when the user double-clicks the System Control menu in the top-left corner of the Form1 window. When this event occurs, instead of enabling the window to close down naturally (which is the standard way this closing is done) I inserted the statement POST(EVENT:Accepted,?CancelButton). This effectively pushes the Cancel button and executes the code for the EVENT:Accepted within the CASE EVENT() statement of the ?CancelButton control. I used this technique in this window to be consistent with the technique used in the Form2() procedure, but I could have easily used a BREAK statement, which is a simpler method. Notice the CYCLE statement immediately after the POST() statement. The CYCLE statement prevents the EVENT:CloseWindow from continuing with the standard operation of closing the window when the Clarion for Windows library posts an EVENT:CloseWindow.

The `EVENT:CloseDown` stops the `ACCEPT` loop, then the window is closed by the `BREAK` statement. In structured programming, you generally want only one exit point, and you use the `EVENT:CloseDown` for this purpose.

The Clarion for Windows library posts the `EVENT:Completed` after the library has executed a required controls check and successfully passed this validation. To do the required controls check, set the window property to `PROP:AcceptAll = TRUE`. When this message is posted, a `POST(EVENT:CloseDown)` is issued, which will exit the `ACCEPT` loop and terminate the `Form1()` procedure.

Finally, the MDI frame posts the `EVENT:Restore` when the user selects the menu option `?Form1` and this window is already open. In this event, two things are accomplished: The window is brought to the top when you use the `{PROP:Active} = TRUE` statement; and the thread in which this procedure is running is made the active thread when you issue a `POST(EVENT:Resume)` to the window. What this actually does is "wake up" the thread.

Notice that there is no code required for the actual control `?Name`. This is because the validation happens within the control `?OkButton` instead. If you had multiple required controls in the window, you would need only one piece of code to deal with them—you would not need to insert redundant code for each required control. The validation logic is performed only if the user presses the OK button.

The OK button logic uses the `INCOMPLETE()` function to determine if there are any controls that have the Req attribute and have no value, and returns the window `EQUATE` number of the control. If the `INCOMPLETE()` function returns `TRUE`, a message is displayed warning the user of this condition (see the use of the `Junk` variable there), and then a `SELECT(INCOMPLETE())` is issued, followed by a `CYCLE` statement. The `SELECT(INCOMPLETE())` statement essentially selects the control with the required attribute that is in error. The `CYCLE` prevents any other following code from executing, placing the control at the top of the `ACCEPT` loop. If there are no errors detected, the window property `PROP:AcceptAll` is set to `TRUE`, which informs the Clarion for Windows library to post an `EVENT:Accepted` to each control on the window. When this process is completed, an `EVENT:Completed` is posted to the window, which closes the window and terminates the procedure. When the Cancel Button is pressed, the `EVENT:CloseDown` is posted as follows: `POST(EVENT:CloseDown)`.

The result is that if you press the OK button and nothing has been input into the `?Name` control, you will receive an error message and the cursor will be repositioned on that control. If you press the Cancel button, double-click the System Control menu box for the MDI child or MDI frame, or press the `?Exit` menu item on the MDI frame, this window will close without validation.

A Customized Required Control

In the `Form2()` procedure, there is one check box control and one entry control. The first control is identified by the use variable `Check1`; the second control is identified by the use variable

`Entry1`. Both of these controls use real variables (bound data) and neither are required (do not have the Req attribute) in the window structure.

Notice that the `Check1` and `Entry1` variables are declared before the window structure is declared (because they are used within the window structure) and have the Auto attribute. Immediately following the `CODE` statement, these variables are initialized to their default values. Next, notice how the window `wForm2` is opened, then the `PROP:Text` of the `Check1` control is set to the `'&Do You Like To Program?'` literal string. I did this to illustrate how to set the Text property for a check box control at runtime, and also to illustrate that you can only do so after the window has been opened.

As in the `Form1()` example, the first thing to look at is the window (control-independent) events. For the most part these are identical to the `Form1()` implementation except for the `EVENT:CloseWindow` event processing definition. In this procedure, a `POST(EVENT:Accepted,?OkButton)` is used instead of the `POST(EVENT:Accepted,?CancelButton)` that is used in `Form1()`. This is because in `Form1()` there is an explicit required control defined, and in `Form2()` there are no required controls defined (at least I haven't defined one yet), and if a specific condition is present (I'll discuss that in just a moment), validation will conditionally occur. To have a single piece of source code manage the validation process, I used the `?OkButton` using the `EVENT:Accepted` to trigger the validation process.

As stated earlier, there are no required controls defined on the window Form2. However, the window does contain a required control: the `Entry1` entry control. This control is required only when the `Check1` check box control is checked; otherwise it is not required. Therefore, validation will occur only if the check box control is checked.

Look at the code starting with `OF ?Check1`, and notice that if the check box control is checked (`Check1 = TRUE`), the property `REQ` is set to `TRUE` (turned on) in the `Entry1` entry control, making it now a required control. However, when the `Check1` value is set to `FALSE`, the Req attribute on the `Entry1` entry control is turned off. This piece of code conditionally turns a non-required control into a required control and back again. Also, if the value of `Check1` is not checked, the `Entry1` entry control value is cleared. In either case, the `?Entry1` entry control is redisplayed to reflect any changes in value.

The `OF ?Entry1` statement addresses the entry control processing logic. That is, if the `Entry1` has a value and the `Check1` value is not checked, the `Check1` value will be changed to `TRUE` and then redisplayed. This is done because there is no explicit order in which a user might change or enter data in the window (remember, this is Windows, not DOS). So when there is text in the `Entry1` entry control, the validation process assumes that there must also be a checkmark in the check box control as well, and if not, will take care of this for the user automatically. The remainder of the procedure is almost identical to that of the `Form1()` procedure.

So how does this customized required control work differently from a standard required control? If the check box control is checked, the OK button is pressed, and no data has been input for the entry control, the user is warned that the entry control requires a value. This is because of the Req attribute that is conditionally turned on based on the value in the check box control. In other words, the value of the check box control determines whether validation will take place.

The major difference between this customized required control and a standard required control is in how a window is closed. Instead of posting an EVENT:Accepted to the Cancel button, as was done in Form1(), an EVENT:Accepted is posted to the OK button. This is done because by default the Req attribute is not present. If it is present when the OK button is accepted, a condition exists that has not been completed. Simply ignoring this fact and allowing the window to arbitrarily close is likely to produce upset users. A better approach is to give a warning to the user and allow him to either correct the error condition or press the Cancel button. This is a far more "friendly" way to manage this sort of situation, even though it requires a bit more work on your part to achieve the ubiquitous result: user satisfaction. A user believes that if he inputs data and tries to exit, he should be warned before losing everything he has input. That is what this logic provides.

This type of custom closing logic will also help you prevent the MDI frame from closing, which is the topic of the next section.

Managing MDI Frame Closing

In Listing 15.1 there are a few other items that may prove important for you down the road. The first is preventing the MDI frame from closing down automatically. By default, in Clarion for Windows a double-click on the System Control menu will post a message to the MDI frame, which in turn will post a message to each open MDI child, instructing each MDI child window to close. If no action is taken, all windows will close and the application will terminate. But what if you don't want this to happen?

Looking at the window events in the Main() procedure of Listing 15.1, you will see that there is an EVENT:CloseWindow event listed. In this event logic, a variable called AppClosing is set to TRUE when this event is present (this variable is used later by the MDI child procedures) and the Exit menu item is accepted via the POST(EVENT:Accepted,?Exit,1) statement. This results in the execution of the code found in the OF ?Exit case EVENT:Accepted event. The last thing that is done is to CYCLE. The CYCLE statement effectively stops the close-down process as it clears the MDI frame window events.

Look at what happens in the MDI child when the EVENT:CloseWindow is posted to find out how I stopped the MDI frame from closing and warning the user why this happened. In the Form1() procedure, remember that the POST(EVENT:Accepted,?CancelButton) statement is executed when an EVENT:CloseWindow event is present. This will enable the Form1() procedure to end without validation. However, in the Form2() procedure the opposite is true: Validation is forced by the use of the POST(EVENT:Accepted,?OkButton) statement. Notice that if validation fails, the AppClosing variable is set to FALSE; otherwise it is left as-is. This is because the AppClosing variable is used as a flag to tell the MDI frame to close when the AppClosing variable is TRUE. Notice the last line prior to the RETURN statement in the Form2() procedure:

```
IF AppClosing THEN POST(EVENT:CloseDown,,1).
```

Notice the shortcut used for the preceding IF statement. There are two forms of IF statements in Clarion for Windows: one line or multiline.

In this case I used a one-line IF statement that uses a period (.) to terminate the IF statement and a THEN statement to separate the condition and result. A period can be used in place of an END statement in Clarion for Windows syntax.

This logic is executed only when there are no more errors in this particular MDI child. Because I am manually determining the close of the MDI frame, I can post an EVENT:CloseDown to the MDI frame without fear of unexpected results. How's that? If you look at the OF EVENT:CloseDown logic for the MDI frame, you will see the following code:

```
OF EVENT:CloseDown          !  CLOSE DOWN
   IF ~RECORDS(TQ)          !    If NO THREADS
     BREAK                  !      Quit Loop
   ELSE                     !    Else
     CYCLE                  !      Loop at top
   END                      !    End If NO THREADS
```

This checks the thread-management queue, which reflects the actual open MDI child windows. If there are no MDI children open, the MDI frame can close; otherwise, the CYCLE statement effectively clears the EVENT:CloseDown I posted to the MDI frame, preventing it from closing down. For instance, if there were multiple open windows and the EVENT:CloseDown was posted by the MDI child, the MDI frame would not close unless all MDI children were closed first. You can see this actually working if you run this code, because Form1() and Form2() do exactly the same thing prior to the execution of the RETURN statement in each procedure.

Thread Management

To manage the open MDI children windows, a simplified thread-management scheme has been used. This technique is similar to what the Thread Manager does (see Chapter 28 for details). This scheme uses in-line code, and is simplistic and limited in function. The Thread Manager is far more robust, but is a bit of an overkill for this example.

First there is a global queue defined, called TQ (thread queue). This queue has two elements: the actual internal thread number (ThreadId) assigned by the Clarion for Windows library and the logical name or descriptor for the thread (ThreadName) that you designate.

In the Main() procedure at the OF ?Form1 and OF ?Form2 conditions of CASE FIELD(), you will see the method used to limit each MDI child procedure to only one instance. If the user were to press the Form1 menu item and the Form1 window was already open, instead of starting another instance, focus would be changed to this window. The same is true for the Form2 menu item.

How is all this done? It is done in two parts: One portion resides in the MDI frame and the other is in the MDI child itself. First, the TQ queue record buffer area is cleared by the statement `CLEAR(TQ)`. Next the `TQ:ThreadName` is set to the logical thread descriptor name by which you want to reference the thread. Following this assignment, a `GET(TQ:TQ:ThreadName)` statement is executed. This statement actually searches the TQ for the `TQ:ThreadName` (by logical thread descriptor name). This can be done because the TQ record is added in sorted order based on `TQ:ThreadName`. If an error is posted as a result of this operation, a new instance will be started by the use of the `Junk = START(Form1)` statement. Otherwise, a wake-up message is sent to the MDI child with the `POST(EVENT:Restore,,TQ:ThreadId)`. You can use the `TQ:ThreadId` value because you already issued a `GET()` statement and it was successful, which means that the TQ record buffer has been filled with the appropriate record. The `TQ:ThreadId` will contain the actual thread number assigned by the Clarion for Windows library (I'll get to that in just a minute).

Looking into the `Form1()` procedure under the `EVENT:OpenWindow` of the `CASE EVENT()` structure for the window, you will see how the actual instance of a thread is created in the TQ. First, clear the TQ by using the `CLEAR(TQ)` statement. Next fill the record buffer of the TQ, using the following statements:

```
TQ:ThreadId    = THIS{PROP:Thread}
TQ:ThreadName  = 'FORM1'
```

The first statement will get the thread number for this procedure and fill the `TQ:ThreadId` queue field. As an example of another way to obtain the current thread number, in the `Form2()` procedure under the `EVENT:OpenWindow` event, I used the `THREAD()` function instead of the `THIS{PROP:Thread}` method. The second statement will fill the `TQ:ThreadName` field with the literal string of `'FORM1'`. The `ADD(TQ,TQ:ThreadName)` statement adds the TQ record (thread instance record) in sorted order. If an error occurs, a warning is displayed and the `ACCEPT` loop is stopped.

This takes care of how to create a thread instance, but what about when you want to destroy it? Look at the end of the `Form1()` procedure, and immediately following the `CLOSE(wForm1)` statement you will see how to do this. Again, you perform a search by logical thread descriptor name on the TQ, and if the record is found, it is deleted from the TQ. To keep your TQ in sync with the Clarion for Windows library thread manager, you must always remember that before your threaded procedure terminates, you must always destroy (delete) the relative instance (queue record) in the TQ.

The reason for this discussion was to support the statement used in the `EVENT:CloseDown` event of the `Main()` procedure, where the following statement is executed:

```
IF ~RECORDS(TQ)
  BREAK
ELSE
  CYCLE
END
```

The result is simple: If no records exist in the TQ, the program will exit; otherwise, the program cannot exit and will continue to execute.

You have seen several major points at work in this example. The first is the use of required controls and the ACCEPT loop processing of these controls. The second is the robustness of the messaging model, which enables you to do all sorts of nonstandard event processing.

Summary

There is not enough space to cover every detail of Clarion for Windows' hand-coding techniques, and this chapter has only scratched the surface. However, I hope that you have obtained a good feel for the sorts of things that are possible and that you will explore beyond what this chapter has given you and discover the riches and programming freedom that Clarion for Windows provides.

16

Hand Code, Reuse, and the Application Generator

Until now, this book has looked at application generation and hand coding as two separate programming disciplines. Although this is useful from an organizational perspective, it's a some-what artificial distinction. After all, the AppGen generates code the same way your hands do. The difference is that the AppGen is particularly suited to repetitive, generic tasks, and you, a skilled programmer, are better suited to problem solving and innovation.

Of course, soon after you come up with an innovative solution to some problem, you realize that the solution also applies in a number of different areas. Fortunately, you can easily incor-porate your own hand-code solutions in the AppGen, thereby reusing your code rather than constantly re-creating it.

Code reuse is one of those buzzwords that's been bandied about so much that its meaning has become somewhat confused. You will hear it used at least two ways: There is conventional reusability (the ability to use code from one project to the next) and there is object reusability (the ability to reuse objects in the same or another project). For objects or code to be reusable, they must be both granular and generic. *Granular* means that the components are broken down into pieces—you can build a large number of different items out of a relatively small number of component pieces. *Generic* means that the components are designed to apply to as wide a range of situations as possible.

Conventional Code Reuse

Conventional code reuse is as simple as making a line or lines of code available to different parts of the same program or to different programs. Once you've written the code, you don't have to write it again. This helps to minimize bugs, because when a piece of code has been tested and proven, it will (or should, if it is designed generically enough) work as well any-where else in that or in any other program. If the reused code is a procedure or function, it will also code bloat, because instead of compiling the code in each place it is needed, the program simply makes a call to the procedure. An example of this is the standard MESSAGE() function, which you can use at any point in your programs to display a message dialog box. The only penalty you will incur is the small amount of code required to call the procedure.

The largest payback of code reuse is probably the concept—and reality—of a single point of maintenance. To change, fix, or enhance a previously written portion of code, you need to touch only this one piece and recompile. Your reusable code should generally be self-contained, and should not be reliant on global data that may not be available in every project. In order to reach the goal of "code it once and never code it again" you must take care to make your code granular and generic.

Object-Oriented Reuse

Object-oriented reuse involves the creation of an object (a window or control, for example) that can be inherited from code to code or project to project. In object-oriented terms, it might be a base class or object. In Clarion for Windows (CW) you use objects, but you really don't create them—or do you? Say, for example, that you have a window object that you want to use as a base for all window development. This window might have certain buttons and characteristics, such as color, font, size, and window orientation. Because it's a generic object, you will undoubtedly want to add some different controls, along with the associated control-validation logic. In object-oriented programming (OOP) languages this is done through inheritance. *Inheritance* is the ability to retain the attributes of the parent (that is, the original object) in the child. In CW hand code it would require a bit more work than I have space here to show, but in AppGen, you can do this simply by managing the procedure template for a specific window type.

I tend to think of a procedure template as a base object that you inherit from the AppGen when you select the type of window you want to use and then enter the Window Formatter. There is little work involved in creating a new window in this way because the AppGen uses the definitions from the procedure template to create the window itself. Although this is not strict object-oriented programming, it is similar, and it is definitely easier and faster to reuse objects in this manner. In fact, the template system also gives you the ability to blend different objects through the use of control templates. In OOP terms, this is called multiple inheritance. In CW terms, this is called getting the job done.

The template approach also addresses one extremely important factor that OOP languages continually fight with: code performance. In CW's AppGen, there is no inheritance chain or object hierarchy that might create overhead. Therefore, there is absolutely no performance loss associated with using the AppGen development approach. Templates are covered in more detail in Part IV, "Advanced Topics."

Although neither of these examples fully explores code reuse, they both touch on important issues of which developers all need to be aware. The next section explores how this can be done effectively in CW.

Code Reuse in the AppGen

Effective software development demands that you make the best use of your programming resources. For most tasks the AppGen is the best tool, because programming often involves a lot of repetitive work. But what happens when you come across a situation in which a little hand code, or even a lot, is just what the doctor ordered? As it turns out, the difficulty is not in integrating hand code with an application, it's working out which of the many integration options is best for the job. The good stuff doesn't stop there, either. If you find that you're starting to repeat yourself in your hand code, you have several options for letting the AppGen take care of the repetitive portions of that code.

For example, if you're hand coding you probably come across situations in which you need to test for error conditions and display any resulting errors to the user. You could simply make a call to the MESSAGE() function each time, passing the appropriate text as a parameter, and this would already accomplish a certain amount of code reuse. You might, however, wish to provide more detailed information, or to handle a variety of user-defined errors as well as those returned by the ERROR() function. To do this each time the need arises entails a lot of repetitive hand coding. If instead you create a function that displays a standard error message in a standard Windows message dialog box, you can quite easily reuse the function throughout an entire application.

How is this accomplished? First, you need to give some thought to what the function must do (the initial design stage). Second, you must ensure that the function itself intelligently handles all possible information it may receive (intelligent input processing). If the function is to be used in ways as yet undreamed, and by developers as yet unknown, you cannot make any assumptions about what kind of data someone might try to feed it. It's up to you to anticipate invalid data, and either discard it or respond in an appropriate manner (with yet another error message, perhaps, since CW does allow recursion).

In traditional programming practices, this function would be prototyped and called as needed. With the AppGen, this function could also be part of a procedure template, an external source, a library, or a DLL.

As you will see, the AppGen is not just a tool for creating applications, but for reusing your own code. You begin to tailor the AppGen to your own way of working. When you have some working code, you can add it to the template system (which is really the AppGen's programming knowledge base) so that it becomes available to all your applications.

Before you get too excited about all the things you can do with hand code, you should look at where in the application it can go. There are really three general approaches to this idea: using code-embed points, inserting entire source procedures, and creating or modifying various kinds of templates to mimic your hand code.

In the simplest terms, there are only two places to put source code in an application. One is at an embed point, and the other is in a source procedure, which is a kind of template. The options for adding hand code are, in fact, quite complex due to the highly flexible nature of CW's template system. You'll learn more about the template system later in this chapter, but right now it's time for some early experiments in integrating hand code.

Source Embed Points

Embed points are the most straightforward of all hand-code insertion mechanisms. When you create a procedure in the Application Generator, such as a browse, by default that procedure has a large number of available "slots" for hand code. It works like this: Imagine that you've written a demo of your latest and greatest program, and you want to remind your potential customers each time they enter a particular procedure that this is a demo, and if they had any brains at all they'd recognize how wonderful it is, open the vault, and place an order. But how do you get your code in there?

As it turns out, this is a relatively trivial bit of work. On the Procedure (or Function) Properties window in the AppGen there is a button labeled Embeds, which will give you a list of available code embed points for that procedure. Note that there is a difference between *embed points* (the locations in the procedure or function where code may be embedded) and the actual *embeds* themselves (the fragments of source code). You *embed code* at an *embed point*. You do not need to add the embed points themselves (although you can, by modifying and re-registering the templates). Both embed points and the embeds themselves will appear in tree form in the *embed list*, as shown in Figure 16.1.

FIGURE 16.1.

The standard embed list.

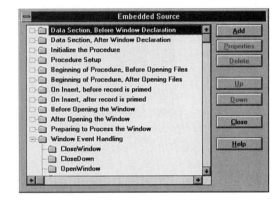

In almost all AppGen procedures the Embed list contains an embed point called Procedure Setup. Select that embed point, click the Add button, choose Source as the embed type, and you will find yourself in the source editor. Type the following line:

```
IF MESSAGE('Impressive, don''t you think? Why not buy, buy, buy now!' ¦
& <10>¦ Call Dave at 555-555-555','Paid Promotional Message'¦
,icon:exclamation).
```

Choose File|Exit, close the Embeds window, and select File|Run. The AppGen will first check for any changed procedures and generate the necessary code before invoking the compiler. When the program loads, choose the procedure in which you embedded the source, and the message shown in Figure 16.2 will appear.

That's really all there is to placing source code in an AppGen procedure. The standard CW templates come littered with embed points—you'll find them in both the data and code sections of procedures, before and after windows are opened, at various points during file input and output (I/O), and particularly for window and control event handling. For instance, a common requirement is entry control validation. The standard templates provide embed points on all controls for all events that pertain to that control.

FIGURE 16.2.
The Message()
function in action.

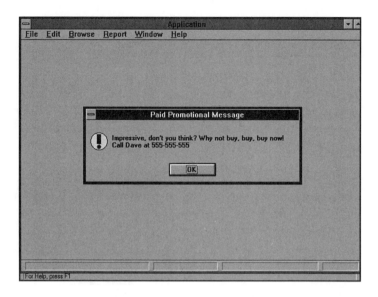

In your Procedure Embeds list is an entry called Control Event Handling. (If the box to the left of the folder icon has a + character showing, click on it to display the list of controls, and click again on the control's folder to display its events.) You will see that for entry controls (and for most other controls) there is an Accepted embed, which allows you to place code where it will be executed whenever that control is accepted (that is, when the user has entered or changed data and moved onto another control).

You can have more than one embed at any embed point. Go back into the application and choose the procedure where you added your source embed. Highlight the embed point (remember that all embeds are attached at embed points) and click on Add. Simply go through the same process of choosing a source embed, type the code in the editor, exit, and save. (If you just want to see the effect, you can try another simple message dialog box, or even just the BEEP() function.) You will now see two embeds under the embed point. You can use the Up and Down buttons to change the order of these embeds if you wish. To make it easier for you to know what your source points contain, the first line of each embed is displayed in the list.

TIP

Since the first line is always used as the descriptor for the embed, use a ! character and some descriptive text on line 1 of the embed point so that you can visually identify the embed point by a phrase instead of by an obscure line of code. For example, the first line of the MESSAGE() example might have been the following:

```
! An example of using the MESSAGE() function
```

You will probably have noticed that when you insert a source embed there are several other types of embeds available. The procedure embed enables you to execute a procedure instead of hand code. The procedure may not have any parameters, and if you wish you can choose one of the already-defined procedures in the application. If you want to call a function or pass parameters, you should use a source embed.

The other types of embeds are code templates, which are covered later in this chapter. The following section deals with the other "pure" hand code insertion point, the source procedure.

Source Procedures

Source procedures are what you use if you want to make a hand-coded procedure or function available within your application. Earlier in this chapter I mentioned a generic error-handling procedure as an example of code reuse. To see how this can be accomplished, you're going to create such a procedure. You will call it ErrorMgr, and you will use it to display either standard CW file-processing errors or developer-defined errors. You could also use it to display technical support information.

First, you need to define an "empty" source procedure in the Application Generator. If you don't happen to have a sample application handy, use Quick Start to create one. (See Chapter 6, "Quick Start: The Two-Minute Application.") Anything with at least one file containing one field and one key will do.

From the application tree window choose Edit|Insert Procedure. Type the name ErrorMgr in the New Procedure entry control, and click OK. Select a procedure type of source. After you do this, the Procedure Properties window appears, as shown in Figure 16.3.

FIGURE 16.3.

The Procedure Properties window.

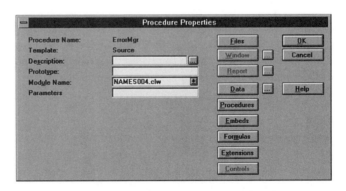

On the Description line type Generic Error Handler. On the Prototype line type (long,<string>,string), which indicates that the procedure takes three parameters, the second of which is optional, as indicated by the angle brackets. The AppGen automatically places this information, along with the module name, in the map. On the Parameters line type

(ErrEvent,ErrTitle,MoreText). This information is combined with the procedure name to create the procedure declaration in the generated source. The names you specify on the Parameters line are what you will use in the source code to refer to the data that has been passed.

Now click on the Embeds button. As you see, there are only two embed points for this procedure. One is for data (Data Section), and the other is for code (Processed Code). Select Processed Code, click on Add, select the source embed type, and enter the code shown in Listing 16.1 (or import it from the file CHAP16\List1.CLW on the book's disk).

Listing 16.1. Generic error-handling code.

pg 276

```
IF OMITTED(2) THEN ErrTitle = 'Data File Problem!'.
IF INRANGE(ErrEvent ,1,100)
   IF  MESSAGE('A File Processing Error Has Occurred' |
                   & '<10>Error: ' & ERROR() |
                   & '<10>Error Code: ' & ERRORCODE() |
                   & '<10>' & MoreText, |
                   ErrTitle, |
                   ICON:EXCLAMATION, |
                   BUTTON:OK)
END
```

There are a couple things to note about this code. First, you are using the vertical bar to split long lines of code. When the compiler reads a vertical bar, provided that it is not inside a string literal, it treats the next line of code as an extension of the current line. You're also using an ASCII 10 character, represented by <10>, to place a line feed in the message dialog box. This lets you neatly split your message into readable sections when the program runs and executes the MESSAGE() function.

If you do a lot of hand coding, you might feel that you could have done this more simply if you just typed the code into a separate source file. The real purpose of the source template is not, however, just to give you a place to put your code. The source template receives the information required for the map and the project system so that the source will be properly integrated into the application.

You now have (assuming no typos) a generic error handler ready to go. Take it for a spin.

Earlier in this chapter, you tested source embed points by inserting a call to MESSAGE(), the standard message handler. You will use this same approach to do a quick-and-dirty test of the error handler. Go to one of your procedures (any one will do) and in the Embed list, find the embed point called Procedure Setup. Insert a source embed with the following code:

```
ErrorMgr(1,,'Serious Problem')
```

When you save your changes and run the program, the message presented in Figure 16.4 will appear as you enter the procedure where the source embed has been placed.

FIGURE 16.4.

The `ErrorMgr()`
procedure in action.

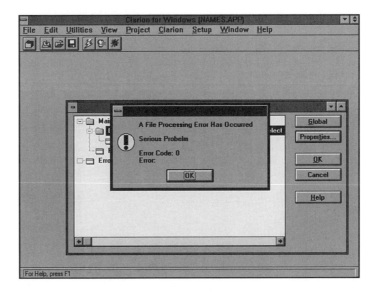

You now have a working error handler, and that's good. The next step is to make this error handler available in other applications. One option is to import this procedure from any other application that might want to use it. That will work, up to a point. The problem with copying procedures usually shows up when you try to make a change to the procedure and you have umpteen copies of it kicking around in your app files. It's a lot of work making sure all those copies now reflect the change.

One way around this problem is to compile the error handler into object code and have all the applications reference it as an external OBJ, LIB, or DLL. There are benefits and drawbacks to this approach, which are described in greater detail in Chapter 31, "Sharing Code: Source, OBJs, and LIBs."

A third solution to the code reuse problem, and one that is covered in the next few chapters, is to integrate the code into a template.

Summary

As you might remember from earlier chapters, the template system is really the heart and soul of the AppGen. It's like a second programming language, but one that you use (in conjunction with the AppGen) to create CW code. The template language is like any other computer language—it has special statements, rules of syntax, various kinds of data declarations, and so on. You'll learn about all that in a little while. In the meantime you'll look at putting your standard error manager in a template; to do that you will need to learn only a few template symbols.

17

Creating Code Templates

The Application Generator (AppGen) is a powerful programming tool that allows you to extend its capabilities to suit your own needs. This chapter explores code templates, which are probably the easiest and quickest way to make your own source code available within the AppGen.

Chapter 16, "Hand Code, Reuse, and the Application Generator," demonstrates that when you inserted a source embed there were a number of embed types, besides procedure and source, listed. These other embed types are called *code templates*. Their purpose is to make the insertion of any standard block of code—whether part of the default procedure templates or created by you or anyone else—as easy as picking that block of code from a list.

The *CloseCurrentWindow* Code Template

Take a moment to open one of your sample applications (any one with a browse procedure will do), go to a browse, open the Properties window, and click on the Embeds button. From the Embedded Source list click on any embed point (excluding folders that contain embed points but are not themselves valid embeds) and then click on Add. You will see a list of embed types similar to that shown in Figure 17.1.

FIGURE 17.1.

The Embedded Source window.

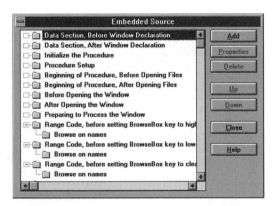

Choose the item called CloseCurrentWindow. This code template will insert some source code at the specified embed point to close down the procedure. After you choose this item, the window shown in Figure 17.2 will appear.

The window you see in this case is strictly informational. It tells you that there are no prompts to fill in (some code templates will have check boxes, entry controls, even file or field lists to choose from) and it gives you some information about the purpose of the template. Because this particular template contains only one line of code, that code is also displayed. Other templates may describe only the functionality. The point is simple—if the code template requires something of you, it will prompt you for what it needs in this window.

FIGURE 17.2.

The Prompts window for the CloseCurrentWindow *code template.*

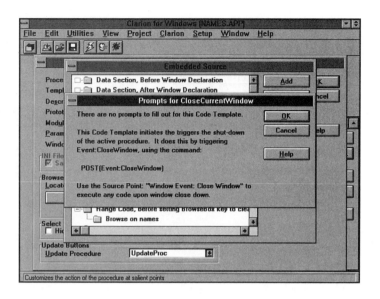

If you select OK, this code template will be hooked into the embed point you have selected. The template itself is not copied at this time—it will be used to generate code when the rest of the procedure is generated, most likely when you do a Make or a Run.

You might wonder, in this case, why bother with a template at all. Wouldn't it be simpler just to write that one line of code? It might be, if you were quite familiar with the language. Even then, however, you would lose one important advantage the template system provides. If, at a later date, the command to close a window changes, you would need to go through all your source embed points and change POST(EVENT:CloseWindow) to whatever the new command might be. If you are using the template system, you would need to change the code template only once, and the next time you generated code all embed points that used that code template would reflect the change. This is similar to object-oriented programming in that through this level of abstraction (code templates) underlying changes such as those just mentioned can be made without any form of hand coding or manual searching and editing of code. It is simply regenerated by AppGen.

The *InitiateThread* Code Template

Most code templates contain more than one line of code. Look at the template called InitiateThread, as shown in Figure 17.3, which is commonly used to call a multiple-document interface child window procedure.

This code template is marginally more complex than the CloseCurrentWindow template. Again, the code fragment itself is short enough that the prompt window displays it in its entirety. The difference in this window from the previous is that there are prompts for you to fill in. You supply the procedure to call (you can type it in or pick one of the existing AppGen procedures), an optional stack size parameter, and a single line of code to execute if the thread cannot be started. (For more information on threads and thread management, see Chapter 28, "Multithreading and Thread Management.")

FIGURE 17.3.

The Prompts window for the InitiateThread *code template.*

> **TIP**
>
> Code templates are code fragments. In other words, they are made up of various portions of code that otherwise could not stand on their own and compile successfully. The rule of thumb is don't code anything more than twice—once to make sure it works, and the second time to place it in an appropriate template.

Writing Code Templates

As you can see, the concept of code templates is quite straightforward. Fortunately, writing code templates can be equally straightforward. Take another look at your ErrorMgr procedure from Chapter 16. Although it's probably a better candidate for a procedure template than a code template, code templates are a little easier to write, and it will make for a useful exercise. (You'll turn it into a procedure template a little later on.) For now, keep in mind that although the code template will contain virtually all the source code in the procedure, in many cases code templates contain only fragments of procedures.

Making Code Maintenance Easy

Your objective is to place all the executable code for ErrorMgr into a code template, and then to create a source procedure, but use the code template, rather than the actual hand code, in the embed. In this way you will be able to update the source for the procedure across multiple applications *simply by changing the template.* It's like having an administrative assistant who will take your changes and absolutely guarantee to apply them wherever they are needed.

Get Your Code Working First

The first step in this process is to make sure you have working code. You should compile and run your original source—it's a lot of trouble to debug template code because you have to go to Setup|Template Registry each time you make a change, reregister the template, then regenerate and test your code.

If you're confident that the code is doing what it should do, copy it to a new source file and save it in the \CW\TEMPLATE directory as CWBOOK17.TPL. You'll need to add a few lines of template code to this file before you can successfully register it. You will use four special template language statements: #TEMPLATE, #CODE, #DISPLAY, and #!.

If you're already familiar with template files, you will have noticed that you are creating a new template chain. Any given set of templates is usually made up of a number of files, only one of which ends in .TPL. This file is, essentially, the master file for that set. All other template files end in .TPW, and are referenced in the TPL file to which they belong. You are going to create an entirely new template chain for the exercises in this book, so you can be sure that your work will not damage any of CW's default functionality. (Not that this would ever happen, right?)

The first statement in any template chain is the #TEMPLATE statement. It takes two parameters: the template class name (which is a way of grouping templates by function or author) and the template description. Enter the following line at the top of the file:

```
#TEMPLATE(CWBookChapter17,'CW Book Exercises')
```

The #CODE statement indicates the beginning of a code template, and takes two parameters. The first is the label of the code template, and it has the same requirements as do labels in the Clarion language. You'll follow the standard template-naming convention and use mixed case for your template name. The second parameter is the text to be displayed in the Select Embed Type window. Add the following line immediately after the #TEMPLATE line:

```
#CODE(ErrorManagerSource,'Error Manager Source Code')
```

The third statement you'll use is the #DISPLAY statement. This simply displays whatever text you specify on the window that appears after you choose the control template embed type. Add the following lines to the top of the file:

```
#DISPLAY('This Code Template contains complete source for a')
#DISPLAY('generic Error Handling Procedure')
#DISPLAY('')
#DISPLAY('This is part of a learning exercise from the book')
#DISPLAY('"Developing Clarion for Windows Applications"')
```

The final statement you'll use is the #! statement. This is just like the ! in the Clarion language—it indicates that the following characters are comments. Add a couple of commented divider lines to separate this code template from any other templates you add to this TPL file later on. Listing 17.1 shows what your completed template should look like.

Listing 17.1. CWBOOK.TPL with the ErrorMgr code template.

```
#TEMPLATE(CWBookExercise,'CW Book Exercises')
#!--------------------------------------------------------------------------------
#!
#!
#!   Developing Clarion for Windows Applications
#!
#!   This set of templates includes the following:
#!
#!   Template Type     Name                     Purpose
#!   ---------------   ---------------------    -----------------------------------
#!   Code              ErrorManagerSource       Source code for error manager
#!
#!
#!
#!--------------------------------------------------------------------------------
#!
#CODE(ErrorManagerSource,'Error Manager Source Code')
#!
#DISPLAY('This Code Template contains complete source for a')
#DISPLAY('generic Error Handling Procedure')
#DISPLAY('')
#DISPLAY('There are no prompts to fill out for this Code Template,')
#DISPLAY('but you will need to fill in the Prototype and Parameter')
#DISPLAY('fields in your source procedure properties as follows:')
#DISPLAY('')
#DISPLAY('  Prototype : (long,<string>,<string>)')
#DISPLAY('  Parameters: (ErrEvent,ErrTitle,MoreText)')
#DISPLAY('')
#DISPLAY('This is part of a learning exercise from the book')
#DISPLAY('"Developing Clarion For Windows Applications"')
  IF OMITTED(2) THEN ErrTitle = 'Data File Problem!'.
  IF INRANGE(ErrEvent ,1,100)
    IF MESSAGE('A File Processing Error Has Occurred' |
& '<10>Error: ' & ERROR() |
              & '<10>Error Code: ' & ERRORCODE() |
              & '<10>' & MoreText,|
              ErrTitle,|
              ICON:EXCLAMATION,|
              BUTTON:OK).
END
#!
#!--------------------------------------------------------------------------------
```

Message function (handwritten annotation pointing to the `& '<10>Error:' & ERROR()` line)

TIP

The MESSAGE() function ordinarily returns a value indicating which of the buttons it displays has been pressed. In this example the only button that will be displayed is the default OK button, and there's no need to check the return value. You could just use the MESSAGE() function the way you use a procedure, since it generates only a compiler warning, not an actual error. On the other hand, the `IF MESSAGE()…` form is a convenient way to discard the result of the `MESSAGE()` function without causing a compiler warning. You'll see the same approach used with `START()` in the template-generated code.

This template also contains some descriptive comments that will appear when the code template is used. As with all other forms of software development, you should develop the habit of commenting your code in such a way that anyone else can understand it with a minimum of effort.

Registering the CWBOOK Template

Save and close the file, and from the main menu select Setup|Template Registry. Click on the Register button and select CWBOOK.TPL in the \CW\TEMPLATE directory. If the template registry reports errors while reading your template, make sure that you have typed the template correctly. As a last resort, you can find the template in the file CHAP17\CWBOOK17.TPL on the accompanying code disk.

Assuming that the template registry didn't find any errors when you registered the template, you should now see CWBookExercises in the template list. (You might have to navigate down the list or collapse the Clarion template chain by clicking on the box to the left of the item called Class Clarion, which should be at the top of the template list.) The template is now registered and is available to any and all applications, so close the template registry, go back to your application file, and give it a shot.

Using the *ErrorMgr* Code Template

To ensure a fresh start, you might wish to begin a new application using QuickStart. If you haven't done this before, see Chapter 6, "Quick Start: The Two-Minute Application."

To add your `ErrorMgr` procedure to this application, create the source procedure the same way you did in Chapter 16. When you have done so, bring up the Procedure Properties window, as shown in Figure 17.4.

Fill in the prototype and parameter lines, but do not add the source embeds. Instead of these, you will now use a code template. From your list of embed points, choose Procedure Setup, and click on Add. From the list of embed types, choose Error Manager Source Code. You'll see the messages you created using `#DISPLAY`, as shown in Figure 17.5.

FIGURE 17.4.

The Procedure Properties window.

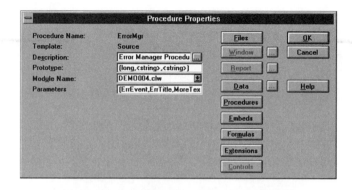

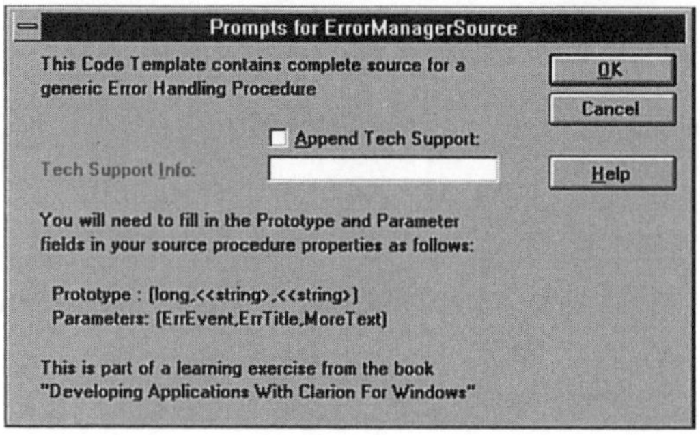

FIGURE 17.5.

The ErrorMgr *code template, as it appears in the AppGen.*

By choosing OK, exiting the embed list, and saving the procedure, you've created ErrorMgr for this application. That's all there is to it.

Because you've moved the code for ErrorMgr into a code template, that source is now available to any applications you might work on. All you need to do is set up the source procedure that will hold that code template in one of its embed points, and whenever the source for that procedure is generated, it will be taken from the template.

It's time to take your code template for a test drive. In the previous chapter, you added a procedure setup source embed with the following line:

```
ErrorMgr(1,,'Serious Problem')
```

Since this is a code template, you can insert it anywhere you have source embed points (except, of course, in a procedure, module, or application data area—only a code template that contains data declarations would be valid in a data embed). To make your testing a little more streamlined, you will create a test button on your main menu that will execute the ErrorMgr test code. Open the Procedure Properties window of your main menu (this will be the procedure that uses the frame template type). Proceed to the Window Formatter by clicking on the Window button.

Creating a Test Button

From the Toolbar menu, choose New Toolbar. As soon as you do this, and the outline of the toolbar appears on the application window, the control toolbox also appears. It was not visible earlier because although you can place controls on an application frame's toolbar, you never can place them on the application frame itself.

From the control toolbox select a button and place it somewhere in the toolbar. Figure 17.6 shows what your window should now look like.

FIGURE 17.6.

Placing a button on an application frame toolbar.

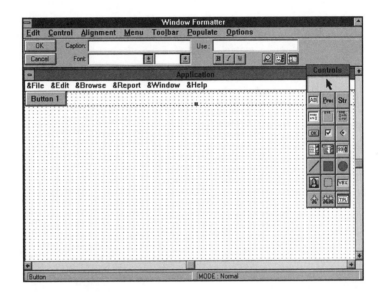

Make sure the button is still selected, and place the cursor in the Caption field (which is in the Window Formatter's toolbar). Change the caption from Button 1 to Test. Then, placing the mouse cursor over the button, click with the right mouse button. Select Action from the Properties menu that appears. You will see the window shown in Figure 17.7.

FIGURE 17.7.

The Prompts for ?Button1 window.

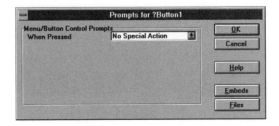

This window provides an easy way to attach procedures to a button. The When Pressed drop-down list box allows you to choose whether you want to call a procedure, run a separate program, or do nothing. If that's not good enough for you, there is an Embed button you can press to get a list of embed points for `Accepted`, `Selected`, and any other events.

Since the purpose of this button is to call the `ErrorMgr` procedure, set When Pressed to Call a Procedure. As you do this, you will see a number of prompts appear on the window. This ability to prompt for certain information based on the user's choice is yet another example of the flexibility of the template language. This window, like many you will see in the AppGen, is created from instructions in the template language. (If you'd like to see what the code looks like, take a moment to view \CW\TEMPLATE\FIELD.TPW and look for the section that begins with the line `#GROUP(%FieldTemplateStandardButtonMenuPrompt)`.)

The Procedure Name field is a combo box—you can either type in the name of a procedure (and if it isn't already in the application tree it will appear as a ToDo procedure) or you can choose it from the available procedures. Either type `ErrorMgr`, or pick it from the list that appears when you click on the down arrow to the right of the field. Now fill the Parameters field with `(30, 'Problem')`. Do not check Initiate Thread. The procedure takes parameters, which is not permitted for threaded procedures, and in any case when an error message pops up you generally want the user to respond to it rather than simply select a different part of the program to work in.

Click on OK in the Prompts window, save your changes in the Window Formatter and the procedure, and click on the Run icon to make and run your program. Click on the Test button on your application's toolbar, and the window shown in Figure 17.8 appears.

FIGURE 17.8.

The `ErrorMgr` *procedure in action!*

Code Maintenance the Easy Way

By placing the code for `ErrorMgr` in a code template, you have not only made it available to all your applications, you have also made code maintenance quite simple. If you have a change to make to `ErrorMgr`, you need to do it only once, in the template. The AppGen will take care of implementing the changes each time you regenerate the source code.

Enhancing Code Templates

The ErrorMgr code template is an example of "bare bones" template programming, but there is a lot more you can accomplish with very little work. For instance, under some circumstances you may want to vary the functionality of the template depending on the circumstances of its use.

This kind of enhancement falls into three categories: the use of template prompts, which request information from the developer; the use of existing (prewritten) template code; and the use of template variables, which provide information pertaining to the current state of the application.

Adding Prompts

When you created the Test button, you were presented with a dialog window that prompted you for the kind of action to take when the button was pressed. Since this dialog window was created from template language statements, and since you, the programmer, have full access to the template language, there's no reason you can't add your own prompts to your own templates, as well. Virtually everything you see the AppGen do you can appropriate for your own uses.

Check Boxes

Check boxes are among the simplest of template language constructs to use. Suppose that after you've used your ErrorMgr procedure for a while you decide that for some of your applications you wish to also display technical support information on the error box. You could create two different code templates, one with tech support information and one without, and switch between them depending on the needs of your application. It would be simplest if you could simply switch tech support on or off for any given application.

The code to modify the template to enable/disable an additional line of tech support information is shown in Listing 17.2.

> **NOTE**
>
> Inserted lines in the template are marked #! New Code, and the display line that contains the text There are no prompts has been removed.

Listing 17.2. The ErrorMgr code template with tech support information added.

```
#CODE(ErrorManagerSource,'Error Manager Source Code')
#!
#DISPLAY('This Code Template contains complete source for a')
#DISPLAY('generic Error Handling Procedure')
#DISPLAY('')
#PROMPT('Append Tech Support:',CHECK),%AppendTechSupport     #! New Line
#DISPLAY('')
#DISPLAY('You will need to fill in the Prototype and Parameter')
#DISPLAY('fields in your source procedure properties as follows:')
#DISPLAY('')
#DISPLAY('  Prototype : (long,<<string>,<<string>)')
#DISPLAY('  Parameters: (ErrEvent,ErrTitle,MoreText)')
#DISPLAY('')
#DISPLAY('This is part of a learning exercise from the book')
#DISPLAY('"Developing Applications With Clarion For Windows"')
  IF OMITTED(2) THEN ErrTitle = 'Data File Problem!'.
  IF INRANGE(ErrEvent ,1,100)
    IF MESSAGE('A File Processing Error Has Occurred' |
#IF(%AppendTechSupport)                                      #! New Line
            & '<10,10>' & MoreText|                          #! New Line
            & '<10,10>Call Tech Support at 555-555-555'|     #! New Line
#ELSE                                                        #! New Line
            & '<10,10>' & MoreText|
#ENDIF                                                       #! New Line
            & '<10,10>Error Code: ' & ERRORCODE()|
            & '<10>Error: ' & ERROR() ,|
            ErrTitle,|
            ICON:EXCLAMATION,|
            BUTTON:OK).
  END
#!
#!-------------------------------------------------------------------------------
```

The check box appears below the first set of #DISPLAY statements, as a #PROMPT with a Check attribute. The template, when you view it in the AppGen, will look like the one shown in Figure 17.9.

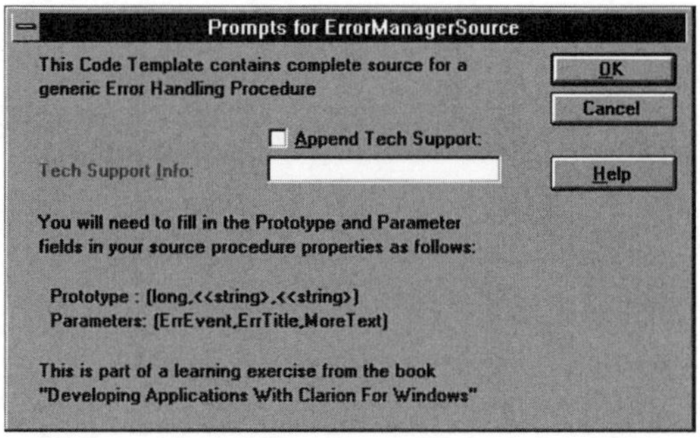

FIGURE 17.9.

The ErrorMgr template, with a tech support check box.

When you check the Append Tech Support box, the template variable `%AppendTechSupport` is set to 1. When the AppGen regenerates the code (as will happen if you change the check box setting) it reads the value of `%AppendTechSupport`. If the variable is set to 1, the code following the line `#IF(%AppendTechSupport)` will be generated, while the code following the `#ELSE` will not, and vice versa if `%AppendTechSupport` is set to 0.

This is conditional compiling, template style. You can use this principle anywhere in the template system to determine which code should or should not be created.

Entry Fields

Entry fields, like check boxes, are an easy way to get information from the programmer. While check boxes are often used to determine which pre-existing features will be included in a particular template, entry fields are generally more appropriate to information that is completely unknown prior to the templates being used. In the case of `ErrorMgr`, you might decide that you want different technical support instructions to appear in different applications. Rather than hard coding this information, you can simply place an entry field on the template and collect it when you create the procedure.

The modifications to make the `ErrorMgr` template support an entry field for the tech support information look like what is shown in Listing 17.3.

> **NOTE**
>
> New lines are marked with `#!NEW` and changed lines are marked with `#<!CHANGED`.

Listing 17.3. The `ErrorMgr` code template with optional tech support information.

```
#CODE(ErrorManagerSource,'Error Manager Source Code')
#!
#DISPLAY('This Code Template contains complete source for a')
#DISPLAY('generic Error Handling Procedure')
#DISPLAY('')
#PROMPT('&Append Tech Support:',CHECK),%AppendTechSupport
#ENABLE(%AppendTechSupport)                           #! New Line
  #PROMPT('Tech Support &Info:',@s255),%TechSupportInfo    #! New Line
#ENDENABLE                                            #! New Line
#DISPLAY('')
#DISPLAY('You will need to fill in the Prototype and Parameter')
#DISPLAY('fields in your source procedure properties as follows:')
#DISPLAY('')
#DISPLAY('  Prototype : (long,<<string>,<<string>)')
#DISPLAY('  Parameters: (ErrEvent,ErrTitle,MoreText)')
#DISPLAY('')
#DISPLAY('This is part of a learning exercise from the book')
#DISPLAY('"Developing Applications With Clarion For Windows"')
```

continues

Listing 17.3. continued

```
  IF OMITTED(2) THEN ErrTitle = 'Data File Problem!'.
  IF INRANGE(ErrEvent ,1,100)
    IF MESSAGE('A File Processing Error Has Occurred' ¦
#IF(%AppendTechSupport)
            & '<10,10>' & MoreText¦
            & '<10,10>' & '%TechSupportInfo' ¦              #<! Changed Line
#ELSE
            & '<10,10>' & MoreText¦
#ENDIF
            & '<10,10>Error Code: ' & ERRORCODE()¦
            & '<10>Error: ' & ERROR() ,¦
            ErrTitle,¦
            ICON:EXCLAMATION,¦
            BUTTON:OK).
  END
#!
#!-----------------------------------------------------------------------------
```

These changes introduce another new template statement: #ENABLE. It is used to enable or disable fields, based on the value of template variables. In this example, the field that is to receive the technical support information is disabled (grayed out and inaccessible to the user) as long as the value of %AppendTechSupport is set to 0.

TIP

You may have noticed a subtle change in the way the changed line is marked. Instead of a #! prefix to indicate a comment, the changed line is marked with a #<! prefix. The extra < character ~~is needed because this line, unlike all the others that have comments, is actual source code that will be generated.~~ TABS to position and then prints the comment (!) in the generated code.

When you go to the embed list in the AppGen and select the template, you will see the window shown in Figure 17.10.

NOTE

Note that there is now a check box called Append Tech Support, and if you check it, the entry field below will be enabled, allowing you to type in the text you want displayed on the message box.

FIGURE 17.10.

The ErrorMgr *code template Properties window.*

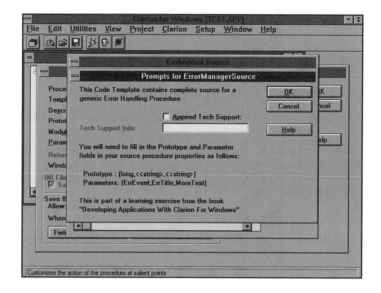

Summary

You've seen some of the benefits of creating a code template. In fact, this example has probably pushed code templates farther than you will probably want to, since their real purpose is to give you a library of code fragments, rather than entire procedures. You can apply the principles learned here to any code fragment that you think might be used in more than one instance in any application you create.

You have also seen the benefits of code reuse and code abstraction, which make for an even higher level of code reusability. There are, however, many ways you can go from here. It's possible to streamline the process of creating shared source procedures even further, and you'll examine that in Chapter 18, "Creating Procedure Templates." It's also possible to extend your own templates by tapping into some of the AppGen's internal data, which is covered in greater detail in Chapter 18, Chapter 19, "Creating Control Templates," and Chapter 20, "Creating Extension Templates."

18

Creating Procedure Templates

As discussed in Chapter 17, "Creating Code Templates," code templates are excellent replacements for commonly used code fragments. That chapter also shows an example of a code template that makes up all the source code for a particular procedure. Under these circumstances, it is usually best to take another step and expand the code template into a procedure template.

Just as you can create as many code templates as you like, you can create as many procedure templates as you like, and each one will appear in the procedure template list when you create a new procedure in the AppGen. Procedure templates do not have to be as complex as the browse or form templates (although they can be). This chapter shows how to create a simple procedure template that can serve as a base for your own explorations.

The *ErrorMgr()* Procedure Template

In Chapter 17 you created a template to display error information at any given time in a program. Although it is a workable solution if the code to display the error is quite brief, if the code is longer than a few lines you should seriously consider placing it in its own procedure to avoid repetition of code in your program. Although maintainability isn't an issue, code bloat is. You will probably still call the procedure using a code template, but this will ordinarily amount to only a single line of code—everything else will be in the called procedure. This chapter walks you through creating an ErrorMgr procedure template.

The *#PROCEDURE* Statement

Just as code templates begin with a #CODE statement, procedure templates begin with a #PROCEDURE statement, which takes at least two parameters: a name, which conforms to standard rules for Clarion labels, and a description.

When you register a template with the following line in it:

```
#PROCEDURE(CWBookErrorMgr,'Error Manager Procedure--CW Book')
```

the AppGen will add a procedure type of CWBookErrorMgr to the procedure type list that appears whenever you create a new procedure. It will then use the information that follows to determine how the procedure is to be built and what information it needs to collect from you.

There are four optional parameters for the #PROCEDURE statement. The Report and Window attributes tell the AppGen to make the report and window formatters available. If these attributes are not present, their respective buttons will be grayed out on the Procedure Properties window. The Hlp attribute allows you to specify a standard Windows keyword or context string. The Help file that will be invoked is the one specified with the #HELP statement, which should occur at the beginning of your template, if you have created a help file. For more on Windows help, see Chapter 10, "Assigning and Building Your Help Files."

The Primary attribute, which is discussed in more detail later in this chapter, specifies that at least one file must be specified for this procedure in the file schematic window, or an error message will be displayed when you attempt to save the procedure. It takes one parameter—a string constant that will be displayed beside the file in the file schematic window.

At this point, you do not need to use any of these attributes. The procedure you will create does not (yet) need a file, window, or report, and it ought to have an associated help file, but that isn't the subject of this chapter.

> **TIP**
>
> A fifth optional parameter, which goes right after the procedure description, is a string constant to specify the language for which the procedure is to generate code. This has no effect on code generation other than to change the default extension of the source module, and to make sure procedures of one language aren't lumped into modules together with procedures of another language. It does, however, suggest some interesting future directions for the AppGen.

Two Important Symbols

The #PROCEDURE statement will enable you to create the procedure in the AppGen, which will ensure that it appears in the map and the project data. Everything else, however, must come from the statements following the #PROCEDURE statement.

You will need to make the name of the procedure appear in the module. The AppGen uses a multivalued symbol called %Procedure to contain the names of all procedures in the currently active application. As each procedure is generated, %Procedure is set to that procedure name. Another multivalued symbol, %ProcedureType, contains either the string FUNCTION, if the procedure returns a value, or PROCEDURE, if it does not return a value. The line

```
%Procedure %ProcedureType
```

will place the procedure name and type in your source code. Listing 18.1 shows a minimal procedure template.

Listing 18.1. A simple procedure template.

```
#TEMPLATE(CWBookChapter18,'CW Book Exercises')
#!-------------------------------------------------------------------------
#!
#!  Developing Applications with Clarion for Windows
#!
#!  This set of templates includes the following:
#!
#!  Template Type      Name                   Purpose
#!  ---------------------------------------------------------------------
#!  Procedure          CWBookErrorMgr         Display Error Messages
#!
```

continues

Listing 18.1. continued

```
#!-----------------------------------------------------------------------
#!
#PROCEDURE(CWBookErrorMgr,'Error Manager Procedure--CW Book')
#!
#DISPLAY('')
#DISPLAY('This procedure is based on the CWBookErrorMgr')
#DISPLAY('procedure template, from the book "Developing')
#DISPLAY('Applications with Clarion for Windows"')
%Procedure %ProcedureType
  CODE
  RETURN
#!-----------------------------------------------------------------------
```

Note the addition of a CODE statement to make this a valid procedure, and of a RETURN statement. The RETURN statement is not technically required but is helpful.

Type in Listing 18.1 (or obtain it from the \CHAP18 directory on the sample disk) and save it in your \CW\TEMPLATE directory as CWBOOK18.TPL. From the main menu, choose Setup|Template Registry, and register the template in the same way that you registered the CWBOOK17.TPL template in Chapter 17. Then create a small application using Quick Start (if you haven't done this before, see Chapter 6, "Quick Start: The Two-Minute Application")— this will be your test bed for the template.

With your test application loaded, choose Edit|Insert Procedure to create a new procedure. Call it ErrorManager, and choose as the type CWBookErrorMgr. It may be well down in the list, and it will be under the Class heading CWBookChapter18. You may want to collapse the Class Clarion list to better see your own procedure types. The Procedure Properties window for the ErrorManager procedure is shown in Figure 18.1.

FIGURE 18.1.

The Procedure Properties window for the ErrorManager procedure.

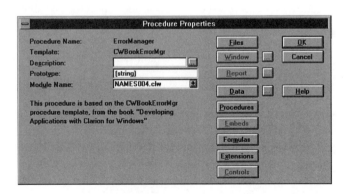

The interesting thing about this window is that it has a Prototype entry but no Parameters entry. This is an oversight in version 1.0, and as it only matters to template writers and is easily fixed, it isn't really a problem. But fix it you must, because if you enter a prototype, such as

(STRING), which indicates that you are passing in a string parameter, and you don't have a variable declared in the parameter list, such as (MyString), then you'll get compiler errors. You can solve the problem two ways—either by putting a prompt in the template or by specifying both the prototype and the parameters in the template, in which case the user can change neither.

A Parameters Prompt

To add a prompt for parameters, add the following line just above the first #DISPLAY statement:

```
#PROMPT('Parameter List',@s255),%ParameterList
```

Then add the %ParameterList symbol to the end of the %Procedure line so it looks like this:

```
%Procedure %ProcedureType%ParameterList
```

Your procedure template will now have the same functionality the standard CW procedure templates have. The prototype will appear in the map, and the parameter list in the procedure, and if the procedure returns a value, the %ProcedureType symbol will replace PROCEDURE with FUNCTION at code-generation time.

The problem with this approach arises when you want to always pass certain parameters to the procedure. You will then have to specify what those parameters should be (typically by using the #DISPLAY statement) and rely on the user to enter them correctly.

The *#PROTOTYPE* Statement

The second way to solve the procedure prototype problem is to hard code it into the template. The #PROTOTYPE statement will place a prototype you specify in the map and display it on the Procedure Properties window in place of the usual prototype entry. In the case of the ErrorManager procedure, you will be passing in a long variable and two optional variables of dynamic type (which will actually be strings but which are prototyped as dynamic parameters since you may want to change the length of those strings in the procedure). Replace the %ParameterList prompt with this line:

```
#PROTOTYPE('(long,<?>,<?>)')
```

and remove the %ParameterList symbol from the %Procedure line. Replace it with (ErrEvent,ErrTitle,MoreText). Your template should now be the same as the one shown in Listing 18.2.

Listing 18.2. The CWBookErrorMgr template with a hard-coded prototype and parameter list.

```
#TEMPLATE(CWBookChapter18,'CW Book Exercises')
#!---------------------------------------------------------------------
#!
#!  Developing Applications with Clarion for Windows
#!
#!  This set of templates includes the following:
```

continues

Listing 18.2. continued

```
#!
#! Template Type      Name                   Purpose
#! ------------------------------------------------------------------
#! Procedure          CWBookErrorMgr         Display Error Messages
#!
#!------------------------------------------------------------------
#!
#PROCEDURE(CWBookErrorMgr,'Error Manager Procedure--CW Book')
#!                   <?>,<?>
#PROTOTYPE('(long,*?,*?)')
#DISPLAY('')
#DISPLAY('This procedure is based on the CWBookErrorMgr')
#DISPLAY('procedure template, from the book "Developing')
#DISPLAY('Applications with Clarion for Windows"')
   CODE     %Procedure   %ProcedureType
   RETURN
#!------------------------------------------------------------------
```

Reopen your application and go to the ErrorManager Procedure Properties window, which is shown in Figure 18.2.

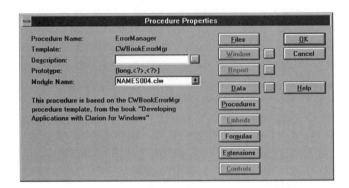

If you generate the code for that procedure, you will get something like Listing 18.3.

Listing 18.3. The code generated by the template in Listing 18.2.

```
MEMBER('NAMES.clw')           ! This is a MEMBER module
ErrorMgr PROCEDURE(ErrEvent,ErrTitle,MoreText)
   CODE
   RETURN
```

Manager

Obviously, this procedure doesn't do anything yet. It doesn't even make use of the passed variables. Add the code in Listing 18.4 to the template, just after the CODE statement and before the RETURN statement.

Listing 18.4. Source code to add to the `CWBookErrorMgr` procedure template.

```
IF OMITTED(2) THEN ErrTitle = 'Data File Problem!'.
IF INRANGE(ErrEvent ,1,100)
  IF MESSAGE('A File Processing Error Has Occurred' |
          & '<10,10>' & MoreText|
          & '<10,10>Error Code: ' & ERRORCODE()|
          & '<10>Error: ' & ERROR() ,|
          ErrTitle,|
          ICON:EXCLAMATION,|
          BUTTON:OK).
END
```

The template, with the addition of this code, will not look any different from the ProcProp window, but it will now generate some usable code, as shown in Listing 18.5.

Listing 18.5. The code generated by the `ErrorManager` procedure.

```
MEMBER('NAMES.clw')            ! This is a MEMBER module
ErrorMgr PROCEDURE(ErrEvent,ErrTitle,MoreText)

  CODE
  IF OMITTED(2) THEN ErrTitle = 'Data File Problem!'.
  IF INRANGE(ErrEvent ,1,100)
    IF MESSAGE('A File Processing Error Has Occurred' |
            & '<10,10>' & MoreText|
            & '<10,10>Error Code: ' & ERRORCODE()|
            & '<10>Error: ' & ERROR() ,|
            ErrTitle,|
            ICON:EXCLAMATION,|
            BUTTON:OK).
  END
  RETURN
```

Testing and Debugging Templates

As discussed in Chapter 17, it's always best when you're placing code in a template to have it thoroughly debugged beforehand. If you find yourself making changes after your code is already in a template, you can debug without cutting out the code, using it as source code somewhere else, and then pasting it back in.

When the Make window stops with a compile error, click on Edit Errors. You will get a dialog window that warns you that errors in embedded source code must be fixed in the application, not in the generated source code, as shown in Figure 18.3.

FIGURE 18.3.

The Edit Errors warning dialog box.

Clicking on OK at this message will take you to the generated source code. Correct the errors but *do not exit the source window.* Make (or Run) your application as you would normally from the application tree window, either by choosing Project|Make or Project|Run from the main menu, or by clicking the appropriate icon. Go through this process until you've solved your code problems, and then copy and paste the good code back into your template. Close the source window, close and reopen the application (to re-register the templates), and regenerate and compile your code to make sure everything now works properly.

Code Templates Redux—Calling the *ErrorManager* Procedure

Now that you have a working ErrorManager procedure, with a little modification you can use the code template you created in Chapter 17. This modified template is shown in Listing 18.6.

Listing 18.6. The code template used to call the ErrorManager procedure.

```
#CODE(CWBookCallErrorMgr,'Call the ErrorManager procedure')
#PROMPT('Auto Error Checking',CHECK),%AutoErrorCheck,DEFAULT(%True)
#BOXED('Custom Errors'),WHERE(%AutoErrorCheck=%False)
  #PROMPT('Error Number to Pass',@n4),%CustomError
#ENDBOXED
#PROMPT('Error Name',@s80),%ErrorName
#PROMPT('Additional Text',@s80),%AdditionalText
#IF(%AutoErrorCheck)
  IF ERRORCODE()
    ErrorManager(ERRORCODE(),'%ErrorName','%AdditionalText')
  END
#ELSE
    ErrorManager(%CustomError,'%ErrorName','%AdditionalText')
#ENDIF
```

When you insert this code template, you will see the window shown in Figure 18.4.

FIGURE 18.4.

The code template used to call the ErrorManager *procedure, set to trap standard errors.*

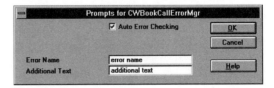

The default setting traps the standard Clarion error codes, using the ERRORCODE() function. The generated code looks (more or less) like this:

```
IF ERRORCODE()
     ErrorManager(ERRORCODE(),'Big Problem!','Call Tech Support')
END
```

If you uncheck this selection when viewing the Code Template Prompts window, the Error Number to Pass prompt appears, as shown in Figure 18.5.

FIGURE 18.5.

The code template used to call the ErrorManager *procedure, set to display existing errors.*

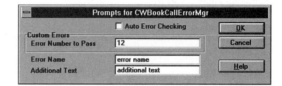

The generated code from this setting, without automatic checking for errors and using a custom error number, may look something like the following:

```
ErrorManager(0012,'Small Problem','Don''t Call Us, We''ll Call You')
```

As you can see, the more times you call this ErrorManager procedure, the more benefit you will get from placing all the duplicated code in one procedure.

Verifying the Existence of the *ErrorManager* Procedure

You've created your code template, and now you go to a new application and you want to use that code template. The only problem is that the code template requires that a specific procedure be present in your application. Leaving aside for now the pros and cons of duplicating procedures between applications (this topic is covered in some detail in Chapter 31, "Sharing Code: Source, OBJs, and LIBs"), it would be useful if the code template could determine if the required procedure already exists, and warn you if it doesn't.

Naturally, this is not only possible, but quite easy to do, and the template in Listing 18.7 demonstrates just how to do that.

Listing 18.7. The CWBookCallErrorMgr code template, with statements to check for the existence of a valid ErrorManager procedure.

```
#CODE(CWBookCallErrorMgr,'Call the ErrorManager procedure')
#PROMPT('Auto Error Checking',CHECK),%AutoErrorCheck,DEFAULT(%True)
#BOXED('Custom Errors'),WHERE(%AutoErrorCheck=%False)
  #PROMPT('Error Number to Pass',@n4),%CustomError
#ENDBOXED
#PROMPT('Error Name',@s80),%ErrorName
#PROMPT('Additional Text',@s80),%AdditionalText
#DECLARE(%ErrorMgrProcFound)
```

continues

Listing 18.7. continued

```
#SET(%ErrorMgrProcFound,%False)
#FOR(%Procedure)
  #IF(%ProcedureTemplate='CWBookErrorMgr')
    #IF(UPPER(%Procedure) = 'ERRORMANAGER')
      #SET(%ErrorMgrProcFound,%True)
      #BREAK
    #ENDIF
  #ENDIF
#ENDFOR
#IF(%ErrorMgrProcFound = %False)
#ERROR('The code template CWBookCallErrorMgr in the procedure '
➡& %Procedure & ' could not find an ErrorManager() procedure.')
#ERROR('Create the ErrorManager() procedure using the CWBookErrorMgr
➡procedure template.')
#END
#IF(%AutoErrorCheck)
  IF ERRORCODE()
    ErrorManager(ERRORCODE(),'%ErrorName','%AdditionalText')
  END
#ELSE
    ErrorManager(%CustomError,'%ErrorName','%AdditionalText')
#ENDIF
```

The part of this template that checks for the existence of the ErrorManager procedure is the
following:

```
#DECLARE(%ErrorMgrProcFound)
#SET(%ErrorMgrProcFound,%False)
#FOR(%Procedure)
  #IF(%ProcedureTemplate='CWBookErrorMgr')
    #IF(UPPER(%Procedure) = 'ERRORMANAGER')
      #SET(%ErrorMgrProcFound,%True)
      #BREAK
    #ENDIF
  #ENDIF
#ENDFOR
```

The #DECLARE statement simply declares a suitable variable for tracking whether the procedure
in question has been found, and the following #SET statement sets it to 0. The template language uses two built-in symbols for true/false checking—%False is 0, and %True is 1.

The #FOR loop processes the multivalue %Percent symbol, which contains the names of all the
procedures in the application. For each procedure name, the #IF statement that follows the
#FOR statement tests for a procedure with the correct template type, and if one is found, it makes
sure that it has the name the code template expects. Note the use of the UPPER function to ensure that the procedure will be found by name even if the case is different. You can use many
CW language expressions within the template language itself.

If a procedure of the correct type and name is found, the template sets the %ErrorMgrProcFound
variable to 1 (%True). The following code then determines which action to take depending on
the value of that variable:

```
#IF(%ErrorMgrProcFound = %False)
#ERROR('The code template CWBookCallErrorMgr in the procedure '
➥& %Procedure & ' could not find an ErrorManager() procedure.')
  #ERROR('Create the ErrorManager() procedure using the CWBookErrorMgr
➥procedure template.')
#END
```

The #ERROR statement presents an error message to the user at code-generation time and stops the compile process from going ahead automatically (although you can override this by simply doing a Make or Run following the errors). When displaying an error message, particularly in a code template, you should provide as much information to the user as possible about where the error occurred. In this case, the first #ERROR statement tells the user the name of the code template and the procedure (by way of the %Procedure symbol) where the error occurred. The second line contains additional information. In most cases it is preferable to have just one error message.

> **TIP**
>
> You may have noticed that although the template loops through the %Procedure symbol and breaks at the ErrorManager procedure, when the symbol is next used it correctly references the current procedure. Built-in multivalued symbols reset themselves outside loops. This means that you can safely loop through all procedures, and when you exit the loop you don't have to worry about resetting values. It also means that if you want to reference a symbol that is not the current value, and you want to do it outside the loop, you have to save it. You will frequently see the #SET statement used within loops to save a particular symbol value, and the #FIX statement used outside loops to set a multivalued symbol to the saved value.

Adding Data Files

Now that you have a working ErrorManager procedure template, you may want to log those errors to a file. You really have two options: You can use a predefined file to hold the error messages, in which case you might declare it local to the ErrorManager procedure, or you can allow the user to determine which file and fields to use. The former is a simple matter of hand coding, and while that's useful, it's not the subject of this chapter. The latter option means enhancing the procedure template, and that's where the good stuff is.

The Primary Attribute

The first change you'll need to make to the template is to add the Primary attribute to the #PROCEDURE declaration:

```
#PROCEDURE(CWBookErrorMgr,'Error Manager Procedure--CW Book'),PRIMARY('Error Log
➥File')
```

This requires the procedure to have at least one file in the file schematic. The message parameter will be displayed in the schematic as the file description, as shown in Figure 18.6.

FIGURE 18.6.

The File Schematic Definition window, showing the Primary file description.

The Field Attribute

Step 1 is picking a file to log the error information to, and Step 2 is choosing which fields in that file will contain the fields passed to the ErrorManager procedure. You do this using a special attribute in the #PROMPT statement, called Field:

```
#PROMPT('Field for Error Code:',FIELD),%ErrorCodeField
```

The Field attribute will place an ellipsis button next to the prompt entry. That button will take you to the Select New Field window, where you can access the fields in the file in which you have chosen to store the error information.

Add three additional prompts to cover the error description, the date and time of the error, and a bit of code to write the fields to the file, and your template should look like the one in Listing 18.8. The #BOXED statement has been used simply to improve the appearance of the window, and the Req attribute on the prompts forces the user to choose fields to use.

Listing 18.8. The CWBookErrorMgr procedure template, with prompts for file fields.

```
#PROCEDURE(CWBookErrorMgr,'Error Manager Procedure--CW Book')
➥,PRIMARY('Error Log File')
#!
#PROTOTYPE('(long,<<?>,<<?>)')
#DISPLAY('')
#DISPLAY('This procedure was created using a procedure template from')
#DISPLAY('"Developing Applications with Clarion for Windows"')
#DISPLAY('')
#BOXED('Log File Fields')
  #PROMPT('Field for Error Code:',FIELD),%ErrorCodeField,REQ
  #PROMPT('Field for Error Description:',FIELD),%ErrorDescField,REQ
```

```
  #PROMPT('Field for Date:',FIELD),%ErrorDateField,REQ
  #PROMPT('Field for Time:',FIELD),%ErrorTimeField,REQ
#ENDBOXED
%Procedure %ProcedureType(ErrEvent,ErrTitle,MoreText)
  CODE
  IF OMITTED(2) THEN ErrTitle = 'Data File Problem!'.
IF INRANGE(ErrEvent ,1,100)
    IF MESSAGE('A File Processing Error Has Occurred' |
              & '<10,10>' & MoreText|
              & '<10,10>Error Code: ' & ERRORCODE()|
              & '<10>Error: ' & ERROR() ,|
              ErrTitle,|
              ICON:EXCLAMATION,|
              BUTTON:OK).
  END
  %ErrorCodeField = ErrEvent
  %ErrorDescField = ErrTitle
  %ErrorDateField = TODAY()
  %ErrorTimeField = CLOCK()
  ADD(%File)
RETURN
```

You can create a suitable log file in your Data Dictionary, create (or update) an `ErrorManager` procedure in your app, and successfully generate your code. You may, however, not be able to compile yet without errors, and if you compile, the procedure will almost certainly not work as advertised. If it won't compile, it's because the application doesn't yet know about the file you've listed in the file schematic and hasn't included the declaration in global data. If it does compile, it's only because you have that file listed in another file schematic in your application. If it compiles but won't run properly, it's because you haven't included the standard template code used to open the file. That code is also dependent on the code used to tell the AppGen about the file(s) used by the procedure, and will be discussed shortly.

The *%FileControlInitialize* Group

Among the CW templates is one called FILECTRL.TPW, which contains a number of blocks of template code, each of which begins with a #GROUP statement. These code groups (which appear in other templates, as well) can be added to your code at any time with the #INSERT (*group*) statement.

The first of the groups you need to insert is `%FileControlInitialize`, as shown in Listing 18.9.

Listing 18.9. The `%FileControlInitialize` group from FILECTRL.TPW.

```
#GROUP(%FileControlInitialize)
#MESSAGE('Initializing File Control',3)
#IF(%Primary)
  #ADD(%ProcFilesUsed,%Primary)
#ENDIF
#FOR(%Secondary)
```

Listing 18.9. continued

```
  #ADD(%ProcFilesUsed,%Secondary)
#ENDFOR
#FOR(%OtherFiles)
  #ADD(%ProcFilesUsed,%OtherFiles)
#ENDFOR
```

This code looks through all the files listed in your file schematic (their names are stored in the %Primary, %Secondary, and %OtherFiles multivalued symbols) and adds them to the %ProcFilesUsed multivalued symbols.

The *%FileControlUpdate* Group

Once the used files are stored in the %ProcFilesUsed symbol, they must be added to the %ModuleFilesUsed multivalued symbol, and you do that by inserting the %FileControlUpdate group, as shown in Listing 18.10.

Listing 18.10. The %FileControlUpdate group from FILECTRL.TPW.

```
#GROUP(%FileControlUpdate)
#FOR(%ProcFilesUsed)
  #ADD(%ModuleFilesUsed,%ProcFilesUsed)
#ENDFOR
```

When you add these two groups to your template, just before the %Procedure %ProcedureType line, you will need to do it in the following format:

```
#INSERT(%FileControlInitialize(Clarion))
#INSERT(%FileControlUpdate(Clarion))
```

When you reference a group from one template class in another template class, you have to tell the AppGen which class it's coming from. In this case you are borrowing a group from the standard Clarion templates, so you must use the (Clarion) parameter. If you make modifications to the standard templates themselves, and use these groups, you will not need the parameter at all.

So far, so good. If you generate code at this point, you will find that your application is now aware of your ErrorManager files, and it ensures that they are declared in global data. Everything should compile properly, but you will not be able to write the record to the file if it isn't open. And the best way to open a file is to piggyback on the standard templates again.

The *%FileControlOpen* Group

The %FileControlOpen group in FILECTRL.TPW is the standard code group used by AppGen procedures to open any required files. (See Listing 18.11.) It consists of an instruction to the

AppGen to display a message while generating code, and insert another code group for each file to be opened.

Listing 18.11. The %FileControlOpen group from FILECTRL.TPW.

```
#GROUP(%FileControlOpen)
#MESSAGE('File Control Open Code',3)
#EMBED(%BeforeFileOpen,'Beginning of Procedure, Before Opening Files')
#FOR(%ProcFilesUsed)
#INSERT(%FileControlOpenFile,%ProcFilesUsed)
#ENDFOR
#EMBED(%AfterFileOpen,'Beginning of Procedure, After Opening Files')
```

The *%FileControlClose* Group

The %FileControlClose group in FILECTRL.TPW is the standard code group used by AppGen procedures to close any required files. (See Listing 18.12.) Like %FileControlOpen, it consists of an instruction to the AppGen to display a message while generating code and to insert another code group for each file to be closed.

Listing 18.12. The %FileControlClose group from FILECTRL.TPW.

```
#GROUP(%FileControlClose)
#MESSAGE('File Control Close Code',3)
#EMBED(%BeforeFileClose,'End of Procedure, Before Closing Files')
#FOR(%ProcFilesUsed)
#INSERT(%FileControlCloseFile,%ProcFilesUsed)
#ENDFOR
#EMBED(%AfterFileClose,'End of Procedure, After Closing Files')
```

To insert these groups in your code, you must again use the Clarion attribute since they belong to the Clarion template class.

Your template should now look like the one in Listing 18.13.

Listing 18.13. The CWBookErrorMgr procedure template with file control groups added.

```
#PROCEDURE(CWBookErrorMgr,'Error Manager Procedure--CW Book'),
➥PRIMARY('Error Log File')
#PROTOTYPE('(long,<<?>,<<?>)')
#DISPLAY('')
#DISPLAY('This procedure was created using a procedure template from')
#DISPLAY('"Developing Applications with Clarion for Windows"')
#DISPLAY('')
#BOXED('Log File Fields')
  #PROMPT('Field for Error Code:',FIELD),%ErrorCodeField,REQ
  #PROMPT('Field for Error Description:',FIELD),%ErrorDescField,REQ
  #PROMPT('Field for Date:',FIELD),%ErrorDateField,REQ
```

continues

Listing 18.13. continued

```
    #PROMPT('Field for Time:',FIELD),%ErrorTimeField,REQ
    #ENDBOXED
    #INSERT(%FileControlInitialize(Clarion))
    #INSERT(%FileControlUpdate(Clarion))
    %Procedure %ProcedureType(ErrEvent,ErrTitle,MoreText)
      CODE
      #INSERT(%FileControlOpen(Clarion))
      IF OMITTED(2) THEN ErrTitle = 'Data File Problem!'.
      IF INRANGE(ErrEvent ,1,100)
        IF MESSAGE('A File Processing Error Has Occurred' |
                & '<10,10>' & MoreText|
                & '<10,10>Error Code: ' & ERRORCODE()|
                & '<10>Error: ' & ERROR() ,|
                ErrTitle,|
                ICON:EXCLAMATION,|
                BUTTON:OK).
      END
      %ErrorCodeField = ErrEvent
      %ErrorDescField = ErrTitle
      %ErrorDateField = TODAY()
      %ErrorTimeField = CLOCK()
      ADD(%File)
      #INSERT(%FileControlClose(Clarion))
      RETURN
```

The code generated by this procedure template, using a log file called ERRLOG, is shown in Listing 18.14.

Listing 18.14. The generated code from the CWBookErrorMgr procedure template.

```
MEMBER('NAMES.clw')          ! This is a MEMBER module
ErrorManager PROCEDURE(ErrEvent,ErrTitle,MoreText)
  CODE
  IF ErrLog::Used = 0
    CheckOpen(ErrLog,1)
  END
  ErrLog::Used += 1
  IF OMITTED(2) THEN ErrTitle = 'Data File Problem!'.
  IF INRANGE(ErrEvent ,1,100)
    IF MESSAGE('A File Processing Error Has Occurred' |
            & '<10,10>' & MoreText|
            & '<10,10>Error Code: ' & ERRORCODE()|
            & '<10>Error: ' & ERROR() ,|
            ErrTitle,|
            ICON:EXCLAMATION,|
            BUTTON:OK).
  END
  ERR:code = ErrEvent
  ERR:description = ErrTitle
  ERR:date = TODAY()
  ERR:time = CLOCK()
  ADD(ErrLog)
```

```
ErrLog::Used -= 1
IF ErrLog::Used = 0 THEN CLOSE(ErrLog).
RETURN
```

As described in Chapter 17, the code in Listing 18.14 (and in earlier listings) uses the IF statement to discard the result of the MESSAGE() function, thereby preventing a compiler warning. The alternative to using IF is to use a variable of some kind to receive the value, and to use such a variable you will have to declare it either globally or locally.

Adding Local Data

You can add local data to a procedure in two ways. First, you can add it to the procedure's local data list, which is available to the user within the AppGen. You use #LOCALDATA and #ENDLOCALDATA statements to bracket the declarations you want to make, as follows:

```
#LOCALDATA
L:JUNK        USHORT
#ENDLOCALDATA
```

The #LOCALDATA declarations appear before the %Procedure declaration in the template. In order for these declarations to make their way into generated code, you must include the following code after the %Procedure declaration and before the CODE statement:

```
#FOR(%LocalData)
%[20]LocalData %LocalDataStatement
#ENDFOR
```

> **TIP**
>
> The bracketed numbers after the leading percent sign are a tab indicator. The next symbol will begin at the 20th character position on the line, if possible. This makes it easy to line up your code. This kind of formatting information is used extensively in the templates.

If you want to use data in your procedure and not have it visible to the AppGen, simply declare it as you would in any procedure, making sure to place your declarations between the %Procedure declaration and the CODE statement.

Adding Embed Points

You can, if you wish, add your own embed points to your procedures (as you can to any of the standard templates). The #EMBED statement, in its simplest form, uses the following format:

```
#EMBED( identifier, descriptor )
```

For example, to add an embed point at the beginning of the `CWBookErrorMgr` procedure template, you might place something like the following right after the `CODE` statement:

```
#EMBED(%ProcedureSetup,'Procedure Setup')
```

When you next reference a procedure that uses the template, you will see that one embed point listed in the procedure embed window.

Summary

Procedure templates are another one of the template language's powerful features. The example in this chapter is a fairly simple one, but even the statements and approaches discussed here can be used to accomplish complex tasks in short order. In particular, procedure templates are suited to those situations in which a code template would introduce too much repetitive code, and the design of the procedure itself is too dynamic for it to be placed in a LIB or DLL, as discussed in Chapter 31 and Chapter 32, "Sharing Code: Creating Clarion DLLs."

Procedure templates, whether they are standard issue or custom creations, usually do most of their work in conjunction with control templates, and that is the subject of Chapter 19, "Creating Control Templates."

19

Creating Control Templates

As earlier chapters have shown, the Clarion for Windows template language is a powerful tool for automating the job of writing code. By writing code templates (as discussed in Chapter 17, "Creating Code Templates"), you can not only reuse source code fragments, but you can easily tailor those fragments to the varying needs of your applications. It's a relatively short step from creating code templates to writing base procedure templates (as discussed in Chapter 18, "Creating Procedure Templates"). While both of these template types are vital to CW, neither really addresses the issue of collecting information from the user, or presenting it to the user. Control templates fill that gap.

A control template is a template that populates your window (or report) with one or more Windows controls. You don't have to use a control template to place a control on a window. If you open the Window Formatter and simply place, say, a button control using the Toolbox, you have not invoked any control templates.

Control templates provide enhanced functionality to the standard (and VBX) controls. They are like control wrappers. You can use them to populate multiple controls in particular positions, attach code to various points in whichever procedure they are being used, and even specify particular files, fields, or other application elements to be used with the control(s).

A Simple Control Template

The control template in Listing 19.1 is just about the simplest control template imaginable. The listing also contains a template header, and must be registered as its own template class.

Listing 19.1. A template class containing a very simple control template.

```
#TEMPLATE(CWBookChapter19,'CW Book Exercises')
#!---------------------------------------------------------------------------
#!
#!   Developing Applications with Clarion for Windows
#!
#!   This set of templates includes the following:
#!
#!   Template Type     Name                     Purpose
#!   --------------------------------------------------------------------
#!   Control           CWBookSimpleControl      Place a Button on the Window
#!
#!---------------------------------------------------------------------------
#!
#CONTROL(CWBookSimpleControl,'A Simple Control Template')
  CONTROLS
    BUTTON
  END
```

The distinguishing characteristic of a control template is the #CONTROL statement. Like the #PROCEDURE and #CODE statements, it takes two parameters: a label and a description.

The Control List

The beginning of the list of controls is marked by the CONTROLS keyword, and the end by the END statement. Although this example uses only one control—a button—there can be any number of controls here of any type.

Register the template in Listing 19.1 and create a small application with at least one procedure. (If you're not familiar with creating applications quickly, see Chapter 6, "Quick Start: The Two-Minute Application"). It doesn't matter which kind of procedure you use as long as you can place a button on it.

Go to the Procedure window and choose Populate|Control Template, or click on the TPL icon on the toolbox. From the class CWBookChapter19 choose the CWBookSimpleControl template. The cursor will turn into a cross-hair Populate cursor. Click somewhere on the window. A button will appear on the window, much as if you'd placed it using the Toolbox, except that it has no attributes of any kind, whereas the toolbox normally provides some defaults. You can provide the defaults also. Change the BUTTON declaration so that it conforms to Listing 19.2.

Listing 19.2. The simple control template with defaults.

```
#CONTROL(CWBookSimpleControl,'A Simple Control Template')
   CONTROLS
     BUTTON('A Button'),AT(,,50,14),USE(?AButton)
   END
```

When you populate this control on the window, several things will be different. First, the button now has some text associated with it. It also has several of its AT() parameters set, specifically length and height. The remaining parameters will be determined by where you place the control. The template also specifies the USE variable, and if it's reasonably distinctive there isn't too much likelihood it will cause a name collision with any other use variables on the window.

You can specify the actual position of the button if you wish. If you fill in the first two AT() parameters so the declaration looks something like BUTTON('A Button'),AT(1,1,50,14), the button will automatically appear at the specified location without any input from you, as soon as you select it from the list of control templates.

You can place more than one control at a time, if you wish. Listing 19.3 shows the code template modified to place four buttons.

Listing 19.3. The simple button template with four buttons.

```
#CONTROL(CWBookSimpleControl,'A Simple Control Template')
   CONTROLS
     BUTTON('A Button'),AT(,,50,14),USE(?AButton)
     BUTTON('Button #2'),AT(,,50,14),USE(?Button2)
     BUTTON('Button #3'),AT(,,50,14),USE(?Button3)
     BUTTON('Last Button'),AT(,,50,14),USE(?LastButton)
   END
```

When you place these buttons on the window, you are prompted each time for the button's location, which means that if you aren't careful you will probably end up with the mess shown in Figure 19.1.

FIGURE 19.1.

The result of letting the programmer decide where buttons go.

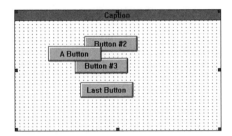

You probably don't like this arrangement, and you're going to learn how to avoid this in a moment, so go ahead and delete one of these controls. As you do, you will be asked if you want to remove the control template. If you answer yes, all the buttons in the control template will be deleted. You will then be asked if you want to delete any related controls. It doesn't matter what you say here, since there are no related control templates.

NOTE

It is possible to create a control template that requires another control template to already be populated on the window. For instance, there is a control template called BrowseSelectButton that only appears on the control template list if there is a browse box control on the window. If you place a BrowseSelectButton control and then delete the browse box control, answering yes to the query to delete related controls will automatically remove the BrowseSelectButton control as well. Control dependencies are established with the Req attribute. For more information, see the CW Help topic #CONTROL.

In the same way you specified where the individual control was to go, you can specify how a sequence of controls should be placed. All X and Y position AT() parameters, after the first control, are relative to the control just placed. To place the controls in a neat vertical row, separated by 5 DLUs, you would use the code in Listing 19.4.

Listing 19.4. Placing controls in a vertical row.

```
#CONTROL(CWBookSimpleControl,'A Simple Control Template')
  CONTROLS
    BUTTON('A Button'),AT(,,50,14),USE(?AButton)
    BUTTON('Button #2'),AT(0,19,50,14),USE(?Button2)
    BUTTON('Button #3'),AT(0,19,50,14),USE(?Button3)
    BUTTON('Last Button'),AT(0,19,50,14),USE(?LastButton)
  END
```

This results in a somewhat more orderly (and automatic) placement of controls, as shown in Figure 19.2. Note that an offset of 0 DLUs is specified rather than a missing parameter. If either of the first two parameters is missing, the window formatter will ask you to place the control.

FIGURE 19.2.

A vertical row of controls, automatically placed following the first control.

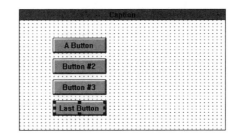

To place the controls in a neat little 2×2 grid, use Listing 19.5.

Listing 19.5. A simple control template.

```
#CONTROL(CWBookSimpleControl,'A Simple Control Template')
  CONTROLS
    BUTTON('A Button'),AT(,,50,14),USE(?AButton)
    BUTTON('Button #2'),AT(50,0,50,14),USE(?Button2)
    BUTTON('Button #3'),AT(-50,14,50,14),USE(?Button3)
    BUTTON('Last Button'),AT(50,0,50,14),USE(?LastButton)
  END
```

This ability to specify control locations is quite useful when you have a large number of controls to populate in a standard configuration. It is, however, only one of the many capabilities of control templates.

Some Control Template Examples

Clarion for Windows comes with a number of standard control templates for common situations. Since control templates can also place code statements at embed points, most of these go well beyond the simple placement of controls. They include the following:

- ASCIIBox—View an ASCII text file in a list box.
- ASCIIPrintButton—Print the contents of an ASCII box.
- ASCIISearchButton—Search for a string in an ASCII box.
- BrowseBox—Browse records from a data file, one page at a time.
- BrowseSelectButton—Select a record from a browse box.
- BrowseUpdateButtons—Update a record from a browse box.

- `CancelButton`—Cancel the current operation.
- `CloseButton`—Close the window.
- `DOSFileLookup`—Look up a DOS filename (using `FileDialog()`).
- `FieldLookupButton`—Trigger an entry control lookup.
- `FileDrop`—Load a file's records into a drop-down list box.
- `SaveButton`—Write a record to a data file.

As you can see, these control templates are used for more than just placing controls—they all have some effect on other processing. One of the simplest is the `Closebutton` template.

The *CloseButton* Control Template

The `CloseButton` control template presented in Listing 19.6 is used to place a Close button on any window. When the user selects the button, the window receives a `CloseWindow` event, which is the recommended way to terminate a procedure.

Listing 19.6. The `CloseButton` control template.

```
#CONTROL(CloseButton,'Close the Window'),WINDOW,HLP('~TPLControlCloseButton')
  CONTROLS
    BUTTON('Close'),USE(?Close)
  END
#ATSTART
  #DECLARE(%CloseControl)
  #FOR(%Control),WHERE(%ControlInstance=%ActiveTemplateInstance)
    #SET(%CloseControl,%Control)
  #ENDFOR
#ENDAT
#AT(%ControlEventHandling,%CloseControl,'Accepted')
LocalResponse = RequestCancelled
POST(Event:CloseWindow)
#ENDAT
```

The first part of the control template should look quite familiar. There is a #CONTROL statement, and a list of controls, in this case containing only a single button with the use variable ?Close. The rest of the code template can be divided into two sections. The first section begins with the #ATSTART statement and ends with #ENDAT:

```
#ATSTART
  #DECLARE(%CloseControl)
  #FOR(%Control),WHERE(%ControlInstance=%ActiveTemplateInstance)
    #SET(%CloseControl,%Control)
  #ENDFOR
#ENDAT
```

The #ATSTART statement is a template-processing instruction that indicates the next code is to be executed before actual code generation begins. Typically, template symbols that will be important to code generation are initialized here, and that is in fact just what happens.

The #DECLARE statement creates a symbol called %CloseControl, which will be used to store the Close button's internal identifier. That symbol is set in the #FOR loop that cycles through all the controls in the window, which are stored in the multivalued %Control symbol. You do not have to do anything to get %Control to contain the correct values—all that is handled automatically by the AppGen.

The #FOR loop is a bit of a special case. In order to set the %Control symbol to this particular button at generation time, you use a WHERE clause that compares two symbols, %ActiveTemplateInstance and %ControlInstance. The former is dependent on the procedure; the latter is dependent on the window. Because it is possible to have more than one window in a procedure, this code is required to make sure that the symbol is set to the correct value.

The final part of the control template is where the code is actually generated:

```
#AT(%ControlEventHandling,%CloseControl,'Accepted')
LocalResponse = RequestCancelled
POST(Event:CloseWindow)
#ENDAT
```

The #AT statement specifies an embed point called %ControlEventHandling, which you can find in the %StandardControlHandling group in STANDARD.TPW.

The second and third parameters of the #AT statement correspond to the symbols at the end of the #EMBED statement:

```
#EMBED(%ControlEventHandling,'Internal Control Event Handling'),
➥%Control,%ControlEvent,HIDE
```

In this case, the code following the #AT will be generated at the specified embed point for the Close button and the Accepted event. The generated code will look like this:

```
CASE FIELD()
  OF ?Close
    CASE EVENT()
    OF EVENT:Accepted       ← LocalResponse = RequestCancelled
      POST(Event:CloseWindow)
    END
  END
```

There is actually a bit of extra code generated by other templates, but this is the bit that gets put in because of the code template.

Much of the power of control templates comes from the #AT statement's ability to hook code into existing embed points. Once you combine that with the template language's flexibility in obtaining information from the user, control templates start to look quite powerful.

The *DOSFileLookup* Control Template

Listing 19.7 shows the DOSFileLookup control template from CODE.TPW. This template is used to prompt the user for a filename.

Listing 19.7. The DosFileLookup control template.

```
#CONTROL(DOSFileLookup,'Lookup a DOS file name'),WINDOW,
➥HLP('~TPLControlDOSFileLookup')
CONTROLS
                        BUTTON('...'),AT(,,12,12),USE(?LookupFile)
                    END

#BOXED('DOS File Lookup Prompts')
  #PROMPT('File Dialog Header:',@S60),%DOSFileDialogHeader,
➥REQ,DEFAULT('Choose a File')
#PROMPT('DOS FileName Variable:',FIELD),%DOSFileField,REQ
  #PROMPT('Default Directory:',@S80),%DOSInitialDirectory
  #PROMPT('Variable File Mask',CHECK),%DOSVariableMask
  #ENABLE(%DOSVariableMask)
    #PROMPT('Variable Mask Value:',FIELD),%DOSVariableMaskValue
  #ENDENABLE
  #ENABLE(NOT %DOSVariableMask)
    #PROMPT('File Mask Description:',@S40),%DOSMaskDesc,
➥REQ,DEFAULT('All Files')
#PROMPT('File Mask',@S12),%DOSMask,REQ,DEFAULT('*.*')
    #BUTTON('More File Masks'),MULTI(%DOSMoreMasks,%DOSMoreMaskDesc
➥& '--' & %DOSMoreMask)
#PROMPT('File Mask Description:',@S40),%DOSMoreMaskDesc,REQ
      #PROMPT('File Mask',@S12),%DOSMoreMask,REQ
    #ENDBUTTON
  #ENDENABLE
#ENDBOXED
#LOCALDATA
DOSDialogHeader       CSTRING(40)
DOSExtParameter       CSTRING(250)
DOSTargetVariable     CSTRING(80)
#ENDLOCALDATA
#ATSTART
  #DECLARE(%DOSExtensionParameter)
  #DECLARE(%DOSLookupControl)
  #FOR(%Control),WHERE(%ControlInstance = %ActiveTemplateInstance)
    #SET(%DOSLookupControl,%Control)
  #ENDFOR
  #IF(%DOSVariableMask)
    #SET(%DOSExtensionParameter,'!' & %DOSVariableMaskValue1)
  #ELSE
    #SET(%DOSExtensionParameter,%DOSMaskDesc & '¦' & %DOSMask)
    #FOR(%DOSMoreMasks)
      #SET(%DOSExtensionParameter,%DOSExtensionParameter & '¦'
➥& %DOSMoreMaskDesc & '¦' & %DOSMoreMask)
#ENDFOR
  #END
#ENDAT
#AT(%ControlEventHandling,%DOSLookupControl,'Accepted')
```

```
IF NOT %DOSFileField
  #INSERT(%StandardValueAssignment,'DOSTargetVariable',%DOSInitialDirectory)
ELSE
  DOSTargetVariable = %DOSFileField
END
#INSERT(%StandardValueAssignment,'DOSDialogHeader',%DOSFileDialogHeader)
#INSERT(%StandardValueAssignment,'DOSExtParameter',%DOSExtensionParameter)
IF FILEDIALOG(DOSDialogHeader,DOSTargetVariable,DOSExtParameter,0)
  %DOSFileField = DOSTargetVariable
  DO RefreshWindow
END
#ENDAT
```

To use the template, you would typically place an entry control on a form and then place the control template to the right of the entry. In this way the user can either fill in the filename or choose it from the standard Windows file dialog box, which is invoked from the DOSFileLookup control. Figure 19.3 shows one example of how this control can be used.

FIGURE 19.3.

The DOSFileLookup
control placed beside an
entry field.

If the user presses the lookup button (a button with an ellipsis is conventional for lookups), a standard File dialog window appears, as shown in Figure 19.4.

FIGURE 19.4.

The Windows File
dialog window.

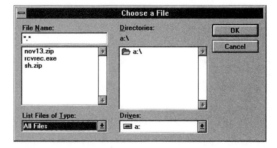

As long as the entry control and the File dialog window are using the same variable, the filename chosen by the user will appear in the entry. The control template provides prompts to set the name of the variable, as well as a number of other features.

In the Window Formatter, double-click on the DOSFileLookup control or choose the Actions menu item. The Prompts window shown in Figure 19.5 appears.

FIGURE 19.5.

The Prompts window for the DOSFileLookup *control template.*

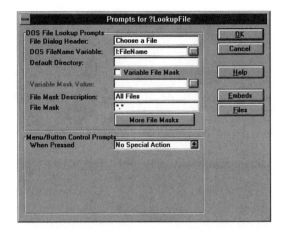

As with other templates, this one has recognizable sections. First come the #PROMPT statements, which collect information from the user about which options are to be used. Following the #PROMPT statements is the local data section. The four variables declared under #LOCALDATA will appear in the procedure's Data window, and are therefore available to the programmer.

> **TIP**
>
> If you want to use local variables in a control (or other) template, but you don't want them to be visible to the user, don't place them in #LOCALDATA. Instead, use the #AT statement to insert them in one of the procedure's data embed points. To place 1:MyVariable in the data section before the window declaration, you would use this code:
>
> ```
> #AT(%DataSectionBeforeWindow)
> 1:MyVariable      STRING(20)
> #ENDAT
> ```
>
> Don't rule out the benefits of making your data available to the user, however. Someone might want to write code that is dependent on your code, or reference those local variables from within the Window Formatter or Report Formatter.

The #ATSTART statement, as discussed earlier, indicates that the next code is to execute before code generation begins. In this case, the template needs to process the information collected from the user. Is this code going to use a variable for the file mask? Or will the file masks come from a list entered by the user from the Template Prompts window? Before the code to call FileDialog() can be written, the template has to determine the parameters.

The actual code that gets placed in your source file is typically the last part of the template. Here it amounts to only a few lines—a call to FileDialog(), the assignment of the returned value to a variable, and a call to the RefreshWindow routine.

The Standard File-Drop Template

One of the big differences between DOS and Windows programming is field validation. In a DOS program, particularly a Clarion for DOS program, lookups to verify that a field value exists in another file usually involve invoking a separate lookup procedure. While you can still do that in Windows, it's more common to use a drop-down list box (DDLB). (For more on DDLBs, see Chapter 5, "Unlearning DOS: Old Habits Die Hard.") The challenge is getting your data into this DDLB. As of version 1.0 of CW, simply placing a paged browse box with the drop attribute will not do the trick, since events are handled differently for DDLBs than for standard list boxes, and you will be unable to view more than the first page of data.

One approach to using a DDLB for field validation is demonstrated in the `FileDrop` control template, which ships with CW 1.0. This template is shown in Listing 19.8.

Listing 19.8. The `FileDrop` control template from CONTROL.TPW.

```
#CONTROL(FileDrop,'File-Loaded Drop Box'),
➥PRIMARY('File Loaded Drop Box',NOKEY),DESCRIPTION('File Loaded Drop Box on ' &
%Primary),WINDOW,MULTI,HLP('~TPLControlFileDrop')
  CONTROLS
    LIST,DROP(5),FROM('File¦Drop')
  END
#BOXED('File Drop Control Prompts')
  #PROMPT('Field to fill:',FIELD(%Primary)),%FillField
  #PROMPT('Default to first entry if USE variable empty',CHECK),
➥%DefaultFill,AT(10,,180)
#ENDBOXED
#ATSTART
  #INSERT(%FileControlInitialize)
  #DECLARE(%DropControl)
  #DECLARE(%DropQueue)
  #DECLARE(%LoadOrder)
  #DECLARE(%MemoPresent)
  #SET(%MemoPresent,%False)
  #FIX(%File,%Primary)
  #SET(%LoadOrder,%File)
  #FOR(%Key),WHERE(%KeyPrimary)
    #SET(%LoadOrder,%Key)
  #ENDFOR
  #FOR(%Field),WHERE(%FieldType='MEMO')
    #SET(%MemoPresent,%True)
    #BREAK
  #ENDFOR
  #DECLARE(%InstancePrefix)
  #SET(%InstancePrefix,'FLD' & %ActiveTemplateInstance & ':')
  #SET(%DropQueue,%InstancePrefix & ':Queue')
  #FOR(%Control),WHERE(%ControlInstance=%ActiveTemplateInstance)
    #SET(%DropControl,%Control)
  #ENDFOR
#ENDAT
#AT(%DataSectionBeforeWindow)
%[20]DropQueue QUEUE
```

continues

Listing 19.8. continued

```
    #FIND(%Field,%FillField)
    #SET(%ValueConstruct,%InstancePrefix & ':Value')
%[22]ValueConstruct STRING(SIZE(%Field))
%[20]Null END
    #SET(%ValueConstruct,%InstancePrefix & ':String')
%[22]ValueConstruct STRING(512)
    #SET(%ValueConstruct,%InstancePrefix & ':CurrentValue')
%[22]ValueConstruct STRING(SIZE(%Field))
#ENDAT
#AT(%BeforeAccept)
DO %InstancePrefix:FillList
#ENDAT
#AT(%WindowEventHandling,'GainFocus')
DO %InstancePrefix:FillList
#ENDAT
#AT(%ProcedureRoutines)
  #FIX(%Control,%DropControl)
%InstancePrefix:FillList ROUTINE
 !Control %Control
  %InstancePrefix:CurrentValue = %ControlUse
  %InstancePrefix:String = ''
  FREE(%DropQueue)
  SET(%LoadOrder)
  LOOP
    #IF(%MemoPresent)
    NOMEMO(%Primary)
    #ENDIF
    NEXT(%Primary)
    IF ERRORCODE() THEN BREAK.
    %InstancePrefix:Value = %FillField
    ADD(%DropQueue)
  END
  IF RECORDS(%DropQueue)
    SORT(%DropQueue,%InstancePrefix:Value)
    LOOP
      GET(%DropQueue,1)
      IF ERRORCODE() THEN BREAK.
      #IF(%DefaultFill)
      IF NOT %InstancePrefix:CurrentValue
        %InstancePrefix:CurrentValue = %InstancePrefix:Value
      END
      #ENDIF
      %InstancePrefix:String = CLIP(%InstancePrefix:String)
➥& '|' & %InstancePrefix:Value
DELETE(%DropQueue)
    END
    %InstancePrefix:String = SUB(%InstancePrefix:String,2,
➥LEN(%InstancePrefix:String)-1)
%Control{Prop:From} = %InstancePrefix:String
    %ControlUse = %InstancePrefix:Currentvalue
  ELSE
    %Control{Prop:From} = ''
    CLEAR(%ControlUse)
  END
#ENDAT
#!--------------------------------------------------------------
#CONTROL(FieldLookupButton,'Trigger an Entry Control Lookup'),
```

```
➥DESCRIPTION('Trigger an Entry Control
Lookup'),WINDOW,MULTI,HLP('~TPLControlFieldLookupButton')
    CONTROLS
      BUTTON('...'),AT(,,12,12),USE(?CallLookup)
    END
#BOXED('Field Lookup Button Prompts')
  #PROMPT('Control with lookup:',CONTROL),%ControlToLookup
#ENDBOXED
#ATSTART
  #DECLARE(%LookupControl)
  #FOR(%Control),WHERE(%ControlInstance=%ActiveTemplateInstance)
    #SET(%LookupControl,%Control)
  #ENDFOR
  #FIX(%Control,%ControlToLookup)
  #IF(%ControlType<>'ENTRY')
    #ERROR(%Procedure & 'Error: File Lookup needs to refer to Entry Control')
  #ENDIF
  #IF(NOT %PreLookupKey AND NOT %PostLookupKey)
    #ERROR(%Procedure & 'Error: File Lookup needs Entry Control to
➥perform a Pre or Post-Edit lookup')
  #ENDIF
#ENDAT
#AT(%ControlEventHandling,%LookupControl,'Accepted')
  #FIX(%Control,%ControlToLookup)
  #IF(NOT %PostLookupKey)
%PreLookupField = %ControlUse
GlobalRequest = SelectRecord
%PreLookupProcedure
LocalResponse = GlobalResponse
IF LocalResponse = RequestCompleted
  %ControlUse = %PreLookupField
  DISPLAY(%Control)
END
  #ELSE
%PostLookupField = %ControlUse
GlobalRequest = SelectRecord
%PostLookupProcedure
LocalResponse = GlobalResponse
IF LocalResponse = RequestCompleted
  %ControlUse = %PostLookupField
  DISPLAY(%Control)
END
  #ENDIF
ForceRefresh = True
LocalRequest = OriginalRequest
#ENDAT
```

In brief, this control template places a DDLB on the window and asks the user for the field from the associated file with which it is to populate the list box. It then declares some local data, including a queue and a few variables. The code it generates goes through a two-stage process to populate the list box. This code is executed whenever the window gains focus, so if you're in a multiple-document interface application and you've used another procedure to update the list of options to display in the DDLB, the changes will appear when you return to the window with the DDLB. All clear so far?

The first part of the DDLB populating process involves reading the file and placing records in the queue so they can be easily sorted in alphabetical order. Once this is done, the records in the queue are concatenated into a string, separated by vertical bars, like this:

```
'String1¦String2¦String3...'
```

List boxes can get their data either from a queue or from a string such as this one. The string, which for purposes of discussion is stored in a string called FLD5::String, is "attached" to the list box validating NAM:State, using the property syntax

```
?NAM:State{PROP:From} = FLD5::String
```

In the standard control template, the list box data string is 512 bytes. If the amount of data you have is small (and it ordinarily should be for a DDLB), this value will probably suffice. There may be situations, however, in which that's just not enough.

Another problem with this DDLB is that it contains only one column of data. While you may be validating only a single field, you might want to display additional information, such as a description of the item being chosen.

As you've probably guessed, there is another alternative to the standard DropList code template. In fact, there are as many as you can imagine, but only one is presented here. The remainder of this chapter looks at adapting the DropList control template to work directly from the queue and support multiple fields.

A True Populated DDLB Control Template

Listing 19.9 shows a modified drop box control template that improves on the standard DropList control template in several ways. Instead of loading values from a field into a 512-byte string, it loads them into a queue, which is limited in size only by available memory (although for practical purposes you probably will not want to use this approach with more than tens of or perhaps a few hundred records, due to the time required to load the queue). The template also allows you to place more than one field in the queue.

Listing 19.9. The CWBookFileDrop control template.

```
#CONTROL(CWBookFileDrop,'File-Loaded Drop Box from queue'),
➥PRIMARY('File Loaded Drop Box'),DESCRIPTION('File Loaded Drop Box on ' &
➥%Primary),WINDOW,MULTI
    CONTROLS
      LIST,DROP(5)
    END
#BOXED('File Drop Control Prompts')
  #PROMPT('Default to first entry if USE variable empty',CHECK),
➥%DefaultFill,AT(10,,180)
  #BUTTON('Range and Filter'),AT(10,,180),HLP('~TPLProcProcess')
    #PROMPT('&Record Filter:',@S255),%RecordFilter
    #ENABLE(%PrimaryKey),CLEAR
```

```
            #PROMPT('Range Limit &Field:',COMPONENT(%PrimaryKey)),%RangeField
        #ENDENABLE
        #ENABLE(%RangeField)
            #PROMPT('&Range Limit Value:',FIELD),%RangeLimit
        #ENDENABLE
    #ENDBUTTON
#ENDBOXED
#ATSTART
#INSERT(%FileControlInitialize(Clarion))
#DECLARE(%DropControl)
#DECLARE(%DropQueue)
#DECLARE(%LoadOrder)
#DECLARE(%MemoPresent)
#DECLARE(%QueueField),MULTI
#SET(%MemoPresent,%False)
#FIX(%File,%Primary)
#SET(%LoadOrder,%File)
#FOR(%Key),WHERE(%KeyPrimary)
  #SET(%LoadOrder,%Key)
#ENDFOR
#FOR(%Field),WHERE(%FieldType='MEMO')
  #SET(%MemoPresent,%True)
  #BREAK
#ENDFOR
#DECLARE(%InstancePrefix)
#SET(%InstancePrefix,'FLD' & %ActiveTemplateInstance & ':')
#SET(%DropQueue,%InstancePrefix & ':Queue')
#FOR(%Control),WHERE(%ControlInstance=%ActiveTemplateInstance)
  #SET(%DropControl,%Control)
  #FOR(%ControlField)
    #ADD(%QueueField,%ControlField)
  #ENDFOR
#ENDFOR
#SET(%DropQueue,%InstancePrefix & ':DropQueue')
#DECLARE(%FirstQueueField)
#ENDAT
#AT(%DataSectionBeforeWindow)
  #MESSAGE('BrowseBox Control Declarations',3)
%[20]DropQueue QUEUE                          #<! Browsing Queue
  #FOR(%QueueField)                           #! FOR each field in list
    #FIND(%Field,%QueueField)          #! FIND Field to control field
    #IF(%FieldType = 'GROUP')                 #! IF component is a group
%InstancePrefix:%[22]QueueField LIKE(%QueueField),PRE(%InstancePrefix)
➥#<! Queue Display field
    #ELSE                                     #! ELSE (component NOT a group)
%InstancePrefix:%[22]QueueField LIKE(%QueueField) #<! Queue Display field
    #ENDIF                                    #! END (IF component is a group)
  #ENDFOR                                     #! END (FOR each field in list)
%InstancePrefix:Ptr    LONG
                       END                    #<! END (Browsing Queue)
  #SELECT(%QueueField,1)
  #SET(%FirstQueueField,%QueueField)
  #FIND(%Field,%FirstQueueField)          #! FIND Field to control field
  #SET(%ValueConstruct,%InstancePrefix & ':CurrentValue')
  #IF(%FieldType = 'GROUP')                   #! IF component is a group
%[20]ValueConstruct LIKE(%FirstQueueField),PRE(%InstancePrefix)
➥#<! Queue Display field
```

continues

Listing 19.9. continued

```
 #ELSE                                      #! ELSE (component NOT a group)
%[20]ValueConstruct LIKE(%FirstQueueField) #<! Queue Display field
 #ENDIF                                     #! END (IF component is a group)
#ENDAT
#AT(%BeforeAccept)
DO %InstancePrefix:FillDropBox
#ENDAT
#AT(%WindowEventHandling,'GainFocus')
DO %InstancePrefix:FillDropBox
#ENDAT
#AT(%ControlEventHandling,%DropControl,'NewSelection')
  #FIX(%File,%Primary)
GET(%DropQueue,CHOICE(%DropControl))
GET(%File,%InstancePrefix:ptr)
#ENDAT
#AT(%ProcedureRoutines)
  #FIX(%Control,%DropControl)
%InstancePrefix:FillDropBox ROUTINE
  %InstancePrefix:CurrentValue = %ControlUse
  FREE(%DropQueue)
  #FIX(%File,%Primary)
  CLEAR(%FilePrefix:RECORD)
  #IF(%PrimaryKey)
    #FIX(%Key,%PrimaryKey)
    #IF(%RangeField)
  %RangeField = %RangeLimit
    #ENDIF
  SET(%Key,%Key)
  #ELSE
  SET(%File)
  #ENDIF
  LOOP
    #IF(%MemoPresent)
    NOMEMO(%Primary)
    #ENDIF
    NEXT(%File)
    IF ERRORCODE() THEN BREAK.
    #IF(%RangeField)
    IF %RangeField <> %RangeLimit THEN BREAK.
    #ENDIF
    #IF(%RecordFilter)
    IF NOT (%RecordFilter) THEN CYCLE.
    #ENDIF
    #FOR(%QueueField)                       #! FOR each field in list
      #FIND(%Field,%QueueField)             #! FIND Field to control field
    %InstancePrefix:%QueueField = %QueueField
    #ENDFOR                                 #! END (FOR each field in list)
    %InstancePrefix:Ptr = pointer(%File)
    ADD(%DropQueue)
  END
  IF RECORDS(%DropQueue)
    SORT(%DropQueue,%InstancePrefix:%FirstQueueField)
    GET(%DropQueue,1)
    GET(%File,%InstancePrefix:ptr)
  END
  %Control{PROP:From} = %DropQueue
```

```
  #IF(%DefaultFill)
  IF NOT %InstancePrefix:CurrentValue
    %InstancePrefix:CurrentValue = %InstancePrefix:%FirstQueueField
    %ControlUse = %InstancePrefix:CurrentValue
  ELSE
    %InstancePrefix:%FirstQueueField = %InstancePrefix:CurrentValue
    GET(%DropQueue,%InstancePrefix:%FirstQueueField)
    IF NOT ERRORCODE()
      GET(%File,%InstancePrefix:ptr)
    ELSE
      CLEAR(%FilePrefix:Record)
    END
  END
  #ENDIF
#ENDAT
```

Theory of Operation

Like the `FileDrop` template, this template creates a queue; but instead of a simple one-field queue, this one is a (potentially) multifield queue.

You populate the list box exactly the same way you populate ordinary browse boxes—using the Populate feature. You will also need to select a file and the key order in which to display records. All this is done in the List Box Formatter.

Each time you populate a field onto the list box, a `%ControlField` record, linked to the control's instance, is automatically created by the AppGen for that field. When you finish populating the list box and generate the code, the template first sets a `%DropQueue` variable to a unique value based on the current instance, then loops through all the `%ControlField` records for the control and adds them to a temporary symbol called `%QueueField`.

Next, these `%QueueField` records are used to build a queue declaration that will hold the data from the fields you select in the List Box Formatter. Listing 19.10 shows the complete process of determining the fields and building the queue. Note that the first field in the queue is always assumed to be the one the user will load into the drop box's use variable, and so it is obtained after the queue is declared and is used to create the variable to hold the current value of the list box.

Listing 19.10. Template code to declare the queue(s).

```
#SET(%InstancePrefix,'FLD' & %ActiveTemplateInstance & ':')
#SET(%DropQueue,%InstancePrefix & ':Queue')
#FOR(%Control),WHERE(%ControlInstance=%ActiveTemplateInstance)
  #SET(%DropControl,%Control)
  #FOR(%ControlField)
    #ADD(%QueueField,%ControlField)
  #ENDFOR
#ENDFOR
#SET(%DropQueue,%InstancePrefix & ':DropQueue')
```

continues

Listing 19.10. continued

```
#DECLARE(%FirstQueueField)
#ENDAT
#AT(%DataSectionBeforeWindow)
  #MESSAGE('BrowseBox Control Declarations',3)
%[20]DropQueue QUEUE                        #<! Browsing Queue
  #FOR(%QueueField)                         #! FOR each field in list
    #FIND(%Field,%QueueField)               #! FIND Field to control field
    #IF(%FieldType = 'GROUP')               #! IF component is a group
%InstancePrefix:%[22]QueueField LIKE(%QueueField),PRE(%InstancePrefix)
➥#<! Queue Display field
    #ELSE                                   #! ELSE (component NOT a group)
%InstancePrefix:%[22]QueueField LIKE(%QueueField) #<! Queue Display field
    #ENDIF                                  #! END (IF component is a group)
  #ENDFOR                                   #! END (FOR each field in list)
%InstancePrefix:Ptr    LONG
                   END                      #<! END (Browsing Queue)
  #SELECT(%QueueField,1)
  #SET(%FirstQueueField,%QueueField)
  #FIND(%Field,%FirstQueueField)            #! FIND Field to control field
  #SET(%ValueConstruct,%InstancePrefix & ':CurrentValue')
  #IF(%FieldType = 'GROUP')                 #! IF component is a group
%[20]ValueConstruct LIKE(%FirstQueueField),PRE(%InstancePrefix) #<! Queue Display
➥field
    #ELSE                                   #! ELSE (component NOT a group)
%[20]ValueConstruct LIKE(%FirstQueueField)  #<! Queue Display field
    #ENDIF                                  #! END (IF component is a group)
#ENDAT
```

You can use the List Box Formatter to set the appearance of the fields in the list box (in its dropped-down mode only). If you do not explicitly format the appearance of the list box, the fields in the queue will be shown in columns, with no headings or special formatting.

The CWBookFileDrop template also allows you to specify a range and filter for the chosen file. The code to accomplish this is fairly straightforward and uses #PROMPT and #ENABLE statements in ways already described.

The CWBookFileDrop template will generate code that looks something like that in Listings 19.11 and 19.12.

Listing 19.11. Data declarations generated by the CWBookFileDrop template.

```
FLD1::DropQueue    QUEUE                      ! Browsing Queue
FLD1::NAM:name                LIKE(NAM:name)      ! Queue Display field
FLD1::NAM:address             LIKE(NAM:address)   ! Queue Display field
FLD1::NAM:city                LIKE(NAM:city)      ! Queue Display field
FLD1::Ptr                     LONG
                   END                         ! END (Browsing Queue)
```

Listing 19.12. The routine code generated by the `CWBookFileDrop` template.

```
FLD1::FillDropBox ROUTINE
  FLD1::CurrentValue = loc:name
  FREE(FLD1::DropQueue)
  CLEAR(NAM:RECORD)
  SET(NAM:Key_name,NAM:Key_name)
  LOOP
    NEXT(name)
    IF ERRORCODE() THEN BREAK.
    IF NOT (upper(sub(nam:name,1,1)) = 'D') THEN CYCLE.
    FLD1::NAM:name   = NAM:name
    FLD1::NAM:address  = NAM:address
    FLD1::NAM:city  = NAM:city
    FLD1::Ptr = pointer(name)
    ADD(FLD1::DropQueue)
  END
  IF RECORDS(FLD1::DropQueue)
    SORT(FLD1::DropQueue,FLD1::NAM:name)
    GET(FLD1::DropQueue,1)
    GET(name,FLD1::ptr)
  END
  ?loc:name{PROP:From} = FLD1::DropQueue
```

Additionally, a call to the `FileDropBox` routine gets added both on an `Event:GainFocus` and when the window first opens. This is clearly one case where the generated code looks like a lot less bother than the template itself. Of course, the more times you use the template, the more you begin to realize the benefit of placing the code in a template.

Disadvantages

Although this drop list template offers some features not found in the standard drop list template, it still doesn't address the problem of large files that might take too long to load into memory. With these you are probably better off using a standard lookup procedure. If you're thinking about using a browse box template with a drop attribute to get around this problem, think again. In CW version 1.0, events are handled differently once a drop attribute is added to a list box, and you will not be able to page through your data unless you write additional code to do the paging.

Summary

Control templates bridge the gap between code templates and procedure templates. They are like wrappers for controls, associating particular functionality with the control or controls and permitting you to place multiple controls on the window at one time. Although you do not need to use control templates to place controls, they can save you writing a lot of repetitive control-related code.

20

Creating Extension Templates

Extension templates bear a resemblance to code templates. Like code templates, you use them to insert code at particular places in a procedure (or the program section). You can also use them to associate code with specific controls, although the official description of extension templates points out that this is not their real purpose.

Rather, extension templates are one-stop shopping for added functionality not (usually) related to any one control. They can intelligently insert code at various points within your procedure or application global area, whereas code templates often insert code at only one point. If you find yourself using several code templates to accomplish one task, chances are you can do the job better with an extension template.

> **TIP**
>
> If the extension code is designed to work with a particular control, it might be better if you incorporate that functionality, along with the control, into a control template.

Flavor of the Month

Extension templates come in two basic flavors: procedure and application. You load application extension templates from the Extensions button on the application's Global Properties window, and you load procedure extension templates from the Procedure Properties window. The two types have, for the most part, separate scope. That is, application extensions aren't used to generate code in procedures, and procedure extensions aren't (usually) used to generate code in the application's program section. Application extension templates ordinarily don't intrude on procedure functionality, and procedure functions seldom change any global code or data.

This chapter primarily discusses procedure extension templates, including the `DateTimeDisplay` extension template that is provided with CW 1.0, and two sets of custom extension templates, which are included on the disk accompanying this book. The first custom example, `CWBookDragAndDrop`, demonstrates adding drag and drop processing to a procedure, as discussed in Chapter 23, "Using Drag and Drop."

The second custom example uses a combination of a procedure extension, an application extension, and code templates to implement the complex thread management approach described in Chapter 28, "Multithreading and Thread Management."

The template language basics have already been covered, so this chapter discusses only features of special interest.

The *DateTimeDisplay* Extension Template

You can find the DateTimeDisplay procedure extension template in the EXTENS.TPW file in your CW\TEMPLATE directory. Its purpose is to add the display of the current date and/or time to the status bar of any procedure. You'll commonly use this on the application's main menu, which will probably be a frame-type procedure. Listing 20.1 shows the complete template extension.

Listing 20.1. The DateTimeDisplay procedure extension template.

```
#!--------------------------------------------------------------------------------
#EXTENSION(DateTimeDisplay,'Display the date and/or time in the current
➥window'),HLP('~TPLExtensionDateTimeDisplay'),PROCEDURE,LAST
#BUTTON('Date and Time Display'),AT(10,,180),
➥HLP('~TPLExtensionDateTimeDisplay')
#BOXED('Date Display...')
    #PROMPT('Display the current day/date in the window',CHECK),
➥%DisplayDate,DEFAULT(0),AT(10,,150)
    #ENABLE(%DisplayDate)
        #PROMPT('Date Picture:',DROP('October 31, 1959|OCT 31,1959|10/31/59
➥|10/31/1959|31 OCT 59|31 OCT 1959|31/10/59|31/10/1959|Other')),
➥%DatePicture,DEFAULT('October 31, 1959')
        #ENABLE(%DatePicture = 'Other')
            #PROMPT('Other Date Picture:',@S20),%OtherDatePicture,REQ
        #ENDENABLE
        #PROMPT('Show the day of the week before the date',CHECK)
➥,%ShowDayOfWeek,DEFAULT(1),AT(10,,150)
        #PROMPT('&Location of Date Display:',DROP('Control|Status Bar')),
➥%DateDisplayLocation
        #ENABLE(%DateDisplayLocation='Status Bar')
            #PROMPT('Status Bar Section:',@n1),%DateStatusSection,REQ,DEFAULT(1)
        #ENDENABLE
        #ENABLE(%DateDisplayLocation='Control')
            #PROMPT('Date Display Control:',CONTROL),%DateControl,REQ
        #ENDENABLE
    #ENDENABLE
#ENDBOXED
#BOXED('Time Display...')
    #PROMPT('Display the current time in the window',CHECK),%DisplayTime,
➥DEFAULT(0),AT(10,,150)
    #ENABLE(%DisplayTime)
        #PROMPT('Time Picture:',DROP('5:30PM|5:30:00PM|17:30|17:30:00|1730|
➥173000|Other')),%TimePicture,
DEFAULT('5:30PM')
        #ENABLE(%TimePicture = 'Other')
            #PROMPT('Other Time Picture:',@S20),%OtherTimePicture,REQ
        #ENDENABLE
        #PROMPT('&Location of Time Display:',DROP('Control|Status Bar')),
➥%TimeDisplayLocation
        #ENABLE(%TimeDisplayLocation='Status Bar')
            #PROMPT('Status Bar Section:',@n1),%TimeStatusSection,REQ,DEFAULT(2)
        #ENDENABLE
        #ENABLE(%TimeDisplayLocation='Control')
```

continues

Listing 20.1. continued

```
          #PROMPT('Time Display Control:',CONTROL),%TimeControl,REQ
        #ENDENABLE
      #ENDENABLE
    #ENDBOXED
  #ENDBUTTON
#ATSTART
  #DECLARE(%TimerEventGenerated)
  #IF(%DisplayDate)
    #DECLARE(%DateUsePicture)
    #CASE(%DatePicture)
    #OF('10/31/59')
      #SET(%DateUsePicture,'@D1')
    #OF('10/31/1959')
      #SET(%DateUsePicture,'@D2')
    #OF('OCT 31,1959')
      #SET(%DateUsePicture,'@D3')
    #OF('October 31, 1959')
      #SET(%DateUsePicture,'@D4')
    #OF('31/10/59')
      #SET(%DateUsePicture,'@D5')
    #OF('31/10/1959')
      #SET(%DateUsePicture,'@D6')
    #OF('31 OCT 59')
      #SET(%DateUsePicture,'@D7')
    #OF('31 OCT 1959')
      #SET(%DateUsePicture,'@D8')
    #OF('Other')
      #SET(%DateUsePicture,%OtherDatePicture)
    #ENDCASE
  #ENDIF
  #IF(%DisplayTime)
    #DECLARE(%TimeUsePicture)
    #CASE(%TimePicture)
    #OF('17:30')
      #SET(%TimeUsePicture,'@T1')
    #OF('1730')
      #SET(%TimeUsePicture,'@T2')
    #OF('5:30PM')
      #SET(%TimeUsePicture,'@T3')
    #OF('17:30:00')
      #SET(%TimeUsePicture,'@T4')
    #OF('173000')
      #SET(%TimeUsePicture,'@T5')
    #OF('5:30:00PM')
      #SET(%TimeUsePicture,'@T6')
    #OF('Other')
      #SET(%TimeUsePicture,%OtherTimePicture)
    #ENDCASE
  #ENDIF
#ENDAT
#AT(%DataSectionBeforeWindow)
  #IF(%DisplayDate AND %ShowDayOfWeek)
DisplayDayString STRING('Sunday    Monday    Tuesday  Wednesday
➥Thursday Friday    Saturday ')
DisplayDayText   STRING(9),DIM(7),OVER(DisplayDayString)
  #ENDIF
```

```
#ENDAT
#AT(%BeforeAccept)
  #IF(%DisplayTime OR %DisplayDate)
IF NOT INRANGE(%Window{Prop:Timer},1,100)
  %Window{Prop:Timer} = 100
END
#INSERT(%DateTimeDisplayCode)
  #ENDIF
#ENDAT
#AT(%WindowEventHandling,'Timer')
  #SET(%TimerEventGenerated,%True)
  #IF(%DisplayDate OR %DisplayTime)
#INSERT(%DateTimeDisplayCode)
  #ENDIF
#ENDAT
#AT(%WindowOtherEventHandling)
  #IF(%DisplayDate OR %DisplayTime)
    #IF(NOT %TimerEventGenerated)
IF EVENT() = Event:Timer
  #INSERT(%DateTimeDisplayCode)
END
    #ENDIF
  #ENDIF
#ENDAT
#GROUP(%DateTimeDisplayCode)
  #IF(%DisplayDate)
    #IF(%ShowDayOfWeek)
      #CASE(%DateDisplayLocation)
      #OF('Control')
  %DateControl{Prop:Text} = CLIP(DisplayDayText[(TODAY()%%7)+1]) & ', ' &
➥FORMAT(TODAY(),%DateUsePicture)
  DISPLAY(%DateControl)
      #ELSE
  %Window{Prop:StatusText,%DateStatusSection} =
➥CLIP(DisplayDayText[(TODAY()%%7)+1]) & ', ' & FORMAT(TODAY(),%DateUsePicture)
      #ENDCASE
    #ELSE
      #CASE(%DateDisplayLocation)
      #OF('Control')
  %DateControl{Prop:Text} = FORMAT(TODAY(),%DateUsePicture)
  DISPLAY(%DateControl)
      #ELSE
  %Window{Prop:StatusText,%DateStatusSection} =
➥FORMAT(TODAY(),%DateUsePicture)
      #ENDCASE
    #ENDIF
  #ENDIF
  #IF(%DisplayTime)
    #CASE(%TimeDisplayLocation)
    #OF('Control')
  %TimeControl{Prop:Text} = FORMAT(CLOCK(),%TimeUsePicture)
  DISPLAY(%TimeControl)
    #ELSE
  %Window{Prop:StatusText,%TimeStatusSection} =
➥FORMAT(CLOCK(),%TimeUsePicture)
    #ENDCASE
  #ENDIF
```

All extension templates begin with the #EXTENSION statement, which is similar in format to the #CODE, #CONTROL, and #PROCEDURE statements discussed in the preceding chapters.

To use this extension, go to the Main() procedure of a Quick Start application (if you're not familiar with using Quick Start to create applications, see Chapter 6, "Quick Start: The Two-Minute Application"). Quick Start applications actually use this extension by default, so when you select Extensions from the Procedure Properties window you'll see that this extension is already on the list.

> **NOTE**
>
> If you're using an application that doesn't have the extension template loaded, click Add from the Edit Extensions window and choose DateTimeDisplay under Class Clarion.

Bring up the Properties window for the extension template. There's not much here, actually, except a button to display the rest of the settings. Click on it, and you'll see the window shown in Figure 20.1.

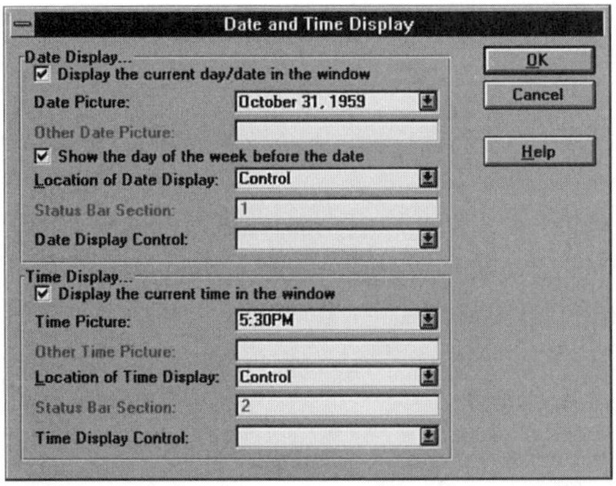

FIGURE 20.1.

The prompts for the DateTimeDisplay extension template.

Most of the #PROMPT logic should be familiar to you from the previous three chapters. Something you may not have noticed before is the CONTROL parameter on the #PROMPT statement:

```
#PROMPT('Time Display Control:',CONTROL),%TimeControl,REQ
```

This displays a list of equates for all controls on the windows, as shown in Figure 20.2.

FIGURE 20.2.

An equates list generated by the CONTROL *parameter.*

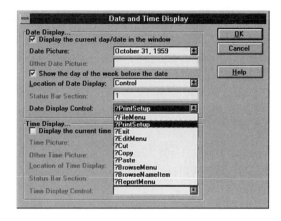

The code generation statements are much like those found in code templates. There is an #ATSTART...#ENDAT pair that denotes template code to execute before any CW source is generated; in this case it's used to translate the date/time strings chosen by the user into the standard date/time pictures about which the compiler knows.

Following this are a series of #AT...#ENDAT pairs that plug code into various embed points, including local data, before the ACCEPT() loop, at the timer event, and so on. Functionally, the template accomplishes the following changes to the procedure's source code:

■ Declares some local data for translating dates into actual days of the week (as needed).

■ Gives the window a Timer attribute (using the property syntax) if it doesn't already have one.

■ Inserts the date/time display code either at the window's timer event handling embed point, if the window already had a timer, or at Other Event Handling, if it had to assign a timer using the property syntax (the AppGen creates the timer embed point only if there is a Timer attribute on the window at generation time).

■ Creates date/time display code that conforms to the user's choice of where and what to display. Because this code is called more than once, it has been placed in a GROUP following the main body of the extension, where it can be referenced by a single call.

This is a pretty typical structure for a procedure extension. As with a lot of template coding, it's not the only possible alternative. If you regularly used a particular control to display dates and times, rather than either a control or the status bar, you could write a control template to accomplish much the same thing. Because this template has a broader application, it's designed as an extension.

The Drag and Drop Extension Template

The details of drag and drop processing are discussed in Chapter 23. The CWBookDragAndDrop template, found in CHAP23\CWBOOK23.TPL, is a companion piece that wraps the functionality described in that chapter into a single template extension that makes it easy to add drag and drop capabilities to any procedure.

The purpose of the template, as shown in Listing 20.2, is to write the repetitive drag and drop code and prompt the user only for the information that changes from one implementation to another.

Listing 20.2. The CWBookDragAndDrop extension template.

```
#EXTENSION(CWBookDragAndDrop,'Drag and Drop Processing'),MULTI,PROCEDURE
#PROMPT('Drag/Drop ID to use:',@s80),%DragDropID
#PROMPT('Enable Drag Control:',CHECK),%DragControlUsed,DEFAULT(1)
#BOXED('Drag Control Settings'),WHERE(%DragControlUsed=%True)
  #PROMPT('Drag Control Equate:',CONTROL),%DragFromControl,REQ
  #PROMPT('Data Transfer Method',
➥DROP('Set DropID()¦Copy to Clipboard¦Embedded Hand
➥Code')),%DragTransferMethod,DEFAULT('Set DropID()')
  #ENABLE(%DragTransferMethod = 'Set DropID()' OR
➥%TransferMethod = 'Copy to Clipboard')
    #PROMPT('Value to transfer:',@s255),%DragTransferValue,REQ
  #ENDENABLE
  #PROMPT('Edit Drag Embed Code',EMBEDBUTTON(%StoreDragDropDataToTransfer)),
➥AT(,,180,)
#ENDBOXED
#PROMPT('Enable Drop Control:',CHECK),%DropControlUsed,DEFAULT(1)
#BOXED('Drop Control Settings'),WHERE(%DropControlUsed=%True)
  #PROMPT('Drop Control Equate:',CONTROL),%DropToControl,REQ
  #PROMPT('Data Transfer Method',
➥DROP('Read DropID()¦Paste from Clipboard¦Embedded
➥Hand Code')),%DropTransferMethod,DEFAULT('Read DropID()')
  #ENABLE(%DropTransferMethod = 'Read DropID()' OR
➥%DropTransferMethod = 'Paste from Clipboard')
    #PROMPT('Copy value to:',FIELD),%ReceiveField,REQ
  #ENDENABLE
  #PROMPT('Edit Drop Embed Code',EMBEDBUTTON(%ReceiveDragDropData)),
➥AT(,,180,)
#ENDBOXED
#LOCALDATA
PropNdx      BYTE
#ENDLOCALDATA
#AT(%AfterWindowOpening)
  #IF(%DragControlUsed)
LOOP PropNdx = 1 TO 16
  IF %DragFromControl{prop:dragid,PropNdx} = ''
    %DragFromControl{prop:dragid,PropNdx} = '%DragDropID'
    BREAK
  END
```

```
END
  #ENDIF
  #IF(%DropControlUsed)
LOOP PropNdx = 1 TO 16
  IF %DropToControl{prop:dropid,PropNdx} = ''
    %DropToControl{prop:dropid,PropNdx} = '%DragDropID'
    BREAK
  END
END
  #ENDIF
#ENDAT
#AT(%ControlEventHandling,%DragFromControl,'Selected')
OF EVENT:DRAG
  ! FOR drag CONTROL %DragFromControl
  IF DRAGID()
  #EMBED(%StoreDragDropDataToTransfer,
➡'Store the drag/drop data to be transfered'),%Control
  #IF(%DragTransferMethod = 'Set DropID()')
    SETDROPID(%DragTransferValue)
  #ELSIF(%DragTransferMethod = 'Copy to Clipboard')
    SETCLIPBOARD(%DragTransferValue)
  #ENDIF
  END
#ENDAT
#AT(%ControlEventHandling,%DropToControl,'Selected')
OF EVENT:DROP
  ! for drop control %DropToControl
  #IF(%DropTransferMethod = 'Read DropID()')
  %ReceiveField = DROPID()
  #ELSIF(%DropTransferMethod = 'Paste from Clipboard')
  %ReceiveField = CLIPBOARD()
  #ENDIF
  #EMBED(%ReceiveDragDropData,'Receive the drag/drop data'),%Control
#ENDAT
```

When this template is loaded, the window shown in Figure 20.3 appears.

FIGURE 20.3.

The Prompts window for the CWBookDragAndDrop extension template.

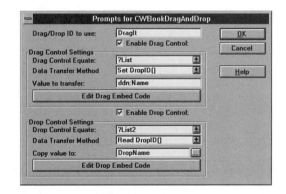

To use this template, you specify the unique Drag/Drop ID that connects the controls in the drag and drop operation. For both controls you specify which control to use, and the information transfer method. You also specify the value to be loaded from the Drag control, and the variable in which to load that value on the Drop side of the operation. All of this can be enhanced with embedded code. (For details on how drag and drop actually works, refer to Chapter 23.)

In addition to the usual business of prompting for user input and writing code at embed points, this extension template introduces two new embed points into the procedure by using the #EMBED statement. Code and control templates can do this, as well, using a statement similar to the one employed here:

```
#EMBED(%StoreDragDropDataToTransfer,
➥'Store the drag/drop data to be transfered'),%Control
```

In addition, by using either the EMBED or EMBEDBUTTON parameter on a #PROMPT, you can edit that embed point directly from the template. The only problem is that when you first enter the procedure and add the extension, the AppGen hasn't yet added the embed to its embed list, and the EMBEDBUTTON prompt in the Template Properties window is grayed out.

Consequently, there's one little trick to using this template. You have to exit to the application tree window, then re-enter the Procedure Properties window and go back to Extensions. At that point, the newly created embed points will be visible to the template, and they'll also show up in the list of embed points.

The Thread Management Templates

The thread management templates discussed here incorporate the complex thread management (CTM) code discussed in Chapter 28. As you may recall, the purpose of thread management is to give you programmatic control over the procedures you launch using the START() function.

CTM makes use of a library of functions to do things such as close threads that are related to a threaded procedure that is being shut down, or minimize one or more windows, or bring a window to the top whenever a user selects a menu item, rather than start another copy of that same procedure.

The first step in getting all this code into the templates, then, is grafting in the appropriate map and project data. This is one of the tasks application extension templates are designed to carry out.

The *CWBookTM_SetupThreadManager* Application Extension

Listing 20.3 shows an application-level extension that adds the CTM library prototypes to the application's map and adds the required LIB to the project. If you intend to supply toolkits to other developers who need them to use your own compiled source code, this is the recommended method because it does not require you to make any changes to the user's template set. Note that the #EXTENSION statement has an Application attribute. This tells the AppGen to display it in only the Global Extensions list. An extension may also have the Procedure attribute, in which case it is visible only in the Procedure Extensions lists.

> **WARNING**
>
> You must have CW 1.001 or later to use this kind of application extension. In CW 1.0, the extension would not add code to global embed points.

Listing 20.3. Using an application extension to add the CTM global data, map, and project information to an application.

```
#EXTENSION(CWBookTM_SetupThreadManager,'Thread Manager Map and Project
➥Additions'),APPLICATION
#DISPLAY('')
#DISPLAY('This extension adds the Thread Management DLL and ')
#DISPLAY('its function prototypes to your application. It is')
#DISPLAY('required for all the thread management functions')
#DISPLAY('')
#PROJECT('TM.LIB')                  adds it to the PROJECT
#AT(%GlobalMap)
MODULE('TM.LIB')        MAP belongs to the TM.DLL (cf TM.INC)
  TmCreate(LONG,STRING,<STRING>,<USHORT>,<STRING>),LONG
  TmDebug()
  TmDestroy(LONG),LONG
  TmDestroyGroup(<STRING>),LONG
  TmGetHWnd(LONG),USHORT
  TmGetId(STRING,<STRING>,<STRING>),LONG
  TmQuery(*QUEUE,<STRING>,<STRING>,<STRING>),LONG
END
#ENDAT
#AT(%GlobalData)
NIL                EQUATE('')                       !Program Equates
ONE                EQUATE(1)                        !One value
SPACE              EQUATE(' ')                      !Space
THIS               EQUATE(0)                        !Current Window
ZERO               EQUATE(0)                        !Zero value
EVENT:CloseQuery   EQUATE(402h)                     !Close and Query Event
gJunk              STRING(20)                       !Junk variable
gThreadNo          LONG,THREAD                      !Thread Number
QTM                QUEUE, PRE(QTM),EXTERNAL         !Thread Manager
➥Queue Definition
  Id                 LONG                           !  Thread Id
  Name               STRING(30)                     !  User Control Name
  Reference          STRING(80)                     !  Name Reference
  HWnd               USHORT                         !  Windows Window Handle
  GroupId            STRING(80)                     !  Thread Group Id
END
#ENDAT
```

The first statement after the extension declaration and the #DISPLAY statements is #PROJECT. This tells the AppGen to load the specified file into the project system. In this case, the LIB file that corresponds to the Thread Manager DLL is added.

Note the use of the %GlobalMap embed point to insert data. This embed location is the same one you see in the Global Properties Embed list. If you want to add data to the Global Data window so it will be available from AppGen pick lists, you should use #GLOBALDATA and #ENDGLOBALDATA instead of the embed point.

TIP

Using #GLOBALDATA and #ENDGLOBALDATA is a handy way to copy variables among applications. Create an application-level extension and enclose the data declarations you want to copy in #GLOBALDATA and #ENDGLOBALDATA. Declarations added to the data list are persistent, so you can load the extension and unload it, and the new variables will be in the list.

The *CWBookTM_ManageThread* Procedure Extension

This extension (shown in Listing 20.4) is one of two pieces of template code required to implement thread management. It's loaded for every procedure that needs to be handled by the thread management library (TM.DLL).

Listing 20.4. The CWBookTM_ManageThread procedure extension.

```
#EXTENSION(CWBookTM_ManageThread,'Manage this procedure with the
➥Thread Manager'),PROCEDURE
#BOXED('Thread Management')
  #DISPLAY('')
  #DISPLAY('This extension should be used for any procedure')
  #DISPLAY('that either STARTs a Thread Manager-monitored ')
  #DISPLAY('procedure (using the code template by that name)')
  #DISPLAY('or IS a Thread Manager-monitored procedure.')
  #DISPLAY('')
#ENDBOXED
#PROMPT('Auto-closed by Parent:',CHECK),%ClosedByParent,DEFAULT(%False)
#BOXED('Parent Group Name'),Where(%ClosedByParent)
  #DISPLAY('')
  #DISPLAY('Specify a text string that the parent procedure')
  #DISPLAY('can use to identify instances of this procedure.')
  #DISPLAY('This string must also be specified on the parent')
  #DISPLAY('procedure''s extension template in the "Child"')
  #DISPLAY('Group Name field')
  #DISPLAY('')
  #PROMPT('Parent Group Name:',@s40),%ParentGroupName,REQ
#ENDBOXED
```

```
#PROMPT('Auto-close Children',CHECK),%CloseChildren,DEFAULT(%False)
#BOXED('Child Group Name'),Where(%CloseChildren)
  #DISPLAY('')
  #DISPLAY('Specify the text string that identifies the ')
  #DISPLAY('instances of child procedures that are to be ')
  #DISPLAY('closed when this procedure closes. This string')
  #DISPLAY('must also be specified on the child procedure's')
  #DISPLAY('extension template in the "Parent Group Name" field')
  #DISPLAY('')
  #PROMPT('Child Group Name:',@s40),%ChildGroupName,REQ
#ENDBOXED
#!---------- procedure startup --------------------------------------------
#AT(%WindowEventHandling,'OpenWindow')
#IF(%ClosedByParent)
  gThreadNo=TMCreate(THIS{PROP:Thread},'%Procedure','%ProcedureDescription',¦
                THIS{PROP:Handle},'%ParentGroupName')
#ELSE
  gThreadNo=TMCreate(THIS{PROP:Thread},'%Procedure','%ProcedureDescription',¦
                THIS{PROP:Handle})
#ENDIF
#ENDAT
#!---------- iconize/restore ----------------------------------------------
#AT(%WindowOtherEventHandling)
CASE EVENT()
OF EVENT:Iconize
  THIS{PROP:Iconize} = TRUE
OF EVENT:Restore
  IF THIS{PROP:Iconize} = TRUE
    THIS{PROP:Iconize} = FALSE
    THIS{PROP:Active}  = TRUE
  ELSE
    THIS{PROP:Active}  = TRUE
  END
  POST(EVENT:Resume)
END
#ENDAT
#!---------- shutdown -----------------------------------------------------
#AT(%WindowEventHandling,'CloseWindow')
#ENDAT
#AT(%AfterFileClose)
  #IF(%CloseChildren)
gJunk = TMDestroyGroup('%ChildGroupName')
  #ENDIF
gJunk = TMDestroy(THIS{PROP:Thread})               !Destroy the logical Thread
#ENDAT
```

This extension adds three blocks of code to any procedure. First, when the procedure starts up, it registers the procedure name in the Thread Manager's internal thread queue, via the TMCreate() function.

The second block of code handles Iconize and Restore messages posted to the procedure by the Thread Manager. This code is inserted in the WindowOtherEventHandling embed point, because there are no default embeds for those events.

The final block of code is executed when the procedure shuts down. The call to TMDestroyGroup()
is made only if the user has designated this procedure as a parent with child procedures that
need to be shut down. It passes the child group name as a parameter to identify those procedures. Just before procedure shutdown, the TMDestroy() function is called with the current thread
ID as a parameter, thereby removing the current thread from the Thread Manager's queue.

One other template is part of this whole scheme, and it's used to initiate threads. It's a code
template, and although those are discussed in another chapter, its use here illustrates the different applications that the various kinds of templates have.

And Finally, Another Code Template

The remaining piece of this template set is a code template used to initiate new threads. You
use this in place of any of the standard methods of calling procedures. As you can surmise, an
extension template would be too awkward a way to start more than a single procedure, and
even that would be clumsy. The template is shown in Listing 20.5.

Listing 20.5. The `CWBookTM_InitiateThread` code template.

```
#CODE(CWBookTM_InitiateThread,'Start a Thread under Thread Manager Control')
#DISPLAY('This code template requires the application extension')
#DISPLAY('CWBookThreadManagerGlobal. For this procedure,')
#DISPLAY('specify how many copies of the procedure can be')
#DISPLAY('executed at one time. If the procedure is already ')
#DISPLAY('running and the maximum number of instances is')
#DISPLAY('reached, the Thread Manager will bring the first')
#DISPLAY('copy run to the foreground')
#DISPLAY('')
#PROMPT('Procedure to call:',PROCEDURE),%CalledProcedure
#PROMPT('Thread Stack:',SPIN(@n7,5000,64000,500)),%ThreadStack,DEFAULT(25000)
#PROMPT('Maximum instances:',SPIN(@n2,1,40,1)),%MaxInstances,DEFAULT(1)
FREE(QTM);CLEAR(QTM)
gJunk = TmQuery(QTM,'%CalledProcedure')
IF gJunk => %MaxInstances
  GET(QTM,1)
  POST(EVENT:Restore,,QTM:Id)
ELSE
  gJunk = START(%CalledProcedure,%ThreadStack)
END
FREE(QTM);CLEAR(QTM)
```

In addition to the usual thread-related information, this template collects one more parameter: the maximum number of instances of that procedure you can initiate using START(). It
uses the TMQuery() function to determine the number of copies that are already running, and
if the limit has been reached, it posts a Restore event to the procedure instead of starting it.
That code is inserted by the CWBookTM_ManageThread extension, and if you look at Listing 20.4
you'll notice that an EVENT:Restore causes the window to minimize and maximize. This has
the effect of bringing the window to the front if it was already maximized.

CWBOOK20.TPL contains several other code templates designed to make it easier to call functions in the Thread Manager. CWBookTM_ThreadDebugger calls the debugger procedure, CWBookTM_MaximizeAll posts Restore messages to all the managed procedures, and CWBookTM_Minimize posts Iconize messages to all the managed procedures. You can use these code templates at embed points on buttons or menu items.

Summary

Extension templates round out the basic set of template types available in CW 1.0. They are particularly well suited for third-party add-ons to the template set, particularly when the add-on requires the use of compiled source code and global data.

When you want to add functionality that isn't related to any one control, extension templates are a good choice. If you find yourself adding multiple code templates to accomplish one thing, chances are you can wrap them all up in an extension template.

This is the last of four chapters on writing templates. By now you should have a good idea of what code, control, procedure, and extension templates are, and where and when they are used. You've probably also realized that there's some blurring of the lines between these types; they share capabilities, and sometimes which one you use to get the job done is simply a matter of preference. This is a tribute to the remarkable flexibility of the template language.

If this chapter has whetted your appetite for template programming, be sure to read Chapter 21, "The AppGen: The Ultimate Hand Coding Tool."

21

The AppGen:
The Ultimate
Hand Coding Tool

The title of this chapter might sound like an oxymoron. Traditionally, application generation and hand coding have been seen as opposite ends of the pole. So why is Clarion for Windows any different from those other application development environments? How can you possibly consider it a hand coding tool? It all comes down to the template language.

Almost all of what the AppGen does is controlled by the templates. This means that in the templates you have access not just to a few default values or some code hooks, but you also have access to the appearance and behavior of the AppGen itself. And at this time, the main way you code templates is—you guessed it—by hand. If you're a skilled hand coder, you stand to benefit from the AppGen more than anyone else. Think of the template language as another programming language to learn. The only difference is that this one will enable you to write programs that write your programs for you.

If you like the idea of templates but don't care for the standard implementation, read on. This chapter will get you started in re-creating the AppGen to suit your own style.

Now You Can Clone Yourself

Learning how to write templates is a lot like cloning yourself, and how many times have you wished you could do that? You are probably aware that you spend a considerable amount of your programming time doing things that in one form or another you have done before. (If you don't, then there are a lot of people out there who would like to have your job.)

That repetitive code may be something as simple as an often-used function call, where four out of the five parameters are identical 98 percent of the time you call it. It might be something as complex as a browse engine that needs some minor customization for particular situations. It might be something as ordinary as writing field editing code.

Handling repetitive code is something at which the template language excels. As Chapter 17, "Creating Code Templates," suggests, you should never write any block of code more than twice. You write it the first time to make sure it works, and the second time you put it in a template. Depending on the nature of the template, that might be as simple as copying in the code. For more complex coding situations, as you have seen, the template language provides a wide range of user input and conditional code-generation options.

With the template language, there's no excuse for wasting time going over the same territory again and again. You write the code once, and you maintain it in one location. When you need to make a change to your applications, you let the AppGen do it. Code reuse is the most obvious benefit of using a template approach to programming.

Think More, Code Less

A second major benefit of the template language is the opportunity it gives you to spend more time designing solutions, and less time actually coding them. Consider the problem of maintaining an audit trail of changes made to individual records within a file. One option, fairly simple from a hand-coding perspective, is to keep historical records, so that each time the record is changed you write a copy of the new record out to the history file. There will still be some work to do at report generation time, when it comes time to ferret out the actual fields that have changed, but you'll worry about that later.

Another option, which requires a little less data storage and a little more work, is to write some code to do a byte-by-byte comparison between the old and new records, determine the individual bytes that have changed, and then work up some kind of indexing scheme based on a known file layout to determine which fields are affected. This lets you store just the changed fields, and makes reporting a little easier, as well. Of course, if someone changes the file layout, you have to rewrite your code to accommodate the new structure. If you want to apply this scheme to another file, you're in for a partial rewrite as well.

No doubt you've seen enough TV commercials to know when you're being set up, so it should come as no surprise that the template language eats this kind of problem for breakfast. In the first place, it's easy to get a list of all the fields in any given file. It has to be easy—that's how the file declarations get laid out in your source code.

It's all done, not with mirrors, but with template language statements (although the effect is often equally magical). The multivalued global symbol %File contains names of all the file declarations in the currently used data dictionary. It's much like a queue, and if you get the record that corresponds to the file you want to use, you'll discover that there are a large number of symbols that are linked to %File, which give you more detailed information about the file in question. These include the %Field symbol, which, like %File, is multivalued. For any given setting of %File, %Field will contain a list of all the fields in the file.

As it turns out, %Field also explodes down into a number of other interesting symbols, including %FieldType, which will have values such as SHORT, STRING, MEMO, and so on. Once you can process all the fields in any given file and actually use that information to build code, it's no big deal to generate a function that can process a file's record and write out to another file one record for each field changed, complete with the name of the field, the old and new values, the date and time, and probably some field identifying the person who made the change.

This solution extends your programming ability considerably. Now, instead of doing the analysis of the file in question yourself, you are applying your energies to a methodology, and you are letting the template statements apply that methodology. This also comes back to the point I made previously: The templates are doing the grunt work, the repetitive coding.

Re-Creating the AppGen in Your Own Image

For most programmers, the AppGen offers enough benefits in its default configuration to keep the software factory humming along. If you're a hand coder, however, you undoubtedly have your own ideas about how you like to code, and you bristle at the thought of having to write code the way the standard templates write it. It might just be sheer cussedness on your part, or it might be a realization that the standard templates have to be everything to everyone, and that doesn't always translate into optimum code for your purposes.

Whatever your reasons, if you decide you want to design a set of templates around your coding style rather than bend your style to the templates, there are some core pieces of the templates that you should think seriously about keeping, at least at the start.

The Core Template Technology

By *core template technology* I mean those aspects of the template language that control code generation and the retrieval of data from the various windows and editors that hang off the procedure and application property windows. In this section I'll survey that code and suggest what to cut and what to keep. As with any template modifications, you're well advised to make changes to a copy of the original. If you want to register both the original and the copy, you'll need (and probably want) to give your original a class name other than Clarion.

Application Management: CW.TPL

The starting point for any template chain is the TPL file, and in the case of the standard templates it's CW.TPL. Listing 21.1 shows the Application Global Properties prompts from CW.TPL.

Listing 21.1. The Application Global Properties section of CW.TPL.

```
#PROMPT('Program &Author:',@s40),%ProgramAuthor
#PROMPT('Use field description as MSG() when MSG() is
➥blank',CHECK),%MessageDescription,DEFAULT(%True),AT(10,,180)
#PROMPT('Generate global data as EXTERNAL',CHECK),%GlobalExternal,AT(10,,180)
#BUTTON('.INI File Settings'),AT(10,,180)
  #PROMPT('&Use .INI file to save and restore program settings',CHECK)
➥,%INIActive,AT(10,,180)
#ENABLE(%INIActive)
    #PROMPT('.&INI File to use:',DROP('Program Name.INI¦Other')),%INIFile
    #ENABLE(%INIFile='Other')
      #PROMPT('&Other File Name:',@S255),%ININame
    #ENDENABLE
  #ENDENABLE
#ENDBUTTON
#BUTTON('File Control Flags'),AT(10,,180)
  #PROMPT('Generate all file declarations',CHECK),%DefaultGenerate,AT(10,,180)
  #PROMPT('When done with a File:',DROP('Close the File¦Keep the File
➥Open')),%DefaultCloseFile,DEFAULT('Close the File')
```

```
   #PROMPT('Enclose RI code in transaction frame',CHECK),
➡%DefaultRILogout,DEFAULT(1),AT(10,,180)
   #ENABLE(%DefaultRILogout)
     #PROMPT('Issue template warning if LOGOUT() not
➡allowed',CHECK),%WarnOnLogoutError,DEFAULT(%True),AT(10,,180)
   #ENDENABLE
   #BOXED('File Attributes')
     #PROMPT('Threaded:',DROP('Use File Setting¦All Threaded¦None
➡Threaded')),%DefaultThreaded,DEFAULT('Use File Setting')
     #PROMPT('Create:',DROP('Use File Setting¦Create All¦Create None')),
➡%DefaultCreate,DEFAULT('Use File Setting')
     #PROMPT('External:',DROP('All External¦None External')),
➡%DefaultExternal,DEFAULT('None External')
     #BOXED('External Files'),WHERE(%DefaultExternal = 'All External'),AT(,90)
       #PROMPT('Declaring Module:',@S255),%DefaultExternalSource
       #PROMPT('All files are declared in another .APP',CHECK),
➡%DefaultExternalAPP,AT(15,,140)
     #ENDBOXED
     #BOXED('Export Files'),WHERE(%DefaultExternal = 'None External' AND
➡%ProgramExtension='DLL'),AT(,90)
       #PROMPT('Export all file declarations',CHECK),%DefaultExport,AT(25,,140)
     #ENDBOXED
   #ENDBOXED
   #BOXED('File Access')
     #PROMPT('File Open Mode:',DROP('Share¦Open¦Other')),
➡%DefaultOpenMode,DEFAULT('Share')
     #ENABLE(%DefaultOpenMode='Other')
       #BOXED('Other Open Mode')
         #PROMPT('User Access:',DROP('Read/Write¦Read Only¦Write
➡Only')),%DefaultUserAccess,DEFAULT('Read/Write')
         #PROMPT('Other Access:',DROP('Deny None¦Deny Read¦Deny Write¦Deny All
➡¦Any Access')),%DefaultOtherAccess,DEFAULT('Deny None')
       #ENDBOXED
     #ENDENABLE
   #ENDBOXED
   #BUTTON('Individual File Overrides'),FROM(%File,%File & ' - ' &
➡%FileDescription),AT(10,,180),HLP('~TPLApplication')
     #PROMPT('Generate file declaration',CHECK),%OverrideGenerate,AT(10,,180)
     #PROMPT('When Done with the File:',DROP('Use Default¦Close the File¦
➡Keep the File Open')),%OverrideCloseFile,DEFAULT('Use Default')
     #PROMPT('Enclose RI code in transaction frame',CHECK),%OverrideRILogout,
➡DEFAULT(1),AT(10,,180)
     #BOXED('File Attributes')
       #PROMPT('Threaded:',DROP('Use Default¦Threaded¦Not Threaded')),
➡%OverrideThreaded,DEFAULT('Use Default')
       #PROMPT('Create:',DROP('Use Default¦Use File Setting¦Create File¦
➡Do Not Create File')),%OverrideCreate,DEFAULT('Use Default')
       #PROMPT('External:',DROP('Use Default¦External¦Not External')),
➡%OverrideExternal,DEFAULT('Use Default')
       #BOXED('External File'),WHERE(%OverrideExternal = 'External'),AT(,80)
         #PROMPT('Declaring Module:',@S255),%OverrideExternalSource
         #PROMPT('The file is declared in another .APP',CHECK),
➡%OverrideExternalAPP,AT(15,,140)
       #ENDBOXED
       #BOXED('Export File'),WHERE(%OverrideExternal =
➡'Not External'  AND %ProgramExtension='DLL'),AT(,80)
```

continues

Listing 21.1. continued

```
        #PROMPT('Export file declaration',CHECK),%OverrideExport,AT(20,,110)
      #ENDBOXED
    #ENDBOXED
    #BOXED('File Access')
      #PROMPT('File Open Mode:',DROP('Use
➥Default¦Share¦Open¦Other')),%OverrideOpenMode,DEFAULT('Use Default')
      #ENABLE(%OverRideOpenMode = 'Other')
        #BOXED('Other Open Mode')
          #PROMPT('User Access:',DROP('Use Default¦Read/Write¦Read Only¦
➥Write Only')),%OverrideUserAccess,DEFAULT('Use Default')
          #PROMPT('Other Access:',DROP('Use Default¦Deny None¦Deny Read¦
➥Deny Write¦Deny All¦Any Access')),%OverrideOtherAccess,DEFAULT('Use Default')
        #ENDBOXED
      #ENDENABLE
    #ENDBOXED
  #ENDBUTTON
#ENDBUTTON
```

Of these settings, the INI prompts and the RI prompts, and their associated code later in the template, most likely fall into the category of "if you like them, keep them." They're not what I'd consider essential. Most hand coders have their own ways of doing these things, particularly relational integrity. The file control flags settings, however, are worth serious consideration.

At some point you'll probably end up putting in most of these flags yourself. Besides, there may be some room to optimize these symbols for your particular uses, but you probably won't find a big payoff here. It's better to concentrate your energy elsewhere.

The rest of CW.TPL you can probably leave as-is. Everything following this prompts section is taken up with managing source generation. You might consider things such as adding explicit flags to control source generation of individual procedures, but again, most of your work will be elsewhere.

Program Generation: PROGRAM.TPW

Like CW.TPL, PROGRAM.TPW is concerned with global issues: building the map, declaring global data, and so on. It also does a lot of symbol gathering, such as determining which files are actually used in the program, and bases some of its code generation on that information.

TIP

To help you get a grasp of what's happening in the flow of a template, look for the #MESSAGE statements. These cause messages to appear during code generation, and are usually a good indication of what's happening at that time in the template code.

Also like CW.TPL, PROGRAM.TPW is reasonably lean. There isn't a lot of room for discussion here, although if you're cutting out the RI code you'll want to remove the references to the %RIGather and %RIDelete groups. You may also want to look at the code for the CheckOpen(), ReportPreview(), StandardWarning(), INIRestoreWindow(), and INISaveWindow() procedures, if you use these. You probably have your own schemes for error handling and the like, and you may or may not want to have these generated for each application anyway. Because the code is always identical for comparable setups, it's generally best to put this sort of code in a LIB or DLL. That's not done in the standard templates because it would unnecessarily complicate things for less-experienced developers.

Get to Know Your #GROUPs

In the template language, a #GROUP denotes code that can be referenced from elsewhere in the template. A #GROUP is like a procedure in the Clarion language—it can even receive parameters, which may be passed by value or address. Treat the #GROUPs (which are found throughout the templates, but particularly in STANDARD.TPW and FILECTRL.TPW) as your template procedure library. There's quite a lot of useful stuff out there.

The file control groups will be of immediate interest to you if you plan to make any use of the AppGen's capability to track which files are used by which procedures. This has so many benefits it's hard to imagine anyone not using this feature.

Any time you add a file to a procedure property file schematic window (which is a requirement for populating fields anywhere in the AppGen), that file gets stored in either the %Primary, %Secondary, or %Other multivalued symbol. It's then up to the template code to propagate this knowledge to the rest of the templates in such a way that, among other things, the application knows which files are used and therefore which to generate declarations for. This knowledge is also used to determine which files need to be opened or possibly closed, if conditional file opening is turned on.

The #GROUP statements in FILECTRL.TPW handle these functions. Chapter 18, "Creating Procedure Templates," covers their use and is recommended reading if you set about creating your own procedure templates.

> **TIP**
>
> If, as this chapter suggests, you have created your own template class (a TPL file with #INCLUDE statements pointing to any member TPW files) and you wish to use a #GROUP that is part of another class (such as the Clarion class), just add the class name to the end of the #GROUP name, in parentheses. For example, to use the %FileControlInitialize group in another chain, you would use the statement #INSERT(%FileControlInitialize(Clarion)).

Where Do I Go from Here?

Once you've decided on the overall path your application design will take, you can get down to the business of creating the individual template components that suit your needs. All procedures need some sort of procedure template, and as just mentioned, a basic one is described in the latter part of Chapter 18. How elaborate you get with your procedure templates is entirely up to you and the type of programming you do. You might find that one procedure type with a multitude of Prompts windows covers your needs nicely, or you may end up mimicking the standard templates by creating a few basic procedure templates, and then do all the rest with the various code, control, and extension templates the AppGen lets you plug in. Much also depends on your use of embed points, as the next section explains.

Using Embeds

Perhaps all this talk of radically rewriting the templates is a bit extreme for your taste. In that case, there is one other option you may want to consider: embeds.

The implementation of the embed list as a tree structure was one of the most interesting evolutionary changes between the third and fourth betas of Clarion for Windows. In Beta 3 the embed list simply showed the embed points, and you had to go to the embed to see what was in it. In Beta 4 the tree control appeared, which lets you see, at a glance, not just the embed points, but all the source embeds, procedure calls, and code templates attached to those points. You can also switch the order of all embeds attached to any embed point.

This embed view presents some interesting opportunities. Most procedures can be broken down into segments, some of which are quite regular in construction. This suggests that even a completely hand-coded application could benefit from being reconstructed entirely as a combination of code templates and embedded source, and based on simple procedure templates with custom embed points.

If you could reduce the amount of actual source code by even half, that could have a tremendous maintenance benefit. You also have the benefit of seeing an outline view of your code, procedure by procedure, as well as the relationships between procedures. An application tree can be a big help in maintaining a design.

The embed approach to code organization can also be an opportunity to migrate code, which never used to be possible inside previous application-generation tools. Once you start making use of the benefits the AppGen has to offer, you'll be hooked.

Drawbacks and Future Developments

Despite everything I've said here, the AppGen still remains a little short of perfection for hand coders. Perhaps the biggest complaint about having to use embed points for source code is that you can't see all your source code, embedded and generated, at once. What the AppGen really needs is an embed editing mode that lets you see and edit all your embed points in one editor window, while preventing you from changing any of the interleaved generated code.

Such an enhancement appears to be in the works for CW. If and when it arrives, the last reason any hand coder has for not using the AppGen will fade into oblivion.

Summary

If you're one of those meat-eating, nail-spitting, hard-core hand coders who wouldn't be caught dead using an application development tool, maybe it's time for you to get into the templates and make the AppGen dance to your tune. Whether you take it slow and start by migrating your hand-coded application into embed points, or rewrite the template system from the ground up, there is a world of productivity out there just waiting to be discovered.

IV

Advanced Topics

22

Using Dynamic Data Exchange

Dynamic data exchange (DDE) is an inter-process communication (IPC) protocol used in Windows programs to communicate between one Windows program and another. An IPC is a mechanism that provides a communication protocol (similar to that of a modem communications package) through which each program communicates in a predictable and standard way, requesting and responding to requests appropriately. DDE enables your program to communicate with another program via messaging or events and DDE functions and DDE procedures. It enables your program to request data from another program or request the other program to invoke some internal process (which may affect the data you ultimately wish to receive).

Clarion for Windows supports the full use of DDE within the Windows programs you create. A Clarion for Windows program can be a DDE server, a DDE client, or both at the same time. A DDE server or client can partake in many different conversations at any given time. DDE can be extremely complicated in a traditional programming language such as C or C++ because of the intricacies of the IPC requirements; however, in Clarion for Windows it is really straightforward to use, as you will soon see.

This chapter explores the intricacies of the DDE communication process. Various example programs will help you see the simplicity that Clarion for Windows provides for dealing with this form of IPC technology.

The Conversation

The DDE communication process is generally referred to as a DDE *conversation*. To have a conversation, there must be at least two parties involved. The terms client and server are used to describe the communicating programs. A *client* requests data from the *server*, and can also request that a process be invoked in the server. A client can also send unsolicited data to a server. A server provides data (sends data back to the client) or executes the process requested by the client.

There are three methods defined for communicating under DDE: a *cold link* (an on-demand communication process), a *hot link* (a continuous, ongoing communication process), and a *warm link* (a periodic communication process). Clarion for Windows supports each of these methods, hiding the complexities and details of much of the work required to initiate, acknowledge, and terminate the conversation. DDE conversations utilize an application name, topic, and item in order to identify the unique conversation between the server and client. Each component (server and client) communicates through a dedicated communication connection known as a *DDE channel* (this is similar to having a phone line running between a server and a client).

Basic Requirements

Both a DDE server and client must have a window and an ACCEPT loop. This is a basic requirement because in Clarion for Windows, an ACCEPT loop is the mechanism that provides the capability to read and write messages to the Windows message queue, upon which DDE relies.

> **TIP**
>
> Although a window is required, it can be hidden using the Hide attribute of the window or by using the Hide property.

The DDE Server

A DDE server is the party in the DDE conversation that serves data or processes the requests of the client. A program that is identified as a server must register itself with Windows so that other programs can find and communicate with it. Registering the server is simple: Your program must issue the DDE function DDESERVER(); the server is then registered in Windows.

All of the DDE functions and procedures are prototyped in a file called DDE.CLW, which is found in your \cw\libsrc directory. You must include the DDE.CLW file in the map of your program to use these functions and procedures.

Finding Active DDE Servers

The sample program in Listing 22.1 queries Windows for any active DDE servers. To best see the results of this program, you should first execute it, then start other Windows programs you have available, switching back and forth between them and this program. If any of the Windows programs you have started have a DDE server capacity, you will see them appear on the DDE Query (Viewer) list.

Listing 22.1. A DDE Query (Viewer) sample program.

```
CWDDEQ              PROGRAM

                    INCLUDE('Equates.CLW')
                    INCLUDE('Keycodes.CLW')
                    INCLUDE('Errors.CLW')

                    MAP
                      DDEViewer()
                      INCLUDE('DDE.CLW')
                    END
```

continues

Listing 22.1. continued

```
DDEServerQue            QUEUE,PRE(DSQ)
Server                    STRING(80)
                        END

COLSEP                  EQUATE(',')
Ndx                     LONG
Pos1                    LONG
Pos2                    LONG
ServerList              STRING(50000)

wDDEViewer WINDOW('DDE Query (Viewer)'),AT(82,52,182,109),¦
          FONT('Arial',10,,FONT:regular),¦
          MSG('Find Servers and list for viewing'), ¦
        TIMER(1),SYSTEM,GRAY,DOUBLE
        BUTTON('&Stop'),AT(128,92,49,13),FONT('Arial',8,,FONT:bold),¦
        USE(?StopButton),STD(std:close),DEFAULT
        STRING(' '),AT(5,94,119,10),¦
        FONT('Arial',10,0800000H,FONT:bold),USE(?LastUpdate),CENTER
        LIST,AT(3,2,176,86),FONT('Arial',8,,FONT:regular),¦
        MSG('View DDE Servers/Functions'),USE(?List1), ¦
            VSCROLL,LEFT,VCR,¦
            FORMAT('43L(1)¦_~Servers From DDEQUERY~@s80@'),¦
            FROM(ddeserverque)
      END

 CODE
 DDEViewer()

!==============================================================================
DDEViewer               PROCEDURE
!==============================================================================
 CODE
 OPEN(wDDEViewer)
 DISPLAY()
 ACCEPT
   CASE EVENT()
   OF EVENT:OpenWindow
      ServerList = DDEQUERY()
      DO BuildServerQue
      DISPLAY()
      wDDEViewer{PROP:Timer} = 400
   OF EVENT:CloseDown
      BREAK
   OF EVENT:Timer
      ServerList = DDEQUERY()
      DO BuildServerQue
      DISPLAY()
   END
   CASE FIELD()
   OF ?StopButton
     CASE EVENT()
     OF EVENT:ACCEPTED
       POST(EVENT:CloseDown)
     END
   END
 END
```

```
  CLOSE(wDDEViewer)
  RETURN

!----------------------------------------------------------------------
BuildServerQue            ROUTINE
!----------------------------------------------------------------------
  FREE(DDEServerQue);CLEAR(DDEServerQue)
  Pos2 = 1
  Ndx  = 0
  LOOP UNTIL Ndx = LEN(ServerList)
    Ndx += 1
    Pos1 = Pos2
    IF ServerList[Ndx] = COLSEP
        Pos2          = Ndx -1
        DSQ:Server    = ServerList[Pos1 : Pos2]
        Pos2          = Ndx + 1
        ADD(DDEServerQue)
        CLEAR(DDEServerQue)
    END
  END
  IF Ndx > Pos2
     DSQ:Server    = ServerList[Pos1 : Ndx]
     ADD(DDEServerQue)
     CLEAR(DDEServerQue)
  END
  ?LastUpdate{PROP:Text} = 'Last Update: ' & |
                            FORMAT(CLOCK(),@t6)
  EXIT
```

In this program you will see the use of only one specific DDE function call, DDEQUERY(<*ApplicationName*>,<*Topic*>). Notice that there is a timer value set in the EVENT:OpenWindow event. This causes the following statements to be executed periodically (about every 4 seconds), updating the list of active DDE servers.

Because both parameters were omitted in the DDEQUERY() DDE function, a comma-delimited string of active DDE servers is returned to the ServerList variable. The routine BuildServerQue is then executed and strips apart this string by the delimiter (which is a comma), filling the DDEServerQue queue that is used by the list box in the DDEViewer window. The timer value is set to accommodate the start time of other Windows programs so that each time a new program is started, if you switch back from that program to the DDE Query (Viewer) window, you should see the updated server list. Your results will vary from machine to machine, so if the list has not been updated, just wait a second to see the new results.

This example is provided so you can get an idea of how to query for multiple active DDE servers at any given time. Of course, there are other ways to do this, which you will see shortly.

Creating a DDE Server

Creating a DDE server in a C or C++ program is quite an exercise; however, in Clarion for Windows it is as simple as making one function call. To create a DDE server, issue the following statement:

```
DDEChannel = DDESERVER('Application Name','Topic')
```

DDEChannel is the unique communication line between your program and another. The parameters of this function call will determine what the conversation is about. The DDEChannel returned is a LONG variable type. The 'Application Name' is generally the name by which your program is called (for example, the EXCEL.EXE program is known as Excel). The 'Topic' parameter identifies the topic of conversation for this DDE server. (For example, the topic might be VENDORS, which might indicate that this conversation is based on and for the VENDORS database table in the DDE server program.)

Listing 22.2 is the Clarion for Windows DDE server example program. It illustrates how to create a fairly robust DDE server that can converse with cold, hot, and warm DDE requests.

Listing 22.2. The CWDDES: DDE server sample program.

```
CWDDES                  PROGRAM

                        INCLUDE('Equates.CLW')
                        INCLUDE('Keycodes.CLW')
                        INCLUDE('Errors.CLW')

                        MAP
                          ServerProc()
                          INCLUDE('DDE.CLW')
                        END

DDEChannel              LONG
DDEMode                 STRING(20)
FullName                STRING(41)
Phone                   STRING(11)
Interval                LONG(5)

wServer WINDOW('CW DDE Server'),AT(89,40,182,32),¦
        FONT('Arial',8,,FONT:regular),¦
        MSG('Find Servers and list for viewing'), ¦
        SYSTEM,GRAY,DOUBLE
      PROMPT('Name'),AT(2,4,25,10),USE(?Prompt1)
      ENTRY(@s40),AT(30,2,144,12),USE(FullName)
      PROMPT('Phone'),AT(2,16,25,10),USE(?Prompt2)
      ENTRY(@P(###)###-####P),AT(30,16,56,11),USE(Phone)
      BUTTON('E&xit'),AT(130,16,44,13),FONT('Arial',8,,FONT:bold),¦
      USE(?ExitButton),STD(STD:Close),DEFAULT
    END

  CODE
  ServerProc()

  !=============================================================================
  ServerProc              PROCEDURE
  !=============================================================================
  CODE
  OPEN(wServer)
  DDEChannel = DDESERVER('CWDDES')
  ACCEPT
    CASE EVENT()
```

```
OF EVENT:CloseDown
  BREAK
OF EVENT:DDEExecute
  DDEMode = DDEVALUE()
  IF DDEMode = '[EXIT]' THEN BREAK.
  CYCLE
OF EVENT:DDERequest
  DDEWRITE(DDEChannel,DDE:Manual,'COLDNAME',FullName)
  DDEWRITE(DDEChannel,DDE:Manual,'COLDPHONE',Phone)
  CYCLE
OF EVENT:DDEAdvise
  DDEWRITE(DDEChannel,DDE:Auto,'HOTNAME',FullName)
  DDEWRITE(DDEChannel,DDE:Auto,'HOTPHONE',Phone)
  DDEWRITE(DDEChannel,INTERVAL,'WARMNAME',FullName)
  DDEWRITE(DDEChannel,INTERVAL,'WARMPHONE',Phone)
  CYCLE
END
CASE FIELD()
OF ?FullName
  CASE EVENT()
  OF EVENT:Accepted
    DDEWRITE(DDEChannel,DDE:Auto,'HOTNAME',FullName)
    CYCLE
  END
OF ?Phone
  CASE EVENT()
  OF EVENT:Accepted
    DDEWRITE(DDEChannel,DDE:Auto,'HOTPHONE',Phone)
    CYCLE
  END
END
END
CLOSE(wServer)
RETURN
```

Initiating the DDE Server

The first thing this program does is initiate a DDE server and register the server with Windows, which is done in this statement:

```
DDEChannel = DDESERVER('CWDDES')
```

The application name used is `CWDDES`, which is the name of the server program. If this parameter had been omitted, the application name would have used the same name by default. The second parameter for TOPIC has been omitted, indicating that this server will communicate on all topics.

Events in the DDE Server

DDE relies on events or messaging to inform either the client or server of the next action to take. Recall that a client can send a request to execute a method (command) in the server. The following statement illustrates how to detect when this event happens:

```
OF EVENT:DDEExecute
   DDEMode = DDEVALUE()
   IF DDEMode = '[EXIT]' THEN BREAK.
   CYCLE
```

The `EVENT:DDEExecute` event is generated when a client sends a `DDEEXECUTE()` command to the server. A *method* is simply some action that the DDE server understands and can act on. In many products such as Excel, complete macro commands can be sent through the `DDEEXECUTE()` DDE function, invoking the actual macro that is sent by the client. For instance, you may want to recalculate a spreadsheet periodically. You can do this by sending the appropriate command to an Excel server.

It is standard Windows practice to enclose the method (command) name in brackets ([ ]). The `DDEVALUE()` DDE function returns the value (command) of the `DDEEXECUTE()` DDE function. In this case, the only value the DDE server is concerned with is '[EXIT]'. When this value is sent to the server, the server's `ACCEPT` loop is exited. Notice the `CYCLE` statement following the `IF` statement. This `CYCLE` statement sends an acknowledgment back to the client after the `EVENT:DDEExecute` has been received and acted on, creating two-way conversation. In the case of the [EXIT] method, it is not necessary to `CYCLE` because the server will also terminate, and each client will receive an `EVENT:DDEClosed` event instead.

The next event, `EVENT:DDERequest`, is received whenever a client requests data from the server using a cold link. When this event is received by the server, the server issues a `DDEWRITE()` DDE procedure and sends the data back to the client. This process is seen in the following code snippet:

```
OF EVENT:DDERequest
   DDEWRITE(DDEChannel,DDE:Manual,'COLDNAME',FullName)
   DDEWRITE(DDEChannel,DDE:Manual,'COLDPHONE',Phone)
   CYCLE
```

Notice the `CYCLE` statement. Again, the `CYCLE` statement is issued to acknowledge or inform the client that the data has actually been sent by the server. The `DDEWRITE()` procedure takes four parameters: From left to right they are DDE channel, DDE mode, Item name, and Item value. The DDE mode in this case has been set to `DDE:Manual`, indicating a cold link.

When the client establishes a hot or warm link, the event `DDE:Advise` is issued to the server. On a hot link, the data is continuously sent back to the client whenever it is changed, until either the server is stopped or the client informs the server to stop sending the data. The following code snippet illustrates how this is done:

```
OF EVENT:DDEAdvise
   DDEWRITE(DDEChannel,DDE:Auto,'HOTNAME',FullName)
   DDEWRITE(DDEChannel,DDE:Auto,'HOTPHONE',Phone)
   DDEWRITE(DDEChannel,INTERVAL,'WARMNAME',FullName)
   DDEWRITE(DDEChannel,INTERVAL,'WARMPHONE',Phone)
   CYCLE
```

The DDE mode in this case has two different values: `DDE:Auto` and `INTERVAL`. `DDE:Auto` is used for hot links and automatically sends data to the client the first time (more on hot links shortly). The `INTERVAL` is a defined time interval for sending periodic data on a warm link to the client.

In this case, the INTERVAL is set to periodic updates every five seconds after a change to the items FullName and Phone has taken place. To ensure that hot link data is sent whenever data is changed, the server needs to monitor the data to be sent, and when it is changed, resend the data to the client. This is shown in the following statements:

```
CASE FIELD()
   OF ?FullName
     CASE EVENT()
     OF EVENT:Accepted
        DDEWRITE(DDEChannel,DDE:Auto,'HOTNAME',FullName)
        CYCLE
     END
   OF ?Phone
     CASE EVENT()
     OF EVENT:Accepted
        DDEWRITE(DDEChannel,DDE:Auto,'HOTPHONE',Phone)
        CYCLE
     END
   END
```

Notice that after each EVENT:Accepted for the data components that are to be sent to the client, a new DDEWRITE() DDE procedure is issued that is identical to the one used in the EVENT:DDEAdvise shown earlier. In this case, whenever the data is changed, the new values are sent automatically to the client, updating the data in the client from the server.

Terminating the Conversation

Terminating the conversation between the server and client is really quite simple and can be done in one of two ways: You can either use the DDECLOSE() DDE procedure or close the server's window. When the server terminates a conversation, an EVENT:DDEClosed is sent to the client, informing the client that the server has closed the DDE channel.

Some events have not been covered in this example because of space constraints, but I think you get the idea of how the DDE server works and can figure out how to effectively use the remaining events.

The DDE Client

A DDE client is the party in the DDE conversation that requests data from the DDE server or requests that an internal method (command) be executed in the server. The DDE client can also send unsolicited data to the server using the DDEPOKE() DDE procedure, which is not covered in this chapter.

Listing 22.3 shows the Clarion for Windows DDE client example program, which illustrates how to create three separate DDE clients, each conversing in a specific DDE mode. Additionally, there is a toolbox that provides an external mechanism to request the server to close using the DDEEXECUTE() DDE procedure, thereby closing all the clients as well.

Listing 22.3. The CWDDEC: DDE client sample program.

```
CWDDEC                   PROGRAM

                         INCLUDE('Equates.CLW')
                         INCLUDE('Keycodes.CLW')
                         INCLUDE('Errors.CLW')

                         MAP
                           ClientColdProc()
                           ClientHotProc()
                           ClientWarmProc()
                           ClientTBProc()
                           INCLUDE('DDE.CLW')
                         END

ThreadNo                 LONG

     CODE
     ThreadNo = START(ClientColdProc)
     ThreadNo = START(ClientHotProc)
     ThreadNo = START(ClientWarmProc)
     ThreadNo = START(ClientTBProc)


!===============================================================================
ClientColdProc           PROCEDURE
!===============================================================================
DDEChannel               LONG
FullName                 STRING(40)
Phone                    STRING(10)
ExePath                  STRING(80)

wClient WINDOW('CW DDE [COLD] Client'),AT(89,90,182,31),¦
        FONT('Arial',8,,FONT:regular),                 ¦
         MSG('Find Servers and list for viewing'),GRAY,DOUBLE
        PROMPT('Name'),AT(2,4,25,10),USE(?Prompt1)
        STRING(@s40),AT(30,4,144,10),¦
        FONT('Arial',8,0800000H,FONT:bold),USE(FullName)
        PROMPT('Phone'),AT(2,16,25,10),USE(?Prompt2)
        STRING(@P(###)###-####P),AT(30,16,52,10),¦
        FONT('Arial',8,0800000H,FONT:bold),USE(Phone)
        BUTTON('&Get Data'),AT(126,16,47,12),¦
        FONT('Arial',8,,FONT:bold),USE(?GetDataButton)
     END

   CODE
   OPEN(wClient)
   ACCEPT
     CASE EVENT()
     OF EVENT:OpenWindow
        DDEChannel = DDECLIENT('CWDDES')
        IF ~DDECHannel
           ExePath = CLIP(PATH())
           RUN(CLIP(ExePath) & '\CWDDES.EXE')
           DDEChannel = DDECLIENT('CWDDES')
           IF ~DDECHannel
              MESSAGE('DDE Server could not be started', ¦
                      0{PROP:Text},ICON:Hand)
```

```
                       POST(EVENT:CloseDown)
              END
          END
      OF EVENT:CloseDown
        BREAK
      OF EVENT:DDEData
        DISPLAY()
      OF EVENT:DDEClosed
        POST(EVENT:CloseDown)
        CYCLE
      END
      CASE FIELD()
      OF ?GetDataButton
        CASE EVENT()
        OF EVENT:Accepted
          DDEEXECUTE(DDEChannel,'[COLD]')
          DDEREAD(DDEChannel,DDE:Manual,'COLDNAME',FullName)
          DDEREAD(DDEChannel,DDE:Manual,'COLDPHONE',Phone)
        END
      END
  END
  CLOSE(wClient)
  RETURN


!===============================================================================
ClientHotProc            PROCEDURE
!===============================================================================
DDEChannel               LONG
FullName                 STRING(40)
Phone                    STRING(10)
ExePath                  STRING(80)

wClient WINDOW('CW DDE [HOT] Client'),AT(89,140,182,31),¦
        FONT('Arial',8,,FONT:regular),¦
        MSG('Find Servers and list for viewing'),GRAY,DOUBLE
       PROMPT('Name'),AT(2,4,25,10),USE(?Prompt1)
       STRING(@s40),AT(30,4,144,10),¦
       FONT('Arial',8,080H,FONT:bold),USE(FullName)
       PROMPT('Phone'),AT(2,16,25,10),USE(?Prompt2)
       STRING(@P(###)###-####P),AT(30,16,52,10),¦
       FONT('Arial',8,080H,FONT:bold),USE(Phone)
     END

  CODE
  OPEN(wClient)
  ACCEPT
    CASE EVENT()
    OF EVENT:OpenWindow
      DDEChannel = DDECLIENT('CWDDES')
      IF ~DDECHannel
        ExePath = CLIP(PATH())
        RUN(CLIP(ExePath) & '\CWDDES.EXE')
        DDEChannel = DDECLIENT('CWDDES')
        IF ~DDECHannel
          MESSAGE('DDE Server could not be started', ¦
                  0{PROP:Text},ICON:Hand)
          POST(EVENT:CloseDown)
        END
```

continues

Listing 22.3. continued

```
      END
      DDEEXECUTE(DDEChannel,'[HOT]')
      DDEREAD(DDEChannel,DDE:Auto,'HOTNAME',FullName)
      DDEREAD(DDEChannel,DDE:Auto,'HOTPHONE',Phone)
  OF EVENT:CloseDown
      BREAK
  OF EVENT:DDEData
      DISPLAY()
  OF EVENT:DDEClosed
      POST(EVENT:CloseDown)
      CYCLE
  END
 END
 CLOSE(wClient)
 RETURN


!===============================================================================
ClientWarmProc          PROCEDURE
!===============================================================================
DDEChannel              LONG
FullName                STRING(40)
Phone                   STRING(10)
Interval                LONG(5)
ExePath                 STRING(80)

wClient WINDOW('CW DDE [WARM] Client'),AT(89,190,182,31),¦
        FONT('Arial',8,,FONT:regular),¦
        MSG('Find Servers and list for viewing'),GRAY,DOUBLE
        PROMPT('Name'),AT(2,4,25,10),USE(?Prompt1)
        STRING(@s40),AT(30,4,144,10),¦
        FONT('Arial',8,08000H,FONT:bold),USE(FullName)
        PROMPT('Phone'),AT(2,16,25,10),USE(?Prompt2)
        STRING(@P(###)###-####P),AT(30,16,52,10),¦
        FONT('Arial',8,08000H,FONT:bold),USE(Phone)
      END

 CODE
 OPEN(wClient)
 ACCEPT
   CASE EVENT()
   OF EVENT:OpenWindow
      DDEChannel = DDECLIENT('CWDDES')
      IF ~DDEChannel
         ExePath = CLIP(PATH())
         RUN(CLIP(ExePath) & '\CWDDES.EXE')
         DDEChannel = DDECLIENT('CWDDES')
         IF ~DDEChannel
            MESSAGE('DDE Server could not be started', ¦
                    0{PROP:Text},ICON:Hand)
            POST(EVENT:CloseDown)
         END
      END
      DDEEXECUTE(DDEChannel,'[WARM]')
      DDEREAD(DDEChannel,Interval,'WARMNAME',FullName)
      DDEREAD(DDEChannel,Interval,'WARMPHONE',Phone)
   OF EVENT:CloseDown
```

```
        BREAK
   OF EVENT:DDEData
       DISPLAY()
   OF EVENT:DDEClosed
       POST(EVENT:CloseDown)
       CYCLE
   END
 END
 CLOSE(wClient)
 RETURN


!==============================================================================
ClientTBProc            PROCEDURE
!==============================================================================
DDEChannel              LONG
ExePath                 STRING(80)

wClient WINDOW('KILL'),AT(341,91,24,17),¦
        FONT('Arial',8,,FONT:regular),IMM,¦
        MSG('Find Servers and list for viewing'), ¦
        TOOLBOX,GRAY,DOUBLE,AUTO
        BUTTON('&Ok'),AT(1,1,21,15),¦
        FONT('Arial',8,,FONT:bold),USE(?killEmButton)
      END

 CODE
 OPEN(wClient)
 ACCEPT
   CASE EVENT()
   OF EVENT:OpenWindow
      DDEChannel = DDECLIENT('CWDDES')
      IF ~DDECHannel
         ExePath = CLIP(PATH())
         RUN(CLIP(ExePath) & '\CWDDES.EXE')
         DDEChannel = DDECLIENT('CWDDES')
         IF ~DDECHannel
            MESSAGE('DDE Server could not be started', ¦
                    0{PROP:Text},ICON:Hand)
            POST(EVENT:CloseDown)
         END
      END
   OF EVENT:CloseDown
      BREAK
   OF EVENT:DDEClosed
      POST(EVENT:CloseDown)
      CYCLE
   END
   CASE FIELD()
   OF ?KillEmButton
     CASE EVENT()
     OF EVENT:Accepted
       DDEEXECUTE(DDEChannel,'[EXIT]')
     END
   END
 END
 CLOSE(wClient)
 RETURN
```

In Listing 22.3, the first thing to note is that each client is multithreading in a non-MDI window mode. The first four lines of executable code (following the first CODE statement) start each client in a separate execution thread. For more information on multithreading see Chapter 28, "Multithreading and Thread Management." Four execution threads will be started, representing the following procedures: ClientColdProc (a cold-linked client), ClientHotProc (a hot-linked client), ClientWarmProc (a warm-linked client), and ClientTBProc (a special form of a cold-linked client).

Initiating the DDE Client

The first thing this program does is initiate the DDE client in each procedure during the EVENT:OpenWindow. Note that for each client the DDE server that we wish to link to is 'CWDDES' (the same program in Listing 22.2). This is illustrated in the following statements:

```
OF EVENT:OpenWindow
   DDEChannel = DDECLIENT('CWDDES')
   IF ~DDECHannel
      ExePath = CLIP(PATH())
      RUN(CLIP(ExePath) & '\CWDDES.EXE')
      DDEChannel = DDECLIENT('CWDDES')
      IF ~DDECHannel
         MESSAGE('DDE Server could not be started', ¦
                 0{PROP:Text},ICON:Hand)
         POST(EVENT:CloseDown)
      END
   END
```

The first thing that happens is that the client issues a DDECLIENT() DDE function that returns the DDEChannel variable. Because the DDEChannel variable is a LONG variable type, the next thing the client does is check whether there is a non-zero value in this variable. If the value is zero, the client program will execute the server program using the RUN() command, thereby registering the server with Windows so the client can link to it.

If the DDE channel is not obtained, the same logic is executed a second time to again try to obtain a DDE channel. If this attempt is not successful, an EVENT:CloseDown is posted to the client, and the program is stopped. Otherwise, if a DDE channel is obtained the client program continues.

The DDECLIENT() DDE function takes two arguments: application and topic. The application name used is 'CWDDES', which is the name of the server program. If this parameter had been omitted, the first server found that was registered in Windows would have been used, which is not what we wanted. The second parameter for topic has been omitted, indicating that this client will communicate with the server on all topics.

The Cold Link (*ClientColdProc*)

A cold link is simply a "retrieve data on demand" concept. To implement this, there is a Get Data button on the CW DDE [COLD] client window. When this button is pressed, any data in the requested items will be obtained in the server and passed to the client. The client will redisplay these values in its window string controls. In Listing 22.3, notice two different DDE procedures: DDEEXECUTE() and DDEREAD().

Ignore DDEEXECUTE() for now, and focus on the DDEREAD() DDE procedure. The DDEREAD() DDE procedure takes four arguments: DDE channel, DDE mode, item, and the value to be updated. I've already discussed the use of the DDEChannel, which provides the communication link between the client and server programs. The DDE mode that is used is DDE:Manual, which indicates that this process is a cold DDE link. The client will generate an EVENT:DDERequest for each DDEREAD() DDE procedure call in the server program, requesting the values (FullName and Phone) in the items (COLDNAME and COLDPHONE). When the server receives the EVENT:DDERequest event, a corresponding DDEWRITE() DDE procedure is performed, as seen in Listing 22.2. The following code snippet illustrates the client's cold link request:

```
OF ?GetDataButton
   CASE EVENT()
   OF EVENT:Accepted
     DDEEXECUTE(DDEChannel,'[COLD]')
     DDEREAD(DDEChannel,DDE:Manual,'COLDNAME',FullName)
     DDEREAD(DDEChannel,DDE:Manual,'COLDPHONE',Phone)
   END
```

The Hot Link (*ClientHotProc*)

A *hot link* is a continuous retrieval of data by the client as its value changes in the server. It is actually simpler for the client to do a hot link than to do a cold link. All that is needed is a one-time call to the DDEREAD() DDE procedure using the proper DDE mode, and the communication thereafter is automatic; when data changes in the requested items in the server, it is automatically passed back to the client. The client will redisplay these values in its window string controls. In Listing 22.3, notice two different DDE procedures: DDEEXECUTE() and DDEREAD().

In Listing 22.3, ignore DDEEXECUTE() for now and focus on the DDEREAD() DDE procedure. Unlike the cold link, the hot link will issue the DDEREAD() DDE procedure statement in the EVENT:OpenWindow event because it needs to be issued only one time to enable this mode of operation. The DDE mode used is DDE:Auto, which indicates that this process is a hot DDE link. The client will generate an EVENT:DDEAdvise for each DDEREAD() DDE procedure call in the server program, requesting the values (FullName and Phone) in the items (HotName and HotPhone). When the server receives the EVENT:DDEAdvise event, a corresponding DDEWRITE() DDE procedure is performed, as shown in Listing 22.2. Additionally, whenever the data value is changed in the server, the server will update the client through another DDEWRITE() DDE procedure call. When the data is sent from the server to the client, an EVENT:DDEData is generated in the client, at which point the string control values are redisplayed to reflect any changes in data values. The following code snippet illustrates the client's hot link request:

```
DDEEXECUTE(DDEChannel,'[HOT]')
DDEREAD(DDEChannel,DDE:Auto,'HOTNAME',FullName)
DDEREAD(DDEChannel,DDE:Auto,'HOTPHONE',Phone)
```

The Warm Link (*ClientWarmProc*)

A *warm link* is a periodic (interval) retrieval of data by the client as its value changes in the server. This concept is identical to that of a hot link, with one primary exception: The DDE mode is set to a numeric value that is used as a timer, which determines the separation between updates from server to client. In all other respects, it looks almost identical to a hot link. In this example, I have set the interval to five seconds. The following code snippet illustrates the client's warm link request:

```
DDEEXECUTE(DDEChannel,'[WARM]')
DDEREAD(DDEChannel,Interval,'WARMNAME',FullName)
DDEREAD(DDEChannel,Interval,'WARMPHONE',Phone)
```

Terminating a DDE Conversation from the Client (*ClientTBProc*)

To illustrate how to terminate a "group" or "party line" (more than one conversation on the same DDE channel) DDE conversation from a client, the ClientTBProc() procedure is provided. This is a special form of DDE client; its only purpose is to establish communication with the server and then terminate the server when the OK button is pressed, terminating all the clients as well. Of course, in a real-world program you might never want to do this sort of thing, but in case you do, the following is a simple example illustrating just how easily it is done.

The DDE initialization in this process is the same as that of the other DDE clients. The main difference is that this client doesn't "listen" to the data messages being sent from the server to the other clients. Instead, this process will always stay on top of the other client windows (because it is a window with the Toolbox attribute), and if the button is pressed, a DDEEXECUTE() DDE procedure is executed that effectively stops the server program, which stops the clients as well. This is done with the following code:

```
OF ?KillEmButton
   CASE EVENT()
   OF EVENT:Accepted
     DDEEXECUTE(DDEChannel,'[EXIT]')
   END
```

Recall from Listing 22.2 that in the server program, when the EVENT:DDEExecute is received and the DDEVALUE() function returns '[EXIT]', the server will stop. When this occurs, an EVENT:DDEClosed is sent to all clients, informing them that this has happened. As you can see in Listing 22.3, each client is listening for this event, and when it occurs, each client stops as well.

TIP

In the \CW\LIBSRC\EQUATES.CLW file, the EVENT:DDEClosed and EVENT:DDEPoke hex values are reversed. The correct values should be the following:

```
EVENT:DDEpoke      EQUATE (210H)
EVENT:DDEclosed    EQUATE (211H)
```

Using the Client and Server Programs

To use the client and server example programs, simply execute the client program, which will start the server program automatically. Type some data into the entry controls in the server. You will see the result appear immediately in the hot client, and about five seconds later you will see the result appear in the warm client. To see the result in the cold client, you must press the Get Data button. To stop the server and clients, push the OK button in the `ClientTBProc()` (Toolbox) client.

Summary

DDE is a difficult subject to master in traditional languages and even in many high-level languages. Clarion for Windows makes DDE child's play. This is primarily due to the Clarion for Windows messaging model and the high level of encapsulation in the Clarion for Windows DDE functions and events. I encourage you to explore DDE with the various other Windows programs, and see for yourself what amazing things you can do with this incredible technology.

23

Using Drag and Drop

Drag and drop is a procedure that lets you move information from one control to another control by clicking and dragging with the mouse. You position the mouse over the data you want to move (or copy), click and hold with the mouse, and drag the data to the new location, releasing the mouse to "drop" the data. If you've ever used the Windows File Manager to copy files, you know the process. The effect is quite striking—it appears as if you, the user, can actually grab data with the mouse and move it to a new location. As with most magic acts, however, the reality is a little more mundane, and the code to accomplish the feat is actually quite simple.

A drag and drop operation has three parts: The user selects a control by pressing the mouse button, the user drags away from the control, and the user releases the mouse button over a destination control (which may or may not be in the same program, by the way). These are represented in Clarion code by the DRAG event, the DRAGGING event, and the DROP event.

The *DRAG, DRAGGING,* and *DROP* Events

The user would appear to be generating EVENT:DRAG, EVENT:DRAGGING, EVENT:DROP, but your CW program sees these events happening in a subtly different order: EVENT:DRAGGING, EVENT:DRAG, EVENT:DROP. Whenever the user clicks and drags on a control, EVENT:DRAGGING (not EVENT:DRAG) gets posted to the control. This is primarily so that you, the programmer, can change the mouse cursor if you wish.

Drag and Drop Cursors

When you are dragging and dropping, you need to give the user some idea of what a valid drop target is. CW provides two default cursors to do this: One is a circle with a slash through it—a form of the international symbol for no—to indicate that the area under the cursor is not a valid drop destination. The other is a solid black down-pointing arrow, indicating a valid drop destination.

Every time the cursor moves over a new control there is the possibility that the destination will be either valid or invalid, so you also get a DRAGGING event each time.

When you release the mouse over a valid drop destination, two things happen. EVENT:DRAG is posted to the control where the drag started. This happens whether or not the control over which the mouse was released is a valid target for the host control. If the target is valid (determined through the use of drag and drop IDs, which are explained shortly), it then receives EVENT:DROP.

These two events, DRAG and DROP, are nothing more than triggers for code that you, the programmer, will write. They do not, themselves, transfer data. There are some built-in functions in CW to help you accomplish dragging and dropping, but they are not an essential part of the process.

Drag and Drop IDs

Dragging and dropping data in a procedure is much like dragging and dropping things in real life. You may need to do laundry and take out garbage on the same day, but if you drop your laundry into the garbage bin and drop your garbage into the washing machine, I guarantee you are going to regret it.

The same goes for Windows applications. You can drag and drop data all over the place, but not every place is appropriate for every piece of data. In your home, common sense determines what is an appropriate receptacle for your stuff. In Windows, because it's easy to make a slip with a mouse, controls that have drag capabilities are assigned one or more drag IDs, and controls that have drop capabilities are assigned one or more drop IDs. A drag and drop operation can complete only if the controls have at least one common drag/drop ID between them.

Writing the Code

For the sake of discussion, imagine that you have a browse that shows a list of names, and you'd like to add a small list box beside it to which you can drag names for some special purpose—perhaps you're thinking of hitting these people up for a loan so you can buy yourself a faster computer.

To carry out this exercise (writing the software, I mean, not begging for money), create an application using Quick Start. (If you haven't yet done this, refer to Chapter 6, "Quick Start: The Two-Minute Application." You can also find the completed application in the \Chap23 directory on the source code disk.) Call the application DragDrop and the file NAMES (with a prefix of NAM). One field in the file called NAM:Name should have a picture token of @S20 and should be a Duplicate key.

Adding a Drop Target List Box

Once you've created the application, you'll need to add a few useful bits. Go to the `BrowseByNames` procedure and bring up the Window Formatter. Move the right margin of the list box to the left about 20 percent of the way, and place a list box to its right, as shown in Figure 23.1.

On the new list box's Properties window, set the From attribute to `DropQueue`. You'll create that queue in a moment. Also, set the horizontal and vertical scroll bars on, and make sure Immediate is not selected. When you do the drag from the browse box to this list box, you will write a couple lines of code that add the name from the browse to `DropQueue`, the contents of which will be automatically displayed in this list box.

FIGURE 23.1.

The BrowseByNames
*procedure with a list box
added to hold the dragged
names.*

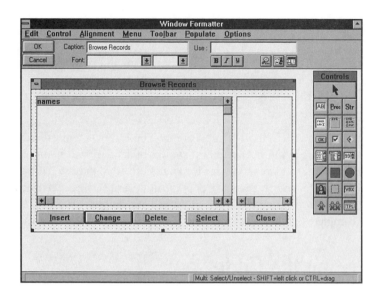

Save your changes, and return to the Procedure Properties window. Go to the data window, and at the bottom of the list of data items insert a new item. Call it DropQueue, and make it a type Queue. When you click OK, you'll immediately get another New Field Properties window, which enables you to add elements to the queue. Give the field the name DropName, and make it a STRING(30). Click OK, and on the next New Field Properties window click on Cancel. Your data window should look like the one in Figure 23.2.

FIGURE 23.2.

The data window for the
BrowseByNames *pro-
cedure, with the local queue
added to support the list of
dragged and dropped
names.*

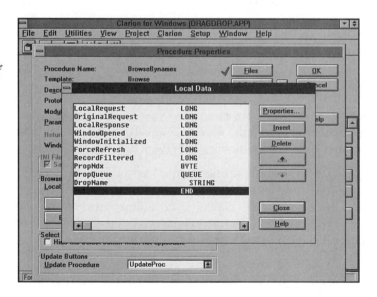

Assigning IDs to the Controls

The next step is to assign a drag ID to the main list box (the one showing the records from your benefactors' file), and to assign a drop ID to the list box that holds the names of those you want to give special attention. This ID will need to be the same for both drag and drop IDs.

There is no way in CW 1.0 to assign a drag or drop ID directly in the Window Formatter. You can do it by accessing the window structure directly from the Procedure Properties window (click the ellipsis button to the right of the Window button) or you can assign the ID at runtime, using the property syntax. This example uses the latter technique, which is simple:

```
?List{PROP:dragid} = 'PatsyName'
?List2{PROP:dropid} = 'PatsyName'
```

Add this code to the After Opening The Window embed point. (For help on adding embedded code, see Chapter 16, "Hand Code, Reuse, and the Application Generator.")

Even though this code will work just fine for this example, I encourage you to consider a slightly more complicated approach. It is possible to have up to 16 IDs on a control. Although it isn't readily obvious, the drag and drop ID properties are arrays. If you don't specify the array index when assigning the property, the compiler will assume you are assigning the first element of the array, and you will overwrite any previous assignments. A better code technique, which checks for the first empty array element and assigns the property there, is shown in Listing 23.1, but for the purposes of this exercise you do not need to code it.

Listing 23.1. Assigning drag and drop IDs in a way that allows for multiple assignments.

```
LOOP PropNdx = 1 TO 16
  IF ?List{prop:dragid,PropNdx} = ''
    ?List{prop:dragid,PropNdx} = 'dragdrop'
    BREAK
  END
END
LOOP PropNdx = 1 TO 16
  IF ?List2{prop:dropid,PropNdx} = ''
    ?List2{prop:dropid,PropNdx} = 'dragdrop'
    BREAK
  END
END
```

Trapping the *DRAG* and *DROP* Events

Now you have to trap the events that occur when the user successfully drags and drops. In the standard templates (at least in CW 1.0) there is no embed point for DRAG or DROP events, so you have to resort to a little trickery. The generated code to handle event processing will look something like that in Listing 23.2.

Listing 23.2. Event processing for a list control.

```
CASE FIELD()
  OF ?List
    CASE EVENT()
    OF EVENT:Accepted
    OF EVENT:NewSelection
      IF RECORDS(Queue:Browse)
        DO BRW1::FillBuffer
        DO RefreshWindow
      END
    OF EVENT:ScrollUp
      DO BRW1::ScrollUp
    OF EVENT:ScrollDown
      DO BRW1::ScrollDown
    OF EVENT:PageUp
      DO BRW1::PageUp
    OF EVENT:PageDown
      DO BRW1::PageDown
    OF EVENT:ScrollTop
      DO BRW1::ScrollTop
    OF EVENT:ScrollBottom
      DO BRW1::ScrollBottom
    OF EVENT:AlertKey
      DO BRW1::AlertKey
    OF EVENT:Selected
    END
```

What you really want to do is add an OF EVENT:Drag to the list. You can simply add a source embed at the Control Event Handling, After Generated Code embed point for any event, and it will work fine. Don't put it before the generated code, or something like a ScrollDown routine may be executed only when the user drags and drops, which probably wouldn't be too impressive, unless you sell to a lot of surrealists. A good choice is the Selected event, because it often has no other code associated with it, and it's common to almost all controls.

Find the appropriate Selected embed point for the ?List control, and add the code shown in Listing 23.3.

Listing 23.3. The code to execute the drag half of the drag and drop operation.

```
OF EVENT:Drag
  IF DRAGID()
    do SyncWindow
    SETDROPID(NAM:Name)
  END
```

There is one bit of hocus-pocus here, and one function to learn. The SyncWindow routine, as a study of AppGen code will tell you, is a standard routine that updates the file buffer with the record currently selected in the browse box. You need this because the NAM:Name field is going to be transferred to the list box, and it wouldn't do to get the wrong record.

The SETDROPID() function works as a courier of the information to be dropped. It loads the value of NAM:Name into a global buffer, where it can be retrieved by the control that gets the drop.

When the code in Listing 23.3 is generated, it will look something like Listing 23.4.

Listing 23.4. Drag event handling as it appears under selected event handling.

```
OF EVENT:ScrollBottom
   DO BRW1::ScrollBottom
OF EVENT:AlertKey
   DO BRW1::AlertKey
OF EVENT:Selected
   OF EVENT:Drag
      IF DRAGID()
         do SyncWindow
         SETDROPID(NAM:Name)
      END
         END
```

The alignment is pretty messed up, which makes the code difficult to read. If you take a moment to align everything, you'll see that you've neatly added another OF to the case statement.

The code for the drop is pretty compact, too. Add Listing 23.5 to the Selected, Control Event Handling, After Generated Code embed for ?List2, which is the field equate for the DropQueue list box.

Listing 23.5. The code to execute the drop half of the drag and drop operation.

```
OF EVENT:Drop
   DropName = DROPID()
   ADD(DropQueue)
```

The DROPID() function retrieves the value set by SETDROPID(), and this value is assigned to the queue element. Adding the queue record automatically displays the name you selected from the browse box, in the list box.

To test your application, make and run it, and add a name or two to the file. Then click and drag one of those names into the DropQueue list box. If you've done everything as specified, the name should appear in the DropQueue list box. (Because there's no code in place at this point to regulate duplicates, you can add to the list as many copies of as many names as you like.)

Dragging Between Procedures

The previous example demonstrates how to drag and drop within a procedure. You can also drag and drop between procedures (and even between applications). Dragging something from one procedure into another can be done exactly as described. In fact, the process shown for dragging and dropping within a procedure is overkill. There is really no need to use SETDROPID() and DROPID() to save and retrieve the values, because all the data is visible to both the drag and drop sides of the operation.

Global Variables and the Clipboard

In addition to SETDROPID(), you can use global variables or the Clipboard to copy data between procedures.

In the example just discussed, the NAM:Name variable is global to the application, and as long as you're not using threaded files, it would be a safe bet as the repository for the name during a drag and drop procedure. It would not, of course, do for copying data between applications.

The SETCLIPBOARD() function enables you to stuff a string or the contents of a variable into the Windows Clipboard, and the CLIPBOARD() function retrieves the current contents of the Clipboard. You can use these functions, or SETDROPID() and DROPID(), to copy data between applications.

Who's Invited to the Party?

Not all controls can participate in drag and drop. You can drag only from regions and list boxes, but you can drop to just about any control. Under some circumstances, you might be able to fake the use of other controls by placing a transparent region over the control. This is possible only when you don't need to actually get access to the underlying control with the mouse. If you do need to get at the control with the mouse, any time you click over the control you'll get it and not the region, and you won't be able to do a drag.

For a region to be on top of a control, it must appear before that control in the window structure. You can make this happen by using the SetOrder option in the Window Formatter and specifying an earlier number for the region than for the control it covers.

> **TIP**
>
> If you have any difficulty getting the region to cover the control, you can verify its position in the window structure by pressing the ellipsis button next to the Window button on the Procedure Properties window. If the region isn't before the control, you can cut and paste the line so that it is. Be careful when you cut and paste in the

window editor—some structures in the window may be several lines long, and if you break these you will get Window Formatter errors.

Dragging Between Applications

If you want to drag and drop between applications, prefix the drag/drop ID with a tilde (~) character. This simply indicates to the drag and drop mechanism that the signature is global to all applications.

File Manager Drops

The drop ID of ~FILE is a special case. You can use it to receive drags of filenames from the File Manager. The result will be a comma-delimited string of filenames, returned by the DROPID() function. For instance, if instead of dragging names from the browse box, you wanted to receive names from the File Manager, use the following code in the After Opening The Window embed point in BrowseByName to set the drop ID for the DropQueue list box.

```
?List2{PROP:dropid} = '~FILE'
```

Be sure you type FILE in uppercase. Now run the Windows File Manager and the sample application so you can see them both on your screen. Run the BrowseByName procedure, then click a file in the File Manager and drag it to the DropQueue list box. You will see the filename appear in the list. If you select multiple files, they will be returned in a string, separated by commas. The filenames you get in this exercise will probably be too long to fit in the list box, but you can easily fix that by making a bigger list box with a larger string as the queue element.

The Drag and Drop Extension Template

To make the business of dragging and dropping a little easier, this book includes a drag and drop extension template. The construction and use of that template is discussed in Chapter 20, "Creating Extension Templates."

Summary

Drag and drop is one of those things that can look positively magical at times, but it is really quite ordinary under the covers. You get a notification that a successful drag and drop has occurred, at which point you can take the appropriate action for copying or moving data, and you have the option of changing the cursor during the drag operation.

Most of the work in drag and drop is in moving data around, and to help you with that, CW provides the SETDROPID(), DROPID(), SETCLIPBOARD(), and CLIPBOARD() functions. You can also drag filenames from the Windows File Manager to any control with the drop ID -FILE.

24

Using Open Database Connectivity

Open database connectivity (ODBC) is a standard common data access methodology developed by Microsoft Corporation for MS Windows. ODBC is no longer just a Windows standard; it can be used across various platforms, including mainframes, minis, and even Macs. This chapter discusses what ODBC means and how it can be used effectively within your Clarion for Windows programs.

The Concept Behind ODBC

ODBC is not a database driver, nor is it a database engine. ODBC is a vendor-neutral database access application programming interface (API) that functions as middleware between your application and the data source (database) of your choice.

In many development environments, native database drivers are not always available for the database engine you wish to use. Microsoft Corporation recognized this fact and created an API that database vendors could support at the database driver level, enabling those environments that cannot directly talk to the database driver to communicate via the ODBC API. Developers needed a standard data access language in order to communicate with the ODBC middleware API. This common data access language had to be acceptable and supported by all development environments in a way that was common to the industry standard. Microsoft chose Structured Query Language (SQL) because it was an industry standard and was in widespread use.

ODBC resides somewhere between your application code and the specific database driver, thus it is considered middleware. ODBC is not responsible for communicating directly with the data source, but with the specific database driver that does communicate directly with the data source. More specifically, ODBC is more like a messaging API than anything else; that is, it obtains a command from your program, translates it into common ODBC driver messages, then passes these messages along to the ODBC driver manager (a component within ODBC), which then communicates with the database driver specified for the data source. The database driver then translates these messages into database-specific calls, performs the desired action, and returns the data through the ODBC layer back to your program. Of course, there is error handling within the ODBC layer that will be invoked when a database request fails for some reason. It is the job of the database driver specified for a data source to directly communicate with the database engine.

ODBC needs you (the developer) or your users to already have the necessary database driver(s) to access the data source. ODBC does not provide a database driver; rather, it provides the capability to communicate with database drivers when your development environment does not support a database natively. Because of the overhead this process involves, ODBC should be used only when there are no native database drivers available. However, it is better to have slower access than no access at all.

Database Drivers

Most database drivers are installed in the \Windows\System directory and are in the form of a dynamic link library (DLL). Some database drivers may install themselves into specific directories so they do not replace other ODBC-compliant components. When you install a database driver, or any other Windows program for that matter, it is always wise to back up your Windows INI files, just to be on the safe side.

When you install a new database driver to your system, it is installed into the ODBCINST.INI file and as well into a related Windows registry database reflecting the installed ODBC drivers. Listing 24.1 shows an example of an ODBCINST.INI file. As you can see immediately, there is a section of text that warns you not to make changes to this file manually. This is because the ODBC installation information is not contained solely in the ODBCINST.INI file, but in the ODBCINST registry database as well. If the two components get out of sync, you may need to re-install the database drivers to correct this situation. Therefore, heed this warning.

As you can see, the first section of the ODBCINST.INI file contains the heading [ODBC Drivers]. This section informs Windows which database drivers are installed and what the default file extension for these databases are. Following this section are individual sections for each database driver listed in the [ODBC Drivers] section. Under each specific database driver section, [Oracle] for example, are two entries: Driver= and Setup=. The Driver= entry informs the ODBC drive manager of the name of the database driver, and to use it for ODBC processing. The Setup= entry is used by the ODBCADM.EXE program when configuring the ODBC data source.

Listing 24.1 contains an example ODBCINST.INI file. Notice the [WATCOM SQL] database driver entry. In this example the database driver is installed in a directory other than the \Windows\System directory.

Listing 24.1. The ODBCINST.INI sample file.

```
;--------------------------------------------------------------------
; WARNING:  Do not make changes to this file without using the ODBC Control
;           panel device or other utilites provided for maintaining data
;           sources.
;
;           Incorrect changes to this file could prevent ODBC from
;           operating or operating correctly.
;--------------------------------------------------------------------

[ODBC Drivers]
Oracle=Installed
SQL Server=Installed
Access Data (*.mdb)=Installed
FoxPro Files (*.dbf)=Installed
dBase Files (*.dbf)=Installed
Paradox Files (*.db )=Installed
```

continues

Listing 24.1. continued

```
Text Files (*.txt; *.csv)=Installed
Excel Files (*.xls)=Installed
Btrieve Data (file.ddf)=Installed
Access 2.0 for MS Office (*.mdb)=Installed
WATCOM SQL=Installed

[Oracle]
Driver=C:\WINDOWS\SYSTEM\sqora.dll
Setup=C:\WINDOWS\SYSTEM\sqorastp.dll

[SQL Server]
Driver=C:\WINDOWS\SYSTEM\SQLSRVR.DLL
Setup=C:\WINDOWS\SYSTEM\SQLSRVR.DLL

[WATCOM SQL]
Driver=c:\WSQL\wsqlodbc.dll
Setup=c:\WSQL\wsqlodbc.dll

[Access Data (*.mdb)]
Driver=C:\WINDOWS\SYSTEM\SIMBA.DLL
Setup=C:\WINDOWS\SYSTEM\SIMADMIN.DLL

[FoxPro Files (*.dbf)]
Driver=C:\WINDOWS\SYSTEM\SIMBA.DLL
Setup=C:\WINDOWS\SYSTEM\SIMADMIN.DLL

[dBase Files (*.dbf)]
Driver=C:\WINDOWS\SYSTEM\SIMBA.DLL
Setup=C:\WINDOWS\SYSTEM\SIMADMIN.DLL

[Paradox Files (*.db )]
Driver=C:\WINDOWS\SYSTEM\SIMBA.DLL
Setup=C:\WINDOWS\SYSTEM\SIMADMIN.DLL

[Text Files (*.txt; *.csv)]
Driver=C:\WINDOWS\SYSTEM\simba.dll
Setup=C:\WINDOWS\SYSTEM\simadmin.dll

[Excel Files (*.xls)]
Driver=C:\WINDOWS\SYSTEM\simba.dll
Setup=C:\WINDOWS\SYSTEM\simadmin.dll

[Btrieve Data (file.ddf)]
Driver=C:\WINDOWS\SYSTEM\simba.dll
Setup=C:\WINDOWS\SYSTEM\simadmin.dll

[Access 2.0 for MS Office (*.mdb)]
Driver=C:\WINDOWS\SYSTEM\ODBCJT16.DLL
Setup=C:\WINDOWS\SYSTEM\ODBCJT16.DLL
```

Defining a Data Source

A data source is equivalent to a database. A *database* can be one physical file, as seen in many desktop databases, or it can be one physical file that contains many tables, as seen in SQL RDBMSs. In any event, a *data source* is always the data you wish to access.

When you use ODBC in Windows, you must first define or register a data source. This can be done using the ODBC Administrator program (ODBCADM.EXE).

Figure 24.1 shows the ODBCADM data source window that is used for defining a database in Windows. There are a few important items in this window to note.

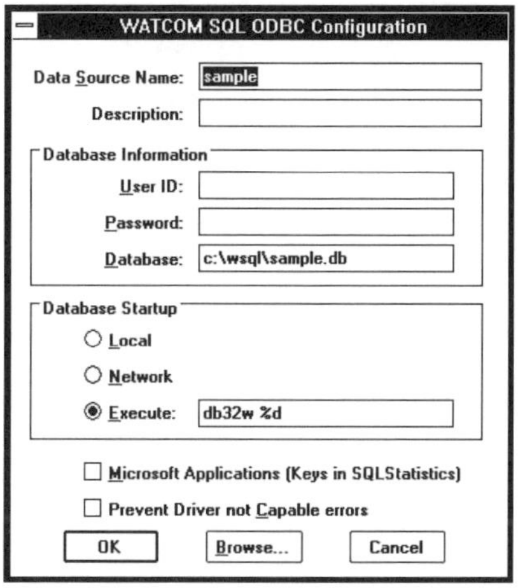

FIGURE 24.1.
ODBCADM.EXE data source window.

- Data Source Name: The Data Source Name is the name by which the ODBC driver will identify the database you wish to use. If you specify this name incorrectly, you will not be able to connect to the database.

- User ID: Many databases enable you to assign the owner of the database in the startup process so that you do not need to log in to the database explicitly when connecting to it. The User ID entry is used for this purpose.

- Password: In conjunction with the User ID entry, a password can be associated with the connection process. Like the User ID entry, the Password entry enables you to automatically connect to the database without explicitly logging in to the database itself.

- Database: Many database engines must have a physically defined database. That is, the database file must be specified in the data source description in order for the engine to start the correct copy of your database. The Database entry is used for this purpose. In server-based database engines, this designation is generally superseded by the use of a server database name instead of a hard-coded path and filename.

■ Database Startup: The Database Startup entry is used to inform the ODBC driver manager how to start the specific data source. A data source can be started locally or on the network. For example, the WATCOM database called SAMPLE.DB can be started locally using a single-user version of the WATCOM SQL engine, or it can execute a client-based component on a PC that communicates with the server-based SQL engine on a network. These options and the parameters they may take are completely database engine specific; therefore, I will not cover them in detail here, because they are beyond the scope of this chapter.

When the data source is defined, another INI file is updated. This file is the ODBC.INI file, which contains the registered data sources. There is an example of an ODBC.INI file in Listing 24.2. As you will notice again, the ODBC.INI file sports the same warning and adheres to the same principles as stated for the ODBCINST.INI file.

The ODBC.INI file contains the registered data sources and their respective definitions, which are defined using the ODBCADM.EXE program. The first section, [ODBC Data Sources], lists all the registered data sources in Windows which correlates the data source name with a specific database driver, and which optionally defines the default file extension for the database.

The following sections each represent a specific data source name. Contained within these sections are entries that represent parameters used for connecting to the specific data source. These parameters vary depending on the actual database driver.

Listing 24.2. The ODBC.INI sample file.

```
;--------------------------------------------------------------------------
; WARNING:  Do not make changes to this file without using the ODBC Control
;           panel device or other utilites provided for maintaining data
;           sources.
;
;           Incorrect changes to this file could prevent ODBC from
;           operating or operating correctly.
;--------------------------------------------------------------------------

[ODBC Data Sources]
PowerBuilder Demo DB=WATCOM SQL
MS Access Databases=Access Data (*.mdb)
FoxPro Files=FoxPro Files (*.dbf)
dBase Files=dBase Files (*.dbf)
Paradox Files=Paradox Files (*.db )
NWind=dBase Files (*.dbf)
sample=WATCOM SQL

[WATCOM SQL]
driver=c:\wsql\wsqlodbc.dll

[MS Access Databases]
Driver=C:\WINDOWS\SYSTEM\SIMBA.DLL
FileType=RedISAM
```

```
SingleUser=False
UseSystemDB=False
DataDirectory=c:\cw\examples\sample.mdb

[FoxPro Files]
Driver=C:\WINDOWS\SYSTEM\SIMBA.DLL
FileType=FoxPro 2.5
SingleUser=False

[dBase Files]
Driver=C:\WINDOWS\SYSTEM\SIMBA.DLL
FileType=dBase4
SingleUser=False

[Paradox Files]
Driver=C:\WINDOWS\SYSTEM\SIMBA.DLL
FileType=Paradox
SingleUser=False

[NWind]
Driver=C:\WINDOWS\SYSTEM\SIMBA.DLL
FileType=dBase4
DataDirectory=C:\WINDOWS\MSAPPS\MSQUERY
SingleUser=False

[sample]
Driver=c:\WSQL\wsqlodbc.dll
UID=
Database=c:\wsql\sample.db
Start=db32w %d
```

Database Definition

In general, an ODBC database utilizes three very important parameters that are required in order to connect with an SQL RDBMS engine. These parameters are Database Name, User Id, and Password. In some databases this information is not required, but in many others it is. Look at the table definition in Listing 24.3 to see how to set up these values when your database needs them.

Listing 24.3. The ODBC table definition.

```
People      FILE,PRE(PEO),DRIVER('ODBC'),¦
            OWNER('DataSourceName','UserId','Password'),¦
            THREAD,BINDABLE,NAME(TableName)
K_PeoNo     KEY(+PEO:PeopleNo),PRIMARY
K_Name      KEY(+PEO:LastNane,+PEO:FirstName),DUP,NOCASE
RECORD      RECORD
LastName      STRING(25)
FirstName     STRING(20)
            END
          END
```

First, you must specify the label of the database table you wish to define; in this case it is `People`. In the `FILE()` parameter, you must use the physical name of the database table. A variable containing the physical location of the database may be used for the `FILE()` parameter. The Name attribute defines the table in the database you are defining and is required. The `DRIVER()` parameter must state that this definition is of an ODBC type. The `OWNER()` parameter specifies the actual data source name, and optionally the user ID and password, each separated by commas. A variable containing the data source, user ID, and password may be used for the `OWNER()` parameter. By definition, most ODBC databases are created externally from Clarion for Windows; therefore, the Create attribute is omitted. The Thread attribute is used to provide separate data buffers for each thread that opens the ODBC data source. And finally, the Bindable attribute is required by the Clarion for Windows ODBC driver.

The Clarion for Windows compiler will normally optimize the amount of data used by your program by not storing column names. However, the ODBC driver needs to use SQL to communicate with the ODBC manager, so it needs to know the names of the columns. The Bindable attribute stops the compiler from performing this name space optimization inherent with other data definitions. An alternative to using the Bindable attribute is to supply external names for all table columns. This enables you to use different names in your Clarion for Windows program than are used by the back-end database engine. This is important for column names that are not valid labels in Clarion for Windows. For example, an MS Access column called `my field` (notice the space) could be used in the Name attribute. You cannot have a space in a column name in Clarion for Windows, so you would need to use the following:

```
MyField   STING(10),NAME('"my field"').
```

This is a very powerful feature that enables you to do computed columns in your record definition. You could therefore use something like the following:

```
Price      DECIMAL(7,2),NAME('Price')
Discount   DECIMAL(7,2),NAME('Discount')
TotField   DECIMAL(7,2),NAME('Price-Discount')
```

where the `Price-Discount` column is a computed column value returned by the ODBC driver to your Clarion for Windows program.

Connecting, Using, and Disconnecting

In languages where SQL is the only data access language, there are specific statements that are used for connecting to and disconnecting from the data source. Additionally, in these environments the only way to access, insert, update, or delete data is with SQL. In Clarion for Windows, you are not limited to just using SQL (set-oriented operations), but you are also given the option of using record-level operations as well.

Connecting

If you are familiar with SQL operations, you are familiar with the CONNECT statement. Essentially you specify the database to which you wish to connect in the CONNECT statement. If a user or password is required, you must also supply this information in some form (that is, in a login screen or an INI file). The CONNECT statement will establish the connection via the ODBC data source information described previously. Once the connection is made, the user requesting access is verified and authorized, and access is either granted or revoked. At this point the user can access any data he or she has been given rights to access.

In Clarion for Windows, this process is handled much differently. Use the OPEN() statement just as you would for any other database, and the Clarion for Windows ODBC driver will pass all connection information to the database. This is the reason for specifying the OWNER() parameter on a database table definition, as seen in Listing 24.3.

To be thorough, after opening a table, you should always issue the FILEERRORCODE() function to ensure that no errors have been encountered. If any errors are encountered, use the FILEERROR() function for textual information about the specific error. Note that this is not the ERRORCODE() function, it is the FILEERRORCODE() function. You should always use ERRORCODE() to check whether an error has been posted; if the error code is 90 (file driver error), you should use the FILEERRORCODE() function to determine which file driver–specific error code has been posted.

Using

Using ODBC is the same as using any other database driver. However, there are a few additional benefits available. For instance, if you wanted to update or delete all records that have a specific value in a given column, you could issue an SQL UPDATE or DELETE statement, respectively. These are strictly non-result set-oriented (performs an action without returning values to your program) commands. In the current version of Clarion for Windows, you can issue any SQL statement that does not return a result set to the user. This limitation will be remedied in another upcoming release of Clarion for Windows, where complete result-set SQL statements may be issued.

Listing 24.4 shows an example of what happens in the ODBC database driver when issuing Clarion for Windows data access syntax. As you can see, the SQL syntax is rather compact in comparison to the Clarion for Windows data access method, which makes SQL beautiful. Rest assured, SQL statements can get extremely complicated (more so than Clarion data access syntax) when joins and nested subqueries get involved. The point here is that you will issue the same familiar syntax for an SQL RDBMS, and the ODBC driver will translate it appropriately for the ODBC data source.

Listing 24.4. Turning Clarion for Windows syntax into SQL syntax.

```
Clarion Data Access:

CLEAR(PEO:Record,-1)
PEO:LastName = 'SANTOS'
PEO:FirstName = 'ROSS'
SET(PEO:K_Name,PEO:K_Name)
NEXT(PEOPLE)

SQL Data Access:

SELECT LastName, FirstName FROM People WHERE LastName > 'SANTOS' OR (LastName =
'SANTOS' AND FirstName >= 'ROSS')
```

For all intents and purposes, you will use normal Clarion for Windows data access statements and they will be translated as needed for the ODBC data source.

As already mentioned, you can send UPDATE and DELETE SQL statements to an ODBC data source. Listing 24.5 shows an example of how this is accomplished.

Listing 24.5. UPDATE and DELETE SQL statements.

```
SEND(PEOPLE,'UPDATE People SET PEO:LastName = ''HARMS'' WHERE PEO:LastName =
''SANTOS''')
SEND(PEOPLE,'DELETE People WHERE PEO:LastName = ''SANTOS''')
```

Notice the use of the SEND() statement. This statement sends a driver-specific command (in this case, a non-result SQL statement) to a database driver. The first statement will change to Harms the last name of each record (row) that has a last name of Santos. The second statement will delete any records (rows) where the last name is Santos. After issuing a SEND() statement, you should always check for errors using the FILEERRORCODE() function.

The best use of the SEND() statement in this version of Clarion for Windows is for mass updates or deletes. Otherwise you should use standard Clarion for Windows data access syntax as you would for any other direct database driver.

Disconnecting

Again, if you are familiar with SQL operations, you are familiar with the DISCONNECT statement. The DISCONNECT statement will log the current user out of the data source, and in most cases will commit all outstanding transactions for this user.

In Clarion for Windows, this process is handled much differently. You use the CLOSE() statement as you would for any other database, and the Clarion for Windows ODBC driver will pass all disconnect information to the database, performing exactly the same functionality as the SQL DISCONNECT statement.

Summary

Other languages need specific syntax to handle record- and set-based database access, but Clarion for Windows keeps it simple and elegant. By using the same language function for all databases, Clarion for Windows hides from the developer the underlying complexities of database-specific access.

25

Using the Windows API

The Windows Application Programming Interface, or API, is the heart of Windows programming. Every Clarion for Windows (CW) program makes massive use of the API. In fact, it used to be that the only way to get real power out of a programming environment was to call the API, and you, the programmer, had to manage this.

The Windows API covers just about every conceivable action a programmer might want to take. There are API calls to create and destroy windows, create and destroy controls, process messages, draw graphics, manage memory, play music, display help information, and so on. Much of CW's functionality is in giving you easy access to the hundreds of API calls; by using Clarion language statements, which in turn call API functions, you get the power without the pain.

There are times, however, when you want to call the API. What CW does it does well and quickly, but there are some esoteric API functions that are not worth putting into the language. This chapter focuses on a group of serial communications API functions you will use to create a telephone autodialer using the serial communications API calls.

The AutoDialer Example

Serial communications is a bit of a tricky business, and particularly so in Windows. Data coming into the serial port needs to be read in a timely manner, and in a cooperative multitasking environment where one program can easily hog the CPU, problems frequently occur. For serious serial communications, such as creating a terminal program or doing file transfers, you probably won't want to use the API. There are a number of DLLs and VBXs available that incorporate thoroughly tested serial communications code with a lot more functionality than the API alone offers.

On the other hand, if you just need to do something such as dial a phone number or send a block of data to a device on the serial port, the code in this chapter will do quite nicely.

Prototyping Functions

One of the first challenges you'll face in calling the Windows API is prototyping functions. Most documentation for the API is written for C programmers and uses C data types; you need to understand how to convert those declarations to something suitable for CW. This subject is dealt with in some detail in Chapter 26, "Using VBXs and Non-CW DLLs."

The *OpenComm( )* Function

The OpenComm() function is essential to serial communications in Windows. It opens for use a communications device, such as a serial port, and it allocates memory to the buffers that will store incoming and outgoing data. The C language procedure prototype looks this:

```
int    WINAPI OpenComm(LPCSTR, UINT, UINT);
```

The CW prototype for the same function is a little different:

```
OpenComm(*CSTRING,USHORT,USHORT),SHORT,RAW,PASCAL
```

In C, the function's return type is declared before the function; in CW, the function's return type is declared after the parameter list. The int, or integer type in the C declaration, corresponds to SHORT in CW. The first parameter is type LPCSTR in C, which means a long pointer to a CSTRING. In CW, LPCSTR is declared as *CSTRING, which is a CSTRING data type prepended with the pointer character. The pointer character simply means that the address of the CSTRING, rather than the string itself, will be passed to the function.

The last two parameters are both declared as UINT in C, which means that they are unsigned integers. You can probably guess that this corresponds to a USHORT declaration in CW.

There are two very important additional keywords on the CW declaration. The PASCAL keyword specifies the calling convention. All TopSpeed languages, including CW, pass parameters in registers, which is considerably faster than passing parameters on the stack. For compatibility with other libraries, such as the Windows API, you must tell the compiler to use the stack-based convention, and in particular the PASCAL (left-to-right) stack-based convention.

The second keyword is RAW. You are required to use it when passing strings by address, because CW normally passes both the address of the string and the length. The API expects only the address, and the RAW strips out the length information. If you aren't passing any strings by address, you don't need the Raw attribute.

Creating a Module for the Map

Once you've prototyped the functions you need, the next step is to place them in a module so the compiler knows they're available. Listing 25.1 shows the standard serial communications functions prototyped for use by Clarion for Windows. The module to contain these functions is declared in much the same way any other module is declared. There's a little twist here, however. If you declare source modules, the MODULE statement's parameter must be the name of the source file. If you declare a library module, that parameter can contain any unique identifier. In this case, I've used WINAPI, but COMSTUFF or any other text would have served the purpose just as well.

NOTE

Listings 25.1 through 25.6 are partial source code listings. To see where the code in these listings fits into the big picture, refer to the complete source code in Listing 26.7.

Listing 25.1. The basic Windows API functions required to do serial communications, prototyped for Clarion for Windows.

```
MODULE('WINAPI')
  OpenComm(*CSTRING,USHORT,USHORT),SHORT,RAW,PASCAL
  CloseComm(SHORT),SHORT,PASCAL
  WriteComm(SHORT,*STRING,SHORT),SHORT,RAW,PASCAL
  ReadComm(SHORT,*STRING,SHORT),SHORT,RAW,PASCAL
  SetCommState(*STRING),SHORT,RAW,PASCAL
  GetCommState(SHORT,*STRING),SHORT,RAW,PASCAL
  BuildCommDCB(*CSTRING,*STRING),SHORT,RAW,PASCAL
  FlushComm(SHORT,SHORT),SHORT,PASCAL
  GetCommError(SHORT,*STRING),SHORT,RAW,PASCAL
END
```

Peek Message (*CSTRING, USHORT, USHORT, USHORT, USHORT), SHORT, PASCAL

Each of these functions is discussed in more detail as it is used in the following code examples.

WINDOWS.LIB

You might not be aware that there is a library called WINDOWS.LIB that is automatically included in any CW application's project. The serial communications functions reside in the Windows file USER.EXE, and WINDOWS.LIB contains the hooks that enable your program to access those functions, in the same way that linking a LIB into your program enables you to use functions in a corresponding DLL. (For more information on LIBs and DLLs, see Chapter 32, "Sharing Code: Creating Clarion DLLs.")

TIP

If you want to use functions that are available only in Windows 3.1, you will need to obtain the TopSpeed Tech Kit, which contains a 3.1 library called WIN31.LIB, or use a library importer to create your own LIB. For more on creating import LIBs, see Chapter 26.

Declaring Structures

API functions often involve the use of C structs, or structures, which are roughly analogous to Clarion's GROUPs. Windows serial communication functions use a struct of the type DCB, which contains port configuration information. This means you can create an organized location for all information relative to serial communications for a given port, and all internal functions can reference it as needed. The process of initializing this structure is described in the following sections. Listings 25.2 and 25.3 show the required source code.

Listing 25.2. The C `tagDCB` comm port structure, taken from `WINDOWS.H`.

```
typedef struct tagDCB
{
    BYTE Id;
    UINT BaudRate;
    BYTE ByteSize;
    BYTE Parity;
    BYTE StopBits;
    UINT RlsTimeout;
    UINT CtsTimeout;
    UINT DsrTimeout;

    UINT fBinary        :1;
    UINT fRtsDisable    :1;
    UINT fParity        :1;
    UINT fOutxCtsFlow   :1;
    UINT fOutxDsrFlow   :1;
    UINT fDummy         :2;
    UINT fDtrDisable    :1;

    UINT fOutX          :1;
    UINT fInX           :1;
    UINT fPeChar        :1;
    UINT fNull          :1;
    UINT fChEvt         :1;
    UINT fDtrflow       :1;
    UINT fRtsflow       :1;
    UINT fDummy2        :1;

    char XonChar;
    char XoffChar;
    UINT XonLim;
    UINT XoffLim;
    char PeChar;
    char EofChar;
    char EvtChar;
    UINT TxDelay;
} DCB;
```

The corresponding CW data structure is shown in Listing 25.3.

Listing 25.3. The CW version of the comm port structure (declared as a `GROUP`).

```
g:PortStruct   GROUP,PRE(PTS)
 ID                BYTE(1)
 BaudRate          USHORT(19200)
 BYTESize          BYTE(8)
 Parity            BYTE(0)
 StopBits          BYTE(1)
 RLSTimeout        USHORT(100)
 CTSTimeout        USHORT(100)
```

continues

Listing 25.3. continued

```
DSRTimeout       USHORT(100)

fBinary          USHORT(1)
fRTSDisable      USHORT(1)
fParity          USHORT(1)
fOutXCTSFlow     USHORT(0)
fOutXCTSFlow     USHORT(0)
fDummy           USHORT
fDTRDisable      USHORT(0)

fOutX            USHORT(0)
fInX             USHORT(0)
fPEChar          USHORT(0)
fNull            USHORT(0)
fChevt           USHORT(0)
fDTRFlow         USHORT(0)
fRTSFlow         USHORT(0)
fDummy2          USHORT

XOnChar          BYTE
XOffChar         BYTE
XOnLim           USHORT
XOffLim          USHORT
PeChar           BYTE
EOFChar          BYTE
EVTChar          BYTE
TxDelay          USHORT
                 END
```

The `GetCommState()`, `PutCommState()`, and `BuildCommDCB()` functions all take the `g:PortStruct` group as a parameter. In CW, GROUPs are passed as strings, and because the C functions are prototyped with a long pointer to the struct, you need to prototype the CW parameter as a string passed by address (remember to add the Raw attribute so that only the address is passed).

Calling the API—The *AutoDialer* Function

Now that you understand the idea of prototyping API functions and declaring C-compatible structures (GROUPs), it's time to put everything together into an autodialer function.

Communications software generally follows a three-step process. Step one is initializing the port for use. In a multitasking environment such as Windows, this is particularly important because several programs may need to use the serial port. There has to be some mechanism for arbitrating which program gets access.

The second step in the process is to conduct the communications session, and the third step is to shut down the comm port. This ensures that the next application that needs to use the port will be able to do so.

Initializing the Comm Port

Listing 25.4 shows the code used to initialize the communications port. The local variable l:PortString is a CSTRING(5), which holds the standard comm port designation COM*n*, where *n* is the port number. This is one of two values you will pass to the function that will contain this code; the other is the phone number. Also note that l:PortString gets its value via PortString, which is the name of the first parameter in the function declaration (see Listing 25.7 for the complete listing including function declarations).

Listing 25.4. Code to initialize the communications port. *OpenComm Function*

```
l:PortString = PortString
l:Port = OpenComm(l:PortString,128,128)
IF l:Port < 0
  r# = MESSAGE('Error opening port: ' & l:Port,'Problem',icon:exclamation)
  RETURN(0)
END
l:ModeStr = PortString & ':2400,n,8,1'
l:Result = BuildCommDCB(l:ModeStr,l:PortStruct)
IF l:Result < 0
  l:Junk = MESSAGE('Error building dcb: ' &¦
    l:Result,'Problem',icon:exclamation)
DO ReturnError
END
l:Result = SetCommState(l:PortStruct)
IF l:Result < 0
  l:Junk = MESSAGE('Error setting port: ' & ¦
    l:Result,'Problem',icon:exclamation)
DO ReturnError
END
l:Result = FlushComm(l:Port,0)      ! Transmit Buffer
l:Result = FlushComm(l:Port,1)      ! Receive Buffer
```

The code shown in Listing 25.4 is contained in a function called OpenComm(), which makes sure that the port is available and allocates receive and transmit buffers. The buffers are there because serial communications in Windows is interrupt driven; that is, your program doesn't actually need to sit by the port and collect each byte as it comes in, or send each byte out. It does need to clear out the receive buffer before it gets filled up, and it needs to make sure it doesn't overfill the transmit buffer, but all the nasty little byte-by-byte details are handled by the communications driver.

Once the port is open, the next step you take is initializing the structure, or GROUP in CW terms, that contains all the port settings. You could do this by individually setting each of the values in the GROUP, but it's far easier (and safer) to use the BuildCommDCB() function. You pass the l:PortStruct group to the function, by address, and it loads all the appropriate values into the group's elements. You can then modify the individual elements if you wish (although, in the sample code, there is no need to do this).

Note the error checking after the call to GetCommDCB() (*Build*). Instead of simply exiting the procedure, it calls a routine that first closes down the port, ensuring that another program might still be able to use it.

After you've built a suitable port settings group using GetCommDCB() (*Build*), you need to tell the port to use it, via the SetCommState() function, which takes the port settings group as a parameter. If this is successful, use the FlushComm() function to make sure the transmit and receive buffers are empty of data, and get ready to send your dialing command.

Dialing the Number

Dialing a number with the modem usually involves only sending a single string to the modem. If the modem conforms to the conventional Hayes command set, the first two characters will be AT (the attention command). The next two characters will be either DT or DP. The D stands for dial, the T for tone, and the P for pulse. To dial the ever-popular 555-5555 on a touch-tone phone, your dial string would be ATDT555-5555. Listing 25.5 shows the code that dials the number.

Listing 25.5. Code used to dial a number.

```
  1:SendString = 'ATDT' & clip(PhoneNumber) & ';<13>'
  1:Result = WriteComm(1:port,1:SendString,len(clip(1:SendString)))
  IF 1:Result <> len(clip(1:SendString))
    1:Junk = MESSAGE('Error sending data to port: ' ¦
    & 1:Result,'Problem',icon:exclamation)
DO ReturnError
  END
  1:Result = GetCommError(1:Port,1:comstat)
  IF 1:Result <> 0
    1:Junk = MESSAGE('GetCommError returns ' & ¦
    1:Result,'Debug',icon:exclamation)
DO ReturnError
  END
```

Before the number is dialed, it's concatenated into a string beginning with ATDT and ending with a semicolon and a carriage return character. The semicolon is a dial command that tells the modem to go back into command mode as soon as it has dialed the number. The ASCII 13 carriage return character tells the modem to execute the dial command.

The WriteComm() function, which is the next function called, takes three parameters: the port identifier (which will be 0 for COM1, 1 for COM2, and so on), the dial string, and a value for the number of characters to be sent. This last number is determined by clipping the dial string and counting its characters with the LEN() function.

The WriteComm() function returns the number of characters that were actually sent. If this is not the same as the number of characters that were to be sent, the DialNumber() function will display an error message.

As an added precaution, you should make a call to GetCommError() after writing any data to the serial port, just in case there was an unexpected problem. Again, this is a bit of overkill for a dialing program, and you'll most likely just discard any error, but it's a good habit to get into when you're writing communications software.

Cleaning Up

After you've sent the dial string to the modem, all you really need to do is shut down the port and get out. This may leave some data behind, however, because most modems by default echo commands back to the serial port. The code in Listing 25.6 pauses one second for the command to be echoed back, then flushes both the transmit and receive buffers.

Listing 25.6. Code to flush commands echoed back from the modem and shut down the port.

```
  l:StartTime = CLOCK()
  LOOP
    IF CLOCK() - l:StartTime > 100 OR CLOCK() < l:StartTime THEN BREAK.
  END
!------------------flush the port ----------------------------------------
l:Result = FlushComm(l:Port,0)
  l:Result = FlushComm(l:Port,1)
  l:Result = CloseComm(l:Port)
  IF l:Result <> 0
    l:Junk = message('Error closing port: ' ¦
    & l:Result,'Problem',icon:exclamation)
END
```

> **TIP**
>
> Take a close look at the code used to pause for 1 second. Most of the time only the left-hand IF statement, IF CLOCK() - l:StartTime > 100, will execute. Imagine what would happen if this code executed less than a second before midnight? Clarion times are stored in hundredths of a second since the start of the day. You could conceivably have a situation in which l:StartTime is set to a value such as 8640000 (immediately prior to midnight), and the next number out of the CLOCK() function is 17. In this case your loop will run 24 hours before breaking. The right-hand IF statement ensures that this will never happen.

The Complete *DialNumber()* Function

Listing 25.7 shows the dialer function in its entirety. If you're hand coding, you shouldn't have any trouble incorporating it into your applications as-is.

If you're using the AppGen, you can create a source procedure. Copy everything below the function declaration and above the CODE statement into a source embed at the data embed point. Then copy everything below the CODE statement into a source embed at the code embed point. Give the procedure a prototype of ~~(STRING,STRING),SHORT~~ and a parameter list of ~~(PortString,PhoneNumber)~~.

Listing 25.7. The complete DialNumber() function.

```
DialNumber      FUNCTION(PortString,PhoneNumber)

1:PortStruct   GROUP,PRE(PTS)
ID                BYTE(1)
BaudRate          USHORT(19200)
BYTESize          BYTE(8)
Parity            BYTE(0)
StopBits          BYTE(1)
RLSTimeout        USHORT(100)
CTSTimeout        USHORT(100)
DSRTimeout        USHORT(100)

fBinary           USHORT(1)
fRTSDisable       USHORT(1)
fParity           USHORT(1)
fOutXCTSFlow      USHORT(0)
fOutXDSRFlow      USHORT(0)
fDummy            USHORT
fDTRDisable       USHORT(0)

fOutX             USHORT(0)
fInX              USHORT(0)
fPEChar           USHORT(0)
fNull             USHORT(0)
fChevt            USHORT(0)
fDTRFlow          USHORT(0)
fRTSFlow          USHORT(0)
fDummy2           USHORT

XOnChar           BYTE
XOffChar          BYTE
XOnLim            USHORT
XOffLim           USHORT
PeChar            BYTE
EOFChar           BYTE
EVTChar           BYTE
TxDelay           USHORT
                END

1:ModeStr       cstring(51)


1:comstat         group
status            BYTE
cbinq             USHORT
cboutq            USHORT
                END
```

```
l:Junk            USHORT
l:PortString      CSTRING(5)
l:Result          SHORT
l:Port            SHORT
l:ModeString      CSTRING(51)
l:SendString      STRING(100)
l:StartTime       LONG

  CODE
  l:PortString = PortString
!-----------------open the comm port for use----------------------------
l:Port = OpenComm(l:PortString,128,128)
  IF l:Port < 0
    r# = MESSAGE('Error opening port: ' & l:Port,'Problem',icon:exclamation)
    RETURN(0)
  END
! l:Result = GetCommState(l:Port,l:PortStruct)
  l:ModeStr = PortString & ':2400,n,8,1'
!-----------------set the comm struct values to defaults-----------------
l:Result = BuildCommDCB(l:ModeStr,l:PortStruct)
  IF l:Result < 0
    l:Junk = MESSAGE('Error building dcb: ' ¦
      & l:Result,'Problem',icon:exclamation)
DO ReturnError
  END
!-----------------load the comm struct values----------------------------
l:Result = SetCommState(l:PortStruct)
  IF l:Result < 0
    l:Junk = MESSAGE('Error setting port: ' ¦
      & l:Result,'Problem',icon:exclamation)
    DO ReturnError
  END
!-----------------flush the send and receive buffers--------------------
l:Result = FlushComm(l:Port,0)
  l:Result = FlushComm(l:Port,1)
!-----------------send the number to the modem--------------------------
  l:SendString = 'ATDT' & clip(PhoneNumber) & ';<13>'
  l:Result = Writecomm(l:port,l:SendString,len(clip(l:SendString)))
  IF l:Result <> len(clip(l:SendString))
    l:Junk = MESSAGE('Error sending data to port: ' ¦
      & l:Result,'Problem',icon:exclamation)
    DO ReturnError
  END
  l:Result = GetCommError(l:Port,l:comstat)
  IF l:Result <> 0
    l:Junk = MESSAGE('GetCommError returns ' ¦
      & l:Result,'Debug',icon:exclamation)
DO ReturnError
  END
!-----------------wait one second for the modem to echo back-------------
l:StartTime = CLOCK()
  LOOP
    IF CLOCK() - l:StartTime > 100 OR CLOCK() < l:StartTime THEN BREAK.
  END
!-----------------flush the port ----------------------------------------
l:Result = FlushComm(l:Port,0)
```

continues

Listing 25.7. continued

```
  l:Result = FlushComm(l:Port,1)
  l:Result = CloseComm(l:Port)
  IF l:Result <> 0
    l:Junk = message('Error closing port: ' ¦
    & l:Result,'Problem',icon:exclamation)
END
  RETURN(1)


ReturnError        ROUTINE
  l:Result = CloseComm(l:Port)
  IF l:Result <> 0
    l:Junk = message('Error closing port: ' ¦
    & l:Result,'Problem',icon:exclamation)
END
  RETURN(0)
```

Whether you're hand coding or using the AppGen, you will need to include the API functions in your map. Refer to Listing 25.1 for a map include file. If you're using the AppGen, you should copy the code in that listing to a source embed at the Global Map source embed point.

Summary

Most of the difficulty in using the Windows API involves translating C/C++ function and data declarations to Clarion for Windows equivalents (this is discussed in more detail in Chapter 26). Once you get those wrinkles ironed out, almost the entire API is there for your use. You won't need most of it, because CW does a terrific job of embodying most of its functionality, but if there's something you want to do in Windows, and CW doesn't do it, the API is one of the first places you should look.

26

Using VBXs and Non-CW DLLs

Clarion for Windows is a pretty amazing package that will do just about anything you want, but you won't necessarily choose to use it for all aspects of your applications. After all, if somebody has written the code you want to use, perhaps to read images from a scanner or use network services, it's usually cheaper to buy it than to build it yourself.

Most likely, you will obtain such a product in the form of a Visual Basic custom control (VBX) or a Windows dynamic link library (DLL).

NOTE

This chapter uses the terms *VBX* and *custom control* interchangeably.

DLLs are discussed in some detail in Chapter 32, "Sharing Code: Creating Clarion DLLs." Although this chapter is concerned with DLLs created in other languages, the principles are the same, because CW creates Windows standard DLLs. See Chapter 32 for more on the theory and use of DLLs.

Decisions, Decisions

Deciding whether you will use a VBX or a DLL is only an issue if the particular toolset you want comes in both formats. DLLs tend to be oriented toward managing processes, and VBXs tend to be oriented toward user interface features. DLLs are libraries of procedures, whereas a VBX is specifically a control (actually, it can be more than one control, but for the purposes of this discussion it is a single control).

A control, as explained in Chapter 4, "Concepts You Should Know," is an object on the window that collects information from the user and/or displays information to the user. A list box is a control, a button is a control, a prompt is a control...you get the idea. VBXs are controls as well, and while some of them resemble the familiar objects on a Windows screen, many of them are quite different. And that, after all, is the point of having a custom control—to do things or appear in ways the standard controls can't manage.

In fact, VBXs are also DLLs, but a special kind with a well-defined interface that makes them somewhat easier to use than ordinary DLLs. As you can probably see, the DLL, in one form or another, is common currency in the Windows programming world.

If your choice does come down to a VBX versus a DLL, in general you will find that the VBX is easier to use, particularly in the Window Formatter, but it may not offer you all the flexibility that a DLL can. Also, even though prototyping a DLL can be more difficult than using a VBX, your chances of getting sophisticated functionality out of the DLL are greater. If you're an API hotshot, go for the DLL.

The VBX: Thank You, Visual Basic

Clarion programmers have a lot to thank Visual Basic for. VB's massive popularity led to a phenomenal growth in custom controls, covering just about every aspect of programming you can imagine. Some of the most popular categories include the following:

- Grid controls, which provide spreadsheet-type functionality
- Word processing (handy for editing memo fields)
- Data access (not a big plus for CW, but something to keep in mind)
- Report writing (some products, such as Crystal Reports, come with VBXs that work together with the standalone report-writing tools)
- CD-ROM access
- Scanning and optical character recognition
- Image display, editing, and manipulation
- Data compression and archiving
- Graphing and charting
- Network access
- Serial communications
- Animation
- Tab (container) controls for multipage display
- Financial and scientific functions

The list goes on and on. Unfortunately, not everything on that list will work with CW.

Level with Me

You might have heard talk about which VBXs CW is compatible with, and that means you might have heard a lot of wrong information. For the record, there are currently three "levels" of VBXs, which correspond to the first three versions of Visual Basic. You should be able to use any level one VBX with Clarion for Windows. I say "should" because not all VBXs are well behaved.

Level one is the basic level of compatibility, however, and if you feel that isn't sufficient, keep in mind that it's all you get from virtually every development environment but Visual Basic. Microsoft has effectively published the level one API by demonstrating how to call VBXs in its own C compilers, and that is the model that language vendors such as TopSpeed have used. Level two and three VBXs, however, make use of the Visual Basic runtime environment, which is not available when you use VBXs in another language.

Having said that, you may find some level two or three VBXs that work with CW. VBXs can be written to require post–level one functionality, or just take advantage of it if it's available. If the VBX prefers to have post–level one functionality, but doesn't require it, you're probably in luck. Sometimes the only way to find out is to try. If you do find a VBX that is C++ compatible, but won't work with CW, notify TopSpeed at once so the development team can make it work.

TIP

When you're shopping for VBXs, you'll probably have the best success if you ask vendors if their controls support C++, rather than which level the control is. Not only do you stand a chance of getting a level three control that really works with CW, but a significant number of vendors don't have a very clear idea of what "level" means when applied to a control.

Assuming you've fought your way through the valley of the shadow of VBX compatibility and have found the control of your dreams, you need to do a couple things to make use of it.

The VBX Registry

Before you can place any custom control using the Window Formatter, you need to register it. From the main menu, choose Setup|VBX Registry, as shown in Figure 26.1.

FIGURE 26.1.

The VBX custom control registry.

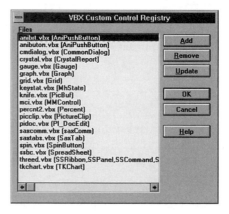

To register a VBX, click Add, then select the appropriate VBX using the standard file dialog box.

Registering a VBX accomplishes two things. First, the registry does a quick check to verify that the VBX is compatible with CW. Second, it stores information on the VBX that makes it possible for the Window Formatter to display the control and allow you to set its properties.

> **NOTE**
>
> CW version 1.0 comes with two VBXs that you can use in your own development:
> The SaxTab VBX is a tab control and the graph VBX is a chart control. Both of these
> controls come with special licenses. The SaxTab VBX can only be used to run the
> COOKBOOK sample application, and the graph VBX is crippled and may only be
> distributed with the sample graphing program. If you want to use either of these VBXs
> in your distributed applications, you will need to contact the vendors. See the file
> README.WRI in your DOC directory.

Container (Tab) Controls

Container controls are controls that can have other controls placed on them and linked to them.
A popular example of this is the tab control (an example of which, the SaxTab VBX, is discussed shortly), which uses a notebook tab metaphor to organize multiple pages of information. A control is placed on one page of the tab, and the programmer selects another page and
places other controls. At runtime, the user sees the same kind of behavior.

Faking Tab Controls

Clarion for Windows does not, as of version 1.0, support container controls. That is, it doesn't
support their automatic functionality. If you place a control on one page of a tab control, and
then change the tab or page, the control remains where you placed it, fully visible.

You can get around this in several ways. You can trap the event that is triggered when the user
selects a different tab, and hide all the controls except the ones belonging to that page of the
tab. This works, but it's a little messy in the design stage because all your controls are stacked
on top of each other.

You can get around *that* problem by making your window large enough to hold the separate
groups of controls, then move them onto the tab when everything is working. Again, it's a little
messy when maintenance time comes. So you might want to experiment with leaving the various
groups spread around your window (beyond the margins of what will display), then size
your window at runtime and hide/unhide/move the various groups of controls as needed.

> **NOTE**
>
> It is expected that there will be a tab control that supports containers in a future
> version of CW.

Placing VBXs in the Window Formatter

Because VBXs are controls, you place them on a window the way you place any other control. This can be a bit confusing, depending on the nature of the control. For instance, MSCOMM.VBX is a communications control that ships with the Visual Basic Professional Edition. There's no need to actually display it, however, because its purpose is to receive instructions from the program (dial a number, send some data, receive some data, and so on) rather than to display information on the window. In a case like that, you can give the control the Hide attribute. Whether or not you display the control, you have to place it on a window to use it. DLLs, which are discussed later in the chapter, do not have this limitation.

The SaxTab VBX

Most custom controls display information. For example, the SaxTab VBX that ships with CW shows a series of file folder–style tabs you can click to display different pages of information.

Make sure you have SaxTab.VBX registered and load an application (or create one using Quick Start—for more on this see Chapter 6, "Quick Start: The Two-Minute Application"). Open a window, and click the VBX button on the toolbar. The cursor turns into a crosshair, prompting you for the placement of the VBX. Click a suitable location, and the VBX list appears, as shown in Figure 26.2.

FIGURE 26.2.

Placing a custom control (VBX) list in the Window Formatter.

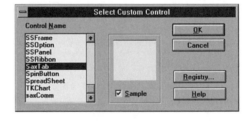

After you've placed the control, you can size and move it the same way you do any other control. You can also get at its properties, and of course this is where things get both interesting and potentially confusing.

VBX Properties

Visual Basic custom controls have properties in the same way standard CW controls have properties, but they're implemented a little differently. For starters, the Properties window looks quite a bit different. Take a look at Figure 26.3.

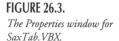

FIGURE 26.3.

The Properties window for SaxTab.VBX.

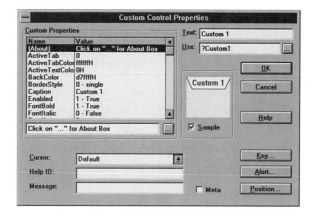

A few of these properties, such as Text and Use in the upper-right corner, and Cursor, Help ID, and Message in the lower-left corner, are familiar to you. The list of custom properties in the upper-left quadrant of the window is probably new to you.

This list varies from control to control, and is obtained from the VBX itself. There are some standard properties that most VBXs share, such as BackColor, BorderStyle, the various font properties, and so on, but there are others that are unique to individual controls.

You can set these properties two ways: by using the property syntax, or by specifying a new value in this dialog box. Values specified here become default values for when the procedure opens.

Default Properties

Documentation is always a big help when you are working with VBXs. For instance, it might not be immediately obvious that the way to add additional tabs to the control is to add the text for the additional tabs to the Text property, and separate them with vertical bars. Enter the line A¦B¦C¦D¦E in the Text entry, and click OK. Your control will now look something like the one in Figure 26.4.

FIGURE 26.4.

The tab VBX with five tabs.

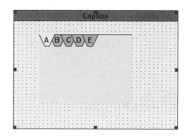

The default (highlighted) tab is probably the A tab. To change it to D, return to the tab's property window and set the ActiveTab property to 3 by typing that number in the entry control that is displayed just below the Custom Properties list. (In this case, tab numbering begins with 0 rather than with 1.)

Each time you set a default property on a custom control, the appropriate information is added to its declaration in the window structure. An unadulterated SaxTab control looks like the following in the window:

```
CUSTOM('Custom 1'),AT(139,30,50,50),USE(?Custom1),CLASS('SaxTabS.VBX','SaxTab')
```

The same control, with the changes just discussed to the Text and ActiveTab properties, looks like the following:

```
CUSTOM('A¦B¦C¦D¦E'),AT(24,12,88,63),USE(?Custom1),CLASS('SaxTabS.VBX','SaxTab'),¦
'ActiveTab'('3'), ¦
```

Runtime Properties

You can also set properties at runtime. Some properties, such as the control's text, are handled exactly the same as for standard CW controls. To give the tab control five tabs at runtime, use this:

```
?Custom1{prop:text}='A¦B¦C¦D¦E'
```

It's possible to use an equate label here (PROP:Text) because just about all controls have a Text property. Most do not, however, have an ActiveTab property. In that case, and for most VBX properties, the syntax is the following:

```
?Custom1{'ActiveTab'} = 3
```

That's the simple solution. Instead of an equate label, you use the property name in single quotes.

Multivalued Properties

Some controls have properties with multiple values. For example, you use this syntax:

```
?Custom{'PropertyName,2'} = Value
```

to assign the value to the second element of the PropertyName value.

As with other property assignments, you can retrieve the value of any current property by placing the variable on the left side of the equals sign and the property on the right.

Detecting VBX Events

In addition to using properties to communicate information back to the program, VBXs may also generate events. The SaxTab VBX generates a VBX event whenever the user selects a different tab control, and to detect it you use code similar to that shown in Listing 26.1.

Listing 26.1. Detecting a VBX event in the ACCEPT loop.

```
ACCEPT
  CASE FIELD()
    OF ?Custom1
      CASE EVENT()
      OF EVENT:VBXevent
         ! do something
      END
    END
  END
END
```

TIP

If you need to know which particular event occurred, you can use something like
`IF ?Custom1{prop:VBXEvent} = 'EventName'` to find out. Events may also indicate that
the VBX has returned one or more values. If they do, you can get at them with
something similar to `SaveValue = ?Custom{PROP:VBXEventArg,2}`, which would load
the second element of a multivalued event property into the `SaveValue` variable.
Whether any of this type of code is needed is entirely dependent on the control, and
any requirement should be fully documented by the vendor.

VBX Methods

In addition to properties, you can also exchange information with custom controls by using
methods. *Methods* are really just another name for procedures and functions, but because these
are custom controls the syntax is a little different from that of usual procedure calls. In fact, the
syntax is identical to the property syntax. You simply substitute the method name for the property name, as in `?Custom1{'MethodName'} = Value`.

If the method takes multiple parameters, you can do them one at a time, specifying the number of each parameter, as in the following:

```
?Custom1{'MethodName',1} = Value1
?Custom1{'MethodName',2} = Value2
```

The parameters will be stored, and the method will be executed the next time the `ACCEPT()`
statement is encountered.

Control Templates Revisited

Although assigning properties to custom controls isn't all that difficult a task, it's not something that is immediately obvious to someone using the AppGen. Although you can assign
properties at design time by using the Window Formatter, that won't always suit all your needs.

The template language makes it possible to create template "wrappers" for Visual Basic custom controls. Instead of assigning a complex series of properties, you can use a template to provide all the defaults and simplify the assignment of the remaining properties. You can even use code templates and template extensions, or additional control templates, to provide a complete set of tools that remove any need to set the controls' properties directly. An example of this is the use of the SaxTab VBX to provide range limits on recipes, in the COOKBOOK.APP example program.

As Clarion for Windows matures and its use becomes more widespread, expect to see a number of third-party developers providing control templates for popular VBXs. You may even want to check with the VBX supplier directly.

Non-CW DLLs

DLLs that are created in Clarion for Windows for Clarion for Windows are discussed in some detail in Chapter 32. This section deals with another animal: the third-party, non-Clarion Windows DLL. If you're a little unclear about what a DLL is or why you'd want to use one, look at Chapter 32 (and possibly Chapter 31, "Sharing Code: Source, OBJs, and LIBs," which discusses some basic issues of code sharing).

For most developers, DLLs are probably the second most important source of add-on compiled libraries of code. They tend to be more general-purpose than VBXs, more powerful, and also somewhat more difficult to use, because there are more variations in the interfaces they use.

Prototyping Considerations

Before you can use a non-CW DLL in your program, you need two things. You must declare a prototype for each DLL procedure you wish to call, and you have to have a LIB that corresponds to the DLL, which you can link into your program. The trickiest part of this business is usually getting the prototyping right.

Passing Parameters

TopSpeed languages, by default, use a different scheme than most other languages for passing parameters between procedures. The vast majority of languages pass parameters on the stack, but TopSpeed uses registers by default, which makes for faster operations. When you interface to a Windows library created in another language, you must use the PASCAL keyword on the procedure prototype. This tells the compiler to pass parameters on the stack, using the PASCAL convention (which is standard for Windows DLLs).

Numeric Parameters

When passing numeric parameters, your only real difficulty will be determining the appropriate data type. Most DLLs are documented for C programmers, so if you're not familiar with the language you might want to browse a reference book just to get up to speed on the declarations. Table 26.1 shows some common equivalents.

Table 26.1. Translating numeric parameters from C to CW.

C Data Type	CW Equivalent
UNSIGNED CHAR	BYTE
HWND	USHORT
HDC	USHORT
HANDLE	USHORT
UINT	USHORT
BOOL	SHORT
INT	SHORT
WORD	SHORT
ULONG	ULONG
DWORD	ULONG
LONG	LONG
FLOAT	SREAL
DOUBLE	REAL

Pointers

Long pointers can usually be prototyped simply as the variable type they point to. For instance, a LPSTR type will be prototyped as *STRING, and LPCSTR will be prototyped as *CSTRING.

The Problem of Strings

Strings that are passed by address require a Raw attribute on the declaration. By default, Clarion for Windows passes both the address of a string and its length, even when you pass by address. The Raw attribute tells the compiler to strip out the length information.

Strings that are passed by value are a language-specific problem. You will need to find out how the compiler that created the library expects to receive the string. Where in memory does the string reside? Is the called function expecting a length as well? Is it worth the trouble of trying to make it work? Probably not.

If you're the one writing the DLL in another language, and it's to be called by CW, make sure you pass the string by address, not by value. If you wish to pass the length of the string as well, leave off the Raw attribute and prototype your string in the called procedure as two parameters. The first, a USHORT, is the length, and the second is the pointer to the string.

Passing Structures

When a function requires a complex set of parameters, it's often easiest to pass in a struct, or structure, that contains the appropriate elements. The equivalent in CW to a struct is a group. These are normally passed in by address, and you should prototype them as *STRING, because a group is handled as a string internally. For an example of passing a struct to a non-CW DLL, see Chapter 25, "Using the Windows API." The auto-dialer example in that chapter passes a structure that contains all the communications port settings required by the Windows communications library.

Multimedia Fun: The *sndPlaySound()* Function

If your computer has a sound card, you've probably fooled around with some of the different sounds you can attach to standard Windows functions. These sounds are stored in WAV files, and you can easily add the capability to play WAV files to your CW applications.

Prototyping the *sndPlaySound()* Function

All you need to make noise is a sound card and the sndPlaySound function. The latter is tucked away in MMSYSTEM.DLL in your WINDOWS\SYSTEM directory, and it's prototyped in C like this:

```
BOOL sndPlaySound(LPCSTR lpszSoundName, UINT uFlags)
```

This function returns a Boolean value (USHORT, from Table 26.1), and takes two parameters. The first is a long pointer to a CSTRING, and the second is an unsigned integer. The CW declaration looks like the following:

```
sndPlaySound(*CSTRING,USHORT),USHORT,RAW,PASCAL
```

The second parameter is a flag that tells the function how to behave. The values are usually shown as constants, which are equivalent to CW equates, so you'll need to set up comparable equates or just use the numeric value. Some of these values can be added together with a logical OR.

Table 26.2. Possible values for the second parameter of the sndPlaySound() function.

Flag Name	Hex Value	Description
SND_SYNC	0H	Function returns only when the sound has finished playing. In the meantime, your program can do nothing.

Flag Name	Hex Value	Description
SND_ASYNC	1H	The function returns immediately; the sound plays while your program does other things.
SND_NODEFAULT	2H	If the filename is invalid the program won't play anything.
SND_MEMORY	4H	The filename parameter references a waveform sound already in memory.
SND_LOOP	8H	Used with SND_ASYNC. This tells the library to play the sound continuously until the function is called with the filename set to null (ASCII 0; in CW this would be a string declared as '<10>').
SND_NOSTOP	10H	Do not interrupt an already playing sound—the specified sound is not played.

Making the LIB File

As with just about all DLL calls, you need a corresponding LIB file to link into your program. You don't do this with a lot of Windows API calls because they're already in WINDOWS.LIB, which is automatically linked into every application. The multimedia calls are not part of this library, however, so you'll need to procure a LIB file for MMSYSTEM.DLL.

The easiest way to do this is with a library importing program, such as TSIMPLIB.EXE, which comes with the TopSpeed Tech Kit, or IMPLIBW.EXE, which comes with Borland's Windows compilers. The Borland tool is a Windows program and is particularly easy to use. All you do is tell it which DLL (or EXE) to create the LIB for, and in a blink of an eye you have one.

Calling the Procedure

Listing 26.2 shows a small hand-coded program that enables you to select WAV files and play them.

Listing 26.2. A small program for playing WAV files.

```
PROGRAM

     MAP
       PlayWavFile()
       MODULE('MMSYSTEM.LIB')
         sndPlaySound(*CSTRING,USHORT),USHORT,RAW,PASCAL
       END
     END
```

continues

Listing 26.2. continued

```
        INCLUDE('EQUATES.CLW')


  CODE
  PlayWavFile()
  RETURN



PlayWavFile       PROCEDURE

WavFileName       CSTRING(81)

window WINDOW('WAV Player'),AT(52,20,226,67),GRAY,DOUBLE
        MENUBAR
          ITEM('E&xit!'),USE(?exit),STD(STD:CLOSE)
        END
        BUTTON('...'),AT(196,21,12,12),USE(?FileLookup)
        PROMPT('File Name:'),AT(24,21,,),USE(?Prompt1)
        ENTRY(@s30),AT(64,21,,),USE(WavFileName)
        BUTTON('Play'),AT(96,45,35,14),USE(?PlayWav),DISABLE,DEFAULT
      END


  CODE
  OPEN(WINDOW)
  ACCEPT
    CASE FIELD()
    OF ?FileLookup
      CASE EVENT()
      OF EVENT:Accepted
        IF NOT FileDialog('Open Sound File',WavFileName,
                        ➥'WAV Files¦*.wav',0)
          BEEP
          DISABLE(?PlayWav)
        ELSE
          ENABLE(?PlayWav)
        END
        DISPLAY(?WavFileName)
      END
    OF ?PlayWav
    OROF ?WavFileName
      CASE EVENT()
      OF EVENT:Accepted
        IF NOT sndPlaySound(WavFileName,1)   ! Return From Function Immediately
          BEEP
          DISABLE(?PlayWav)
        ELSE
          ENABLE(?PlayWav)
        END
      END
    END
  END
```

The DLL *CALL()* Function

There is one other way to call DLL functions that does not require a LIB file. You can use the CALL() function. It takes two parameters: the name of the DLL (including its extension, and optionally the full path) and the name of the procedure. This procedure cannot receive any parameters, and it cannot return any value.

Optionally, you can specify the procedure number instead of the procedure name when you make the call. This number corresponds to the order in which the procedure appears in the DLL.

> **NOTE**
>
> As of CW version 1.001, the CALL() function, though documented, is not fully implemented. If you attempt to use it you will get a linker error. CALL() is expected to be available in a subsequent release.

Summary

Smart programmers buy all the tools they can afford, because it's almost always cheaper to buy common functionality than it is to reinvent it yourself. VBXs are the tool of choice when you want to extend your library of available controls. If you need to add functionality that isn't necessarily related to displaying or retrieving information from the user, or if you need to pass a wide range of data types, you'll probably end up using a DLL.

Whether you're calling Windows DLLs that are not supported by CW's WINDOWS.LIB or DLLs that you purchase from some other vendor, the principles are the same: You translate the procedure prototypes to CW equivalents, obtain or create a library, link the library into your application, and go!

Between the ease of use offered by VBXs and the power of DLLs, chances are you can find a tool to extend CW's power just as you like.

27

Using Initialization Files

An *initialization file*, or INI file, is a place to store information your program needs to know when it starts up. This information cannot be compiled into the program because it might change over time. It could be user information, color settings, window location, file location, or any of a host of other pieces of information.

In DOS, many developers stored this type of data (configuration settings) in proprietary formats so that the user could not manipulate it. However, in Windows, the opposite practice is common; a simple ASCII file, which is known as an INI file, does the trick instead.

This chapter covers the basics of initialization files—when and how to create, update, and delete them.

INIs Defined

What is an initialization file? You may have noticed that each time you add a new program to Windows, a file called WIN.INI in the Windows directory is updated with information that pertains to the newly installed program. Sometimes new initialization files are also created, either in the Windows directory or in the program's root directory. Don't be alarmed—this is a standard Windows practice.

An initialization file—WIN.INI is a prime example of one—is a simple ASCII file that contains information that is generally used during the startup of a program. An initialization file is not a requirement under Windows; it is purely optional and its use is left to your discretion. An initialization file also does not alleviate the need for registration databases or proprietary initialization files. If you have some information that needs to be kept secret, don't put it in an INI file.

> **TIP**
>
> There are two primary INI files used extensively by Windows itself: WIN.INI and SYSTEM.INI. The WIN.INI file is the Windows initialization file and is used for setting configuration, option, and preference and installation settings. The SYSTEM.INI file contains information and settings about device drivers and other operating system installation options.

INI File Format

INI files are made up of sections of data that contain entry-value pairs. A *section* is an indicator that defines the type of data that will follow. An *entry-value pair* is a variable that contains the data for the section. An entry-value pair can be either a string or a numeric value.

The INI section listed next is from the Clarion for Windows CW.INI file, and is just one of many sections in that file. Clarion for Windows reads this file on startup and configures itself based on the values it finds. If you reconfigure the environment, Clarion for Windows will save the related values in the CW.INI file when you exit, and these values will be used the next time you start Clarion for Windows.

```
;This is a comment line for illustration purposes only
[window formatter]
gridx=2
gridy=2
grid=on
```

The section [window formatter] is used to set the options for the Clarion for Windows Window Formatter. As you can see, the grid entity-value pair has been set to on, indicating that I want to use the grid when using the Window Formatter. If the grid setting is turned off, the next time I exit Clarion for Windows this section in the INI file will read grid=off.

CW INI Functions

There are different methods and uses of initialization files. Clarion for Windows provides two functions that neatly encapsulate most of the INI updating you will ever need to do. These are GETINI() and PUTINI().

GETINI ()

The GETINI() function has the following format:

```
GETINI( Section ,Entry [,Default] [,File] )
```

The GETINI() function returns the value for a specific section and entry value in a specified initialization file. Using the [window formatter] section as an example, the function call might look like the following:

```
GridSetting    STRING(3)
CODE
 GridSetting = GETINI('window formatter','grid','off','c:\cw\bin\cw.ini')
```

To see how this really works, you might want to first look at the prototype of the function call in BUILTINS.CLW, which is found in the \CW\LIBSRC directory.

```
GETINI(STRING,STRING,<STRING>,<STRING>),STRING,NAME('Cla$GETINI')
```

As you can see in the GridSetting example, the first and second parameters are required, but the third and fourth are not. To understand this function, it is easiest to work from right to left in the `GETINI()` function prototype. The fourth or last parameter of the function call tells the `GETINI()` function where to search for the section/entry-value pair. If this parameter is omitted, the `GETINI()` function will search the WIN.INI file for the section/entry-value pair. The third parameter specifies a default value for the entry-value pair in the case where the `GETINI()` function cannot find the value specified in the initialization file (or fourth parameter). If no value is specified and the entry value is not found, an empty string is returned. The second parameter is the entry-value name, which in this case is `'grid'`. The first parameter is the section name, or in this case `'window formatter'`.

You have probably noticed that the brackets have not been placed around the section name, nor has the equals sign been placed between the entry and value. This is because the `GETINI()` function handles this task automatically.

If you were writing this type of code in C, for example, you would need to use one or more of the Windows API calls presented in Table 27.1.

Table 27.1. Windows API calls for retrieving information from INI files.

Function	Description
`GetPrivateProfileInt()`	Retrieves an integer value from the program initialization file
`GetPrivateProfileString()`	Retrieves a string value from the program initialization file
`GetProfileInt()`	Retrieves an integer value from the WIN.INI initialization file
`GetProfileString()`	Retrieves a string value from the WIN.INI initialization file

With this one dedicated function call, Clarion for Windows simplifies the retrieval of initialization settings.

PUTINI()

The `PUTINI()` function has the following format:

```
PUTINI( Section ,Entry [,Value] [,File] )
```

The `PUTINI()` function sets the value for a specific section and entry value in a specified initialization file. For example, using the `[window formatter]` section, the function call might look like the following:

CODE
```
PUTINI('window formatter','grid','on','c:\cw\bin\cw.ini')
```

To see how this really works, you might want to first look at the prototype of the function call in BUILTINS.CLW, which is found in the \CW\LIBSRC directory:

```
PUTINI(STRING,STRING,<STRING>,<STRING>),NAME('Cla$PUTINI')
```

As you can see in the Window Formatter example, the first and second parameters are required, but the third and fourth are not. To understand this function, it is easiest to work from right to left in the PUTINI() function prototype. The fourth, or last, parameter of the function call tells the PUTINI() function where to search for and write the section/entry-value pair. If this parameter is omitted, the PUTINI() function will search and write the section/entry-value pair to the WIN.INI file. The third parameter specifies the value for the entry-value pair. This parameter has multiple meaning; if a value is specified or an empty string is specified, it will replace the value accordingly, but if the parameter is omitted, the entry-value pair will be deleted altogether. This is a handy feature that enables you to effectively delete an entry-value pair. The second parameter is the entry-value name—in this case it is 'grid'. The first parameter is the section name, or in this case 'window formatter'. When the section or the entry-value pair is not found in the initialization file, it will be created for you.

You have probably again noticed that the brackets have not been placed around the section name, nor has the equals sign been used between the entry and value. This is because the PUTINI() function handles this task.

If you were writing this type of code in C, for example, you would need to use one or more of the Windows API calls presented in Table 27.2.

Table 27.2. Windows API calls for writing to INI files.

Function	Description
WritePrivateProfileString()	Write a string to the program initialization file
WriteProfileString()	Write a string to the WIN.INI initialization file

Again, with this one dedicated function call, Clarion for Windows simplifies the insertion, updating, and deletion of initialization information.

Strategies for Managing INI Files

There are several ways to manage initialization files. This chapter covers three basic concepts that you could implement in your programs: using WIN.INI, using a program.INI in the Windows directory, and using a program.INI in the program's root directory. Each method has its benefits and drawbacks.

This chapter covers three basic functionalities using these three methods: creating and initializing your initialization settings, maintaining your initialization settings, and uninstalling your program's initialization settings.

Creating and Initializing Your Initialization Settings

Assuming that the user can install your program wherever he or she desires, there must be a way to create and initialize the default settings for your program.

If the user moves the program after installation, your program must be able to regenerate the initialization file when an initialization file does not exist. In this example, you will take the easy way out and simply re-create the initialization file and default settings when the program has been moved. You could modify this example and attempt to locate a previous initialization file for the program and copy it to the new directory for the program.

Maintaining Your Initialization Settings

In Clarion for Windows, when you reconfigure the environment, you may have noticed that your last used settings and file selections were memorized by Clarion for Windows. This was done so that the next time you enter the program, things appear as you left them. This is a professional touch that is simple to attain and is increasingly expected by the end user.

In order to provide this capability in your programs, you will need to first have an entry-value pair defined for the data you wish to have your program memorize for the user. You will then need to update the entry-value pair as the user changes the setting. And don't forget that once you save a value you must also remember to retrieve it on startup and your program should respond accordingly.

Adding this aspect to your program makes it more professional and friendly for the end user. The following example illustrates how easy it is to do this.

Uninstalling Your Program's Initialization Settings

One thing most programs do not often do is clean up after themselves. They may write to several initialization files, adding to the volume of information stored in these files. Yet many programs offer no way to remove themselves from these files. With newer technology on the horizon and myriads of complaints over the years about this exact problem, in the near future you will be required to clean up when your program is uninstalled. To help prepare for this scenario, I will provide a code template for you to place on a menu item, giving you the ability to delete the program's initialization data from the initialization file.

Using WIN.INI

In the beginning, and as Windows matured, most if not all programs installed their initialization information in the WIN.INI file in the Windows directory. The WIN.INI file is an initialization file that is designed for Windows startup itself, not for your program. However, it has been a convenient place for a Windows program to save its program initialization information as well because software developers knew that the WIN.INI file would be there for Windows itself, thus it was a reliable solution. Unfortunately, this has led to many a bloated WIN.INI file.

Updating WIN.INI is straightforward. Simply add a section, such as [MYPROG], to the WIN.INI file, then add all the possible entry-value pairs for the section. Whenever your program starts up, have it read the WIN.INI file using the GETINI() function. The following could be used to create the entry Registered=R&D, under the [MYPROG] section in the WIN.INI file:

```
PUTINI('MYPROG','Registered','R&D',)
```

Conversely, your program could retrieve this information using the following code:

```
Registered  STRING(30)
CODE
Registered = GETINI('MYPROG','Registered','(NONE)',)
```

I have used the default (NONE) to be returned when this information cannot be found in the initialization file. This literal is commonly used in Windows programs when a value is not present. I have used this only to illustrate how the default value of GETINI() works. Notice that the last parameter (the INI filename) in the GETINI() function is omitted. This tells GETINI() to search the WIN.INI file instead of a specific INI file.

Pros

The overriding reason for using WIN.INI is convenience. First, WIN.INI is required by Windows itself, which means that it will always be available for your Windows program. Second, it is easy to find; that is, by omitting the INI filename in both the GETINI() and PUTINI() functions, these functions will always look at the WIN.INI file, wherever it may be. You do not have to know which physical drive and directory Windows is installed in.

Cons

The overriding factor for not using WIN.INI is bloating of the WIN.INI file. Most programs install something into the WIN.INI file during installation, but do not delete it when the program is removed. This leaves you with a largely invalid WIN.INI file, which Windows must nonetheless process every time Windows is started. This can and will slow down Windows' initialization process, sometimes dramatically.

Another problem is the likelihood that some other program may inadvertently use a section of WIN.INI that your program relies on, with the result that your saved settings become mangled.

WIN.INI is also a good candidate for other sorts of damage, such as when a well-meaning user inadvertently removes your information while pruning out code that other programs never uninstalled. Putting all your information in WIN.INI is like never doing backups—sooner or later you're going to come to grief.

Program.INI in the Windows Directory

If you are a bit more conservative and want to protect your investment, the following initialization file approach might work for you. Many programs add a single entry into WIN.INI that tells the program where to look for the program.INI file. In this case the program's INI file is stored in the Windows directory, along with the WIN.INI file.

> **NOTE**
>
> For the next two topics, the term *program.INI* means the name of the program's initialization file. For example, if the program name is MYPROG, then the related initialization file is MYPROG.INI.

This approach is again reasonably simple, but just a bit more involved than using the WIN.INI file alone. First, you will need to write a section/entry-value pair into the WIN.INI the first time the program is started or during the installation process itself. This entry-value pair will simply point to the program.INI file that is stored in the Windows directory. For example, if you want to create an entry in WIN.INI and a program.INI for the program MYPROG.EXE, you could use the following code:

```
PUTINI('MYPROG','INIFileName','c:\windows\MYPROG.INI',)
PUTINI('MYPROG','FirstEntryName','First Entry Value', 'c:\windows\MYPROG.INI')
```

The first PUTINI() statement creates an entry in the WIN.INI file because the fourth parameter, which by default will use the WIN.INI file as its destination, will be left off. The second PUTINI() statement creates the new MYPROG.INI file in the Windows directory, as referenced in the fourth parameter, and adds the entry-value pair specified in the first, second, and third parameters.

Conversely, your program could retrieve this information using the following code:

```
ProgramINI   STRING(255)
FirstEntry   STRING(30)
CODE
ProgramINI = GETINI('MYPROG','INIFileName',,)
FirstEntry = GETINI('MYPROG','FirstEntryName','(NONE)',ProgramINI)
```

As you can see, first I look in the WIN.INI for the section [MYPROG] in order to get the initialization file (the ProgramINI variable) directory and name. I then read the program.INI file for the entry-value pair desired (FirstEntryName).

Pros

This is a good solution that serves the purpose of isolating the program.INI from the WIN.INI. It helps to avoid adding unnecessary information to the WIN.INI file, which might later cause you technical support problems.

Cons

The only drawback to this approach is that the program.INI is separated physically from the installed program. Because the program.INI is stored in the Windows directory, users and other programs might inadvertently delete or mangle your program's initialization file.

Program.INI in the Program Directory

If you would like to provide the most protection for your initialization file, use the following approach. As in the previous example, many programs add a single entry into WIN.INI that tells the program where to look for the program.INI file. In this case, however, the program.INI file is stored in the program's root directory along with the program itself. This approach is again fairly simple, yet it provides the best protection for your initialization files since the initialization files will reside wherever your program is physically installed.

First, you will need to write a section/entry-value pair into the WIN.INI file the first time the program is started, or during the installation process itself. This entry-value pair will simply point to the program.INI file in the program's working directory. For example, if you want to create an entry in WIN.INI and a program.INI for the program MYPROG.EXE, you could use the following code:

```
PUTINI('MYPROG','INIFileName','c:\myprog\MYPROG.INI',)
PUTINI('MYPROG','FirstEntryName','First Entry Value', 'c:\myprog\MYPROG.INI')
```

The first PUTINI() statement creates an entry in the WIN.INI file because the fourth parameter has been left off, which by default will use the WIN.INI file as its destination. The second PUTINI() statement creates the new MYPROG.INI file in the program's working directory, as referenced in the fourth parameter, and adds the entry-value pair specified in the first, second, and third parameters.

Conversely, your program could retrieve the information using the following code:

```
ProgramINI    STRING(255)
FirstEntry    STRING(30)
CODE
ProgramINI  = GETINI('MYPROG','INIFileName',,)
FirstEntry  = GETINI('MYPROG','FirstEntryName','(NONE)',ProgramINI)
```

As you can see, this code is identical to the code used in the section "Program.INI in the Windows Directory." First I look in the WIN.INI for the section [MYPROG] in order to get the initialization file (the ProgramINI variable) directory and name. I then read the program.INI file for the entry-value pair I want (FirstEntryName).

Pros

This solution isolates the program.INI from the WIN.INI, both logically and physically. It helps to avoid adding unnecessary information to the WIN.INI file, which might later cause you technical support problems. It also aids you in determining when the program has been moved from the original installed directory.

Cons

Users are typically the single drawback to this and all approaches listed so far, because they can inadvertently delete, change, or mangle your program's initialization file.

If a user moves the program to another location on the disk and doesn't move the program.INI file, the initialization information will not be found. In this case, your program could create a new program.INI file (using default initialization information) at the new location on disk and then update the WIN.INI file to reflect the new location of the program.

TIP

Earlier I mentioned that you should still possibly keep a file that contains configuration information in a proprietary (protected) format as well. If you did this and saved the program.INI settings in this file as a backup for the program.INI file, your program could create the new program.INI file in the new location using this information instead of some arbitrary default initialization values. This approach would definitely impress your users.

Uninstalling Your Program.INI References from WIN.INI

As mentioned earlier, one of the most aggravating issues surrounding initialization file management is that most programs don't clean up after themselves. Using both of the previous program.INI strategies, you can easily provide a method for cleaning up WIN.INI entries that were added by your program.

If you have added a section/entry-value pair to the WIN.INI file, the following code will delete this entry and clean up for your program:

```
CODE
PUTINI('MYPROG','INIFileName',,)
```

This seems too simple, doesn't it? Because the third parameter has been omitted, this section/entry-value will be deleted. Therefore, you can clean up a WIN.INI entry of this type with one statement.

As an example, Listing 27.1 is a simple hand-coded program that illustrates various techniques in dealing with initialization files, as used in the approach mentioned in the section "Program.INI in the Program Directory" (which is also included on the accompanying disk). This program will, on initial startup, write a section/entry-value pair to the WIN.INI file and write the corresponding program.INI file in the working directory of the program. You may read the program.INI, change entry-value pairs in the program.INI, or re-initialize and delete the WIN.INI and program.INI section/entry-value pairs altogether.

Listing 27.1. The TESTINI program.

```
TESTINI                 PROGRAM

                        INCLUDE('Equates.CLW')
                        INCLUDE('Keycodes.CLW')
                        INCLUDE('Errors.CLW')

ApplicationName         EQUATE('TESTINI')
SectionName             EQUATE('SETTINGS')
WinIniSectionName       EQUATE('IniFileName')

QUE                     QUEUE,PRE(QUE)
SectionName               STRING(40)
EntryName                 STRING(40)
EntryValue                STRING(80)
                        END

EntryName               STRING(40),DIM(5)
IniFileName             STRING(255)

                        MAP
                          Main()
                          InitINI()
                          ReadINI()
                          MaintINI()
                          DeleteINI()
                        END

!===========================================================================
 CODE
!===========================================================================
   Main()

!---------------------------------------------------------------------------
Main                    PROCEDURE
!---------------------------------------------------------------------------
wMdiFrame APPLICATION('TESTINI.EXE'),AT(0,0,317,172),CENTER,STATUS,SYSTEM, |
        MAX,MAXIMIZE,RESIZE
     MENUBAR
       MENU('&File')
         ITEM('&Initialize'),USE(?InitINI),MSG('Initialize INI Settings')
         ITEM('&Read'),USE(?ReadINI),MSG('Read INI Settings')
         ITEM('&Maintain'),USE(?MaintINI),MSG('Maintain INI Settings')
         ITEM('&Delete'),USE(?DeleteINI),MSG('Delete INI settings')
```

continues

Listing 27.1. continued

```
            ITEM('Item&3'),SEPARATOR
            ITEM('E&xit'),STD(STD:CLOSE),MSG('Exit this program')
        END
      END
    END

CODE
!Assign Default array values
EntryName[1] = 'Style'
EntryName[2] = 'Owner'
EntryName[3] = 'Date Last Accessed'
EntryName[4] = 'Time Last Accessed'
EntryName[5] = 'Purpose'

OPEN(wMdiFrame)
ACCEPT
  CASE EVENT()
  OF EVENT:OpenWindow
     InitINI()
  OF EVENT:CloseDown
     BREAK
  END
  CASE FIELD()
  OF ?ReadINI
     CASE EVENT()
     OF EVENT:Accepted
        ReadINI()
     END
  OF ?MaintINI
     CASE EVENT()
     OF EVENT:Accepted
        MaintINI()
     END
  OF ?InitINI
     CASE EVENT()
     OF EVENT:Accepted
        PUTINI(SectionName,EntryName[1],,IniFileName)
        InitINI()
        MESSAGE('Initialization has been completed!', ¦
                'TESTINI.EXE',ICON:EXCLAMATION)
     END
  OF ?DeleteINI
     CASE EVENT()
     OF EVENT:Accepted
        DeleteINI()
     END
  END
END
CLOSE(wMdiFrame)
RETURN

!-----------------------------------------------------------------
InitINI                 PROCEDURE                !Initialize INI File Procedure
!-----------------------------------------------------------------
CODE
!Update WIN.INI
PUTINI(ApplicationName,WinIniSectionName, ¦
       CLIP(PATH()) & '\' & CLIP(ApplicationName) & '.INI',)
```

```
!Get program INI file name
IniFileName = GETINI(ApplicationName,WinIniSectionName,,)

!If no entries then INITIALIZE settings
IF GETINI(SectionName,EntryName[1],'(NONE)',IniFileName) = '(NONE)'
    PUTINI(SectionName,EntryName[1], ¦
           'Using WIN.INI and TESTINI.INI files',IniFileName)
    PUTINI(SectionName,EntryName[2],'R&D',IniFileName)
    PUTINI(SectionName,EntryName[3],FORMAT(TODAY(),@d2),IniFileName)
    PUTINI(SectionName,EntryName[4],FORMAT(CLOCK(),@T3),IniFileName)
    PUTINI(SectionName,EntryName[5], ¦
         'Developing Applications in Clarion For Windows',IniFileName)
END
RETURN


!---------------------------------------------------------------------------
ReadINI                PROCEDURE
!---------------------------------------------------------------------------
Ndx                    BYTE(0)

wReadIni WINDOW('Read TESTINI.INI'),AT(,,260,106),CENTER,SYSTEM,GRAY, ¦
         MAX,DOUBLE
       STRING('WIN.INI:'),AT(5,10,30,10),USE(?String1)
       STRING(@s255),AT(35,10,215,10),FONT('Arial',10,0800000H,FONT:regular), ¦
       USE(IniFileName)
       LIST,AT(3,31,252,50),FONT('MS Sans Serif',10,,FONT:regular), ¦
       MSG('Scroll for initialization information'), ¦
          USE(?List),HVSCROLL, ¦
       FORMAT('80L¦_M-Section~C@s40@80L¦_M-Entry~C@s40@80L¦_M~ Value~C@s80@'), ¦
          FROM(que)
       BUTTON('E&xit'),AT(115,85,,),USE(?Exit),DEFAULT
     END

CODE
!Get program INI File Name
IniFileName = GETINI(ApplicationName,WinIniSectionName,'(NONE)',)
FREE(QUE);CLEAR(QUE)
LOOP Ndx= 1 TO 5
   QUE:SectionName = SectionName
   QUE:EntryName   = EntryName[Ndx]
   QUE:EntryValue  = GETINI(QUE:SectionName,QUE:EntryName,'(NONE)', ¦
                           IniFileName)
   ADD(QUE)
END

OPEN(wReadIni)
DISPLAY()
SELECT(?List,1)

ACCEPT
  CASE EVENT()
  OF EVENT:CloseDown
    BREAK
  END
  CASE FIELD()
  OF ?Exit
    CASE EVENT()
    OF EVENT:Accepted
```

continues

Listing 27.1. continued

```
            POST(EVENT:CloseDown)
        END
    END
END
CLOSE(wReadIni)
FREE(QUE);CLEAR(QUE)
RETURN


!------------------------------------------------------------------------
MaintINI                PROCEDURE
!------------------------------------------------------------------------
Ndx                     BYTE(0)
ValueArr                STRING(80), DIM(5)

wMaintIni WINDOW('Maintain WIN.INI Settings'),AT(,,260,100),CENTER,SYSTEM,¦
        GRAY,MAX,DOUBLE
        STRING(@s40),AT(4,8,84,10),USE(EntryName[1])
        ENTRY(@s80),AT(88,8,168,10),USE(ValueArr[1])
        STRING(@s40),AT(4,20,84,10),USE(EntryName[2])
        ENTRY(@s80),AT(88,20,168,10),USE(ValueArr[2])
        STRING(@s40),AT(4,32,84,10),USE(EntryName[3])
        ENTRY(@s80),AT(88,32,168,10),USE(ValueArr[3])
        STRING(@s40),AT(4,44,84,10),USE(EntryName[4])
        ENTRY(@s80),AT(88,44,168,10),USE(ValueArr[4])
        STRING(@s40),AT(4,56,84,10),USE(EntryName[5])
        ENTRY(@s80),AT(88,56,168,10),USE(ValueArr[5])
        BUTTON('&Cancel'),AT(228,84,26,12),USE(?Cancel)
        BUTTON('&OK'),AT(200,84,26,12),USE(?OK),DEFAULT
    END

CODE
LOOP Ndx = 1 TO 5
  ValueArr[Ndx] = ¦
    GETINI(SectionName,EntryName[Ndx],' ',IniFileName)
END

OPEN(wMaintIni)
ACCEPT
  CASE EVENT()
  OF EVENT:CloseDown
    BREAK
  END
  CASE FIELD()
  OF ?Ok
    CASE EVENT()
    OF EVENT:Accepted
      !Loop Max Entry Times and save values to program INI
      LOOP Ndx = 1 TO 5
        PUTINI(SectionName,EntryName[Ndx],ValueArr[Ndx],IniFileName)
      END
      POST(EVENT:CloseDown)
    END
  OF ?Cancel
    CASE EVENT()
    OF EVENT:Accepted
      POST(EVENT:CloseDown)
    END
  END
```

```
END
CLOSE(wMaintIni)
RETURN

!-----------------------------------------------------------------------
DeleteINI              PROCEDURE
!-----------------------------------------------------------------------
NDX                    BYTE(0)

CODE
!Loop max entry times
! Clear Program INI Entry-Values
LOOP Ndx = 1 TO 5
  PUTINI(SectionName,EntryName[Ndx],,IniFileName)
END
!Clear WIN.INI Entry-value
PUTINI(ApplicationName,WinIniSectionName,,)
MESSAGE('TESTINI.EXE settings removed','DeleteINI Procedure',ICON:HAND)
RETURN
```

On the book's disk there are two code templates that may be of value to you: InsertWININI and DeleteWININI. These code templates can be placed on a menu item or within the code, as you see fit.

The InsertWININI code template will insert and/or update the section/entry-value pair for your program in the WIN.INI file. This code template can be inserted in the EVENT:OpenWindow of your application (frame) window.

The DeleteWININI code template will delete your program's section/entry-value pair in the WIN.INI file. You could place this under a menu item in your program using EVENT:Accepted to trigger this action.

Summary

Initialization processing using the Windows API can be very labor intensive. Clarion for Windows has addressed this issue by providing you with two very sophisticated functions: GETINI() and PUTINI(). Using these functions will help you easily insert, update, and delete your initialization information, as desired. A careful choice of INI file strategies can also keep you out of trouble.

28

Multithreading and Thread Management

One of the most useful, powerful, and complex features of Clarion for Windows is its built-in capability to create multithreaded applications. What are multithreaded applications? In the simplest sense, a *multithreaded application* is a modeless application that enables you to open multiple windows at the same time and switch among them as desired.

You can see multithreading first-hand by using any application created in Quick Start. (If you don't have an application already created in Quick Start or are not familiar with Quick Start, please see Chapter 6, "Quick Start: The Two-Minute Application," and create a simple application to review.) For example, in a Quick Start–generated program, a thread is started whenever you select a browse window from the menu. Selecting multiple browse windows will start multiple threads, each running separately within the application. Each of these browse windows is an instance of the browse window process defined in the browse template; that is, they are cloned and identical, and you can switch between them as you like. If you defined two keys in your Quick Start application, there will be two browse options. Each will execute as a thread and each can be started until you run out of memory or there are 64 threads executing at once.

A traditional example of something that uses multithreading is a word processor. It will open documents; every document might use the same window, but the contents of the document might be different; and when each document is opened, it might obscure the view of the previous one. Therefore, if you have three documents opened, there are three windows running at the same time. Each window is identical in functionality but different in actual content, and you can switch to any window and modify it as necessary, in any order. When threads are used in this fashion, generally you use a multiple-document interface (MDI) window management scheme so that you can manage the document windows (see Chapter 29, "Multiple-Document Interface Versus Non–Multiple-Document Interface," for further information on window management schemes).

Each program you create in Clarion for Windows can be single-threaded or multithreaded. Single-threaded programs are like DOS programs—they have only one execution path, making them *modal* by nature. Multithreaded programs are more common in Windows and have many execution paths, making them *modeless* by nature.

Why might you want to use multithreading? In Windows, users expect to be able to open and select various windows within an application as they wish. In order for this capability to work, you must create modeless applications. The most common use of threading is seen in MDI-style applications. You can see an example of multithreading at work in the Windows Program Manager and File Manager programs. In Clarion for Windows, this capability is available through the use of multithreading.

A *thread*, as you will see later in this chapter, is a separate path of execution within one program. It is like another copy of the program running at the same time, and therefore is a powerful tool. This chapter defines multithreading and explores some effective techniques that can be used to manage and harness this incredible power.

Threads Defined

A thread is an isolated unit of execution; it is like having two instances of the same program run at the same time. This means that a thread knows only about global program data and variables and its own data, and runs independently of all other threads except for the primary program thread itself. A thread has its own stack space, where local data can be defined and allocated for use during the life of the thread. When a thread is started, any locally defined data and variables are instantiated on the thread program stack. When a thread is stopped, any locally defined data and variables are destroyed. Threads can contain a window (MDI or non-MDI) or they can simply process logic.

Syntax

Thread creation is quite simple. The following statement creates a thread:

```
ThreadNo = START(ProcedureName,<StackSize>)
```

This simple statement will start (create or instantiate) a thread. START is a function that takes two parameters: The first is the actual name of a procedure and the second is the optional size for the thread's stack space. The procedure used in the START function must be defined without any parameters, it must be a procedure and cannot be a function. By default, a thread's stack space is 10KB—if you want a smaller or larger stack size, you can specify the size in the second parameter. The START function returns a unique thread number ranging from 2 to 64. What happened to thread number 1? The first thread number (thread number 1) is always reserved for the main program code itself. You can have up to a maximum of 64 threads executing at the same time. If the START function fails, a zero will be returned instead of a unique thread number.

A thread is destroyed when your code returns from the procedure that was started. In other words, when a RETURN statement in a thread is executed or the thread has a logical end, whereby the code stops and control returns to the main program, the thread is destroyed.

Controlling Threads

Now that you have an idea of what threads are and how to create and destroy them, the next thing on your agenda will be to control threads. By control, I mean that you need to make sure that the threads in your programs do what you want them to do when you want them to. This is the first step in managing threads.

Basic Training

Listing 28.1 is a small example program that illustrates some basic thread control practices, the posting and parsing of events (messaging), and various property-setting techniques. The objective of the program in Listing 28.1 is to start a new MDI child thread from a MDI frame's

menu and to disable the menu option until this new thread has been stopped, limiting the user
to only one instance of the MDI child window at any given time.

Listing 28.1. The Multithreading Example 1 (MTI) program.

```
MT1                       PROGRAM

                          INCLUDE('EQUATES.CLW')
                          INCLUDE('ERRORS.CLW')
                          INCLUDE('KEYCODES.CLW')

                          MAP
                            Main()
                            NewThread()
                          END

EVENT:EnableDisableMenu EQUATE(401H)

MdiFrameThreadNo          LONG

NewThreadNo               LONG

wMdiFrame APPLICATION('MT1 - MDI frame'),AT(0,0,316,171),CENTER,¦
          ICON('WINPYR.ICO'),STATUS,SYSTEM,MAX,MAXIMIZE,  ¦
        RESIZE
      MENUBAR
        MENU('&File')
          ITEM('&Start Thread'),USE(?StartThread)
          ITEM('E&xit'),KEY(AltF4),STD(STD:Close)
        END
      END
    END

  CODE
  Main()

!==============================================================================
Main                    PROCEDURE
!==============================================================================
  CODE
  OPEN(wMdiFrame)
  MdiFrameThreadNo = THREAD()
  ACCEPT
    CASE EVENT()
    OF EVENT:EnableDisableMenu
      DO EnableDisableMenu
    END
    CASE FIELD()
    OF ?StartThread
      CASE EVENT()
      OF EVENT:Accepted
        NewThreadNo = START(NewThread)
      END
    END
  END
  CLOSE(wMdiFrame)
  RETURN
```

```
!----------------------------------------------------------------------
EnableDisableMenu               ROUTINE
!----------------------------------------------------------------------
 IF NewThreadNo
   DISABLE(?StartThread)
 ELSE
   ENABLE(?StartThread)
 END


!==============================================================================
NewThread                 PROCEDURE
!==============================================================================

wNewThread WINDOW('MT1 - MDI CHILD'),AT(0,0,104,30),SYSTEM,GRAY,RESIZE,MDI
       BUTTON('&Ok'),AT(38,8,,),MSG('DEFAULT BUTTON'),USE(?Ok), ¦
       STD(STD:CLOSE),DEFAULT
     END

 CODE
 OPEN(wNewThread)
 ACCEPT
   CASE EVENT()
   OF EVENT:OpenWindow
     POST(EVENT:EnableDisableMenu,,MdiFrameThreadNo)
   OF EVENT:CloseWindow
   END
 END
 CLOSE(wNewThread)
 NewThreadNo = 0
 POST(EVENT:EnableDisableMenu,,MdiFrameThreadNo)
 RETURN
```

The first thing to notice is that there is a user-defined event called EVENT:EnableDisableMenu. A *user-defined event* is a message that you create and can use in your programs to accomplish a specific action. It works the same as other Window messages, but it is up to you to determine how it is used in your programs. The event in Listing 28.1 was arbitrarily named and given a hex value of 401H, which is a user-defined event number. User-defined events are special events that you create as an equate label and for which you then develop the related functionality in your program. This gives you a way to send application-specific messages between threads that belong only to your program, not to Windows or to the Clarion for Windows library. Of course, there is a chance that you may never need any user-defined events, but because you may, I have included in Listing 28.1 an example of how to do this. In order to determine which value to assign to this user event, I simply reviewed the EQUATES.CLW file, which is found in the \CW\LIBSRC directory, where the user-definable event range is defined. The following is the section in EQUATES.CLW that defines the range of user-definable hex values:

```
! User-definable events

EVENT:User          EQUATE (400H)
EVENT:Last          EQUATE (0FFFH)
```

I have added my user-defined event equate number after the EVENT:User equate number.

You will also notice two variable declarations in Listing 28.1:

```
MdiFrameThreadNo        LONG
NewThreadNo             LONG
```

These variables are used to record and reference the actual thread numbers assigned in the program. By using descriptive variable names, you can visually determine which thread is being referenced in the variable. As mentioned earlier, I really didn't need to save the MDI frame's thread number because it is assumed to be thread number 1, but to clarify this example I used a variable instead of the numeral 1.

Before you reach the first ACCEPT statement, you can see that the MDI frame's thread number has been saved in the variable MdiFrameThreadNo through the Clarion for Windows library function call THREAD(). This function will return the thread number that is currently executing.

Looking a bit further into the Main() procedure, notice the reference to the CASE EVENT() statement and EVENT:EnableDisableMenu. This is the event (user-defined event) that will trigger the enabling and disabling of the menu items.

After the CASE FIELD() statement, notice the OF ?StartThread equate label, and after this statement yet another CASE EVENT() statement. The difference between the first CASE EVENT() and the second CASE EVENT() is that the first is for window-specific events and the latter is for control-specific events. Beneath the second ?StartThread CASE EVENT() statement notice an EVENT:Accepted, which indicates that the user actually selected the menu item labeled &Start Thread in the MDI frame's menu structure.

Here is where things start to get a bit interesting. When the user selects the Start Thread menu option, the code will issue a NewThreadNo = START(NewThread) statement. This is where the MDI child thread is started, or instantiated. If you are familiar with the Clarion for DOS method of calling a procedure, you will remember that when you call a procedure, you cannot access a previous screen without first closing the current screen you are on, which means that the application is modal. In Windows, the START() statement does not function as a procedure call; START() is a function call to the Clarion for Windows thread management library routine, which will actually allocate, instantiate, and return control to the thread that issued the START() statement. Therefore, what happens is a bit strange if you are familiar with only the DOS modal programming technique. START() will return the thread number from the Clarion for Windows thread management library routine, control will then be given back to the current ACCEPT loop (in this case that of the MDI frame), and when all current ACCEPT loop processing has finished in the current ACCEPT loop and the loop cycles, the new thread you just started will receive focus and become the currently active thread. To see this process, I encourage you to go to the Clarion for Windows Debugger and watch the window messages that are processed until the MDI child window becomes the current or active ACCEPT loop. Frankly, you might not need to know any of this. However, it might appear logical to you to do the following:

```
OF ?StartThread
  CASE EVENT()
  OF EVENT:Accepted
    DISABLE(?StartThread)
    NewThreadNo = START(NewThread)
    ENABLE(?StartThread)
```

Docsn't Work (example)
as desired

You may be thinking that if you disable the menu item before the START() statement occurs, you will not enable this menu item again until the thread has been stopped. I have seen many folks attempt this strategy and wonder why it doesn't work correctly. It fails for the simple reason that START will return the thread number and will continue to execute in the current thread until the ACCEPT loop cycles, at which point the newly started thread will receive focus. The result of this example is that you will in fact disable the menu item and then re-enable it again, immediately after the START function call has been executed. Therefore, you will never see the menu item actually disable.

In Listing 28.1, after executing the START() logic you will soon find yourself in the NewThread() procedure. Again, in this procedure you will see a window-specific CASE EVENT() statement. This time an EVENT:OpenWindow event is being used. This event enables you to insert code to execute when the ACCEPT loop receives the message that the window has opened. Notice that the following statement is inserted:

```
POST(EVENT:EnableDisableMenu,,MdiFrameThreadNo)
```

The POST() function is being used to send a message to another thread—in this case, the MDI frame thread. There is only one message queue, and the Clarion for Windows library manages how the relevant messages are dispatched and read in a given ACCEPT loop process. The event being sent or posted is the user-defined event OF EVENT:EnableDisableMenu (401H) that was previously discussed.

The third parameter of the POST() function instructs the POST() function to send the message to a specified thread number, and if this parameter were to be omitted, the POST() function would send the message to the currently executing thread. If you look back at the MDI frame's window level CASE EVENT() statement, you will see the statement OF EVENT:EnableDisableMenu. After the POST() statement has executed and there are no more messages to process for the currently executing thread's ACCEPT loop, the Clarion for Windows library will recognize that there are messages pending in the message queue for other threads and will dispatch them according to the relevant thread's ACCEPT loop. In the case of the MDI frame, there is a message (EVENT:EnableDisableMenu) waiting in the message queue to be processed, so the MDI frame will gain focus and process that message.

The statement following OF EVENT:EnableDisableMenu will execute a local routine in the MDI frame that will determine what the value in the NewThreadNo variable is—either zero or a number. If it is not zero, there has been a thread number placed into the variable, indicating that the thread has been started (this was done in the NewThreadNo = START(NewThread) statement) and will disable the menu item. Otherwise, if the value is zero, the menu item will be enabled.

But where does the `NewThreadNo` variable get reset to zero? At the end of the `NewThread()` procedure, notice that immediately after the `CLOSE(wNewThread)` statement, `NewThreadNo` is set to zero. This is done safely at this point because the `ACCEPT` loop has finished and the window has been closed. In Clarion for Windows, you can receive Windows messages only within an `ACCEPT` loop structure, so for all intents and purposes, this second thread is ready to stop and it is safe to clear the `NewThreadNo` value to zero. After this assignment is made, you will notice that another `POST(EVENT:EnableDisableMenu,,MdiFrameThreadNo)` is sent to the MDI frame procedure. This time, when the routine `EnableDisableMenu` is executed, the value in the `NewThreadNo` variable is zero and the menu item is enabled again.

Understanding How Threads Work Together

Now that you have an idea how threads work at a simplistic level, it is time to get a little bit more detailed.

The sequence of creating threads is interesting. If you start three threads, you will get thread numbers: 2, 3, and 4, respectively. If you return from thread 3, thread numbers 2 and 4 will remain. If you then start another thread, the next thread number assigned is thread number 3. This process is shown in Listing 28.1. As you can see, if you had hard coded or relied on a specific thread number for something in your code, you could end up with unpredictable results. Therefore, managing threads will become extremely important as you begin to communicate among the various threads your program starts.

Listing 28.2 shows another simplistic thread control scheme that utilizes a small-dimensioned array of long type variables. The first element of the array has purposely not been used and remains a zero value; this is because the program code (in this case the MDI frame) is assumed to be thread number 1. An array was used in this example purely as an example and has no particular meaning other than as a placeholder for the thread numbers themselves.

> **NOTE**
>
> If you were to work with this example for a few moments, you would soon realize a major deficiency: the ability to reference the thread by some logical value other than the thread number itself. In order to keep the array elements in sync with the assigned thread numbers, the numbering scheme was started with array element [2] instead of array element [1].

Listing 28.2. The Multithreading Example 2 (MT2) program.

```
MT2                          PROGRAM

                             INCLUDE('EQUATES.CLW')
                             INCLUDE('ERRORS.CLW')
                             INCLUDE('KEYCODES.CLW')
```

```
                     MAP
                       Main()
                       ThreadProc()
                     END

THIS                 EQUATE(0)
EVENT:CloseQuery     EQUATE(401H)
ThreadNo             LONG, DIM(4)

wMdiFrame APPLICATION('MT2'),AT(0,0,317,190),CENTER,ICON('WINPYR.ICO'),¦
          STATUS,SYSTEM,MAX,MAXIMIZE,RESIZE
        MENUBAR
          MENU('&File')
            ITEM('Start &3 Threads'),USE(?Start3Threads)
            ITEM('Stop  &1 Thread'),USE(?Stop1Thread)
            ITEM('&Start 1 Thread'),USE(?Start1Thread)
            ITEM('&Close All Threads'),USE(?CloseAllThreads)
            ITEM('E&xit      Alt+F4'),KEY(AltF4),STD(STD:Close)
          END
        END
      END

 CODE
 Main()


!===============================================================================
Main                         PROCEDURE
!===============================================================================
 CODE
 OPEN(wMdiFrame)
 ACCEPT
   CASE EVENT()
   OF EVENT:OpenWindow
     MESSAGE('Select the menu items in order to see the effect     <10>' & ¦
             'of multithreading and thread number assignments.  <10>' & ¦
'Code has been added to prevent you from doing things<10>' & ¦
             'out of order so you can simply walk down the menu items ',  ¦
             THIS{PROP:TEXT},ICON:Hand)
     DISABLE(?Stop1Thread)
     DISABLE(?Start1Thread)
     DISABLE(?CloseAllThreads)
   OF EVENT:CloseDown
     BREAK
   OF EVENT:CloseQuery
     MESSAGE('You have just closed threads 2-4, press EXIT to quit', ¦
             THIS{PROP:TEXT},ICON:EXCLAMATION)
   END
   CASE FIELD()
   OF ?Start3Threads
     CASE EVENT()
     !Start 3 Procedures
     OF EVENT:Accepted
       ThreadNo[2] = START(ThreadProc)
       ThreadNo[3] = START(ThreadProc)
       ThreadNo[4] = START(ThreadProc)
       DISABLE(?Start3Threads)
       ENABLE(?Stop1Thread)
```

continues

Listing 28.2. continued

```
      END
    OF ?Stop1Thread
      CASE EVENT()
      OF EVENT:Accepted
        POST(EVENT:CloseDown,,ThreadNo[3])
        DISABLE(?Stop1Thread)
        ENABLE(?Start1Thread)
      END
    OF ?Start1Thread
      CASE EVENT()
      OF EVENT:Accepted
        ThreadNo[3] = START(ThreadProc)
        DISABLE(?Start1Thread)
        ENABLE(?CloseAllThreads)
      END
    OF ?CloseAllThreads
      CASE EVENT()
      ! Post Close Down to all Child Threads
      OF EVENT:Accepted
        POST(EVENT:CloseDown,,ThreadNo[2])
        POST(EVENT:CloseDown,,ThreadNo[3])
        POST(EVENT:CloseDown,,ThreadNo[4])
        POST(EVENT:CloseQuery)

        DISABLE(?CloseAllThreads)
      END
    END
  END
CLOSE(wMdiFrame)
RETURN


!=============================================================================
ThreadProc               PROCEDURE
!=============================================================================

wThreadProc WINDOW('Thread Procedure'),AT(,,127,43),SYSTEM,GRAY,MAX,RESIZE,MDI
      TEXT,AT(2,3,122,37),FONT('Arial',8,0800000H,FONT:regular),USE(?Text1),¦
        VSCROLL,READONLY
      END


CODE
OPEN(wThreadPRoc)
ACCEPT
  CASE EVENT()
  OF EVENT:OpenWindow
    THIS{PROP:TEXT} = THIS{PROP:TEXT} & ' ' & THREAD()
    ?Text1{PROP:TEXT} = 'This is thread ' & ThreadNo[THREAD()] & '<13,10>'
  OF EVENT:CloseDown
    BREAK
  OF EVENT:Restore
    IF THIS{PROP:Iconize} = TRUE
      THIS{PROP:Iconize} = FALSE
      THIS{PROP:Active}  = TRUE
      POST(EVENT:Resume)
    ELSE
      THIS{PROP:Active}  = TRUE
      POST(EVENT:Resume)
```

```
      END
    END
    CASE FIELD()
    END
  END
  CLOSE(wThreadProc)
  !Reset the current Thread Number array value to zero
  ThreadNo[THREAD()] = 0
  RETURN
```

In this example, menu items are disabled and enabled purposely so that if you run this code you will be forced into a specific direction of execution. This was done to prevent array bounds errors and possible misinterpretation of the purpose of the code itself. In normal Windows-based programs, you would not normally control threads in this manner, but if you ever needed to, this is a good example of how you could do it.

As you can see in `'Start &3 Threads'`, the START() function is used to create and instantiate multiple occurrences of the same window object. When the START() function is issued, the Clarion for Windows library will instantiate the new threads, take care of some internal library housekeeping, then yield back to the thread that started these threads. Any code following the START() function will be executed, then the ACCEPT loop will cycle. At this point, the Clarion for Windows library will gain control again and then yield to the newly started thread and give the focus to the last thread started.

When the new thread regains focus, its ACCEPT loop is entered and the EVENT:OpenWindow event is executed where the window title is changed, to denote which thread is actually running. When the thread is exited, note that a strange-looking piece of code has been inserted: ThreadNo[THREAD()]=0. This is a shortcut used to clear the appropriate ThreadNo array element by using the Clarion for Windows function THREAD(). This function returns the number of the thread that is currently executing that has focus, which is used as the offset to the array. By setting the array element to zero you are denoting that the thread is no longer running or active, and decisions in your program could be made based on this information. This happens when you select the menu option Stop 1 Thread.

In the menu option Start 1 Thread, you will see that even though there were four threads running and the third thread has been stopped, the Clarion for Windows library knows that there is a hole in the sequence (only threads 1, 2, and 4 are running at this point). Because the third thread is no longer running, the next thread to be started will be thread number 3 and not thread number 5. In other words, the lowest unused thread number will be assigned. This enables you to track threads fairly easily and straightforwardly, because you know that if a thread is stopped, the number for that thread will be reused in the next START() function call.

In the menu option Close All Threads, you will see that for each thread (threads 2 through 4), an EVENT:CloseDown is posted. When the main ACCEPT loop cycles, each thread will receive the message to close and perform exactly the same process that Stop 1 Thread performed, only it will happen for each thread. I have added a user event called EVENT:CloseQuery, which is posted after the `EVENT:CloseDown` for each thread. This event is used to invoke a subsequent process once the threads have closed and is an example of the power of the event model in Clarion for Windows.

When threads contain an `ACCEPT` loop, they communicate with the other threads via messaging and events, as shown in Listing 28.2. You can see an explicit use of this in the `POST(EVENT:CloseDown,,ThreadNo[3])` statement. What this does is send a message to the third thread, informing it to close down and return, thus destroying that specific thread instance. Although this example is simple, it helps to illustrate why you might need a better way of referencing a thread in your programs. It would be very difficult to know the relative importance of thread number 3 unless you had a way to recognize and refer to it in a logical manner, perhaps by giving it a name you could remember and count on. It is a dangerous practice to arbitrarily count on a thread number value. In this instance, array element 3 will actually equal thread number 3 by design, but I highly advise against this practice. This example was used to illustrate that it is possible to use the array logic technique when tight programmatic control is utilized. All of this leads to the major focus of this chapter: thread management.

Thread Management

As alluded to already, there are various reasons for providing thread management in your programs. There are many methods by which you can manage threads; these methods range from simple to complex depending on your needs. Clarion for Windows does the hard work—it provides physical thread management, memory allocation, initialization, fetching and dispatching of messages, and destruction and memory deallocation. However, Clarion for Windows does not predispose how you might want to logically address threads. Instead, Clarion for Windows provides various language functions so that you can design the scheme most practical and usable for your given situation. This is great news, but flexibility like this comes with a price—you must write some code to deal with a few situations.

By default, in the templates supplied with Clarion for Windows, you can start what may seem like unlimited instances of a given object. However, there is a limit: Clarion for Windows allows you to start 64 threads provided that you have enough memory to do so. Why would this default behavior of automatically starting threads be allowed? The reason is simple: flexibility. There is one side effect, which I call the "unwanted thread," for one obvious reason: Most of the time you will want to start only one or some limited number of instances of a given object, and most likely not as many as 64. So, to avoid this situation, you must insert code to prevent it from occurring. For example, an application created using Quick Start will have at least one browse item on the menu. You could select this menu option repeatedly, over and over again, until you either run out of memory or you hit the 64-thread limitation. But you most likely want the user to be able to start only one instance of the browse at any given time, so how do you limit the instances of the window object? Thread management, of course.

> **NOTE**
>
> The goal of thread management is to relate physical threads with a logical tracking component.

The Thread Attribute

Before getting into the details of thread management, there is a related topic that should be covered because it can affect the work you do in threads: the Thread attribute. The Thread attribute can be placed only on variables, queues, and file definitions.

If the Thread attribute is used on a variable, the result will be a new instance, or shadow copy, of that variable created each time a new thread is started. For example, if you want a new copy of a variable called NDX created for you each time a thread is started, you would use the following definition:

```
NDX     LONG, THREAD
```

You might want to create a variable like this for various reasons, an obvious example being an index variable for an array or queue. Instead of declaring this index variable locally within each thread, you might declare this variable globally with the Thread attribute. This will accomplish the same goal, but without the need to remember to declare it in each thread.

Threaded variables are always treated and allocated as if a Static attribute had been applied to them. The special thing about threaded variables is that upon startup of the thread, the threaded variables are created from the program heap and are paged in and out upon thread swaps. This paging process is further optimized so that if a threaded variable is local to a procedure (that is, it is used only in that procedure), then paging will not occur until the procedure is actually entered.

Variables that are defined with the Thread attribute will always be instantiated automatically whenever a new thread is created. This means that each time a thread is started, the threaded variable will essentially be declared and initialized for you automatically in each thread, whether you want it to or not.

In summary, the Thread attribute is really a modifier for the Static attribute. Variables defined with the Thread attribute are created from the heap. Local variables are always thread specific anyway, because they are allocated from the stack. Depending on the amount and size of the threaded and local variables you use, your thread stack space may need to be increased.

You could avoid the Thread attribute overhead altogether by using a local procedure variable, which is how most efficiency-oriented programmers might do it. The benefits of threaded variables are mostly convenience and consistency, which you get at a calculated cost.

> **TIP**
>
> One thing to keep in mind is that overall program and procedure size has a direct impact on performance and efficiency of the program. So use threaded variables wisely and only as needed.

If the Thread attribute is used on a file definition, the result will be a new instance or new copy of the file's record buffer whenever that file is opened in a started thread. For example, a classic problem is a program that enables multiple instances (copies) of a given browse procedure that uses, for example, a file called PEOPLE. If you do not have the Thread attribute on the file definition, each browse would share the other's record buffer space, which could have some really strange results, depending on what the user does in the browse procedure. However, when you use the Thread attribute on the file definition, each browse will receive its own unique copy of a record buffer for the file, which prevents each thread from affecting the other. In most multithreaded applications, you will want to use the Thread attribute on your file definitions. Your file definition might look like the following:

```
People  FILE,DRIVER('TOPSPEED'),RECLAIM,PRE(PEO),CREATE,THREAD
```

Understanding the benefits and the responsibilities of threaded variables and threaded files will become paramount as you begin writing multithreaded programs. Even more important is how you manage and communicate with threads in your programs. The following two sections deal with thread management, both simple and complex. The terms simple thread management (STM) and complex thread management (CTM) are not standard Windows terms; they are designations I have made to describe the utility of function that each method provides.

Determining which of these two methods is appropriate for your situation is entirely up to you; in many cases, only STM is necessary. Yet, for some situations, you will soon see why CTM is the best option, regardless of program complexity. Once you are familiar with CTM, you most likely will decide to use CTM because of its versatility.

Due to the rapid application development (RAD) nature of Clarion for Windows, simple programs can become complex programs in a matter of minutes, thanks primarily to the AppGen. As program complexity grows, so does the need to manage the threads within your program, and CTM provides the best alternative for small- to large-scale programs.

Simple Thread Management

Listings 28.1 and 28.2 are both example programs that use a technique I call simple thread management. The listings are two different implementations of STM, but both have one common element: a predefined scope for managing threads. *STM* is a method in which threads are managed via global data elements such as a single variable or a variable array. This means that your program knows exactly where to look for the physical thread number for a specific thread instance. Although arrays could be used a bit more dynamically, after you review the principles of CTM later in this chapter, you can make the decision to use STM or CTM.

Listing 28.3 contains an STM example that illustrates some interesting techniques. You will see that there is a specific variable used for the MDI frame, the Splash window, and an MDI child window by which threads are tracked, controlled, and managed. The Splash window will serve two purposes: It will be a standard Splash window that is displayed at program initialization and it will be an About window.

Listing 28.3. The Multithreading Example 3 (MT3) program.

```
MT3                     PROGRAMMultithread

                        INCLUDE('EQUATES.CLW')
                        INCLUDE('ERRORS.CLW')
                        INCLUDE('KEYCODES.CLW')

                        MAP
                          Main()
                          Splash()
                          MdiChild()
                        END

NIL                     EQUATE('')
THIS                    EQUATE(0)
ZERO                    EQUATE(0)

!Is an About window when set to 1
IsAboutWindow           BYTE(0)
ItemMdiChild            LONG
ItemSplash              LONG
MdiChildThreadNo        LONG(0)
MdiFrame                &WINDOW
MdiFrameThreadNo        LONG(0)
SplashThreadNo          LONG(0)

wMdiFrame APPLICATION('MT3'),AT(0,0,317,190),CENTER,ICON('WINPYR.ICO'),|
        SYSTEM,MAX,MAXIMIZE,RESIZE,STATUS(-100,-40,-40,-30,-30)
      MENUBAR
        MENU('&File')
          ITEM('&Start MDI CHILD'),USE(?MdiChild)
          ITEM('&About MT3'),USE(?Splash)
          ITEM('&Close All Threads'),USE(?CloseAllThreads)
          ITEM('Item&5'),USE(?Item5),SEPARATOR
          ITEM('E&xit      Alt+F4'),KEY(AltF4),STD(STD:Close)
        END
      END
    END

CODE
Main()
```

continues

Listing 28.3. continued

```
!=============================================================================
Main                    PROCEDURE
!=============================================================================
 CODE
 MdiFrame             &= wMdiFrame
 OPEN(wMdiFrame)
 ItemMdiChild       = ?MdiChild
 ItemSplash         = ?Splash
 MdiFrameThreadNo   = THREAD()
 THIS {PROP:Timer}  = 120
 ACCEPT
   CASE EVENT()
   OF EVENT:OpenWindow
     SplashThreadNo = START(Splash)
   OF EVENT:Timer
     THIS {PROP:StatusText,4} = FORMAT(TODAY(),@D2)
     THIS {PROP:StatusText,5} = FORMAT(CLOCK(),@T3)
     IF SplashThreadNo OR MdiChildThreadNo
        ?CloseAllThreads {PROP:Disable} = FALSE
     ELSE
        ?CloseAllThreads {PROP:Disable} = TRUE
     END
   OF EVENT:CloseDown
     THIS {PROP:Timer} = ZERO
     BREAK
   END
   CASE FIELD()
   OF ?MdiChild
     CASE EVENT()
     OF EVENT:Accepted
        IF ~MdiChildThreadNo
           MdiChildThreadNo = START(MdiChild)
        ELSE
           POST(EVENT:Restore,,MdiChildThreadNo)
        END
     END
   OF ?Splash
     CASE EVENT()
     OF EVENT:Accepted
        IF ~SplashThreadNo
           IsAboutWindow  = TRUE
           SplashThreadNo = START(Splash)
        ELSE
           POST(EVENT:Restore,,SplashThreadNo)
        END
     END
   OF ?CloseAllThreads
     CASE EVENT()
     OF EVENT:Accepted
        IF MdiChildThreadNo
           POST(EVENT:CloseDown,,MdiChildThreadNo)
        END
        IF SplashThreadNo
           POST(EVENT:CloseDown,,SplashThreadNo)
        END
     END
   END
 END
END
```

```
    CLOSE(wMdiFrame)
    RETURN

!==============================================================================
MdiChild              PROCEDURE
!==============================================================================

wMdiChild WINDOW('Mdi Child Procedure'),AT(,,102,27),SYSTEM,GRAY,MAX,RESIZE,¦
        MDI
      BUTTON('Thread'),AT(4,6,94,14),FONT('MS Sans Serif',8,,FONT:bold),¦
        USE(?ThreadButton),DEFAULT,STD(STD:Close)
    END

  CODE
  OPEN(wMdiChild)
  ACCEPT
    CASE EVENT()
    OF EVENT:OpenWindow
      ?ThreadButton {PROP:TEXT}    = 'Is Thread Number ' & THREAD()
      MdiFrame {PROP:StatusText,2} = 'MDI CHILD=' & THREAD()
      MdiFrame $ ItemMdiChild {PROP:Disable} = TRUE
    OF EVENT:CloseDown
      BREAK
    OF EVENT:Restore
      IF THIS{PROP:Iconize} = TRUE
        THIS{PROP:Iconize} = FALSE
        THIS{PROP:Active}  = TRUE
        POST(EVENT:Resume)
      ELSE
        THIS{PROP:Active}  = TRUE
        POST(EVENT:Resume)
      END
    END
  END
  MdiFrame                {PROP:StatusText,2} = NIL
  MdiFrame $ ItemMdiChild {PROP:Disable}      = FALSE
  CLOSE(wMdiChild)
  MdiChildThreadNo = ZERO
  RETURN

!==============================================================================
Splash                PROCEDURE
!==============================================================================

wSplash WINDOW('Splash Procedure'),AT(5,4,306,157),ICON('WINPYR.ICO'),SYSTEM,¦
        GRAY,MAX,RESIZE,MDI
        STRING('This is a SPLASH! Procedure'),AT(6,14,294,20),¦
        FONT('Times New Roman',24,080H,FONT:bold+FONT:italic), ¦
        USE(?WindowType),TRN,CENTER
        STRING('Developing Applications in CW'),AT(6,64,294,13),¦
        FONT('Arial',14,0800000H,FONT:bold),USE(?String2), ¦
        TRN,CENTER
        IMAGE('MT4.ICO'),AT(139,39,,),USE(?Image1)
        BUTTON('&Ok'),AT(266,102,,),FONT('MS Sans Serif',8,,FONT:bold),¦
        USE(?OkButton),STD(STD:Close),DEFAULT
        STRING('By Ross A. Santos and Dave Harms'),AT(8,136,292,12),¦
        FONT('Times New Roman',12,,FONT:bold+FONT:italic), ¦
        USE(?String3),TRN,CENTER
    END
```

continues

Listing 28.3. continued

```
CODE
OPEN(wSplash)
IF ~IsAboutWindow
    ?OkButton {PROP:Hide}   = TRUE
    THIS      {PROP:Timer}  = 240
ELSE
    THIS        {PROP:TEXT} = ¦
                'This is an ABOUT! Procedure'
    ?WindowType {PROP:TEXT} = THIS{PROP:TEXT}
END
ACCEPT
  CASE EVENT()
  OF EVENT:OpenWindow
    IF ~IsAboutWindow
       MdiFrame {PROP:StatusText,3} = ¦
                'SPLASH=' & THREAD()
       MdiFrame $ ItemMdiChild {PROP:Disable} = TRUE
       MdiFrame $ ItemSplash   {PROP:Disable} = TRUE
    ELSE
       MdiFrame {PROP:StatusText,3} = ¦
                'ABOUT=' & THREAD()
    END
  OF EVENT:Timer
    POST(EVENT:CloseDown)
  OF EVENT:CloseDown
    THIS {PROP:Timer} = ZERO
    BREAK
  OF EVENT:Restore
    IF THIS{PROP:Iconize} = TRUE
      THIS{PROP:Iconize} = FALSE
      THIS{PROP:Active}  = TRUE
      POST(EVENT:Resume)
    ELSE
      THIS{PROP:Active}  = TRUE
      POST(EVENT:Resume)
    END
  END
END
MdiFrame {PROP:StatusText,3} = NIL
IF ~IsAboutWindow
   MdiFrame $ ItemMdiChild {PROP:Disable} = FALSE
   MdiFrame $ ItemSplash   {PROP:Disable} = FALSE
END
CLOSE(wSplash)
SplashThreadNo = ZERO
IsAboutWindow  = ZERO

RETURN
```

It is time to begin dissecting this program. Looking at Listing 28.3, you will see the declarations section of the program, which includes the following items:

```
NIL                  EQUATE('')
THIS                 EQUATE(0)
ZERO                 EQUATE(0)
```

The equates in the listing are special equates used to make the program a bit more readable. The NIL equate is used to clear a string value to an empty string. For example, if you had a variable called NAME that was a STRING(40), you could simply clear the contents of the variable by assigning NAME=NIL. The THIS equate is used to reference the current window name in property settings. The property syntax for a window must include a window name as part of the property setting, or if zero is used, this value indicates the current window as the target for the property assignment statement. Therefore, THIS can be used in place of the window name when you refer to this window. For example, if you wanted to minimize the current window you could use THIS{PROP:ICONIZE} = TRUE. The final equate of ZERO is used in place of the literal zero.

For example, if you had a variable called THREADNO that was a long variable, you could simply clear the contents of the variable by assigning THREADNO=ZERO. Why do I use equates for these purposes? Mostly for readability and ease of maintenance. Because these equates represent a value and are not the value itself, it becomes much easier to do global searches and replaces as needed. If you attempted to search and replace on the literal zero, it might take a long time because many values have a zero associated with them in some form or another, and the possibility of making a mistake when replacing literals such as zero is quite high. This technique of using equates for common values is also used in the AppGen (for example, when you use the equates TRUE and FALSE).

The following are the global variables used in this example:

```
IsAboutWindow           BYTE(0)
ItemMdiChild            LONG
ItemSplash              LONG
MdiChildThreadNo        LONG(0)
MdiFrame                &WINDOW
MdiFrameThreadNo        LONG(0)
SplashThreadNo          LONG(0)
```

There are only a few global variables included in this example, and they are primarily used for the simple thread management process. The IsAboutWindow variable is used to determine which type of window to display—either a Splash window or an About window. If the variable is zero, a Splash window is displayed; otherwise, an About window is displayed. The ItemMdiChild and ItemSplash variables are used as the menu option use variables, so in the program you can reference the menu items within another procedure, out of scope of the procedure in which the menu is defined. The thread number variables, MdiChildThreadNo, MdiFrameThreadNo, and SplashThreadNo, are all defined as long variables because this is the value returned from the START() function. These variables are used for messaging between threads and managing the threads themselves. The MdiFrame variable is known as a *reference variable*. This variable is used to reference the wMdiFrame window in a procedure other than the one in which it is defined. To assign a reference variable you need to use a slightly different assignment statement than you would use for a normal variable. The following statement stores the reference to the window wMdiFrame in the variable MdiFrame:

```
MdiFrame            &= wMdiFrame
```

Reference variables are quite handy, and I'm sure you'll find all sorts of uses for them as you continue to uncover the gems that are hidden in Clarion for Windows.

In the wMdiFrame window definition, notice that I have set up a status line with five widths, or "holes," in the status bar:

```
STATUS(-100,-40,-40,-30,-30)
```

The first width is used for the messages that automatically display when you move from control to control, assuming that there is a MSG() attribute on the controls. The second width is used to display the MdiChild() procedure's related thread number, and the third width is used to display the Splash() procedure's related thread number value. The order in which you open and close these windows will affect the actual thread number that is displayed. For example, if you selected the Start MDI Child menu option first, the value for the MDI child width will be 2, otherwise it will be 3. The final two widths represent the current date and time, respectively, and are updated using an EVENT:Timer in the Main() procedure.

As you will see in the following statements, when the wMdiFrame window is opened, the Splash() procedure is started automatically, saving the value returned from the START() function in the SplashThreadNo variable. The Splash() procedure runs for a time and then stops. This is called a *Splash-style window.* Generally, most commercial programs will not only display the Splash window but will also take care of program initialization at this point, maybe reading INI files and setting up the program environment for the user:

```
OF EVENT:OpenWindow
     SplashThreadNo = START(Splash)
```

In this example, the wSplash window is displayed, and will remain on top of the wMdiFrame window for a short time and then disappear. The first sign of simple thread management appears within the Splash() procedure, as seen in the following statements:

```
OF EVENT:OpenWindow
     IF ~IsAboutWindow
        MdiFrame {PROP:StatusText,3} = ¦
                  'SPLASH=' & THREAD()
        MdiFrame $ ItemMdiChild {PROP:Disable} = TRUE
        MdiFrame $ ItemSplash   {PROP:Disable} = TRUE
     ELSE
        MdiFrame {PROP:StatusText,3} = ¦
                  'ABOUT=' & THREAD()
     END
```

First, when the wSplash window opens, the global variable IsAboutWindow is checked to determine what kind of window functionality is to be employed. In this case, the IsAboutWindow variable is zero and the first part of the IF statement is executed. The first statement will set the third width value to SPLASH=2, then the following two statements will disable both the Start MDI Child and the About MT3 menu items on the wMdiFrame window. Notice the use of the reference variable MdiFrame. The dollar sign ($) must be used between the MdiFrame and the ItemMdiChild and ItemSplash because the MDI frame is not the currently active window. Using this property setting informs the Clarion for Window library that you are making a property assignment to a window other than the current one.

The wSplash window will remain for a short time until the EVENT:Timer event fires, at which point it will post a message to close itself down using the EVENT:CloseDown. At this point the event EVENT:CloseDown will be processed and the ACCEPT loop will be stopped. Immediately after the end of the ACCEPT loop the following statement is executed:

```
MdiFrame {PROP:StatusText,3} = NIL
  IF ~IsAboutWindow
     MdiFrame $ ItemMdiChild {PROP:Disable} = FALSE
     MdiFrame $ ItemSplash   {PROP:Disable} = FALSE
  END
```

The first statement above will clear the third status line width, and here you see the use of the NIL equate. The next statement is similar to the previous IF statement; it checks the value in IsAboutWindow to determine which route it is to take. Because the IsAboutWindow variable is zero, the first portion of the IF statement will be executed. The next two lines re-enable the menu items that were previously disabled. You may be wondering why the menu items were disabled in the first place. The fact that the wSplash window is an MDI child window means that you can select the menu while the wSplash window is displayed and executing, and you most likely wouldn't want these menu items selected until you were finished setting up the program environment.

In the Splash procedure after the CLOSE(wSplash) window, you will see the following statements:

```
  SplashThreadNo = ZERO
  IsAboutWindow  = ZERO
  RETURN
```

These statements clean up for the thread. First, the SplashThreadNo variable must be set back to zero so that this window procedure can be used again later. The IsAboutWindow variable is reset to zero so that if you needed a splash window again you could have one. Finally, the RE-TURN statement is the point where the thread will physically end or be destroyed. What you have seen so far in Listing 28.3 is the starting of a thread, the managing of menu items that are not in the current thread's scope, and the destruction of the thread existence, using specific variables to denote the different threads in your program.

Continuing down the EVENT() process in the MAIN() procedure of Listing 28.3, you will see the line OF EVENT:Timer. Prior to the ACCEPT statement there is a statement THIS {PROP:Timer} = 120. This statement sets the interval value for the Clarion for Windows library to post the

EVENT:Timer event to this ACCEPT loop. There are several things accomplished in the EVENT:Timer. First, the current date and time are updated on the status widths 4 and 5. Second, a check is made to determine if any of the child thread processes are currently executing. This is done by interrogating the values in SplashThreadNo and MdiChildThreadNo, respectively. If either is set to a non-zero value, this means that a child thread is executing.

The following code is used to enable and disable the menu options in the EVENT:Timer:

```
OF EVENT:Timer
    THIS {PROP:StatusText,4} = FORMAT(TODAY(),@D2)
    THIS {PROP:StatusText,5} = FORMAT(CLOCK(),@T3)
    IF SplashThreadNo OR MdiChildThreadNo
        ?CloseAllThreads {PROP:Disable} = FALSE
    ELSE
        ?CloseAllThreads {PROP:Disable} = TRUE
    END
```

I expect you might be asking How can I know for sure if a thread is actually executing? That is a great question. There are various ways to distinguish this, including using the Windows API, but for this case (STM), you will manage this process with global variables. One thing to note is that physical thread creation and logical thread tracking can get out of sync if you forget to do one of the following:

■ Set the thread tracking variable to the value returned from the START() function.

■ Clear the thread tracking variable on return from the procedure that was started.

If there are threads executing, the menu item Close All Threads will be enabled; otherwise, it will be disabled. One thing to note here is that if your EVENT:Timer interval is too long, the menu item will not be enabled or disabled soon enough, which might appear as if you have a bug in the program. A half-second delay on the EVENT:Timer should be sufficient for almost anything.

Now that you have a good idea of what is happening at the start and what is also happening as a timed sequence, it is time to dive into what happens when you select a menu item. For example, if you select the About MT3 menu item, the following code will be executed:

```
OF ?Splash
    CASE EVENT()
    OF EVENT:Accepted
        IF ~SplashThreadNo
            IsAboutWindow  = TRUE
            SplashThreadNo = START(Splash)
        ELSE
            POST(EVENT:Restore,,SplashThreadNo)
        END
```

The basic premise here is that you will be able to start only one About window at a time. The IF statement first checks whether your SplashThreadNo variable has a value, indicating that the process is already running. If SplashThreadNo is zero, then the IsAboutWindow variable is set to TRUE, or 1 (more on this variable in just a moment). Then the Splash() procedure is started, and the thread number is returned from the START() function and is assigned to the

SplashThreadNo variable. If you had already selected this item, the ELSE portion of the IF statement would be executed. If you now look at the Splash() procedure, you will note what happens when IsAboutWindow is set to TRUE. First, the following statements are executed:

```
IF ~IsAboutWindow
    ?OkButton {PROP:Hide}    = TRUE
    THIS      {PROP:Timer}   = 240
 ELSE
    THIS           {PROP:TEXT} = |
                   'This is an ABOUT! Procedure'
    ?WindowType {PROP:TEXT} = THIS{PROP:TEXT}
END
```

If IsAboutWindow is zero, then the OK button will be hidden and the window timer interval is set; otherwise, the title of the window is changed to reflect that the process is now an About window and not a Splash window. Also notice that the OK button appears in this case. When it is pressed, it will process the standard Window action equivalent to the equate STD:Close. If you press the OK button, an EVENT:CloseDown will be generated by the Clarion for Windows library and the ACCEPT loop will stop, following a clean-up process similar to what the Splash window had.

If the Splash() procedure was already executing and you pressed the menu item About MT3, then the MDI frame would post the EVENT:Restore to the SplashThreadNo. In the Splash() procedure the following statements would be executed:

```
OF EVENT:Restore
    IF THIS{PROP:Iconize} = TRUE
      THIS{PROP:Iconize} = FALSE
      THIS{PROP:Active}  = TRUE
      POST(EVENT:Resume)
    ELSE
      THIS{PROP:Active}  = TRUE
      POST(EVENT:Resume)
    END
```

These statements essentially interrogate the current state of the window. If the window is minimized (PROP:Iconize=TRUE), then the wSplash window will be set to normal (PROP:Iconize=FALSE). If the window is not minimized, then it will be set to the active on-top window (PROP:Active=TRUE). Here you see the use of the THIS equate instead of the name of the window itself. This trick is not only easy to use, but it makes your system much more friendly and intuitive for the end user. By default, simply setting focus on a window will not affect the state of the window. In this example, if you set focus to a window (PROP:Restore), it is assumed that you want that window to be accessible and therefore you should make sure that the window is set to normal if it was minimized or to active if it was already set to normal before you selected the menu item. The key to making the window completely active again is to post the EVENT:Resume, which essentially informs the thread to "wake up."

Finally, now that you have seen how to create (instantiate or start) and manage (communicate) threads in various ways, the last thing to learn is how to destroy these executing threads on demand. The following code is used to perform this function:

```
OF ?CloseAllThreads
   CASE EVENT()
   OF EVENT:Accepted
      IF MdiChildThreadNo
         POST(EVENT:CloseDown,,MdiChildThreadNo)
      END
      IF SplashThreadNo
         POST(EVENT:CloseDown,,SplashThreadNo)
      END
   END
```

Pressing the menu item Close All Threads will send the event EVENT:CloseDown to each executing child thread, resulting in the destruction of each of these child threads. The IF statement is used because you are resetting the MDiChildThreadNo and SplashThreadNo variables to zero when each thread is closed. If you post a message and the third parameter of the POST() function is zero or omitted, the Clarion for Windows library assumes that you intend to post the message to the current ACCEPT loop. In this case, the MAIN() procedure's ACCEPT loop would execute the EVENT:CloseDown logic in the wMdiFrame window, closing down all executing child threads, as well, which is not what the menu item was designed to accomplish. By design, only child threads should close, not the MDI frame parent thread.

All this may seem a bit complex, but it really is quite simple once you learn the basics, which I hope you have now learned. CTM is a bit more involved, and the next section explores issues that have not been covered yet—specifically, managing multiple instances of the same procedure, as well as a host of other issues important to developing multithreaded applications.

Complex Thread Management

The term complex thread management implies that the process is somehow more difficult than STM. However, this is not necessarily the case. I call it CTM primarily because what you are trying to accomplish is far more complex, and requires a technique that is far more robust, dynamic, and effective than that of STM.

STM uses global variables to represent a logical thread descriptor (a visible and understandable way of identifying an arbitrary thread number) of the physical thread numbers. This is where CTM and STM begin to diverge. CTM uses a global queue (doubly linked list) to accomplish this task. STM lends itself to managing one instance of a procedure, but CTM provides the robustness to represent multiple instances of the same procedure. STM does not provide capabilities to query which threads are executing, how many threads of a procedure type are executing at a given time, or even the logical record values in a given thread. CTM provides this functionality and much, much more.

The Thread Manager

I have had many requests from developers interested in a tool I created called the *Thread Manager*. Instead of marketing this tool, I decided to place it on the disk included with this book. A subdirectory called \CHAP28 includes the Thread Manager's source code files.

> **WARNING**
>
> You may freely use and modify the Thread Manager as needed for your projects without paying royalties of any type. However, you may not market the Thread Manager as a product in any way, shape, or form. There are no warranties or guarantees expressed or implied and there is no formal technical support available. Use the Thread Manager at your own risk.

In the upcoming example code, the Thread Manager will be used extensively, so the first line of business is to discuss what the Thread Manager can and will do for you.

Thread Manager Defined

The Thread Manager provides mechanisms to create, manage, query, and destroy logical thread descriptors for the physical threads that are executing in your program. For example, when a physical thread is created or destroyed, a logical counterpart must perform similar functionality. What if you needed to determine the count of the instances of a procedure that are currently executing, or what if you needed to know the exact data records that are contained in an executing instance? The Thread Manager provides just this sort of functionality.

The Thread Manager may be used in source, LIB, or DLL format, as desired. The basic components, functionality, and usage are described in full detail in the next section.

Thread Manager Components

The Thread Manager is relatively simple. There is a declaration file that contains the global equates, variables, and queues, as well as a source file that contains all the Thread Manager functions. The Thread Manager includes the following files:

- TM.VAR (Thread Manager variable declarations)
- TM.INC (The program map include file)
- TM.CLW (Thread Manager functions)

Thread Manager Declarations

Listing 28.4 contains the global declarations used in the Thread Manager. Included in this list are the standard equates, the variables, and the queues as they are used in the MT4 example program shown in Listing 28.6.

Listing 28.4. TM.VAR Thread Manager variable include file.

```
!==============================================================================
!NAME     : TM.VAR v1.0
!SYSTEM   : Any CLARION FOR WINDOWS Application
!PURPOSE  : Contains definitions required for the Thread Manager
!==============================================================================


!EQUATES---------------------------------------------------------------------
NIL                     EQUATE('')                      !Program Equates
ONE                     EQUATE(1)                       !One value
SPACE                   EQUATE(' ')                     !Space
THIS                    EQUATE(0)                       !Current Window
ZERO                    EQUATE(0)                       !Zero value
EVENT:CloseQuery        EQUATE(402h)                    !Close and Query Event

!GLOBAL VARIABLES------------------------------------------------------------
gJunk                   STRING(20)                      !Junk variable
gThreadNo               LONG,THREAD                     !Thread Number

!GLOBAL STRUCTURES-----------------------------------------------------------
MdiFrameGroup           GROUP, PRE(MFG)                 !
Reference                 STRING(80)                    !Current Thread
                        END                             !


!GLOBAL QUEUES---------------------------------------------------------------
TMQ                     QUEUE, PRE(TMQ)                 !Thread Manager Queue
Id                        LONG                          ! Thread Id
Name                      STRING(30)                    ! User Control Name
Reference                 STRING(80)                    ! User Control Ref
HWnd                      USHORT                        ! Windows Window Handle
GroupId                   BYTE                          ! Thread Group Id
                        END                             !

QTM                     QUEUE, PRE(QTM)                 !Query TM Queue
                          LIKE(TMQ),PRE(QTM)            ! Like Thread Manager
                        END                             !
```

(handwritten annotations in margins:) MidiChildrenGroup / SystemGroupID; ThreadID, ThreadName, Reference, GroupID; GroupName; QVERyQUE QUEUE LIKE(TMQ), PRE(QQU) END; EQUATE(1); STRING(20); BYTE

The Thread Manager queue (TMQ) is the global queue that contains all the logical thread descriptor information. As you will see in Listing 28.6, you should never address the TMQ directly, but only through the appropriate Thread Manager functions. If you address the TMQ directly, you could render the thread management useless. The QTM (Query Thread Manager) queue is used for interrogating the status of threads instead of the TMQ, as you will see in Listing 28.6.

The following describes the type of data to be inserted into the TMQ. The Thread Manager does this for you via the TmCreate() function.

- ID (Physical thread number)
- NAME (Logical thread descriptor name)
- REFERENCE (Data represented in the thread instance)
- HWND (Windows window handle for the thread's window)
- GROUPID (Relationship identifier for relating threads)

The QTM queue is used as a temporary queue for retrieving results from the Thread Manager. The use of the LIKE operator is important in this queue example because it represents some of the basic object-oriented (OO) functionality in Clarion for Windows. The LIKE operator is discussed in detail in Chapter 15, "Hand-Crafted Code: Principles and Approaches." Essentially, the LIKE operator enables the QTM queue to inherit the field attributes in the TMQ without any additional code. The contents of the data are not inherited—only the attributes or field definitions are inherited.

The Thread Manager Program Map Include File

This file is inserted inside your program MAP statement after the local procedures and functions have been declared using the INCLUDE directive:

```
MAP
  Main()
  INCLUDE('TM.INC')
END
```

The TM.INC file includes the following information, which is discussed in detail later in this chapter:

```
!=============================================================================
!NAME    : TM.INC v1.0
!SYSTEM  : Any CLARION FOR WINDOWS Application
!PURPOSE : The MAP include file for the Thread Manager
!=============================================================================

                       MODULE('TM')
                        TmCreate(LONG,STRING,<STRING>,<USHORT>,<BYTE>),LONG
                        TmDebug()
                        TmDestroy(LONG),LONG
                        TmDestroyGroup(<BYTE>),LONG
                        TmGetHWnd(LONG),USHORT
                        TmGetId(STRING,<STRING>,<BYTE>),LONG
                        TmQuery(*QUEUE,<STRING>,<STRING>,<BYTE>),LONG
                       END
```

Thread Manager Functions

The Thread Manager is a single source file that contains various functions to assist you in creating, managing, and destroying logical thread descriptors. Table 28.1 represents the functionality contained in the Thread Manager.

Table 28.1. The functionality in the Thread Manager.

Function	Description
TmCreate	Create a thread instance
TmDebug	View the thread manager queue

continues

Table 28.1. continued

Function	Description
TmDestroy	Destroy a thread instance
TmDestroyGroup	Destroy a group of thread instances
TmGethWnd	Retrieve a thread's window handle
TmGetId	Get a specific thread-by-thread ID
TmQuery	Query and return specific threads

These functions each have a specific functionality, but you will see as you review these functions in Listing 28.6 that they can be used in various ways.

Now it's time to dig into the Thread Manager. The entire Thread Manager is shown in Listing 28.5. Instead of breaking down each line of code for you, I will comment on each function and describe its highlights, purpose, and use. After reviewing the information in Listing 28.5, you will see how I have used each function to perform the specific task in Listing 28.6. The key to the Thread Manager isn't the functionality, but how you utilize the information it gives you.

Listing 28.5. The Thread Manager.

```
                          MEMBER('MT4')
!===========================================================================
!NAME    : TM.CLW v1.0
!SYSTEM  : Any CLARION FOR WINDOWS Application
!PURPOSE : Creates, manages, queries and destroys logical thread descriptors
!===========================================================================


!===========================================================================
!NAME    : TMCreate
!TYPE    : FUNCTION
!PURPOSE : Create a logical Thread descriptor in the Thread Manager Queue(TMQ)
!SYNOPSIS: ThreadNo=TMCreate(THIS{PROP:Thread} , ¦
!                            ThreadName          , ¦
!                            Reference           , ¦
!                            THIS:{PROP:Handle}, ¦
!                            GroupId             )
!UPDATES : RAS 941113 Created for CWBOOK
!===========================================================================
TMCreate                FUNCTION(ThreadId,ThreadName,Reference,hWnd,GroupId)

iRetVal                 LONG,AUTO                      !Return Value
                                                       !
  CODE                                                 !
  iRetVal = ZERO                                       !Initialize Variables
                                                       !
  CLEAR(TMQ)                                           !Clear the Queue
  TMQ:Id         = ThreadId                            !Set Values To Save
  TMQ:Name       = ThreadName                          !
  IF ~OMITTED(3)  THEN TMQ:Reference = Reference .     !If Reference Passed
  IF ~OMITTED(4)  THEN TMQ:HWnd      = HWnd      .     !If Handle Passed
  IF ~OMITTED(5)  THEN TMQ:GroupId   = GroupId   .     !If Group Passed
```

```
          ADD(TMQ,TMQ:GroupId)                              !Add Queue Record
          IF ~ERRORCODE() THEN iRetVal = TMQ:Id        .   !If NO ERRORS set return
                                                            !value to current
                                                            !thread id

          RETURN(iRetVal)                                   !Return Results


!========================================================================
!NAME    : TMDebug
!TYPE    : PROCEDURE
!PURPOSE : Display values in the Thread Manager Queue (TMQ) which meet
!         : specification
!SYNOPSIS: TMDebug()
!UPDATES : RAS 941113 Created for CWBOOK
!========================================================================
TMDebug                 PROCEDURE

TMD                     QUEUE, PRE(TMD)                   !TM Debug Queue
                          LIKE(TMQ),PRE(TMD)              !LIKE the TMQ
                        END                               !

iNdx                    LONG,AUTO                         !Loop control variable

wTMDEBUG WINDOW('Thread Manager DEBUG'),AT(1,1,257,109), ¦
        FONT('MS Sans Serif',10,,FONT:regular),CENTER, ¦
        MSG('View Active Threads'),SYSTEM,GRAY,DOUBLE
      LIST,AT(6,10,244,74), ¦
      FONT('MS Sans Serif',8,,FONT:regular),USE(?DEBUGList),¦
      VSCROLL, ¦
      FORMAT('13R¦_~ID~@N3@81L¦_~Name~@S20@83L¦_~Reference~S(100)@S60@39R¦
            _~hWnd~@N08@14R¦_~GR'¦'P~@N3@'),FROM(TMD)
      BUTTON('E&xit'),AT(108,90,39,13),¦
      FONT('MS Sans Serif',8,,FONT:bold),STD(STD:Close),DEFAULT
    END

  CODE                                                    !
                                                          !
  DO LoadQue                                              !Load the Que
  OPEN(wTMDEBUG)                                          !Open This Window
  SELECT(?DebugList,ONE)                                  !Select first que
                                                          !record
  DISPLAY()                                               !Display the Window
                                                          !
  ACCEPT                                                  !Accept Loop
    CASE EVENT()                                          !  Window Events
    OF EVENT:CLOSEDOWN                                    !   CLOSE DOWN
      BREAK                                               !    Quit Loop
    END                                                   !
  END                                                     !End Accept Loop
                                                          !
  FREE(TMD);CLEAR(TMD)                                    !Free and clear
                                                          !the Queue
  CLOSE(wTMDEBUG)                                         !Close this Window
  RETURN                                                  !Return to caller

!------------------------------------------------------------------------
LoadQue                 ROUTINE                           !Load Debug Queue
!------------------------------------------------------------------------
```

continues

Listing 28.5. continued

```
iNdx = ZERO                                       !Initialize Variables
FREE(TMD);CLEAR(TMD)                              !Free and clear the
                                                  !Debug queue
                                                  !
LOOP RECORDS(TMQ) TIMES                           !Loop Through TM Recs
  iNdx += ONE                                     ! Increment by one
  GET(TMQ,iNdx)                                   ! Get Next
  CLEAR(TMD)                                       ! Clear Debug queue
  TMD = TMQ                                        ! Assign  Debug Queue
                                                  !   from TMQ
  ADD(TMD,TMD:GroupId)                            ! Add Debug Queue
                                                  ! Record Order
                                                  ! By Group
END                                               !End Record Loop
                                                  !
GET(TMD,ONE)                                       !Get First queue rec
EXIT                                               !Exit Routine


!===========================================================================
!NAME    : TMDestroy
!TYPE    : FUNCTION
!PURPOSE : Destroy a Thread Descriptor in the Thread Manager Queue
!SYNOPSIS: ThreadNo=TMDestroy(THIS{PROP:Thread})
!UPDATES : RAS 941113 Created for CWBOOK
!===========================================================================
TMDestroy               FUNCTION(ThreadId)

bHit                    BYTE,AUTO                 !Entry Found Flag
iNdx                    LONG,AUTO                 !Loop Control
iRetVal                 LONG,AUTO                 !Function Return Value

 CODE                                             !
 bHit    = ZERO                                   !Initialize Variables
 iNdx    = ZERO                                   !
 iRetVal = ZERO                                   !
                                                  !
 CLEAR(TMQ)                                       !Clear the TMQ Area
                                                  !
 LOOP RECORDS(TMQ) TIMES                          !Loop through TMQ
   iNdx += ONE                                    ! Increment by one
   GET(TMQ,iNdx)                                  ! Get Next
   IF TMQ:Id <> ThreadId THEN CYCLE.              ! If NOT SAME, cycle
   bHit = ONE                                     ! Set Hit Flag
   BREAK                                          ! Quit Loop
 END                                              !End Record Loop
                                                  !
 IF bHit                                          !If Hit flag is on
    DELETE(TMQ)                                   !  Delete Entry
    IF ERRORCODE()                                !  If an ERROR
       iRetVal = TMQ:Id                           !     Set to current
                                                  !       Thread Id
    ELSE                                          !  Else
       iRetVal = ZERO                             !     Set to Default
    END                                           !  End if ERROR
 END                                              !End If Hit Flag is on
                                                  !
 CLEAR(TMQ)                                       !Clear TMQ Area
 RETURN(iRetVal)                                  !Return Results
```

```
!===============================================================================
!NAME    : TMDestroyGroup
!TYPE    : FUNCTION
!PURPOSE : Destroy a Group of related Threads in the Thread Manager Queue
!SYNOPSIS: IF TMDestroyGroup(GroupId)
!UPDATES : RAS 941113 Created for CWBOOK
!===============================================================================
TMDestroyGroup          FUNCTION(GroupId)

iNdx                    LONG,AUTO                   !Loop Control Value
iRetVal                 LONG,AUTO                   !Return Value

 CODE                                               !
 iNdx    = ZERO                                     !Initialize Variables
 iRetVal = ZERO                                     !
                                                    !
 CLEAR(TMQ)                                         !Clear TMQ Area
 FREE(QTM);CLEAR(QTM)                               !Free/Clear QTM
                                                    !
 iRetVal = TMQuery(QTM,,,GroupId)                   !Determine if there
                                                    !are groups
                                                    !
 IF iRetVal                                         !If Groups exist
    LOOP RECORDS(QTM) TIMES                         !   Loop QTM Times
      iNdx += ONE                                   !     Increment by one
      GET(QTM,iNdx)                                 !     Get QTM
      IF ERRORCODE() THEN BREAK.                    !     If ERROR/Stop
      POST(EVENT:CLOSEDOWN,,QTM:Id)                 !     Post CLOSEDOWN
                                                    !     to Thread
    END                                             !   End Record Loop
 END                                                !End If Groups exist
                                                    !
 FREE(QTM);CLEAR(QTM)                               !Free/Clear QTM
 RETURN(iRetVal)                                    !Return Result

!===============================================================================
!NAME    : TMGetHWnd
!TYPE    : FUNCTION
!PURPOSE : Find a Threads Window Handle in the Thread Manager Queue
!SYNOPSIS: IF ~TMGetHWnd(ThreadId)
!UPDATES : RAS 941113 Created for CWBOOK
!===============================================================================
TMGetHWnd               FUNCTION(ThreadId)

bHit                    BYTE  ,AUTO                 !Entry Found Flag
iNdx                    LONG  ,AUTO                 !Loop Control
iRetVal                 USHORT,AUTO                 !Return Value (hWnd)

 CODE                                               !
 bHit    = ZERO                                     !Initialize Variables
 iNdx    = ZERO                                     !
 iRetVal = ZERO                                     !
                                                    !
 CLEAR(TMQ)                                         !Clear TMQ area
                                                    !
 LOOP RECORDS(TMQ) TIMES                            !Loop TMQ times
   iNdx += ONE                                      !  Increment by one
```

continues

Listing 28.5. continued

```
   GET(TMQ,iNdx)                                     !  Get Next
   IF TMQ:Id <> ThreadId THEN CYCLE.                 !  If NOT SAME/cycle
   bHit = ONE                                        ! Set Hit flag to on
   BREAK                                             !  and Quit Loop
 END                                                 !End Record Loop
                                                     !
 IF bHit THEN iRetVal = TMQ:HWnd .                   !If Hit flag then
                                                     !set the hWnd value
                                                     !
 RETURN(iRetVal)                                     !Return Results


!==============================================================================
!NAME    : TMGetId
!TYPE    : FUNCTION
!PURPOSE : Find a specific Thread in the Thread Manager Queue
!SYNOPSIS: IF ~TMGetId(ThreadName,Reference,GroupId)
!UPDATES : RAS 941113 Created for CWBOOK
!==============================================================================
TMGetId                    FUNCTION(ThreadName,Reference,GroupId)

bHit                       BYTE,AUTO                 !Entry Found Flag
iNdx                       LONG,AUTO                 !Loop Control
iRetVal                    LONG,AUTO                 !Return Value

 CODE                                                !
 bHit    = ZERO                                      !Initialize Variables
 iNdx    = ZERO                                      !
 iRetVal = ZERO                                      !
                                                     !
 CLEAR(TMQ)                                          !Clear the TMQ area
                                                     !
 LOOP RECORDS(TMQ) TIMES                             !Loop TMQ times
   iNdx += ONE                                       !  Increment by one
   GET(TMQ,iNdx)                                     !  Get Next
   IF TMQ:Name <> ThreadName THEN CYCLE.             !  If NOT SAME/cycle
   IF ~OMITTED(2) THEN                               !  If REF passed
      IF TMQ:Reference <> Reference THEN CYCLE.      !   If NOT SAME/cycle
   END                                               !
   IF ~OMITTED(3) THEN                               !  If GROUP Passed
      IF TMQ:GroupId <> GroupId THEN CYCLE.          !   If NOT SAME /cycle
   END                                               !
   bHit = ONE                                        !  Set Hit flag to on
   BREAK                                             !  and Quit Loop
 END                                                 !End Record Loop
                                                     !
 IF bHit THEN iRetVal = TMQ:Id.                      !If hit is on, set
                                                     !return value to
                                                     !current Thread Id
 RETURN(iRetVal)                                     !Return Results


!==============================================================================
!NAME    : TMQuery
!TYPE    : FUNCTION
!PURPOSE : Find all Threads in the Thread Manager Queue matching the passed
!         : specification
!SYNOPSIS: IF ~TMQuery(QueryQueue,ThreadName,,Reference,GroupId)
!UPDATES : RAS 941113 Created for CWBOOK
!==============================================================================
```

```
TMQuery                     FUNCTION(QueryQue,ThreadName,Reference,GroupId)

iNdx                        LONG,AUTO                !Loop Control
iRetVal                     LONG,AUTO                !Return Value

  CODE                                               !
  iNdx    = ZERO                                     !Initialize Variables
  iRetVal = ZERO                                     !
                                                     !
  CLEAR(TMQ)                                         !Clear TMQ
                                                     !
  LOOP RECORDS(TMQ) TIMES                            !Loop TMQ Times
    iNdx += ONE                                      !  Increment by one
    GET(TMQ,iNdx)                                    !  Get Next
    IF ~OMITTED(2)                                   !  If NAME Passed
       IF TMQ:Name <> ThreadName THEN CYCLE.         !    If NOT SAME/cycle
    END                                              !
    IF ~OMITTED(3) AND Reference <> NIL              !  If REF Passed
       IF TMQ:Reference <> Reference THEN CYCLE.     !    If NOT SAME/cycle
    END                                              !
    IF ~OMITTED(4) AND GroupId <> ZERO               !  If GROUP Passed
       IF TMQ:GroupId <> GroupId THEN CYCLE.         !    If NOT SAME/cycle
    END                                              !
    iRetVal   +=ONE                                  !  Increment Value
    QueryQue = TMQ                                   !  Assign QTM to
                                                     !  TMQ
    ADD(QueryQue)                                    !  Add QTM
  END                                                !End Record Loop
                                                     !
  RETURN(iRetVal)                                    !Return Results
```

Create a Thread Instance

The TmCreate() function instantiates a logical thread descriptor. Generally, TmCreate() is called in the EVENT:OpenWindow of the started procedure. This is done primarily for one reason: If the EVENT:OpenWindow fails, the logical thread descriptor will not be created. The TmCreate() function has the following prototype:

```
TmCreate(LONG,STRING,<STRING>,<USHORT>,<BYTE>),LONG
```

From left to right you must pass the currently executing thread number and thread name, and you may optionally pass the thread reference value, the Windows window handle, and a group ID. The result of this function is to add a queue record to the TMQ using only the passed values. If any values are omitted, they are not placed into the TMQ queue record. If the function is successful, it will return the TMQ:Id, which will be the same value as the thread number you passed into the function; otherwise, it will return a zero, indicating failure.

View the Thread Manager Queue

The TmDebug() procedure is included in the Thread Manager simply as a way to view the contents of the TMQ. This procedure takes no parameters and will list the complete contents of the TMQ. The Thread Manager Debug (TMD) queue uses a LIKE operator to insert the TMQ's field definition attributes via inheritance. The TmDebug() function has the following prototype:

```
TmDebug()
```
← *Actions / Source*

Generally, I will include this procedure on the main menu whenever I am developing an application. I will then remove it later, before I distribute my application.

Destroy a Thread Instance

The TmDestroy() function destroys a logical thread descriptor. Generally, TmDestroy() is called immediately before the RETURN statement in the started procedure. This is done primarily for one reason: The only time it is safe to terminate a logical thread descriptor is after the currently executing ACCEPT loop terminates and prior to the RETURN statement. The TmDestroy() function has the following prototype:

```
TmDestroy(LONG),LONG
```

You must pass the currently executing thread number. The result of this function, if it's successful, will delete the TMQ record that logically represents the thread number that you passed to it. If this function is successful, it will return a zero; otherwise, it will return the thread number that you passed to it, indicating that the thread is still active.

Destroy a Group of Thread Instances

The TmDestroyGroup() function destroys a group of logical thread descriptors. This function will first query the TMQ using the TmQuery() function in the Thread Manager, which will then fill the QTM with any applicable TMQ record values that match the specification of the passed in group ID. From this point on, the QTM, not the TMQ, is used for processing. The TmDestroyGroup() function has the following prototype:

```
TmDestroyGroup(<BYTE>),LONG
```

You may optionally pass in a group ID, but if it is omitted, the TmDestroyGroup() function assumes that you mean *all* threads.

> **TIP**
>
> The group ID is important. It gives you a way to link various threads together into a group that can be managed as a whole.

The return value from this function indicates the count of threads that match the specification in the group ID, or all threads in the case where the group ID is omitted. If there is a return value, it indicates the number of threads that are being destroyed. If the return value is zero, it means there are no more threads matching that specification to destroy.

I chose my words very carefully here, for good reason. I said "are being destroyed," not "are destroyed." There is a subtle but profound difference. Notice in this function that a POST(EVENT:CloseDown,,QTM:Id) is being used outside of the currently executing ACCEPT loop, and it may be posting this message to many different threads. This means that the threads that are being destroyed are not actually destroyed until the next cycle of the current ACCEPT loop where the TmDestroyGroup() function was invoked. This may cause a rare side effect—the threads that are expected to close, may not all close as intended—this can occur if you have more than 40 threads open at any given time. This side effect is due to a limitation of the message queue itself. You can work around this problem by calling the TmDestroyGroup() function multiple times in succession.

The TmDestroyGroup() function is very different from the TmDestroy() function because it doesn't physically perform the deletion of the TMQ record. Rather, this function informs each child thread in the QTM to close down, at which point each child thread, after receiving the EVENT:CloseDown message, will call the TmDestroy() function itself. This is a form of logic indirection, which can become problematic if you forget to code the TmDestroy() function in each child thread. The result is that threads will not close as intended.

Get the Windows Window Handle of a Thread

The TmGetHWnd() function will return the Windows window handle from the TMQ. The obvious question is Why might you want to do this? The short answer is that you don't want to. The long answer is that you might need to address a VBX control from outside the currently executing thread or use a Windows API function that requires the handle of the window. This function will find the TMQ entry and return you the Windows window handle value. The TmGetHWnd() function has the following prototype:

```
TmGetHWnd(LONG),USHORT
```

You must pass in the thread number to obtain the Windows window handle. When this task is successful, the return value will be the Windows window handle for the specified thread number. Otherwise, it will return zero, indicating failure, or that no window handle is available. Please note that once a TMQ entry has been found, the TMQ entry is left in the queue buffer until another Thread Manager function overwrites the queue buffer values.

Get a Specific Thread ID

The TmGetId() function will return the thread number for the logical thread descriptor from the TMQ. If successful, this function will return the TMQ:Id value for your specified criteria;

otherwise it will return a zero, which indicates that it could not find the specified thread. The `TmGetId()` function has the following prototype:

```
TmGetId(STRING,<STRING>,<BYTE>),LONG
```

You must pass in the thread name, and you have the option to further qualify the thread by passing in the thread reference value and/or group ID. Omitted parameters are not used in the query process. Please note that once a TMQ entry has been found, the TMQ entry is left in the queue buffer until another Thread Manager function overwrites the queue buffer values.

Query- and Return-Specific Threads

The `TmQuery()` function will fill the QTM queue with matching TMQ record values and return the count of records that are placed in the QTM as a result of this function. The `TmQuery()` function has the following prototype:

```
TmQuery(*QUEUE,<STRING>,<STRING>,<BYTE>),LONG
```

You must pass in the queue (QTM) that matches the TMQ queue structure definition exactly. You also have the option to pass in the thread name, thread reference value, and group ID in order to narrow the scope of the query to specific TMQ records. If the count returned by the `TmQuery()` function is zero, no matching records were found. Otherwise, it is safe to assume that you can access QTM queue records in your program code, with one caveat: If after you call the `TmQuery()` function you issue another Thread Manager function call, you must always call the `TmQuery()` function again if you are planning on using the QTM entries. This is done because another Thread Manager function call might destroy the integrity of the QTM.

A Thread Manager Sample Program

To see some of the benefits a thread manager that utilizes the CTM concept can provide, please review the program in Listing 28.6. This program is similar to the one used in Listing 28.3, but it has more features and robustness because the Thread Manager and CTM are used.

In Listing 28.6, you will be able to start multiple-instance MDI child threads (`'&Start MDI CHILD'`), single-instance MDI child threads that contain data (`'Start MDI CHILD Reference &1'` and `'Start MDI CHILD Reference &2'`). You also will be able to isolate each thread instance by data; control the number of instances a MDI child may be started (`'Start MDI CHILD &Up To Three'`); start a single About window (`'&About MT4'`); minimize, restore, and close all executing threads; and view the TMQ contents. Only the code added for Listing 28.6 is discussed here, so if you have not reviewed the STM example in Listing 28.3, I highly suggest that you do it now. By the time you finish with this example, it should be apparent just how simple it is to manage physical threads when you apply a logical extension via a tool such as the Thread Manager.

Listing 28.6. Multithreaded Example 4 (MT4.CLW) using the Thread Manager.

```
MT4                       PROGRAM

                          INCLUDE('EQUATES.CLW')
                          INCLUDE('ERRORS.CLW')
                          INCLUDE('KEYCODES.CLW')

                          !Thread Manager Variables
                          INCLUDE('TM.VAR')

                          MAP
                            Main()
                            Splash()
                            MdiChild()
                            SetStatusBar()

                            !Thread Manager Program Map
                            INCLUDE('TM.INC')
                          END                       !

MdiChildrenGroupId        EQUATE(1)                 !group of MDI CHILDREN
SystemGroupId             EQUATE(2)                 !group of SYSTEM

i                         LONG, AUTO
IsAboutWindow             BYTE, AUTO
ItemCloseAllThreads       LONG, AUTO
ItemMdiChild              LONG, AUTO
ItemMdiChildRef1          LONG, AUTO
ItemMdiChildRef2          LONG, AUTO
ItemMdiChildUpTo3         LONG, AUTO
ItemMinimizeAll           LONG, AUTO                !Menu Minimize All
ItemRestoreAll            LONG, AUTO                !Menu Restore All
ItemSplash                LONG, AUTO                !Menu Splash
ItemTMDebug               LONG, AUTO                !Menu Thread Manager Debug
MdiFrame                  &WINDOW          ref variable
MdiFrameThreadNo          LONG, AUTO

wMdiFrame APPLICATION('MT4 - Using The Thread Manager'),AT(0,0,317,190),|
          CENTER,ICON('WINPYR.ICO'),STATUS(-100,-80,-30,-30), |
        SYSTEM,MAX,MAXIMIZE,RESIZE
      MENUBAR
        MENU('&File')
          ITEM('&Start MDI CHILD'),USE(?MdiChild),|
            MSG('Start 1 child thread multiple times')
          ITEM('Start MDI CHILD Reference &1'),USE(?MdiChildRef1),|
            MSG('Start 1 child thread with data reference 1 only')
          ITEM('Start MDI CHILD Reference &2'),USE(?MdiChildRef2),|
            MSG('Start 1 child thread with data reference 2 only')
          ITEM('Start MDI CHILD &Up To Three'),USE(?MdiChildUpTo3),|
            MSG('Start up to 3 child threads only')
          ITEM('Item&4'),USE(?Item4),SEPARATOR
          ITEM('E&xit      Alt+F4'),MSG('Exit System'),KEY(AltF4),|
            STD(STD:Close)
        END
        MENU('&Window')
          ITEM('&Minimize All'),USE(?MinimizeAll),|
            MSG('Minimize all child threads')
```

continues

Listing 28.6. continued

```
                ITEM('&Restore All'),USE(?RestoreAll),¦
                  MSG('Restore all child threads')
                ITEM('&Close All Threads'),USE(?CloseAllThreads),¦
                  MSG('Close all child threads')
                ITEM('Item&13'),USE(?Item13),SEPARATOR
                ITEM('&About MT4'),USE(?Splash),MSG('About MT4 program')
                ITEM('&Thread Manager Debug'),USE(?TMDebug),¦
                  MSG('View Thread Manager Queue')
            END
          END
        END

    CODE
    i                       = ZERO                        !Initialize Variables
    IsAboutWindow           = ZERO
    ItemCloseAllThreads     = ZERO
    ItemMdiChild            = ZERO
    ItemMdiChildRef1        = ZERO
    ItemMdiChildRef2        = ZERO
    ItemMdiChildUpTo3       = ZERO
    ItemMinimizeAll         = ZERO
    ItemRestoreAll          = ZERO
    ItemSplash              = ZERO
    ItemTMDebug             = ZERO
    MdiFrameThreadNo        = ZERO

    Main()

    !==============================================================================
    ! Main Menu Procedure
    !==============================================================================
    Main                    PROCEDURE
    CODE
    MdiFrame                &= wMdiFrame                   !Assign REFERENCE
    OPEN(wMdiFrame)

    ItemCloseAllThreads     = ?CloseAllThreads             !Assign Menu Items
    ItemMdiChild            = ?MdiChild
    ItemMdiChildRef1        = ?MdiChildRef1
    ItemMdiChildRef2        = ?MdiChildRef2
    ItemMdiChildUpTo3       = ?MdiChildUpTo3
    ItemMinimizeAll         = ?MinimizeAll
    ItemRestoreAll          = ?RestoreAll
    ItemSplash              = ?Splash
    ItemTMDebug             = ?TMDebug

    MdiFrameThreadNo    = THREAD()

    THIS {PROP:Timer}   = 120

    ACCEPT

      CASE EVENT()
      OF EVENT:OpenWindow
        gJunk = START(Splash)
      OF EVENT:Timer
        SetStatusBar()
```

```
OF EVENT:CloseDown
    THIS {PROP:Timer} = ZERO
    BREAK
END

CASE FIELD()
OF ?MdiChild
  CASE EVENT()
  OF EVENT:Accepted
     MFG:Reference = NIL                               !Clear reference
     gJunk = START(MdiChild)                           ! Start MDI CHILD
  END
OF ?MdiChildRef1
  CASE EVENT()
  OF EVENT:Accepted
     MFG:Reference = 'Reference 1'                     !Assign Reference
     IF ~TmGetId('MDICHILD'       , |                  !If not running
               MFG:Reference      , |
               MdiChildrenGroupId)
       gJunk = START(MdiChild)                         !  Start MDI CHILD
     ELSE                                              !ELSE
       POST(EVENT:Restore,,TMQ:Id)                     !  Wake up MDI CHILD
     END
  END
OF ?MdiChildRef2
  CASE EVENT()
  OF EVENT:Accepted
     MFG:Reference = 'Reference 2'                     !Assign Reference
     IF ~TmGetId('MDICHILD'       , |                  !If not running
               MFG:Reference      , |
               MdiChildrenGroupId)
       gJunk = START(MdiChild)                         !  Start MDI CHILD
     ELSE                                              !ELSE
       POST(EVENT:Restore,,TMQ:Id)                     ! wake up MDI CHILD
     END
  END
OF ?MdiChildUpTo3
  CASE EVENT()
  OF EVENT:Accepted
     MFG:Reference = 'Up to 3'                         !Assign Reference
     FREE(QTM);CLEAR(QTM)                              !Free/Clear QTM
     i = TmQuery(QTM             , |                   !Count Threads
               'MDICHILD'        , |                   !
               MFG:Reference     , |                   !
               MdiChildrenGroupId)                     !
     IF i = 3                                          !If Count is 3
        GET(QTM,1)                                     ! Get first QTM
        POST(EVENT:Restore,,QTM:Id)                    ! Restore first of 3
     ELSE                                              !ELSE
        gJunk = START(MdiChild)                        ! Start MDI CHILD
     END                                               !
     FREE(QTM);CLEAR(QTM)                              !Free/Clear QTM
  END
OF ?Splash
  CASE EVENT()
  OF EVENT:Accepted
     IF ~TmGetId('SPLASH',,SystemGroupId)              !If not running
        IsAboutWindow = TRUE                           ! Set About Window
```

continues

Listing 28.6. continued

```
              gJunk = START(Splash)                           ! Start SPLASH
          ELSE                                                !ELSE
              POST(EVENT:Restore,,TMQ:Id)                     ! wake up SPLASH
          END
      END
  OF ?MinimizeAll
    CASE EVENT()
    OF EVENT:Accepted
        FREE(QTM);CLEAR(QTM)                                  !Free/Clear QTM
        i = TmQuery(QTM,,,)                                   !Get thread Count
        IF i                                                  !If Threads exist
          LOOP i = 1 TO RECORDS(QTM)                          ! Loop QTM recs
            GET(QTM,i)                                        !  Get Next
            POST(EVENT:Iconize,,QTM:Id)                       !  Post ICONIZE Event
          END
        END
        FREE(QTM);CLEAR(QTM)                                  !Free/Clear QTM
    END
  OF ?RestoreAll
    CASE EVENT()
    OF EVENT:Accepted
        FREE(QTM);CLEAR(QTM)                                  !Free/Clear QTM
        i = TmQuery(QTM,,,)                                   !Get thread Count
        IF i                                                  !If Threads exist
          LOOP i = 1 TO RECORDS(QTM)                          ! Loop QTM recs
            GET(QTM,i)                                        !  Get Next
            POST(EVENT:Restore,,QTM:Id)                       !  Post RESTORE Event
          END
        END
        FREE(QTM);CLEAR(QTM)                                  !Free/Clear QTM
    END
  OF ?CloseAllThreads
    CASE EVENT()
    OF EVENT:Accepted
      gJunk = TmDestroyGroup()                                !Close Down Threads
      !Post Close Query, making sure all threads closed
      POST(EVENT:CloseQuery,?CloseAllThreads,MdiFrameThreadNo)
    OF EVENT:CLOSEQUERY
        FREE(QTM);CLEAR(QTM)                                  !Free/Clear QTM
        IF TMQuery(QTM,,,)                                    !If failing
          gJunk = MESSAGE('WARNING:Threads Open' , ¦          ! Display Warning Message
                          THIS{PROP:Text}         , ¦
                          ICON:Hand               )

          GET(QTM,1)                                          !Get First QTM
          POST(EVENT:RESTORE,,QTM:Id)                         !Post Restore event
        END
        FREE(QTM);CLEAR(QTM)                                  !Free/Clear QTM
    END
  OF ?TMDebug
    TmDebug()                                                 !TM Debug Window
  END
END
CLOSE(wMdiFrame)
RETURN
```

```
!=============================================================================
! MDI CHILD Window Procedure
!=============================================================================
MdiChild                PROCEDURE

wMdiChild WINDOW('Mdi Child Procedure'),AT(,,149,38),ICON('MT4.ICO'),SYSTEM,¦
          GRAY,MAX,RESIZE,MDI
        STRING(NIL),AT(2,8,144,10),FONT('Arial',12,0800000H,FONT:bold),¦
          USE(?Reference),TRN,CENTER
        BUTTON('Thread'),AT(22,20,94,14),FONT('MS Sans Serif',8,,FONT:bold),¦
          USE(?ThreadButton),STD(STD:Close), ¦
            DEFAULT
      END

  CODE
  OPEN(wMdiChild)
  ACCEPT
    CASE EVENT()
    OF EVENT:OpenWindow
        gThreadNo = TMCreate(THIS{PROP:Thread} , ¦              !Instantiate Thread
                             'MDICHILD'         , ¦
                             MFG:Reference      , ¦
                             THIS{PROP:Handle} , ¦
                             MdiChildrenGroupID  )

        ?ThreadButton {PROP:TEXT} = ¦
                      'Thread Number ' & THIS{PROP:Thread}

        ?Reference {PROP:Text} = MFG:Reference
        IF MFG:Reference <> NIL
          THIS{PROP:Text} = THIS{PROP:Text} & ¦
                            ' - ' & MFG:Reference
        END
        SetStatusBar()
    OF EVENT:CloseDown
        BREAK
    OF EVENT:Iconize
        THIS{PROP:Iconize} = TRUE
    OF EVENT:Restore
        IF THIS{PROP:Iconize} = TRUE
            THIS{PROP:Iconize} = FALSE
            THIS{PROP:Active}  = TRUE
        ELSE
            THIS{PROP:Active}  = TRUE
        END
        POST(EVENT:Resume)
    END
  END
  gThreadNo = TMDestroy(THIS{PROP:Thread})                !Destroy Thread
  CLOSE(wMdiChild)
  SetStatusBar()
  RETURN


!=============================================================================
! SPLASH/ABOUT Window Procedure
!=============================================================================
```

continues

Listing 28.6. continued

```
Splash                    PROCEDURE

wSplash WINDOW('Splash Procedure'),AT(5,8,306,155),ICON('MT4.ICO'),SYSTEM,¦
        GRAY,MAX,RESIZE,MDI
        STRING('Developing Applications in CW'),AT(6,64,294,13),¦
        FONT('Arial',14,0800000H,FONT:bold),USE(?String2), ¦
        TRN,CENTER
        STRING('Thread Manager'),AT(6,2,294,28),¦
        FONT('Times New Roman',36,0FFH,FONT:bold),USE(?String4), ¦
        TRN,CENTER
        STRING('By Ross A. Santos and Dave Harms'),AT(6,102,294,12),¦
        FONT('Times New Roman',14,,FONT:bold+FONT:italic), ¦
        USE(?String3),TRN,CENTER
        BUTTON('&Ok'),AT(136,130,,),FONT('MS Sans Serif',8,,FONT:bold),¦
        USE(?OkButton),STD(STD:Close),DEFAULT
     END

CODE

OPEN(wSplash)
IF ~IsAboutWindow
   ?OkButton {PROP:Hide}  = TRUE
   THIS      {PROP:Timer} = 240
   MdiFrame $ ItemMdiChild        {PROP:Disable} = TRUE
   MdiFrame $ ItemMdiChildRef1    {PROP:Disable} = TRUE
   MdiFrame $ ItemMdiChildRef2    {PROP:Disable} = TRUE
   MdiFrame $ ItemMdiChildUpTo3   {PROP:Disable} = TRUE
   MdiFrame $ ItemMinimizeAll     {PROP:Disable} = TRUE
   MdiFrame $ ItemRestoreAll      {PROP:Disable} = TRUE
   MdiFrame $ ItemSplash          {PROP:Disable} = TRUE
   MdiFrame $ ItemTMDebug         {PROP:Disable} = TRUE
ELSE
   THIS      {PROP:TEXT} = ¦
             'This is an ABOUT! Procedure'
END

ACCEPT
  CASE EVENT()
  OF EVENT:OpenWindow
     gThreadNo = TMCreate(THIS{PROP:Thread} , ¦          !Instantiate Thread
                          'SPLASH'           , ¦
                                             , ¦
                          THIS{PROP:Handle} , ¦
                          SystemGroupID      )
     SetStatusBar()
  OF EVENT:CloseDown
     THIS {PROP:Timer} = ZERO
     BREAK
  OF EVENT:Timer
     POST(EVENT:CloseDown)
  OF EVENT:Iconize
     THIS{PROP:Iconize} = TRUE
  OF EVENT:Restore
     IF THIS{PROP:Iconize} = TRUE
        THIS{PROP:Iconize} = FALSE
        THIS{PROP:Active}  = TRUE
```

```
      ELSE
         THIS{PROP:Active}  = TRUE
      END
      POST(EVENT:Resume)
   END
END
IF ~IsAboutWindow
   MdiFrame $ ItemMdiChild        {PROP:Disable} = FALSE
   MdiFrame $ ItemMdiChildRef1    {PROP:Disable} = FALSE
   MdiFrame $ ItemMdiChildRef2    {PROP:Disable} = FALSE
   MdiFrame $ ItemMdiChildUpTo3   {PROP:Disable} = FALSE
   MdiFrame $ ItemMinimizeAll     {PROP:Disable} = FALSE
   MdiFrame $ ItemRestoreAll      {PROP:Disable} = FALSE
   MdiFrame $ ItemSplash          {PROP:Disable} = FALSE
   MdiFrame $ ItemTMDebug         {PROP:Disable} = FALSE
END
gThreadNo = TMDestroy(THIS{PROP:Thread})              !Destroy Thread
CLOSE(wSplash)
IsAboutWindow  = FALSE
SetStatusBar()
RETURN


!=============================================================================
! Set Status Bar Values
!=============================================================================
SetStatusBar            PROCEDURE

iNdx                    LONG,AUTO
 CODE
 iNdx = ZERO
 iNdx = RECORDS(TMQ)

MdiFrame {PROP:StatusText,2} = 'Total Child Threads:' |
         & iNdx
MdiFrame {PROP:StatusText,3} = FORMAT(TODAY(),@D2)
MdiFrame {PROP:StatusText,4} = FORMAT(CLOCK(),@T3)
IF iNdx                                          !If TMQ recs
   MdiFrame $ ItemMinimizeAll     {PROP:Disable}= FALSE
   MdiFrame $ ItemRestoreAll      {PROP:Disable}= FALSE
   MdiFrame $ ItemCloseAllThreads{PROP:Disable}= FALSE
   MdiFrame $ ItemTMDebug         {PROP:Disable}= FALSE
ELSE
   MdiFrame $ ItemMinimizeAll     {PROP:Disable}= TRUE
   MdiFrame $ ItemRestoreAll      {PROP:Disable}= TRUE
   MdiFrame $ ItemCloseAllThreads{PROP:Disable}= TRUE
   MdiFrame $ ItemTMDebug         {PROP:Disable}= TRUE
END
RETURN
```

Notice that there is a new include file INCLUDE('TM.VAR') added beneath the standard includes at the top of the program. This include file contains all the standard global constants, variables, and queues used in conjunction with the Thread Manager and is required for this program to successfully compile and execute.

There has also been a new item included in the program MAP area—INCLUDE('TM.INC')—which contains the module definition for the Thread Manager functions. You also must have this file to use the Thread Manager.

Notice that I have added two new equates within the global program:

```
MdiChildrenGroupId      EQUATE(1)
SystemGroupId           EQUATE(2)
```

These equates are logical representations for groups of related threads and are used in the group ID parameter of various Thread Manager functions, as you will soon see. You could say that these equates are unnecessary in this example, and that would be absolutely true. However, I included them so you could see the effect of having these values present in the TMQ.

Each menu item that is to be addressed outside the scope of the MAIN() procedure has been given a corresponding variable that is used exactly as the menu variables were used in the Listing 28.3 (STM) program.

Notice that there is a difference in the way the status bar is handled in this program than that of the one used in Listing 28.3. Instead of in-line code, I opted to use a procedure on the EVENT:Timer:

```
OF EVENT:Timer
   SetStatusBar()
```

I did this for the simple reason that I wanted to be able to call this procedure from any other procedure in order to update the status bar on demand.

The first menu option is Start MDI Child. When it is selected, this option executes the following statements:

```
OF ?MdiChild
   CASE EVENT()
   OF EVENT:Accepted
      MFG:Reference = NIL
      gJunk = START(MdiChild)
   END
```

There are several interesting points here. First, the MFG:Reference variable is the variable I use to inform the Thread Manager of the data value to be inserted into the TMQ record. In this case, there is no value to be inserted. Because MFG:Reference is a global variable, it must be cleared in this case before a new thread is started in the MAIN procedure. This is because the MdiChild procedure is used by all the Start... menu options, as opposed to each option having a separate procedure. This means that when the MdiChild procedure calls to the Thread Manager functions, the calls will always look the same, but the value passed to the function will differ depending on the menu option selected.

Another point of interest is the use of a "garbage" variable, in this case gJunk. This variable is used to collect data that is of no value and to prevent compiler warnings about calling a function as a procedure.

When this option is selected, the MdiChild procedure is started, and on opening the window wMdiChild in the MdiChild procedure, the following code is executed:

```
OF EVENT:OpenWindow
   gThreadNo = TMCreate(THIS{PROP:Thread} , ¦
                        'MDICHILD'          , ¦
                        MFG:Reference       , ¦
                        THIS{PROP:Handle} , ¦
                        MdiChildrenGroupID  )

   ?ThreadButton {PROP:TEXT} = ¦
             Thread Number ' & THIS{PROP:Thread}

   ?Reference {PROP:Text} = MFG:Reference
   IF MFG:Reference <> NIL
     THIS{PROP:Text} = THIS{PROP:Text} & ¦
                       ' - ' & MFG:Reference
   END
   SetStatusBar()
```

Looking at the TMCreate() function in this code reveals how the magic begins to happen. As you recall from the description of TMCreate() in the Thread Manager discussion, this function will create a new TMQ record to mirror the actual physical thread creation process in the Clarion for Windows library. From left to right in the TMCreate() function call it includes the following information: the thread number (I used the property method to capture the thread number of the currently executing thread), the thread descriptor, the data reference, the Windows window handle (I again used a property method to capture the handle of the current window), and the group ID for relating threads. If this was the first child thread started, the values in the TMQ would look like the following:

```
TMQ:Id    = 2
TMQ:Name  = 'MDICHILD'
Reference = ''
Hwnd      = (some numeric value assigned at run time by Windows)
GroupId   = 1
```

Please note the use of the thread variable gThreadNo in Listing 28.6. The TMCreate() function will return the current thread number to this variable. You can then use gThreadNo in this process as you need, understanding that it has the same value as THREAD() or THIS{PROP:Thread}. After the logical thread descriptor record is created in the TmCreate() function, the button text on this window will be changed to reflect the actual thread number that is executing. The reference string control will be updated with the value in the MFG:Reference variable; in this case it will be empty. The next statement will append to the current title the value stored in MFG:Reference when the value is not empty. In this case, this statement is skipped. Finally, the SetStatusBar() procedure is called. The primary reason for calling SetStatusBar() is to update the holes on the status bar immediately, instead of waiting for the EVENT:Timer event to fire. What this gives you is an instantaneous update on the status bar with no visual delay as the process occurs. You can comment out this call to see its effect.

p 462,3,4   TMCreate   FUNCTION(Thread ID, ThreadName, Reference, hWnd, Group—

In STM example in Listing 28.3, you assigned the variable that held the thread number at the START() function. In CTM, you call the TMCreate() function with the necessary parameters inside the started procedure once the procedure becomes the current thread. This is the first major difference you'll experience between STM and CTM.

The second major difference occurs at the end of the MdiChild procedure. The following code is used to destroy the current thread:

```
gThreadNo = TMDestroy(THIS{PROP:Thread})
CLOSE(wMdiChild)
SetStatusBar()
```

When the ACCEPT loop is stopped, the TMDestroy() function is called with the current thread number as the value for the parameter. Because the ACCEPT loop has been stopped, it is assumed that the thread will also be stopped. A logical destruction must then be done to rid the TMQ of the record for this thread. Because the wMdiChild window has not been closed, I can use the property assignment THIS{PROP:THREAD} again to get the current thread number. After destroying the logical thread descriptor record using the TMDestroy() function, the window is closed and the SetStatusBar() function is again called to update the status bar immediately.

Now for the fun stuff! Look at the menu items Start MDI Child Reference 1 and Start MDI Child Reference 2 to see how the Thread Manager can be used to query for a specific data value in a thread and then determine what action to take. The following statements illustrate this point:

```
OF ?MdiChildRef1
   CASE EVENT()
   OF EVENT:Accepted
      MFG:Reference = 'Reference 1'
      IF ~TmGetId('MDICHILD'         , |
                   MFG:Reference      , |
                   MdiChildrenGroupId)
         gJunk = START(MdiChild)
      ELSE
         POST(EVENT:Restore,,TMQ:Id)
      END
   END
```

The MFG:Reference = 'Reference 1' statement sets the global variable used for data reference to a value for which you want to query in the TMQ. The next IF statement essentially attempts to find the specific instance of a thread in the TMQ that matches the criteria supplied. If the TmGetId() function fails, a new thread (using the MdiChild procedure) is started using the MFG:Reference variable. Otherwise, because the TMGetId() function does not clear the TMQ buffer area after performing the search, the value in the TMQ:Id field is the actual thread number that was found for the supplied criteria. The event EVENT:Restore is posted to the TMQ:Id (thread number), informing it to "wake up." The same process is true for the Start MDI Child Reference 2 menu item, as well.

The key point here is that you can search the TMQ by a unique ID that can also include a data reference. This helps when you want to prevent another instance of a procedure from occurring when an executing thread already includes this information. Say you have a database of patients in a medical program. You allow the user to start many instances of the Patient Information window. The one limitation you might want to impose is that if a patient is already referenced in another executing Patient Information window thread, another instance of the same patient is not started. Instead, a context switch to the thread containing this patient is performed.

Looking at the Start MDI Child Up To 3 menu item, you will see how you can limit the number of instances of a procedure to some value greater than one. The following code illustrates this point:

```
OF ?MdiChildUpTo3
    CASE EVENT()
    OF EVENT:Accepted
        MFG:Reference = 'Up to 3'
        FREE(QTM);CLEAR(QTM)
        i = TmQuery(QTM                ,  |
                    'MDICHILD'          ,  |
                    MFG:Reference       ,  |
                    MdiChildrenGroupId)
        IF i = 3
            GET(QTM,1)
            POST(EVENT:Restore,,QTM:Id)
        ELSE
            gJunk = START(MdiChild)
        END
        FREE(QTM);CLEAR(QTM)
    END
```

The first thing to notice is that the MFG:Reference variable has been set to a specific value that will be used in the TmQuery() function search criteria. Notice that the QTM queue is being freed and cleared immediately before and after this process completes. This is because you can rely on the values in this queue only for the duration of a given process. The next thing that occurs is that the TmQuery() function is called, returning the value of the query (count of records) to the global variable i. In the TmQuery() function the values passed from left to right include the queue to store the results in (QTM), the logical thread descriptor, the data reference, and the group ID. If the TmQuery() function successful, the variable i will have a count greater than zero. The IF statement essentially determines whether the maximum number of threads for this menu option is executing. If there are fewer than three threads matching the TmQuery() function criteria executing, another MdiChild procedure is started; otherwise, the first of the three executing threads is sent an EVENT:Restore.

Now it's time to show some power. The Minimize All and Restore All menu items essentially do the same thing except for the message that is posted. The following statements illustrate the Minimize All functionality:

```
OF ?MinimizeAll
    CASE EVENT()
    OF EVENT:Accepted
        FREE(QTM);CLEAR(QTM)
        i = TmQuery(QTM,,,)
```

```
      IF i
         LOOP i = 1 TO RECORDS(QTM)
            GET(QTM,i)
            POST(EVENT:Iconize,,QTM:Id)
         END
      END
      FREE(QTM);CLEAR(QTM)
   END
```

In this example, you see the TMQuery() function at work again. This time, there are no parameters except the queue itself passed to the function, which implies that all threads are to be
found. If there are threads executing, a loop is performed to the maximum number of threads
in the QTM (which, in this case, is exactly the same as the TMQ). Inside this loop, each record
in the QTM is fetched and the event EVENT:Iconize is sent to each QTM:Id. Again, prior to and
after this process, the QTM is freed and cleared. Why use the QTM instead of the TMQ? As
stated in the discussion about the Thread Manager, you should never directly touch or query
the TMQ queue, to avoid possible side effects. Instead, always use a Thread Manager function
designed for that purpose. If there is a bug in the Thread Manager, you can easily fix it in one
place instead of needing to fix possibly hundreds of lines of code in your application.

One more powerful example is the Close All menu item. This menu item will inform all threads
to close down or stop. The following code illustrates this point:

```
OF ?CloseAllThreads
    CASE EVENT()
    OF EVENT:Accepted
      gJunk = TmDestroyGroup()
      POST(EVENT:CloseQuery,?CloseAllThreads,MdiFrameThreadNo)
    OF EVENT:CLOSEQUERY
      IF TMDestroyGroup()
         gJunk = MESSAGE('WARNING:Threads Open' , |
                         THIS{PROP:Text}          , |
                         ICON:Hand                 )
         GET(TMQ,1)
         POST(EVENT:RESTORE,,TMQ:Id)
      END
    END
```

This example uses a different Thread Manager function: TmDestroyGroup(). By using this function in your application and not passing any parameters, it is assumed that all threads are to be
destroyed. For more information on the TmDestroyGroup() function, refer to prior discussions
in this chapter on the Thread Manager functions. What essentially happens is that all threads
are instructed to close when an EVENT:CloseDown is issued from the TmDestroy() function.
However, because the ACCEPT loop has not yet cycled, the threads have not yet received this
message. In order to see the effect of the EVENT:CloseDown message and then make sure that all
threads in fact did close as desired, a user-defined event called EVENT:CloseQuery is posted to
the current control (?CloseAllThreads) in the current thread (MdiFrameThreadNo). By posting
this message, the ACCEPT loop will cycle, enabling each thread to process its respective messages,
then EVENT:CloseQuery will be executed for the control ?CloseAllThreads. Notice in the
EVENT:CloseQuery logic that the TmQuery() function is executed in an IF construct. The reason

is simple: If the function fails, all threads have been destroyed; otherwise, at least one thread still exists. In this case, the user is warned of this situation and the first record in the QTM is selected and woken up.

Summary

This chapter touches on many different and exciting issues. I invite you to explore the multithreading templates included with this book, as well as the example programs shown. You will undoubtedly find many uses for this information as you continue to build the finest Windows applications using Clarion for Windows.

29

Multiple-Document Interface Versus Non–Multiple-Document Interface

Many applications developed for Windows use multiple-document interface (MDI) because of how easily it helps the developer enforce window management and window standards. However, MDI is not the only style used in Windows applications. Clarion for Windows doesn't force you to use MDI—you can create single or multithreaded applications that use a variety of window styles, using various window management techniques.

This chapter focuses on the standard windows behavior associated with MDI, as well as the other non-MDI styles that can be developed using Clarion for Windows.

MDI: Defined

MDI is a Windows management technique that provides you, the programmer, a framework for managing windows and processes in a structured and standard way. One of the keys to graphic user interface (GUI) development is standardization. Enforcing standards helps you train users to use your program, which ultimately reduces the cost of learning and using your application.

MDI Frame

At the lowest level of the MDI architecture is the MDI frame. Each MDI application begins with a *frame*, which provides the workspace in which all other windows reside in an MDI application. This is an important concept to grasp. I'm sure you have noticed that if you minimize an MDI frame, all windows related to the MDI frame will hide within the minimized application's icon on the Windows desktop. This is one vital function of the MDI frame: to manage the windows in an application.

In Clarion for Windows, the term MDI implies that your application will ultimately be multithreaded by design. The MDI frame is the first thread in a multithreaded application. This means that if you use the THREAD() function or the WindowName{PROP:Thread} property syntax, the value returned in each case will be the number 1.

An MDI-based application manages other related MDI windows. This management is done via messaging. For example, when the user is closing the MDI frame via the System Control Box menu, a message is sent to all related windows within the application informing them that the MDI frame is about to close. Each related window at this point can either comply with the MDI frame's request to close or deny it. If the window denies the request, the MDI frame is prevented from closing, as well. If the window complies with the request, the MDI frame closes, and the application stops execution.

The MDI frame is generally composed of the following components:

■ System Control Box menu: The System Control Box menu (located at the upper-left corner of the window) should be placed on an MDI frame if you plan on following standard Windows design guidelines. This menu provides the user with the basic window functions such as Restore, Move, Size, Minimize, Maximize, Close, and Switch To. These are standard window functions.

■ Minimize button: The Minimize button (located in the upper-right corner of the window) is made visible when you declare an icon for the MDI frame window. This button will minimize the application to an icon on the Windows desktop. Most applications use an iconic representation (usually the one that appears when you place the program into a window group within the Program Manager) of the program so you can minimize it to temporarily get it out of the way.

■ Title bar: The title bar appears at the top of the window and when no other windows are present. The name in the title bar generally represents the name of your application. The value of the title bar should change as other MDI windows are opened (this will be discussed in just a moment). If you double-click the title bar, the MDI frame window will either maximize or restore to the defined default size of the window. This process works like a toggle; if the window is initially maximized, it will be restored, and if the window is not initially maximized, it will be maximized.

■ Menu: A menu resides directly beneath the title bar for the entire width of the MDI frame window. The general minimum requirement for an MDI frame menu includes the File, Window, and Help menus. When document windows are opened, the menu should minimally include the Edit menu. This is done primarily because the standard Edit menu items make sense only when there are items in a window that may be modified.

■ Toolbar: Optionally, an MDI frame can include a toolbar, which is located directly beneath the menu. Toolbars are generally used to provide quick graphical selections of menu items, depicted generally by buttons with images on them. Clarion for Windows does not govern which menu items you can include on the toolbar or how the application should respond to the selection of a toolbar item. This is entirely up to your discretion.

■ Status bar: The status bar is located at the bottom of the MDI frame window for the full width of the window. A status bar is not required, but it is recommended if you plan on displaying messages to the user. A status bar is where you might place information for your users such as the default message for a selected control, the time, the date, or anything else you might be able to dream up. By default, any message defined for a control will automatically show up on the status bar in the first width (hole) on the status bar. A status bar may be made of many widths or holes, which are the sections or dividers on the status bar where text appears. The first width is managed for you by the Clarion for Windows library; all other widths are defined and managed by your application.

■ Workspace: The area between the menu and the status bar, or if a toolbar is present the area between the toolbar and the status bar, is called the workspace. This area is where other related MDI windows within the application reside and are "clipped."

This means that if you attempt to move an MDI window outside of the MDI frame, only the portion not moved outside of the MDI frame will show. The portion of the window moved outside of the MDI frame is hidden, so it appears clipped. If a related MDI window is minimized within the application, the MDI window appears iconized within the MDI frame just above the status bar.

An MDI frame cannot contain any controls. Although you may be tempted to place a graphic on the MDI frame window as a backdrop for your application, you cannot. Instead, you must create a window—usually, a splash window—that contains the desired graphic. A splash window enables you to display a graphic image while an application is starting, but after initialization the image disappears. You see this sort of thing done on almost every commercial program available.

The Window Menu

You should add the Window menu to MDI-based applications. Under the Window menu are the functions necessary to help your users manage the multiple windows in your application. The Window menu might include the following items, which are standard windows actions found in the \CW\LIBSRC\EQUATES.CLW file:

```
STD:WindowList    EQUATE (1)
STD:TileWindow    EQUATE (2)
STD:CascadeWindow EQUATE (3)
STD:ArrangeIcons  EQUATE (4)
```

Use the STD: equates to automatically enable and disable these features depending on the windows that are currently open, and depending on the state of each window (opened, minimized, and so on). For example, if you have no MDI child windows open, none of the items will be enabled. However, if at least one MDI child window is open, the Tile and Cascade items will be enabled. If you have any minimized windows, the Arrange Icons item will be enabled. The Window List item is different from all the rest. This item is assigned to the window menu itself. When MDI child windows are opened, each will appear beneath the other items, which provides a pick list for your users to select a specific open window in your application. The result of adding a Window menu to an MDI child window might look like the following:

```
MENU('&Windows'),STD(STD:WindowList)
  ITEM('&Tile'),STD(STD:TileWindow)
  ITEM('&Cascade'),STD(STD:CascadeWindow)
END
```

MDI Children (Document Windows)

The term used for an MDI-style window that is not an MDI frame is called an MDI child, or document window. In a word processor, a *document* is a single isolated unit of information. You can open many documents in a word processor, switch between each document, and edit the current window. MDI children act this same way, so they are called document windows.

You can open many MDI child windows, which can be the same window (known as multiple instances) containing different information (as a word processor does), or which can be entirely different from each other.

Each MDI child inherits its base functionality from the MDI parent (frame), which means that each child has similar features (known as properties or attributes) as the MDI parent. A primary difference between the two is that MDI children contain controls.

In a sense, an MDI frame owns the MDI child windows. If the frame is minimized, all MDI windows are encapsulated within the MDI frame's icon on the Windows desktop. You can minimize each MDI child independently within the MDI frame by assigning an icon to the MDI child window itself.

In Clarion for Windows, MDI and multithreading go hand in hand. As stated earlier, the MDI frame is the first thread in a multithreaded application. To use an MDI child window from the menu on an MDI frame, you must start the MDI child window procedure using the following statement:

```
ThreadNo = START(MdiChildProc)
```

For more information on multithreading, see Chapter 28, "Multithreading and Thread Management." If you are in an MDI child window procedure, you can call additional procedures that contain MDI child windows; however, only the last window opened will remain on top in the thread. If the window on top is a "called" MDI child window, you will not be able to select the caller's MDI child window until the current MDI child window is closed and that procedure is exited. You can still select a different window that is in another thread, this also includes the MDI frame. The one thing to understand is that only one window can be on top in a thread at any given time; this is why MDI children are threaded.

Each MDI child procedure can contain its own status bar. To do this, check the Status Bar property on the Window Formatter Properties window. If this is done, whatever definition is specified for this status bar will override the MDI frame's status bar properties and contents, essentially replacing the MDI frame's status bar with the MDI child's. Normal MDI child behavior will use the frame's status bar, which is updated through property settings on the MDI frame window. The first status bar width (hole) is always assumed to contain the contents of the MSG attribute on a control, and the other widths may contain whatever you desire. By default, the MSG attribute of the currently selected control is always automatically added to the current status bar for you.

One thing that is not done automatically for you is the management of the title bar. Generally, when you have an MDI-based application, the frame will contain the title of the application in the title bar. As each MDI child window gains focus, the MDI frame's title bar should reflect the default title, plus a reference to the currently focused MDI child window. For example, if you look at the Clarion for Windows MDI frame window, you will see something like this:

```
Clarion For Windows (TEST.PRJ)
```

The default MDI frame's title bar displays Clarion for Windows. When the TEST.PRJ project has been selected, or in this case is created, the literal (TEST.PRJ) is appended to the MDI frame's title bar. If you then open an editor window, for a source document called TEST.CLW, sthe source document name is appended to the MDI frame's title bar using - [C:\CW\EXAMPLES\TEST.CLW]. The result will look something like the following:

```
Clarion For Windows (TEST.PRJ) - [C:\CW\EXAMPLES\TEST.CLW]
```

Say, for example, that you have an application called PHONE MGR. This application can use different databases stored in different directories. After initial display of the MDI frame window, the user might select the database, which in this example is C:\PM\HomeList.DAT. Now the user might want to select a record from a browse window that is called Browse People. The title bar at this point might look like this:

```
Phone Mgr v1.0 (C:\PM\HomeList.DAT) - [Browse People]
```

After the user selects a name from the Browse list, the MDI frame title bar might look like this:

```
Phone Mgr v1.0 (C:\PM\HomeList.DAT) - [Smith, John Doe]
```

This gives the user visual feedback of the current activity on the MDI frame's title bar. There is an added benefit. If the application is minimized on the Windows desktop, the text that appears under the icon reflects the current state of the program when it was minimized, because a minimized application uses the text from the MDI frame's title bar for display under the icon.

This is a general practice used in most MDI-based applications; although not required, it is recommended.

The Edit Menu

In general, the Edit menu should be available whenever a document window is the topmost window. There is no requirement to use an Edit menu, but it has become standard to do so. You might want to provide an Edit menu so the user can cut, copy, and paste data from or to the MDI client window. The Edit menu might include the following items, which are standard Windows actions found in the \CW\LIBSRC\EQUATES.CLW file:

```
STD:Cut        EQUATE (10)
STD:Copy       EQUATE (11)
STD:Paste      EQUATE (12)
STD:Clear      EQUATE (13)
STD:Undo       EQUATE (14)
```

Use the STD: equates to automatically enable and disable these features, depending on the type of control that is receiving focus. For example, if your cursor is placed within an entry control, Cut, Copy, and Clear will be available. If you then either cut or copy, Paste and Undo will be available. The result of adding an Edit menu to an MDI child window might look like the following:

```
MENU('&Edit'),FIRST
  ITEM('&Undo'),STD(STD:Undo)
  ITEM('C&lear'),STD(STD:Clear)
  ITEM('Item&2'),USE(?Item2),SEPARATOR
  ITEM('Cu&t'),STD(STD:Cut)
  ITEM('&Copy'),STD(STD:Copy)
  ITEM('&Paste'),STD(STD:Paste)
END
```

Menu Merging

When you add a menu to an MDI child, the result is a concept known as menu merging. *Menu merging* enables you to logically define menus for each MDI child, which will ultimately be merged with the MDI frame's menu. The default mode for menu merging is ON for each MDI child, unless the Nomerge attribute is checked in the menu editor. The key to menu merging is to identify the name of each menu and each item you want to remain in the MDI frame's menu exactly the same way in the MDI child's menu.

For example, say you have a File menu that contains an Exit menu item when the MDI frame is the only window open. When you open an MDI child, the menu defined in the MDI child might enable you to print the MDI child window's contents. The Print menu item then would need to be added to the File menu. You can do this by creating a menu structure identical to the MDI frame's File menu structure, with the added Print menu item before the Exit menu item.

If you prefer, you can use property syntax on the MDI frame's menu to manage menus without menu merging. This brings up a very important design consideration. Some users feel most comfortable when all menu items are displayed at all times, and those items that are not available are disabled. Other users like only those menu items that are available to be displayed at any given time. Both methods are completely Windows standard, which leaves the decision up to you and your user's taste. There are pros and cons for both ways, and there is no one right decision.

Here's one last note on standard Windows behavior with regards to MDI children: If you specify that you want default behavior for an MDI child window, the MDI child window will act somewhat differently than you might expect. That is, each time an MDI child window is opened with the default attribute, it will open at the next predefined position in the MDI window scheme, creating the effect that each subsequent MDI child window that is opened is sliding down off the MDI frame. When there is no room left to slide down the MDI frame, the next MDI child opened will open at the top of the workspace. The MDI window management scheme remembers the last opened default MDI window position and recalculates the next available position automatically. This is done so that MDI children do not obscure each other when they are subsequently opened. If you do not want this type of behavior, you should not use the Default attribute in the Window Formatter Properties window for an MDI child window. Instead, set the window AT() properties for your window.

Alternatives to MDI (Non-MDI)

Up to this point this chapter covers only MDI concepts, primarily because MDI is the most frequently used in Windows applications. However, there are some alternatives. Some applications do not need the flexibility or the complexity of MDI applications. For these types of applications you can use a single-threaded type of application scheme. Other applications need the benefit of multithreading, but do not need to follow MDI window management behavior. Both of these alternatives are discussed next.

Single-Threaded Applications

A single-threaded application is by nature a small application (similar to DOS programs) with modality in mind. You can create this type of application by simply using a window with a menu that calls various other window procedures. The difference here is that the primary window is not an application window (MDI frame), it is simply a window. Use a single-threaded application if you want a completely modal "feel" that is similar to DOS.

For instance, say you can call two different window procedures from a window with a menu defined on it. Once you have called the first window procedure, you can no longer select the calling procedure's window. Therefore, you cannot select the second window procedure until the current procedure has returned to the calling procedure.

This type of application scheme is not seen very often in most commercial Windows programs because it is not very flexible. Nevertheless, it can be done if desired. Listing 29.1 shows an example of how to create a single-threaded application.

Listing 29.1. A sample single-threaded application.

```
STAPP                   PROGRAM

                        INCLUDE('Equates.CLW')

                        MAP
                          MainMenu()
                          FirstWin()
                          SecondWin()
                        END

wMain WINDOW('Single Threaded Application
Example'),AT(,,425,198),FONT('Arial',8,,FONT:regular),CENTER, |
        ICON('BOOT.ICO'),STATUS,SYSTEM,GRAY,MAX,MAXIMIZE
      MENUBAR
        MENU('&File')
          ITEM('&First Win'),USE(?FirstWin)
          ITEM('&Second Win'),USE(?SecondWin)
          ITEM('Item&3'),USE(?Item3),SEPARATOR
          ITEM('E&xit'),STD(STD:Close)
        END
```

```
        END
      END

  CODE
  MainMenu()


!===========================================================================
MainMenu                 PROCEDURE
!===========================================================================
  CODE
  OPEN(wMain)
  ACCEPT
    CASE EVENT()
    OF EVENT:CLOSEDOWN
      BREAK
    END
    CASE FIELD()
    OF ?FirstWin
      CASE EVENT()
      OF EVENT:ACCEPTED
        FirstWin()

      END
    OF ?SecondWin
      CASE EVENT()
      OF EVENT:ACCEPTED
        SecondWin()
      END
    END
  END
  CLOSE(wMain)


!===========================================================================
FirstWin                 PROCEDURE
!===========================================================================

wFirstWin WINDOW('First Window Procedure'),AT(,,185,34),|
        FONT('Arial',8,,FONT:regular),CENTER,SYSTEM,GRAY,DOUBLE
      BUTTON('OK'),AT(74,11,35,14),USE(?OkButton),STD(STD:Close),DEFAULT
    END

  CODE
  OPEN(wFirstWin)
  ACCEPT
    CASE EVENT()
    OF EVENT:CloseDown
      BREAK
    END
  END
  CLOSE(wFirstWin)
  RETURN


!===========================================================================
SecondWin                PROCEDURE
!===========================================================================

wSecondWin WINDOW('Second Window Procedure'),AT(,,185,34),|
        FONT('Arial',8,,FONT:regular),CENTER,SYSTEM,GRAY,DOUBLE
```

continues

Listing 29.1. continued

```
        BUTTON('OK'),AT(74,11,35,14),USE(?OkButton),STD(STD:Close),DEFAULT
      END

CODE
OPEN(wSecondWin)
ACCEPT
  CASE EVENT()
  OF EVENT:CloseDown
     BREAK
  END
END
CLOSE(wSecondWin)
RETURN
```

Non-MDI Multithreaded Applications

There are many reasons for creating a multithreaded application that doesn't need to be an MDI-based application. To create a non-MDI application, simply start each procedure without an application window defined and use a normal window rather than an MDI-type window.

For instance, say you have a program that displays the time and date in a window, and another window that enables you to change some characteristics about the time and date window. Both windows are running in separate threads and are non-MDI. Listing 29.2 shows an example of how to create a non-MDI multithreading program.

Listing 29.2. A sample non-MDI multithreading program.

```
NMAPP                   PROGRAM

                        INCLUDE('Equates.CLW')

                        MAP
                          TimeDateWin()
                          ToolBoxWin()
                        END

FormatType              BYTE(1)
TimeDateThreadNo        LONG
ToolBoxThreadNo         LONG

 CODE
 ToolBoxThreadNo = START(ToolBoxWin)
 TimeDateWin()


!========================================================================
TimeDateWin             PROCEDURE
!========================================================================
```

```
wTimeDate WINDOW('Time/Date Window'),AT(51,45,178,36),|
         FONT('Arial',8,,FONT:regular),CENTER,TIMER(1),DOUBLE
       STRING(' '),AT(4,4,170,12),FONT('Arial',10,0800000H,FONT:bold),|
       USE(?DateVal),CENTER
       STRING(' '),AT(4,20,170,11),FONT('Arial',10,0800000H,FONT:bold),|
       USE(?TimeVal),CENTER
     END

 CODE
 OPEN(wTimeDate)
 TimeDateThreadNo = THREAD()
 ACCEPT
   CASE EVENT()
   OF EVENT:CloseDown
     BREAK
   OF EVENT:Timer
     EXECUTE FormatType
       BEGIN
         ?TimeVal{PROP:TEXT} = FORMAT(CLOCK(),@T1)
         ?DateVal{PROP:TEXT} = FORMAT(TODAY(),@D1)
       END
       BEGIN
         ?TimeVal{PROP:TEXT} = FORMAT(CLOCK(),@T2)
         ?DateVal{PROP:TEXT} = FORMAT(TODAY(),@D2)
       END
       BEGIN
         ?TimeVal{PROP:TEXT} = FORMAT(CLOCK(),@T3)
         ?DateVal{PROP:TEXT} = FORMAT(TODAY(),@D3)
       END
       BEGIN
         ?TimeVal{PROP:TEXT} = FORMAT(CLOCK(),@T4)
         ?DateVal{PROP:TEXT} = FORMAT(TODAY(),@D4)
       END
       BEGIN
         ?TimeVal{PROP:TEXT} = FORMAT(CLOCK(),@T5)
         ?DateVal{PROP:TEXT} = FORMAT(TODAY(),@D5)
       END
       BEGIN
         ?TimeVal{PROP:TEXT} = FORMAT(CLOCK(),@T6)
         ?DateVal{PROP:TEXT} = FORMAT(TODAY(),@D6)
       END
     END
   END
 END
 CLOSE(wTimeDate)
 RETURN


 !==============================================================================
 ToolBoxWin               PROCEDURE
 !==============================================================================

 wToolBox WINDOW('ToolBox'),AT(263,46,53,36),FONT('Arial',8,,FONT:regular),|
         CENTER,SYSTEM,GRAY,DOUBLE
       BUTTON('&1'),AT(2,2,16,14),FONT('Arial',8,,FONT:bold),USE(?Format1)
       BUTTON('&2'),AT(18,2,16,14),FONT('Arial',8,,FONT:bold),USE(?Format2)
       BUTTON('&3'),AT(34,2,16,14),FONT('Arial',8,,FONT:bold),USE(?Format3)
```

continues

Listing 29.2. continued

```
          BUTTON('&4'),AT(2,18,16,14),FONT('Arial',8,,FONT:bold),USE(?Format4)
          BUTTON('&5'),AT(18,18,16,14),FONT('Arial',8,,FONT:bold),USE(?Format5)
          BUTTON('&6'),AT(34,18,16,14),FONT('Arial',8,,FONT:bold),USE(?Format6)
       END

CODE
OPEN(wToolBox)
ACCEPT
  CASE EVENT()
  OF EVENT:CloseDown
     BREAK
  END
  CASE FIELD()
  OF ?Format1
     CASE EVENT()
     OF EVENT:Accepted
        FormatType = 1
     END
  OF ?Format2
     CASE EVENT()
     OF EVENT:Accepted
        FormatType = 2
     END
  OF ?Format3
     CASE EVENT()
     OF EVENT:Accepted
        FormatType = 3
     END
  OF ?Format4
     CASE EVENT()
     OF EVENT:Accepted
        FormatType = 4
     END
  OF ?Format5
     CASE EVENT()
     OF EVENT:Accepted
        FormatType = 5
     END
  OF ?Format6
     CASE EVENT()
     OF EVENT:Accepted
        FormatType = 6
     END
  END
END
POST(EVENT:CloseDown,,TimeDateThreadNo)
CLOSE(wToolBox)
RETURN
```

Summary

As you can see, you can dream up many permutations (different styles of windows and window-management schemes), and Clarion for Windows provides many different solutions to the problem at hand. However, because MDI is the most common window-management scheme used, and the standard templates provide support for MDI, I suggest that you use MDI whenever possible.

30

Clarion for Windows and Client/Server Computing

In today's world of technology, the most talked-about rave is client/server computing. The mystique, methodologies, processes, and implementation that surrounds this technology are quite thought-provoking for us developers. However, client/server computing is not just a technology exercise; it is a corporate way of life, which must transcend political domains and empires if it is to be successful at all.

Although client/server is a relatively new term, it is anything but a new concept. Rather, it is an awakening that has been ignited by the recent focus on cost containment, customer service levels, rapid delivery of mission-critical applications, the need to solve today's problems today, and of course the recent downsizing-rightsizing-one-size-fits-all phenomenon that is sweeping corporations worldwide.

Whether you believe client/server to be a fad or not is really not the issue. What is important is that you understand this new player so that when it knocks at your door (and that day may come sooner than you think), you will be prepared to tackle the issues head on, without reservation and with confidence.

But isn't this a book about Clarion for Windows? Correct! As client/server technology will become more and more important to Clarion for Windows developers, it is critical to understand what role Clarion for Windows plays in this technology and how to effectively position you and Clarion for Windows for client/server computing.

Client/Server: Defined

Client/server is a fancy new term for shared data access across an organization, with the capability to partition data and processes throughout the organization. This concept has been in place for many years in large corporations that were utilizing mini or mainframe-based systems and solutions. These systems have generally used leased or dedicated communication lines running between various sites to provide online access to information, utilizing either terminals or PCs with some form of emulation software.

The information systems departments (information systems, management information systems, information technology, and so on) in large corporations are generally responsible for the protection (security) and availability (access) of data development. They are also responsible for the deployment of application programs (which provide the data in end-user form) and the management and direction of corporate computing needs, resources, and solutions.

It is well known that in many large corporations the information systems department is bogged down in technology requests (some extending well into the next century), internal bureaucracy, corporate politics, and many outdated technologies, all of which result in lost opportunities and revenues for the organization as a whole. For instance, it's common to find several groups within the technology branch of a large corporation working on the same problem, from different perspectives, for different yet similar purposes, using different tools. They can spend thousands, even millions, of dollars on this work. Sometimes this approach yields good results, but often it is an exercise in futility. Projects are canceled because of costs, and careers are destroyed, and sometimes the knowledge that could have been useful in other projects is lost due to staff attrition and budget cutting.

To combat some of these issues, corporations began the downsizing craze of the late '80s and early '90s. This trend re-allocated information management responsibilities to the local business organization, and enabled them to develop solutions without the oversight and management of the centralized information systems department. The local area could then either hire its own development staff or hire consultants to write the necessary programs. The tasks the information systems department once performed now had to be provided by the local business organization as well. These tasks include data backup, archiving, security, integrity, policies, procedures, and more.

The problem that arose from this downsizing was that the local business organization did not understand the value or the process to get these tasks done properly, if at all. In many cases, nobody even thought about data protection (the primary corporate resource and asset). The PC revolution actually fueled this trend because processors and software tools became more and more capable of handling larger and more robust tasks. For many organizations, this craze created anarchy and self-rule, redundant data, incompatible systems, and general chaos within the organization as a whole. Costs have actually soared in many cases where promises to reduce cost were once the byline. Enter client/server computing.

There are many differences in the way client/server computing is approached and managed, and the only way it is done properly is with great care. No longer is there an ominous ivory tower (the MIS department) dictating "thou shalts" nor are there rogue factions in the organization developing whatever is felt to be required. Instead, client/server focuses on the enterprise as a whole, data as a strategic resource and asset, and the capability to scale and distribute applications developed by the enterprise to the enterprise for the benefit of the enterprise as a whole. In other words, the organization by design reaches its primary goal: to work as a team, reducing costs and potential long-term mistakes. It is still too early to tell whether client/server can reduce overall costs, although this may be the case in the short term. But client/server doesn't promise to reduce cost; rather, this concept promises a better way to use the available money and resources to achieve corporate cooperation.

Clients

A *client* is any workstation or PC that can access corporate data through application programs, report writers, and interactive Structured Query Language (SQL).

In traditional local area networks (LANs) the workstation or PC is responsible for accessing the data on a network server directly. The workstation or PC will use its central processing unit to process the request until data is sent back across the network transport to the workstation or PC. The network is truly used as a transport for data and requests, and does not off-load any processing to the network file server. This means that high volumes of data packets are sent back and forth across the network, affecting the overall performance of the network.

In client/server, the client sends requests (generally through SQL) to a database server. The database server processes the request, formulates the result, and returns to the client only the data requested. This provides an effective cooperative processing environment in which the client handles the front end (application software) and the database server handles the back end (database engine processes).

The client workstation or PC provides the user interface and mechanisms to request data, and the server provides the data access engine to retrieve, store, and manipulate this data. Performance can be considerably faster in a true client/server architecture than in a local LAN-based operation, even across large geographical areas, because far fewer data packets are actually sent back and forth across the wire.

In true client/server operation, data integrity and access security are handled at the database level on a database server, and not within the client. This also provides a far greater level of protection for the prized corporate asset: data.

Clarion for Windows is a definite candidate for use as a client (front-end) development system because Clarion for Windows provides a robust user interface development platform through the AppGen and hand code.

The key to client systems development is a technique known as rapid application development (RAD). RAD embodies a concept that the AppGen so eloquently provides: quick prototyping and usable software. Generally, RAD is used to quickly develop the user's request so that validation of the request, as well as usability studies, can be performed early in the development life cycle (the process of specifying, building, testing, and delivering software), when the cost for doing so is relatively low. Furthermore, sometimes systems are developed once and left as-is because of budgetary constraints. Due to the nature of Clarion for Windows' AppGen, you can be assured that the systems you prototype will certainly work after the prototype is complete. Standard software development life cycle practices are generally also used at later stages of the project. However, these practices are usually modified so that systems accepted by corporations can be created in record time, and Clarion for Windows was made to do just that.

Servers

A *server* is the back-end processor that attaches to the network and processes client requests, ultimately serving data back to the client. The server can access data on several physical machines using a network protocol such as IPX/SPX or TCP/IP. Data can be stored on the server or on other machines, and can be distributed across geographically different sites, on various different hardware platforms and operating systems.

Two-Tier Versus Three-Tier Client/Server

There are currently two schools of thought on serving data. The first is a two-tier architecture approach, which is most common today. Clients will request data and manage the end-user presentation of the data. The server(s) will service the request for data.

The second approach is known as a three-tier client/server architecture. This particular approach enables the developers of application systems to distribute processes across various disparate machines, each best suited for a particular kind of task. This process is similar to that used in many UNIX environments, and is nothing completely new or radical. The new buzzword for this strategy is "application partitioning." In theory, this approach seems quite reasonable.

For example, the client might request and present data only for the end user. You might add an additional processor if you need to do some number crunching, say on a UNIX machine. The client will formulate the request for data and send it to the server, but while the server is locating and preparing to send the data back, the UNIX machine might be calculating some abstract calculation that requires accessing a different set of data on the server. Both the server and the processor send information back to the client. In theory, this would happen in a fraction of the time it would take if all processes were to be serialized and performed by the client itself. Sounds great, doesn't it? Even though today's technology, coupled with excellent programmers, can produce this type of distributed processing system, high-level languages that can accommodate this type of concept in an automated fashion are just now starting to appear. In all reality, the three-tier client/server approach is just now coming up to speed in the Windows marketplace.

The Wide Area Network

A *wide area network* (WAN) is a collection of LANs and/or other machines that together serve the geographical organization. In some instances, a mainframe may be a significant part of the WAN, used as a data storage and retrieval vehicle for the clients on the WAN. To be considered a WAN, there must be at least two networks connected together, sharing data between them in one form or another. In many cases, a "switched" technology (such as SMDS, ISDN, T1, T2, T3) is used to transport data over long distances. Sometimes dial-up or slower-speed lines are used for the rare occasions when they are needed.

In any event, a WAN simply connects the various workgroups in an organization into one large-scale network through some form of communication protocol (for example, phone lines, satellite, microwave).

Database Servers

A *database server* is a machine that is dedicated to running the database engine (such as ORACLE or Sybase). The term database server is sometimes used in conjunction with the database engine, because generally one machine will act as a database server for the database engine. Network file servers are generally middle-of-the-road machines (that is, 486 DX2 66 mHz), but a database server is generally a high-powered machine (such as a Pentium-based or RISC-based machine). This is because the database server not only serves data to the client (as a network server does), but also performs services for the clients such as executing SQL requests from the client, stored procedures, and triggers directly on the database server machine. In comparison, a client on a LAN will execute the SQL statements locally against the data stored on a file server.

Distributed Computing

Distributed computing is a term used to define the domain of data storage, and sometimes the ownership of the data. This means that data can be placed at strategic geographical locations within the organization where it makes the most sense for normal usage. For instance, say you need to access a database that contains vendor and inventory data. The site where you are located might be the sales office that is responsible for those who purchase your products (vendors), while your warehouse (which is geographically located elsewhere) is responsible for shipping and inventory control. The vendor table might reside on your database server, and the inventory table might reside on the warehouse's database. The database engine knows where this data resides, and whenever you request data that includes both tables, the proper data is fetched from the respective tables at their respective locations. The rationale for distributing the data might be convenience or strategic importance. For the most part, you will get a little better data access performance against the localized data than you do for the distributed data.

Another reason to distribute data is to accommodate different needs within the organization. For example, a corporate data model contains some, but not all, of the details of the data you need locally. Distributing the data is a great solution for this purpose. You will use the corporate data model, extending it by appending your localized data model to it. You might add only those elements that make sense for the localized business requirements, therefore reducing the margin for error and data redundancy enterprisewide.

Normalization and Replication

By and large, most large-scale database systems are designed using the relational database model. This model dictates that redundancy cannot exist. However, in some circumstances, this model might hamper performance if data is widely distributed geographically throughout the organization. To solve this problem, the replication server was created.

A replication server will either work on timed intervals, demand requests or triggered events, replicate data from one site to another, storing data redundantly at the local site. For example, you need to provide read-only data to your users when a query is made or a report is run, which could easily be done via replicated data. However, if the user wishes to update this data, the database engine might request the latest snapshot of it from the originating database to ensure integrity, allow the user to make the necessary changes, then transmit those changes back to its place of origin. This activity might trigger an event to update the replicated data stored locally as well, ensuring that the latest information is represented at each local site. "Real" data resides in one place for all intents and purposes, so replication servers can greatly boost performance for the average use of the data.

Politics, Empires, and the New Regime

Of course, nothing comes easy, so client/server has come up against the information systems departments, management, and the organization as a whole, and is slowly becoming victorious. As mentioned at the beginning of this chapter, client/server is not just a technology, it is a way of life for the enterprise. An organization that does not embrace, breathe, and eat the client/server credo from top to bottom will most likely fail if it tries to implement just one workgroup or business unit in isolation.

By definition, client/server is cooperative computing, not empirical computing. This means that all factions of an organization must grapple with and solve computing problems in a common and goal-oriented fashion.

In all organizations there are political domains and empires. If left to their own devices, the ensuing politics can put a stranglehold on the very existence of the organization. We have seen all too many times the childish games that are played when power struggles persist: "It's my ball. If you won't play by my rules, I'm taking my ball and going home." As ridiculous as this may sound, it is shockingly so.

Many organizations have found themselves paralyzed because of one person's view of the "right" solution. Many of these organizations have found that once this "one person" was removed from the equation, the organization could begin to breathe and become a viable working unit once again. There was a time when one person could rule the assets of corporate data, but those days are long gone, and with the state of technology, no one person can know all or be all—it takes a highly skilled team.

The dynasty of the information systems department has been all but shattered with the recent events of client/server computing. No longer is the information systems department the king; rather, the information systems department is now the servant to the organization. Often a complete information systems staff is laid off, replaced by a commercial consulting firm outsourcing the client/server solutions. Why does this happen? For the most part, it is a cleansing process. As most software developers know, you don't fix what isn't broken, but when it's broken, sometimes it takes a complete rewrite to get the desired results. Although this is the current state of affairs, I suspect that we will see another pendulum swing, and we'll see things fall out somewhere in the middle.

So now what's the game plan? This is a much-debated topic, of which I can only share my views. Information systems has traditionally been the keeper of the data, the policymaker, and the insurer against disaster, and it should still hold this responsibility. Information systems should maintain the integrity of database systems, decide on a corporate development policy, design the corporate data model, and protect the investment and strategic asset the data represents.

Over the years, information systems has been the designer, developer, tester, and implementor of systems, as well, but here is where I think some changes can be made. Who better understands the needs of the end users than those who work with the end users every day? These folks are the managers, business analysts, and key decision makers who reside where the work is actually performed. They should specify the new systems needed to solve today's problems. The local area should also provide technical support, software support, and development staff to aid in the delivery and support of RAD-based systems to the local user community. However, herein lies the catch. The local developers must adhere to information systems standards, policies, and procedures for enterprisewide application development, communicate with information systems leaders when changes are necessary at the corporate data model level, and develop systems that can be rapidly deployed to other business groups or units within the organization, providing great strategic benefits for the enterprise. In order to do this, they need a common development plan and architecture.

The result of moving development outside of information systems brings with it some benefits. The end user community can form a closer relationship with the developers, which means that empathy and understanding are more likely to prevail when problems arise (and problems certainly will arise). Developers will also take more ownership of their projects, compelled by this closer relationship to provide the very best solution for the end users.

In all of this, the key to being successful is responsibility. Each party in a client/server development effort must be accountable to the others, as well as to the enterprise for its portion of the work. There are no more islands or secret pacts; it must be an open network of development efforts with the goal of making the organization profitable at all times.

Keep in mind that these are only my views, but I honestly believe these are requirements to have a successful client/server implementation.

The Introduction Game (Considerations)

How does Clarion for Windows fit into this equation? There are several things to consider. First, you've got to get your foot in the door, no matter how small a piece that means you take. If that is writing one special report, then so be it.

Clarion for Windows lacks in one key area today when it comes to client/server computing: SQL drivers and complete SQL compliance. By this I mean that if you have an SQL query written in one language, you should be able to use it in another. This is one goal of SQL: to be a portable scripting language. To address this issue, Clarion for Windows SQL drivers have already begun to appear. The AS400 and GUPTA drivers are available, the ORACLE and Sybase drivers are in testing, and of course you already have ODBC. So this really leaves just SQL compliance. In an upcoming version of CW there will be full SQL support; until then, you may have to do a little dance step or two if the corporation for which you want to develop must have portable nonproprietary SQL support.

I have found that it works to take on departmental projects where Visual Basic, MS Access, Paradox, dBase, and FoxPro have traditionally been used. These projects generally are small in scope and are non–mission critical to the organization. Let the departmental applications prove just how quickly you can produce stable and professional applications using Clarion for Windows.

I have also found that where large-scale client/server development languages have problems, you can slip Clarion for Windows in to solve these problems just as C or C++ have been used in the past. For instance, if you need higher performance for certain processes than you could currently obtain from, for example, PowerBuilder, you could create a standard DLL (very much like you would in C/C++, but in far less time) that can be called by the PowerBuilder language directly. You could use dynamic data exchange as another way to use Clarion for Windows behind the scenes.

Finally, the Clarion for Windows user base is growing like wildfire. As the market acceptance grows, so do your opportunities. Make sure to ask for references and recommendations from any company for which you provide software solutions with Clarion for Windows. The mass appeal may take a while, so showing your depth and how Clarion for Windows has been effectively used to solve someone else's business problems may help the next company decide to use you, Clarion for Windows, or both.

Summary

Client/server computing is not for the weak at heart; it is a large commitment on everyone's part. Client/server computing is a way of life, which can be difficult for many in large organizations to accept. Traditional development methodologies must evolve in order for users to benefit from the newer tools that support client/server computing. Rapid application development is at the heart of productivity in client/server computing, and Clarion for Windows provides a great front-end client development system, utilizing RAD-based tools (such as the AppGen) to effectively build and distribute fast, stable, and robust applications for the enterprise.

31

Sharing Code: Source, OBJs, and LIBs

As you develop applications, you will undoubtedly find yourself using certain code more than once. This could be something as simple as some data declarations, it could be a specialized function, or it could even be a whole group of functions. In an earlier series of discussions (Chapter 16, "Hand Code, Reuse, and the Application Generator," Chapter 17, "Creating Code Templates," Chapter 18, "Creating Procedure Templates," Chapter 19, "Creating Control Templates," and Chapter 20, "Creating Extension Templates") you learned how to use the template language to share uncompiled code and data. In this chapter you'll learn how to use the more traditional code-sharing options: source include files for uncompiled code, and OBJ and LIB files for compiled code and data.

You may have noticed that shared source code functions are absent from this list. This chapter discusses them briefly, though not favorably, because there are a number of better options you can use to share functions.

Uncompiled Source

I admit to a bias against sharing uncompiled code, at least outside of the template system (see Chapters 16 through 20). It requires the use of INCLUDE directives in your code, which tell the compiler where to look for a particular source file. This reduces readability, and also spreads your application's source files over a greater area, because global includes are generally kept in a separate directory from all other application source. It also is somewhat risky to have multiple applications sharing source code that is in a state of flux, which often happens during development.

Despite this, there are clearly circumstances in which sharing global uncompiled source is appropriate. A good example of this is the global shared source code that the AppGen uses, which can be found in the \CW\LIBSRC directory.

Shared Global Data in \CW\LIBSRC

Take a moment to browse through the files in the \CW\LIBSRC directory. The files EQUATES.CLW, ERRORS.CLW, KEYCODES.CLW, and PROPERTY.CLW all contain global equate statements (the EQUATE statement is explained in Chapter 14, "Hand-Crafted Code: A Language Primer"). The following is a partial listing from EQUATES.CLW, showing the labels that have been assigned to some of the events that can occur within a CW program:

```
EVENT:MouseDown      EQUATE (01H)
EVENT:MouseUp        EQUATE (0aH)
EVENT:MouseIn        EQUATE (0bH)
EVENT:MouseOut       EQUATE (0cH)
EVENT:MouseMove      EQUATE (0dH)
EVENT:VBXevent       EQUATE (0eH)
EVENT:AlertKey       EQUATE (0fH)
EVENT:PreAlertKey    EQUATE (10H)
EVENT:Dragging       EQUATE (11H)
EVENT:Drag           EQUATE (12H)
```

```
EVENT:Drop          EQUATE (13H)
EVENT:ScrollDrag    EQUATE (14H)
```

The files DDE.CLW and BUILTINS.CLW contain map statements. BUILTINS.CLW is automatically included in each program's map by the compiler, assuming the program has a map (and all but the simplest one-module programs do). DDE.CLW looks like the following:

```
! DDE.CLW
! CW DDE support map definitions
  MODULE('CWDDE')
      DDEclient(<string>,<string>), ULONG, NAME('Cla$DDEclient')
      DDEserver(<string>,<string>), ULONG, NAME('Cla$DDEserver')
      DDEclose(ULONG), NAME('Cla$DDEclose')
      DDEread(ULONG, SHORT, STRING, <*?>), NAME('Cla$DDEread')
      DDEwrite(ULONG, SHORT, STRING, <*?>), NAME('Cla$DDEwrite')
      DDEpoke(ULONG, STRING, STRING), NAME('Cla$DDEpoke')
      DDEexecute(ULONG, STRING), NAME('Cla$DDEexecute')
      DDEquery(<STRING>,<STRING>), STRING, NAME('Cla$DDEquery')
      DDEchannel(),ULONG,NAME('Cla$DDEchannel')
      DDEitem(),STRING,NAME('Cla$DDEitem')
      DDEapp(),STRING,NAME('Cla$DDEapp')
      DDEtopic(),STRING,NAME('Cla$DDEtopic')
      DDEvalue(),STRING,NAME('Cla$DDEvalue')
```

The files in \CW\LIBSRC are more conspicuous because of what they don't have than because of what they do have. The files contain constants, but virtually no global variables, declared here. Take that as a hint. As much as you can, resist any urge to place variables in global data include files. The more global variables you use, the greater the risk that your functions will interact with each other in unplanned, and undesirable, ways.

If you find that you have global variables that you want all your apps to use, you might want to place them in a file in the \CW\LIBSRC directory, because this directory is searched by the redirection file. If you are developing with the AppGen, you will have to place an INCLUDE statement that points to this file in the global data embed point for the application. This will let you use the declarations in your code, but they will not be available in pick lists, as they would be if you entered the declarations using the Data button on the Application Global Properties window. If you are hand coding, of course, this is not an issue. A future version of CW may provide the capability to store non-file data in the dictionary editor, which will solve most of the problems with declaring global source code. You also may want to explore the use of template extensions to add the required global data to each application (see Chapter 20).

TIP

You can circumvent some of the problems with sharing source code by declaring a file in the Data Dictionary and placing the variables you want to use as fields in the file. You will never do any I/O on this file, although your program will probably create it on disk at some time.

Shared Local Data

Just as you sometimes need to share global data, there might also be times when you want to use a particular Data Declaration in multiple procedures, but you don't want it to be global. Instead of making a copy of the data for each procedure, you might want to put the definition in a separate file and use an INCLUDE statement to pull it into the procedures in question. This approach suffers from the same drawback as using a global data include: You cannot reference any of the variables declared in that way, in the usual AppGen pick lists. As with global data, you may also want to explore how to use template extensions to add commonly used data to a procedure.

> **TIP**
>
> Limit your shared, uncompiled source to global equates, and only use global variables where you really have no other choice.

Shared Functions

Although several of the files in \CW\LIBSRC do contain procedure prototypes, they do not include any source code for procedures or functions, which are not intended to be shared as source code in CW. This might come as a bit of a surprise to you, if, like many Clarion 2.x programmers, you have developed the habit of putting commonly used procedures in a special directory and giving them an empty MEMBER() statement so they can be compiled by any application.

If you try to share procedures with empty MEMBER() statements in CW, you'll get an error message telling you that MEMBER() statements are required.

> **DANGEROUS TIP**
>
> Sharing procedures in source code form is still possible, and just to show you I'm trying to be fair, I'll tell you how. After all, if you want to shoot yourself in the foot, that's your own problem. Probably the most straightforward approach is to create shell source procedures for your apps. These procedures should contain only a MEMBER() statement and an include statement referencing a source file (which is kept in a directory the redirection file will search) with the rest of the procedure in it. You won't normally want to do this because, as you'll see, it's a complete waste of good processor time to keep recompiling source code that you know works.
>
> You can also use compiler directives to conditionally compile the correct MEMBER() statement for the current application, or you can place the MEMBER() statement in an

include file and keep a separate include file in each directory. The redirection file will search the current directory for the source procedure, but it will not locate it. It will then search for shared procedure source in the directory you specify, and will locate the file. Finally, it will begin to look for the map include file, which will be in the current directory and will contain the `MEMBER()` statement for the current application.

Like all good programming languages, CW gives you enough rope to hang yourself, if that's what you really want to do.

In CW, procedures and functions are designed to be shared, but only in compiled form. That is the subject of the next section.

Compiled Source: OBJs and LIBs

If you've done any amount of application development, you've probably run into a situation in which you wanted to reuse some procedure or function. In Chapter 18 you learned about placing procedures to be shared in a template, which is then available to all applications created with the AppGen. This approach has tremendous benefits, but there are still some circumstances in which using compiled code has its advantages.

To Compile or Not to Compile

All source code, as discussed in Chapter 11, "From Here to EXE: The Project System," must be compiled into an optimized, computer-readable form before it can run as a CW program. This optimized code is called *object code*. Object code files typically have the extension OBJ, and are usually referred to as OBJ files.

All code must go through this compile process, which means that by sharing OBJ files instead of source files, you can be one step ahead of the game because you do not need to continually recompile the source code. This is one of the benefits of sharing compiled code instead of uncompiled code. Just how much of an advantage it really is depends on a lot of other factors, such as how much of your code is in OBJ form, how often it changes, how fast your compiles are, and so on.

A more quantifiable benefit is the absence of readable source code. It's pretty difficult for the average (or even above-average) programmer to change an OBJ file. In a workgroup situation, where a number of developers are working on one project, distributing OBJ files removes the temptation individuals may feel to tailor a particular shared piece of code to their own uses. A primary purpose of sharing code is, after all, to ensure that everyone has the same set of tools with which to work.

If you are a third-party developer, you might not want to give your competition access to your source code (unless you are a particularly bad programmer, in which case you have enough troubles of your own). Because of their inherently cryptic nature, OBJ files can be used to distribute code that you want others to be able to use, but for which you don't want others to access the source.

Sharing Source Code

You have two broad options for sharing code between applications, other than templates, which are discussed in Chapters 17 through 20 and Chapter 21, "The AppGen: The Ultimate Hand Coding Tool." First, you can make multiple copies of the code in question (and it doesn't really matter whether you are talking about source code or compiled code; the fact is that you have multiple identical declarations, code blocks, or procedures on your system). It's pretty obvious why this isn't such a great idea—as soon as you have multiple copies of something, it becomes that much more difficult to make changes. How can you be sure you've changed every copy of the information? This gets worse if you've embedded some copies inside applications.

The second option is to have only one copy of the information and have all your applications somehow reference that copy. This makes maintenance a whole lot easier, because you have to go to only one place to make the changes.

However, there are a number of ways to share code, and each method has its place. The following section discusses sharing precompiled source code, in the form of OBJ files and LIB files.

Creating OBJ Files

You don't have to do anything special to create OBJ files—just compile your source code. OBJ files are automatically created in the first directory specified on the OBJ line of your redirection file (CW.RED), and in most cases this will be \CW\OBJ. One OBJ file is created for each module.

> **NOTE**
>
> You can edit the redirection file by choosing Setup|Edit Redirection File.

Whether you set up an additional directory for your shared OBJ files depends somewhat on your working style. If you are working on a multi-application project, where some of your source of OBJ files is likely to change a lot, you might want to manually copy current OBJs to a separate directory so that your other applications are not affected by works in progress. On the other hand, you may want to keep all your applications up-to-date, in which case they should be using OBJ files from the directory where they are automatically created.

An Example of Using OBJ Files

The following example demonstrates how to place an OBJ from one application into another application.

First, you will need to create the application that will provide the OBJ, which you can easily do using Quick Start. (If you haven't used Quick Start yet, refer to Chapter 6, "Quick Start: The Two-Minute Application.")

Using Quick Start, create an application called OBJAPP. You will want one file called NAMELIST, with one field called NAME, which will be a STRING(30) and which will have a unique key. Figure 31.1 shows how your Quick Start window should look just before you press OK.

FIGURE 31.1.

Creating the OBJAPP application using Quick Start.

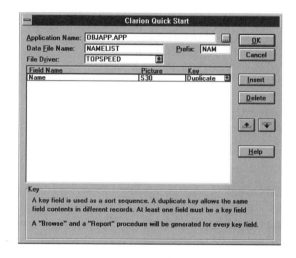

After Quick Start has finished generating the OBJAPP application, select Project|Make. After the make file is complete and you have a working EXE, return to the CW main menu. Use View|Module View to see a display of the application's modules. Make a note of the module that contains the UpdateProc procedure, which will be the subject of this exercise. Now select File|Save As to save the application under the name EXEAPP. You will now have two application files using the same dictionary.

The following section describes how to use an OBJ module from OBJAPP in EXEAPP. The example is somewhat arbitrary, because you are working with what are essentially two identical applications, but it will illustrate the process.

Adding an OBJ Module to an Application

In OBJAPP.APP, select the UpdateProc procedure and choose Edit|Delete to remove it. This will leave a ToDo item, labeled UpdateProc, in the application tree.

NOTE

This is not part of the usual process you would go through to add an OBJ to an application. Using two identical applications and deleting a procedure from one of these applications is simply a convenient way to create a condition in which an OBJ from one application will fill a need in another application.

Ensure that you are in the Module view in the application tree (select View|Module View) and highlight the UpdateProc (ToDo) procedure. Choose Edit|Move Procedure. The dialog box in Figure 31.2 appears.

FIGURE 31.2.

The Select destination module window.

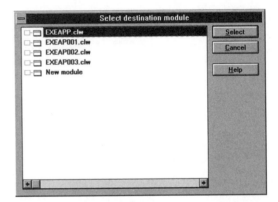

Because you want the UpdateProc procedure to be called from object code (obtained from the OBJAPP application), you will need to select New module. The Module Properties dialog box appears next, as shown in Figure 31.3.

FIGURE 31.3.

The Module Properties dialog box.

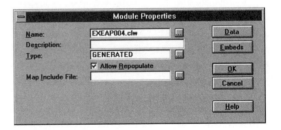

Change the module type from Generated to ExternalObj. Clicking the ellipsis button to the right of the Type entry will bring up a list of valid module types, including ExternalObj. Highlight it, and click Select. Now change the name of the module to the name of the module that contains the UpdateProc procedure in OBJAPP. Fill in a description (for example, Object Code from OBJAPP). Click OK on the Module Properties window, and you will be back at the application tree, which should now look like what is presented in Figure 31.4.

FIGURE 31.4.

The EXEAPP application tree after you add an external source module.

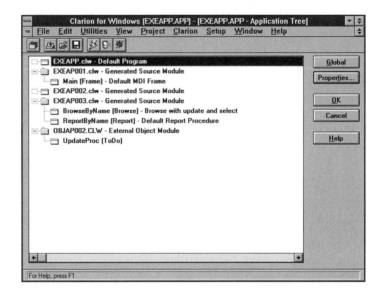

Just to keep everything tidy, you should also select the generated source module (most likely called EXEAPP02.CLW), which is used to contain UpdateProc, and which is now empty, and delete it. (There is no danger of accidentally deleting a procedure this way, because the AppGen will enable you to delete only empty modules.) Then choose Utilities|Renumber Modules to get your numbering back in sequence.

All that remains is to change UpdateProc from a ToDo to an actual procedure. Select it, and click the Properties button. From the Procedure Type list, select External. You will see the now-familiar Procedure Properties window. Because this procedure has no parameters, there is nothing further to be added. Click OK and return to the Application Tree view. At this point, in Module view, your application should look like what is presented in Figure 31.5.

FIGURE 31.5.

The EXEAPP application, with an object module from OBJAPP, ready to be made and run.

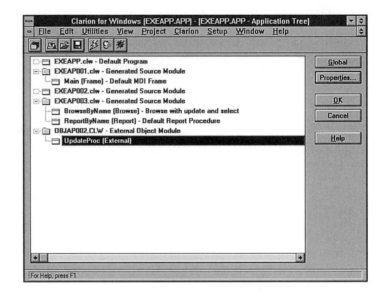

The LIB File: An OBJ Library

Libraries are really just collections of OBJ files, so essentially the same rules apply to their use as apply to OBJ files. They take one more step to create, however. You must set the target type of your application to Library (LIB), which you can do either in Edit|Application Properties, or in the project editor.

Adding LIBs to an Application

Adding library procedures to an application is virtually the same as adding OBJ procedures. The only difference is that when you create the module, you will use the type ExternalLib instead of ExternalObj.

Enforced Modularity

The ability to create OBJ and LIB files can have a profound effect on the way you write code. When you write a procedure that will be going into a LIB, you do not know who is going to be calling it, or under what conditions. This is particularly true if you're in a workgroup situation in which you may be sharing libraries with a number of other programmers.

Sometimes procedures act completely independently of the procedure that calls them. For instance, if you create an About Box procedure for your program, there's really no information that needs to pass between the menu and the about procedure. If you put that procedure in a library, the only thing anyone would need to know is the name of the procedure.

Modularity in the *Message()* Function

Much of the time a procedure or function is useful because it communicates in some way with the calling procedure. This exchange of information can go either way or both ways. For instance, if an error has occurred and you wish to display it to the user with the standard MESSAGE() function, you will need to communicate to the MESSAGE() function the information to display. In this case, you do so by passing a parameter:

```
MESSAGE('An error has occurred: ' & ERROR())
```

The procedure you are calling may also communicate something back:

```
IF MESSAGE('An error has occurred: ' & ¦
  ERROR(),,,Button:OK + Button:Cancel) = Button:Cancel THEN RETURN.
```

In this case, the calling procedure tells MESSAGE() to display not only the specified text, but also to display two buttons, OK and Cancel, and to return the value of the button pressed.

Using Global Variables

Parameters and return values are the safest way to pass information back and forth from library (or any) procedures. They are not, however, the only way.

You can also use global variables to communicate information. For instance, the creators of CW could have written a message function that displayed the contents of a string variable called, for example, GLOBAL:MESSAGE. (There is no such variable in CW as shipped, so don't go looking for it.) In that case, you would set the contents of GLOBAL:MESSAGE, then call MESSAGE to display it. As you can imagine, this a less satisfactory choice because it requires the programmer to know about yet another variable.

If you really wanted to get nasty in your procedure design, you could communicate to the user which button was pressed by setting the value of GLOBAL:MESSAGE to that button. The user would then have to test that global variable to know the response. (You could also pass variables by address, if you didn't want to use global variables.)

As you can see, there is no end to bad design once you get started, so you want to keep things as clean as possible. When you create libraries, always document the procedure calls, parameters, return values, and any and all global variables that are required to make the procedure function. Also, document any global variables that are changed by the procedure, so that calling procedures can be written to take this into account.

If global variables are such a nightmare, why use them at all? Why not just pass all required data as parameters? This is the ideal, but there is one circumstance in particular under which this is not possible, and that is discussed in the next section.

Modularity and Threaded Procedures

When you start a procedure on its own thread using the START command, you are not allowed to pass any parameters. If you are using MDI, you must use START on all MDI children. You can also use START on non-MDI procedures. In either case, the effect you get is multiple procedures that you can switch between using the mouse or equivalent keystrokes. All such procedures, if they require some communication with the procedure which issued the START, must use global (either program or module level) data.

Summary

When applications share code, that code will either be compiled or uncompiled. Uncompiled code, at least outside the template system, should be restricted as much as possible to constants and map declarations. Procedures are better shared as compiled code, in the form of OBJ modules, or library (LIB) files.

The following chapter looks at a very specialized and powerful mechanism for sharing precompiled code: dynamic link libraries.

32

Sharing Code: Creating Clarion DLLs

In Chapter 31, "Sharing Code: Source, OBJs, and LIBs," you saw how LIBs save you the hassle of recompiling procedures that you already know work properly. Those procedures, however, still have to be linked into the main program to be used. What if you could save that step as well? What if you could create a library that could stay separate from the program, but would be available to it while it is executing? If you could do that, you'd have a dynamic link library, or DLL.

DLLs: A Hybrid Strain

DLLs are not replacements for LIBs, but are a special type of LIB with particular benefits and constraints. They occupy the area between LIBs and EXEs. Like LIBs, they provide a common library of procedures and functions to as many programs as need to use them. Like EXEs, they are (or rather, can be) independent of other programs, running in their own memory space. Also, like EXEs, they can have their own global memory, which, as you'll see shortly, can be quite useful.

> **TIP**
>
> If the procedure you are considering for a DLL is small and self-contained, and there will be no difference in functionality if it is in a LIB, then that's probably where it should go. For example, a specialized capitalization function belongs in a LIB, but a set of browses and forms that you use in several different applications is a good candidate for a DLL.

DLLs are particularly useful when you are developing large applications, where certain procedures are heavily reused. They are also useful in a multideveloper environment, where it's convenient to break the application into logical blocks that can be individually developed and tested, and later incorporated into a single program.

Runtime Linking

One of the obvious benefits of using DLLs for shared code is that they are linked only at runtime. This means that, with the restrictions I'll explain shortly, you can make changes to a DLL that is a component of your program, place the new DLL in your program directory, and the next time you start the program the new code will be executed. In large systems, the ability to update individual sections of code can save you a lot of time rebuilding applications and a lot of disks distributing those changes.

This flexibility does come at a price, however. With one exception (the CALL() function, discussed later in this chapter), all DLL functions that you wish to have available from your program (or from other DLLs) must have a small LIB file linked in. This LIB file is created at the same time the DLL is created, and contains only interface code that tells your program how to find the DLL and the functions and data it contains.

Any time you change this interface code, by removing or adding a function, by changing a parameter list, or anything else of that sort, you will have to relink the DLL's LIB file into all the programs or DLLs that use it. That means that if your one small update to the DLL involves a new function, you won't get any immediate benefit, from a distribution point of view, over using a LIB. The payback comes when you discover that you made an uncharacteristic mistake in some processing within a DLL's procedure or function. Because the interface code hasn't changed, you only need to remake the DLL with your correction, and distribute it to your clients.

Global Data

DLLs are more like programs than they are like LIBs when it comes to data storage. A LIB has no global data section; it is really a collection of object code modules. Each procedure in an object code module can have its own local data, and each module can have module data, but there is no way all the procedures in a multimodule LIB can share their own global data that is private to the LIB.

DLLs, like programs, have a global data section. This means, for example, that DLLs that use files in common with other programs or DLLs will, by default, have their own record buffers. That might suit your needs, or it might not. There is a way to make a DLL share data with other DLLs and EXEs, and it's discussed a little later in this chapter.

Creating DLLs

DLLs are remarkably easy to create. The first step is to go to the Application Properties window and change the destination type to Dynamic Link Library, as shown in Figure 32.1.

FIGURE 32.1.

The Application Properties window, with the destination type set to Dynamic Link Library.

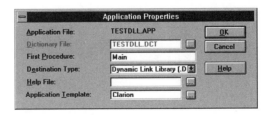

As soon as you make this change, you will notice that all the procedures in the application tree now have the Export: prefix, as shown in Figure 32.2.

FIGURE 32.2.

The application tree, showing procedures marked for export.

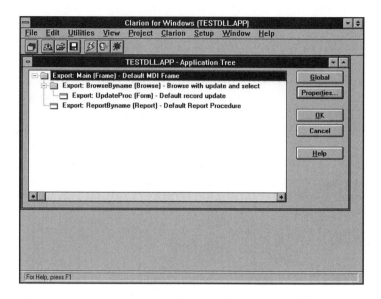

If you look at the Procedure Properties window for any of these procedures, you will notice a new Export Procedure check box under the Module Name drop-down list box. Use this option to decide whether the procedure is to be available to all EXEs and DLLs that use this DLL (that is, whether it will be a public procedure or private to the DLL).

Public and Private Procedures and the EXP File

When you create a DLL, every procedure in your application is linked in. Only those procedures that are marked for export, however, are going to be visible outside the DLL. All this is controlled by the EXP, or Export file, which has the name of the application and the extension .EXP. When you check and uncheck the Export Procedure box, all you're doing is determining whether the procedure gets an entry in the EXP file. Listing 32.1 shows a typical EXP file.

Listing 32.1. A typical EXP file.

```
LIBRARY TESTDLL

CODE MOVEABLE DISCARDABLE PRELOAD
DATA MOVEABLE SINGLE PRELOAD

HEAPSIZE  1024
STACKSIZE 32678

SEGMENTS
    ENTERCODE MOVEABLE DISCARDABLE PRELOAD
```

```
EXETYPE WINDOWS

EXPORTS
  Main
  BrowseByname
  ReportByname
  UpdateProc
  $GlobalRequest
  $GlobalResponse
```

Everything from LIBRARY TESTDLL to EXPORTS is standard header information. The EXP file is created by the AppGen, and if you want to change any of this information you will need to make the appropriate modifications to PROGRAM.TPW, the template file that contains the EXP code.

TIP

If you want to modify the EXP in a way that the AppGen does not support, you can make your changes in the source editor. After saving the file, mark it as read-only using the DOS ATTRIB +R *filename* command. You will not get any error messages telling you the file could not be replaced, and of course any future changes to your application will not be reflected in the EXP file, either.

The EXPORTS list is what will concern you most. All procedures that you've marked for export will appear in the list first, followed by any global data that is marked for export. Each global data name is prefixed with a $ character to differentiate them from procedure names.

If a procedure is in the DLL but not in the EXPORTS list, it is private to that DLL. If you're supplying a DLL as a third-party toolkit, you could use this feature to hide all the good proprietary bits so your competition doesn't get any ideas about how you're doing things. It's also good practice to limit the number of entry points to a DLL to help keep DLL load times to a minimum.

TIP

In CW 1.0 the EXP file is not removed if you change the application target from DLL back to EXE. When you then create the EXE, the linker will read the EXP file that is designed for a DLL, and your program will be corrupt. You need to remove or rename the EXP file so the linker will look for the default EXE-style EXP.

The DLL's LIB File

At link time, CW uses the EXP file information to create a LIB that corresponds to the DLL. As mentioned earlier, other programs get access to the DLL by linking in this corresponding LIB file.

Depending on the modifications you've made to your redirection file (CW.RED), you may experience some initial difficulties finding the LIB and DLL files you create. Take a quick look at CW.RED by choosing Setup|Edit Redirection File from the main menu. You are concerned here with the lines that begin with `*.dll` and `*.lib`. The first entry in the directory list to the right of the equals sign is the directory where any file of that type will be created.

In the standard setup, the DLL will be created in the current directory, and the LIB will be created in the OBJ directory. Because the OBJ directory is probably not on the path, you will need to either specify the full path any time you use it in another application, or copy the LIB to another directory that is on the path. You might also want to create a special LIB and DLL directory, add it to your path, and make sure that this directory is first on the directory list in CW.RED, for both LIBs and DLLs.

To use your new DLL in another DLL or EXE, you will need to add the DLL's LIB file to the application, and declare the procedures that belong to the LIB/DLL in the global map. *↳ use an INC file*
  ↳ in Project Edit
The standard approach to this is exactly the same one you use to add a LIB procedure to the map (see Chapter 31). The other approach is simply to add the LIB file to the project manually and create a map in the global map include, as described in Chapter 25, "Using the Windows API."

Sharing Global Data

As discussed earlier in this chapter, DLLs have their own global data section. This global data capability actually introduces some problems. Imagine that you have an update procedure for a browse, and you wish to call this update procedure in four or five different programs. You place the procedure in a DLL, and in one of your programs you call it when the user presses one of the update buttons on the browse procedure. The first thing you notice is that you can add records, but you seem unable to delete or change records. This is because the DLL has its own global data, which means that it has its own copy of the file's record buffer. It's acting just like a separate program, and because it has its own copy of the record buffer, it has no way of knowing which record is currently active in the browse procedure, and that it should be acting on that record.

Another problem with global data is the global action variables `GlobalRequest` and `GlobalResponse`, which are used to communicate actions such as `InsertRecord` and `DeleteRecord`. If these are allocated their own memory in the DLL, setting their value in an EXE will have no effect on the copy that is active when the procedure in the DLL runs.

The solution to this problem is to set up the DLL and the program so they share the same record buffer. This isn't that hard to do, but it does take a little planning. The two components to any strategy are exporting and declaring data as external.

External and Exported Variables

In order for two program entities (where one is a DLL and the other is either another DLL or an EXE) to share data, one of the entities has to declare the data item as external, and the other has to export its definition of the data item.

In order for any variable to be used by a program or DLL, it has to be allocated memory equal to its size. The External attribute tells the linker not to do this because the memory will be allocated by another program or DLL. If this is the case, why bother with declaring the variable at all? The compiler still needs a label to reference as it's going through your code, and it will use the declaration to do type checking to make sure (as much as the compiler can) that no problems will occur during program execution.

You can put the External attribute on any valid variable, and your program will compile (assuming it is otherwise error free, of course). At link time, any variables declared this way will need to be found in LIBs that are in the project, or you will get an error message telling you that the variable's label is unresolved in whatever module it is referenced. The only way to get those variables into the LIBs is to export them. When you set the application target to DLL, all files used by exported procedures and all global data not allocated as external will be exported.

If you want to share a global variable between an EXE and a DLL, or between two DLLs, that variable will have to be declared as external in one place and exported in the other. The trick is deciding which should be which.

Strategies for Sharing Global Data

Probably the trickiest issue in sharing global data is what to do with file definitions. Imagine a development environment in which you have one EXE that calls four DLLs, and of the files in the application some are used by the EXE and all DLLs, some by a few DLLs, and some by only one DLL.

Each file referenced in any combination of EXEs and DLLs should ideally be declared only once without the External attribute. This will ensure that only one copy of the file definition is allocated memory.

You could have non-external file definitions scattered throughout your EXEs and DLLs, but you'll probably find it easiest if you have them all in one place. Because large applications often have more than one EXE, I suggest you place all your non-external file definitions in a single DLL, and have all your other DLLs and EXEs reference that DLL.

> **TIP**
>
> It's important to keep all your data file definitions consistent, even though only one of them will be allocated memory. If at all possible, you should use the AppGen and Data Dictionary, rather than hand code, to manage your DLLs. Any time you make a change to your Data Dictionary, first rebuild the master file DLL, then rebuild all the DLLs and EXEs that use that DLL.

The AppGen supports this kind of multi-DLL application development environment. In the application's Global Properties window, for the DLL that contains all the file definitions, set the file external attributes to None External, and check the Export All File Declarations box. (This setting becomes visible only when the application type is DLL and the default file external attributes setting is None External.) In order to ensure that all files are exported, create a window procedure (it doesn't have to be called by anything), and load up the Other section of its file schematic with all the files in the dictionary.

For all the other DLLs and EXEs that use these file definitions, set the file external attributes to All External, and check the All Files Are Declared box. You do not need to put a value in the Declaring Module entry, which is only used when you need to specify which module contains the exported (non-external) file definition, and it should be left blank when that module is a DLL.

Resolving Problems

There is one additional pitfall you should watch out for. If your DLLs require that the `GlobalRequest` and `GlobalResponse` variables be passed between your EXE and DLL, they, too, will have to be exported in the file DLL (which they are by default), and declared as external in all the other DLLs and EXEs. (You do this by checking the Generate Global Data as External box.)

Using CW DLLs with Other Windows Programs

You can use CW DLLs with other Windows programs. The biggest problem you're likely to face is prototyping the CW functions in the language of your choice. This is the reverse of the prototyping issues discussed in Chapter 25, where you converted C declarations to Clarion declarations, but you may find some useful information there, as well. Remember to use the PASCAL keyword on any procedures you declare for use by other environments.

The *CALL()* Function

Although the usual way to call a DLL procedure is to link in the associated LIB, you can also use the CALL() function to do this. There are some restrictions; the procedure cannot have any parameters and it can't return a value. This drastically limits your options, but it does offer some interesting benefits.

> **TIP**
>
> Because the CALL statement resolves which DLL it is calling at runtime, you can use it to make a highly configurable system. You might, for instance, build a system out of a number of "plug and play" DLLs, and control which ones are called by means of an INI file.

Summary

DLLs occupy a unique and specialized niche in the world of Windows programming. Although effectively using DLLs in your application design can be complex—mostly involving sharing file definitions—it can be very beneficial as well.

Third-Party Tools

Integral to any software development product are the third-party vendors. Third-party vendors can focus on unique or special product offerings which can enhance your application and the time it takes to build it. Listed in this appendix are a few third-party vendors that support Clarion for Windows.

> **NOTE**
>
> The information in this appendix, especially pricing, is subject to change. The publisher and authors are not responsible for any misquoted prices.

Template Vendors

AVD Ltd.	011 44 61 976 6237
Nigel Moss	
8 Park Avenue	
Timperly	
Altrincham, Cheshire, WA14 5AX	
United Kingdom	
CIS 100272,2431	

MULTIMA CORPORATION	(401)885-1916
One Rosewood Ct	(401)885-2605 FAX
East Greenwich, RI 02818-1543	

HighEdit Word Processing Control Template
Word Processing Instantly! Price $99. Visa, MasterCard, and American Express accepted.
The HighEdit control template enables the developer to place a HighEdit word processing control on a CW window and have an instant SDI or MDI word processor for documents or database memo fields. No code is needed to bring the full power of WYSIWYG word processing and mail merge to your CW applications.

C3 Development Inc.	(708)385-9844
6517 W. 127th, Suite 108	(708)385-8542 FAX
Palos Heights, IL 60463	(708)385-9885 BBS

Tagging Template
Tag, Tag all, Untag, and Reverse Tagging in list box. Tags usable in batch or report. $45 C3 upgrade, $55 Non C3 Upgrade.

In-Place Editing Template
Add, modify, and delete records directly in a list box. $65 C3 upgrade, $75 Non C3 Upgrade.

VCR Form Template
Page thru, add, delete, and change records on a form using multiple keys and locators. $35 C3 upgrade, $45 Non C3 Upgrade.

Many Key Browse Template
Use multiple keys and locators on a single browse, view in forward, or reverse key order. $35 C3 Upgrade, $45 Non C3 Upgrade.

List Resize Template
Resize list box according to window size. $10 All.

Multipage Form Using the FarPoint Tab/Pro VBX
Manage forms with a tab style container control template. $65 C3 upgrade, $75 Non C3 Upgrade.
Bundle discounts apply to the templates when purchased in groups. C3WDEMO.ZIP available on C3's BBS or CompuServe.
There's an extra 5% discount for book owners faxing a copy of this page.

ToolCraft Development Corp.
21040 Homestead Rd., Suite 202
Cupertino, CA 95014
CIS: 75244,2146

(408)732-4300
(408)732-4372 FAX

Order Information
You can place your order by phone, fax, e-mail, or U.S. Mail. Please include your shipping address and payment information. MasterCard, Visa, and American Express cards are accepted. Shipping and handling charges are $9.95 for UPS Second-Day Air delivery. California residents will also need to add 8.25% sales tax.

Book Special
All ToolCraft products are available at 25% off the list price. Please ask for this special when ordering.

Power Templates

Power Browse
Power Browse adds multiple key order displays, resizable list boxes, record marking, in-line editing (edit without a form), and also uses a browse library to dramatically reduce the amount of code generated for each browse procedure. $149.

Power Form
Power Form adds in-line editing for invoice type forms, VCR controls for record paging, and also uses the same browse library as Power Form. $99.

Power Wrappers

Chart Wrapper
Chart Wrapper is an add-on code wrapper for use with Chart Builder's GRAPH.VBX product that provides full end-user graphing capabilities for Clarion applications using a template driven interface. $79.

VBX Vendors

AddSoft, Inc.   (402)491-4141
1065 North 115th St.   (402)491-4152 FAX
Omaha, NE 68154

Gantt/VBX
(See ad at end of book)

Intermedia, Inc.   (603)465-2696
60 Plain Rd.   (603)465-7195 FAX
Hollis, NH 03049
CIS 70444,31 or Internet 70444.31@Compuserve.Com

DynaZip
(See ad at end of book)

MicroHelp Inc.   (800)922-3383
4359 Shallowford Industrial Pkwy.   (404)516-1099 FAX
Marietta, GA 30066

Various VBXs
Please call MicroHelp, Inc., for information

Tools

AJS Publishing   (310)215-9145
P.O. Box 83220   (310)215-9135 FAX
Los Angeles, CA 90083

VBXpress v2.31
Create window control level 1.0 VBXs step by step without writing code. Suggested retail $299, introductory book offer of $239.

Mitten Software   (800)825-5461
10709 Wayzata Blvd.
Minnetonka, MN 55305

Various tools available
(See ad at end of book)

SoftTouch Development   (205)233-5353 FAX
P.O. Box 3667
Huntsville, AL 35810
CIS 74750,1752 or Internet 74750.1752@Compuserve.Com

Clarion for Windows HandiRef
HandiRef is a programmer's quick reference for the Clarion for Windows development environment. It is designed by a programmer for programmers. There is a basic
reference package and a premium package. The premium package will be released in
loose-leaf format to allow updates and will include at least one quarterly update. Plans
are to include a disk of CW demos, CW/VB development shareware and the
SoftTouch Development Basic Function Library for Windows. Mention offer 014A
for a 10% discount. Please fax us your request for information or contact us on
CompuServe.

UDICO   (800)289-1948
4 Commercial Blvd   (415)382-8868 FAX
Novato, CA 94949
CIS 74674,30 or Internet 74674.30@COMPUSERVE.COM

Wysi-Help Composer
(See ad at end of book)

Miscellaneous Third-Party Vendors

The Clarion Technical Journal   (507)452-2824
PC Information Group (PCIG)   (507)452-0037 FAX
1126 E. Broadway
Winona, MN 55987

CTJ
The *Clarion Technical Journal* provides excellent product reviews, product information and technical articles, written by programmers for programmers.

CompuServe
TopSpeed Corporation provides a CompuServe forum. To access this forum which
includes announcements, e-mail, file downloads, and excellent product support, type
`GO CLARION`.

The Internet
Edward Mindlin has put together a World Wide Web site of information relating to
Clarion for Windows. The home page houses all the back issues of CW 'Zine, the
Internet electronic magazine, as well as the VBX Shareware/Freeware Archive.
The URL for the Clarion for Windows home page is `http://www.io.com/`
`~hanover/cw.html`.
Also available is the CW Talk Mailing List. You may subscribe to this mailing list by
sending an Internet e-mail message to `majordomo@io.com`. Use no subject, and a one-
line body that says `subscribe cw-talk`. You will be automatically added to the mailing
list. This mailing list has subscribers from all over the world, in all areas of expertise
relating to Clarion for Windows. You will also receive information on how you can
subscribe to CW 'Zine! There is also an FTP site that houses patches and example
application code. The address is `ftp.io.com`. Log in as `anonymous`, and use your
e-mail address for the password. All Clarion for Windows information is under
the directory \pub\user\hanover\CW.
If you have any questions regarding these sites or other Internet related sites for
Clarion for Windows, send an e-mail message to Edward Mindlin at
`hanover@pentagon.io.com`.

I

Index

PLUG YOURSELF INTO...

MACMILLAN INFORMATION SUPERLIBRARY™

que · SAMS PUBLISHING · Hayden Books · que COLLEGE · NRP · alpha books · Brady · ADOBE PRESS

THE MACMILLAN INFORMATION SUPERLIBRARY™

Free information and vast computer resources from the world's leading computer book publisher—online!

FIND THE BOOKS THAT ARE RIGHT FOR YOU!

A complete online catalog, plus sample chapters and tables of contents give you an in-depth look at *all* of our books, including hard-to-find titles. It's the best way to find the books you need!

- **STAY INFORMED** with the latest computer industry news through our online newsletter, press releases, and customized Information SuperLibrary Reports.

- **GET FAST ANSWERS** to your questions about MCP books and software.

- **VISIT** our online bookstore for the latest information and editions!

- **COMMUNICATE** with our expert authors through e-mail and conferences.

- **DOWNLOAD SOFTWARE** from the immense MCP library:
    - Source code and files from MCP books
    - The best shareware, freeware, and demos

- **DISCOVER HOT SPOTS** on other parts of the Internet.

- **WIN BOOKS** in ongoing contests and giveaways!

TO PLUG INTO MCP: ➔   WORLD WIDE WEB: **http://www.mcp.com**

GOPHER: gopher.mcp.com

FTP: ftp.mcp.com

Home Page · What's New · Bookstore · Reference Desk · Software Library · Macmillan Overview · Talk to Us

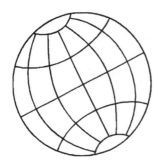

Enter the World Market!

CWIntl - A System of International Support

CWIntl, International Support for CW, opens up the world market to Clarion for Windows programmers. Its number, currency, date, and time functions dynamically change entry and display pictures to match Windows International Settings. Month and day names change without any input from the programmer or end user. *Text functions* makes it easy to display translated text in windows and reports, to move between Ansi and Ascii character sets, and get expected results from upper and lower case functions. A system of *flags* allows the programmer to override individual International Setting components. *Templates* then make it all happen effortlessly. Talk to us also about translation services and program enhancements.

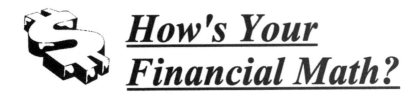

How's Your Financial Math?

CWFin Financial Library will perform financial math in your Clarion for Windows programs. Functions include rate, present value, future value, payment amount, internal rate of return, net present value, amortization, interest, and days duration between dates based on a 360 day calendar. Make calculations based on payments in advance or arrears. Optionally display error messages. Choose different rounding conventions. Available as "try before you buy shareware" (download CWFin.zip from the Clarion Forum). Registered users provided with sample program code, documentation of formulas used, a financial template, discounts on other purchases, and ProDomus e-mail newsletter with CW programming and other tips.

Call (203) 233-0705
MasterCard and Visa Accepted
E-mail: 74650.3623@compuserve.com   Fax: (203) 236-7954

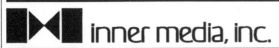

Add to Your Sams Library Today with the Best Books for Programming, Operating Systems, and New Technologies

The easiest way to order is to pick up the phone and call

1-800-428-5331

between 9:00 a.m. and 5:00 p.m. EST.
For faster service please have your credit card available.

ISBN	Quantity	Description of Item	Unit Cost	Total Cost
0-672-30473-2		Client/Server Computing, Second Edition	$40.00	
0-672-30486-4		Rightsizing Information Systems, Second Edition	$40.00	
0-672-30173-3		Enterprise-Wide Networking	$39.95	
0-672-30467-8		Sybase Developer's Guide (Book/Disk)	$40.00	
0-672-30440-6		Database Developer's Guide with Visual Basic 3.0 (Book/Disk)	$44.95	
0-672-30364-7		Win32API Desktop Reference	$49.95	
0-672-30338-8		Inside Windows File Formats	$29.95	
0-672-30507-0		Tricks of the Game-Programming Gurus (Book/CD-ROM)	$45.00	
0-672-30362-0		Navigating the Internet	$24.95	
0-672-30466-X		The Internet Unleashed (Book/Disk)	$44.95	
0-672-30481-3		Teach Yourself NetWare in 14 Days	$29.95	
0-672-30448-1		Teach Yourself C in 21 Days, Bestseller Edition	$24.95	
0-672-30465-1		Developing PowerBuilder 3 Applicaitions	$45.00	
0-672-30590-9		The Magic of Interactive Entertainment, Second Edition (Book/2 CD-ROMs)	$44.95	
❏ 3 ½" Disk		Shipping and Handling: See information below.		
❏ 5 ¼" Disk		TOTAL		

Shipping and Handling: $4.00 for the first book, and $1.75 for each additional book. Floppy disk: add $1.75 for shipping and handling. If you need to have it NOW, we can ship product to you in 24 hours for an additional charge of approximately $18.00, and you will receive your item overnight or in two days. Overseas shipping and handling adds $2.00 per book and $8.00 for up to three disks. Prices subject to change. Call for availability and pricing information on latest editions.

201 W. 103rd Street, Indianapolis, Indiana 46290

1-800-428-5331 — Orders   1-800-835-3202 — FAX   1-800-858-7674 — Customer Service

Book ISBN 0-672-30674-3

Diskette
3.5" • 2HD

Two sided
High density
135 tpi certified

HD

Installing Your Disk

What's on the Disk

The companion disk contains the source code for all complete programs presented in the text.

Software Installation Instructions

1. Insert the disk into your floppy drive.

2. From File Manager or Program Manager, choose Run from the File menu.

3. Type `<drive>`INSTALL and press Enter, where `<drive>` corresponds to the drive letter of your floppy drive. For example, if your floppy is drive A:, type `A:`INSTALL and press Enter.

4. Follow the onscreen instructions in the installation program. Files will be installed to a directory named \DEVCLAR, unless you choose a different directory during installation.